INTELLIGENT KNOWLEDGE-BASED SYSTEMS

BUSINESS AND TECHNOLOGY IN THE NEW MILLENNIUM

VOLUME 3
EXPERT AND AGENT SYSTEMS

INTELLIGENT KNOWLEDGE-BASED SYSTEMS

BUSINESS AND TECHNOLOGY IN THE NEW MILLENNIUM

VOLUME 3
EXPERT AND AGENT SYSTEMS

Edited by

CORNELIUS T. LEONDES
University of California, Los Angeles, USA

KLUWER ACADEMIC PUBLISHERS
BOSTON/DORDRECHT/LONDON

Distributors for North, Central and South America:
Kluwer Academic Publishers
101 Philip Drive
Assinippi Park
Norwell, Massachusetts 02061 USA
Telephone (781) 871-6600
Fax (781) 871-6528
E-Mail <kluwer@wkap.com>

Distributors for all other countries:
Kluwer Academic Publishers Group
Post Office Box 322
3300 AH Dordrecht, THE NETHERLANDS
Telephone 31 78 6576 000
Fax 31 78 6576 474
E-Mail <orderdept@wkap.nl>

Electronic Services <http://www.wkap.nl>

Library of Congress Cataloging-in-Publication Data

Intelligent knowledge-based systems : business and technology in the new millennium. /
edited by Cornelius T. Leondes.

    Includes bibliographical references and index.
    Contents: v. 1. Knowledge-based systems—v. 2. Information technology—
    v. 3. Expert and agent systems—v. 4. Intelligent systems—
    v. 5. Neural networks, fuzzy theory and genetic algorithms.
    ISBN 1-40207-746-7 (set)—ISBN 1-40207-824-2 (v.1)—ISBN 1-40207-825-0 (v.2)—
    ISBN 1-40207-826-9 (v.3)—ISBN 1-40207-827-7 (v.4)—ISBN 1-40207-828-5 (v.5)
    ISBN 1-40207-829-3 (electronic book set)

(LOC information to follow.)

CONTENTS

FOREWORD

Almost unknown to the academic world, and to the general public, the application of intelligent knowledge-based systems is rapidly and effectively changing the future of the human species. Today, human well-being is, as it has been for all of history, fundamentally limited by the size of the world economic product. Thus, if human economic well-being (which I personally define as the bottom centile annual per capita income) is ever soon to reach an acceptable level (e.g., the equivalent of $20,000 per capita per annum in 2004), then intelligent knowledge-based systems must be employed in vast quantities. This is primarily because of the reality that few humans live in efficient societies (such as the United States, Canada, Japan, the UK, France, and Germany, for example) and that inefficient societies, many of which are already large, and growing larger, may require many decades to become efficient. In the meantime, billions of people will continue to suffer economic impoverishment—an impoverishment that inefficient human labor cannot remedy. To create the extra economic output so urgently needed, we have only one choice: to employ intelligent knowledge-based systems in great numbers, which will produce economic output prodigiously, but will consume hardly at all.

This multi-volume major reference work, architected by its editor, Cornelius T. Leondes, provides a wealth of 'case studies' illustrating the state of the art in intelligent knowledge-based systems. In contrast to ordinary academic pedagogy, where 'ivory tower' abstraction and elegance are the guiding principles, practical applications require detailed relevant examples that can be used by practitioners to successfully innovate new operational capabilities. The economic progress of the species depends upon the flow of these innovations, which requires multi-volume major reference works with carefully selected, well-written, and well-edited 'case studies.' Professor Leondes knows these realities well, and the five volumes in this work resoundingly reflect his success in achieving their requirements.

Volume 1 addresses Knowledge-Based Systems. These eleven chapters consider the basic question of how accumulated data and staff expertise from business operations can be abstracted into valuable knowledge, and how such knowledge can then be applied to ongoing operations. Wide and representative situations are considered, ranging from product innovation and design, to intelligent database exploitation, to business model analysis.

Volume 2, Information Technology, addresses in ten chapters the important question of how data should be stored and used to maximize its overall value. Case studies consider a wide variety of application arenas: product development, manufacturing, product management, and even product pricing.

Volume 3 addresses Expert and Agent Systems in ten chapters. Application arenas considered include image databases, business process monitoring, e-commerce, and production planning and scheduling. Again, the coverage is designed to provide a wide range of perspectives and business-function concentrations to help stimulate innovation by the reader.

Volume 4, Intelligent Systems, provides nine chapters considering such topics as mission-critical functions, business forecasting, medical patient care, and product design and development.

Volume 5 addresses Neural Networks, Fuzzy Theory, and Genetic Algorithm Techniques. Its ten chapters cover examples in areas including bioinformatics, product life-cycle cost estimating, product development, computer-aided design, product assembly, and facility location.

The examples assembled by Professor Leondes in this work provide a wealth of practical ideas designed to trigger the development of innovation. The contributors to this grand project are to be congratulated for the major efforts they have expended in creating their chapters. Humans everywhere will soon benefit from the case studies provided herein. Intelligent Knowledge-Based Systems: Business and Technology in the New Millennium, is a reference work that belongs on the desk of every innovative technologist.

It has taken many decades of experience and unflagging hard work for Professor Leondes to accumulate the wisdom and judgment reflected in his editorial stewardship of this reference work. Wisdom and judgment are rare—but indispensable—commodities that cannot be obtained in any other way. The world of innovative technology, and the world at large, stand in his debt.

Robert Hecht-Nielsen
Computational Neurobiology
Institute for Neural Computation
Department of Electrical and Computer Engineering
University of California, San Diego

PREFACE

At the start of the 20th century, national economies on the international scene were, to a large extent, agriculturally based. This was, perhaps, the dominant reason for the protraction, on the international scene, of the Great Depression, which began with the Wall Street stock market crash of October, 1929. After World War II the trend away from agriculturally based economies and toward industrially based economies continued and strengthened. Indeed, today, in the United States, approximately only 1% of the population is involved in the agriculture requirements of the US and, in addition, provides significant agriculture exports. This, of course, is made possible by the greatly improved techniques and technologies utilized in the agriculture industry.

The trend toward industrially based economies after World War II was, in turn, followed by a trend toward service-based economies. In the United States today, roughly over 70% of the employment is involved with service industries—and this percentage continues to increase. Separately, the electronic computer industry began to take hold in the early 1960s, and thereafter always seemed to exceed expectations. For example, the first large-scale sales of an electronic computer were of the IBM 650. At that time, projections were that the total sales for the United States would be twenty-five IBM 650 computers. Before the first one came off the projection line, IBM had initial orders for over 30,000. That was thought to be huge by the standards of that day, and today it is a very miniscule number, to say nothing of the fact that its computing power was also very miniscule by today's standards. Computer mainframes continued to grow in power and complexity. At the same time, Gordon Moore, of "Moore's Law" fame, and his colleagues founded INTEL. Then around 1980 MICROSOFT was founded, but it was not until the early 1990s, not that long ago, that WINDOWS were created—incidentally, after the APPLE computer family started. The first browser was the NETSCAPE browser, which appeared in 1995, also not that long ago. Of course, computer networking equipment, most notably CISCO's, also appeared about that time. Toward the end of the last century the "DOT COM bubble" occurred and "burst" around 2000.

Coming to the new millennium, for most of our history the wealth of a nation was limited by the size and stamina of the work force. Today, national wealth is measured in intellectual capital. Nations possessing skillful people in such diverse areas as science, medicine, business, and engineering produce innovations that drive the nation to a higher quality of life. To better utilize these valuable resources, intelligent, knowledge-based systems technology has evolved at a rapid and significantly expanding rate, and can be utilized by nations to improve their medical care, advance their engineering technology, and increase their manufacturing productivity, as well as play a significant role in a very wide variety of other areas of activity of substantive significance.

The breadth of the major application areas of intelligent, knowledge-based systems technology is very impressive. These include the following, among other areas.

Agriculture	Electronics
Business	Engineering
Chemistry	Environment
Communications	Geology
Computer Systems	Image Processing
Education	Information
Management	Military
Law	Mining
Manufacturing	Power Systems
Mathematics	Science
Medicine	Space Technology
Meteorology	Transportation

It is difficult now to imagine an area that will not be touched by intelligent, knowledge-based systems technology.

The great breadth and expanding significance of such a broad field on the international scene requires a multi-volume, major reference work to provide an adequately substantive treatment of the subject, "Intelligent Knowledge-Based Systems: Business and Technology of The New Millennium." This work consists of the following distinctly titled and well integrated volumes.

Volume I.	Knowledge-Based Systems
Volume II.	Information Technology
Volume III.	Expert and Agent Systems
Volume IV.	Intelligent Systems
Volume V.	Neural Networks

This five-volume set on intelligent knowledge-based systems clearly manifests the great significance of these key technologies for the new economies of the new millennium. The authors are all to be highly commended for their splendid contributions, which together will provide a significant and uniquely comprehensive reference source for research workers, practitioners, computer scientists, students, and others on the international scene for years to come.

Cornelius T. Leondes
University of California, Los Angeles
January 5, 2004

VOLUME 1: KNOWLEDGE-BASED SYSTEMS

N. Bassiliades
Department of Informatics
Aristotle University of Thessaloniki
Thessaloniki
GREECE
Chapter 6. Aggregator: A Knowledge-Based Comparison Chart Builder for eShopping

Peter Bernus
Griffith University
School of CIT
Nathan
Queensland
AUSTRALIA
Chapter 10. Business Process Modeling and Its Applications in the Business Environment

Mariano Corso
Department of Management Engineering
Polytechnic University of Mailand
Milano
ITALY
Chapter 2. Knowledge Management Systems in Continuous Product Innnovation

Eugenio di Sciascio
Dipartimento Elettrotecnica ed Elettronica
Politecnico di Bari
Bari
ITALY
Chapter 11. Knowledge-Based Systems Technology and Applications in Image Retrieval

Francesco M. Donini
Università della Tuscia
Viterbo
ITALY
Chapter 11. Knowledge-Based Systems Technology and Applications in Image Retrieval

Janis Grundspenkis
Faculty of Computer Science and Information Technology
Riga Technical University
Riga
LATVIA
Chapter 7. Impact of the Intelligent Agent Paradigm on Knowledge Management

P. Humphreys
Faculty of Business and Management
University of Ulster
Northern Ireland
UNITED KINGDOM
Chapter 4. Knowledge-Based Systems Technology in the Make-or-Buy Decision in Manufacturing Strategy

Brane Kalpic
ETI Elektroelement Jt. St. Comp.
Izlake
SLOVENIA
Chapter 10. Business Process Modeling and Its Applications in the Business Environment

Marite Kirikova
Faculty of Computer Science and Information Technology
Riga Technical University
Riga
LATVIA
Chapter 7. Impact of the Intelligent Agent Paradigm on Knowledge Management

F. Kokkoras
Department of Informatics
Aristotle University of Thessaloniki

Thessaloniki
GREECE
Chapter 6. Aggregator: A Knowledge-Based Comparison Chart Builder for eShopping

Shian-Hua Lin
Department of Computer Science and Information Engineering
National Chi Nan University
Taiwan
REPUBLIC OF CHINA
Chapter 5. Intelligent Internet Information Systems in Knowledge Acquisition: Techniques and Applications

Antonella Martini
Faculty of Engineering
University of Pisa
Pisa
ITALY
Chapter 2. Knowledge Management Systems in Continuous Product Innovation

R. McIvor
Faculty of Business and Management
University of Ulster
UNITED KINGDOM
Chapter 4. Knowledge-Based Systems Technology in the Make-or-Buy Decision in Manufacturing Strategy

István Mezgár
CIM Research Laboratory
Computer and Automations Research Institute
Hungarian Academy of Sciences
Budapest
HUNGARY
Chapter 9. Security Technologies to Guarantee Safe Business Processes in Smart Organizations

Marina Mongiello
Dipartimento di Elettrotecnica ed Elettronica
Politecnico di Bari
Bari
ITALY
Chapter 11. Knowledge-Based Systems Technology and Applications in Image Retrieval

Ralf Muhlberger
University of Queensland
Information Technology & Electrical Engineering

Queensland
AUSTRALIA
Chapter 10. Business Process Modeling and Its Applications in the Business Environment

Cezary Orlowski
Gdansk University of Technology
Gdansk
POLAND
Chapter 8. Methods of Building Knowledge-Based Systems Applied in Software Project Management

Emilio Paolucci
Department of Operation and Business Management
Polytechnic University of Turin
Torino
ITALY
Chapter 2. Knowledge Management Systems in Continuous Product Innovation

Luisa Pellegrini
Faculty of Engineering
University of Pisa
Pisa
ITALY
Chapter 2. Knowledge Management Systems in Continuous Product Innovation

Ram D. Sriram
Design and Process Group
Manufacturing Systems Integration Division
National Institute of Standards and Technology
Gaithersburg, Maryland
USA
Chapter 1. Platform-Based Product Design and Development: Knowledge Support Strategy and Implementation

Nikos C. Tsourveloudis
Department of Production Engineering and Management
Technical University of Crete
Chania, Crete
GREECE
Chapter 3. Knowledge-Based Measurement of Enterprise Agility

I. Vlahavas
Department of Informatics
Aristotle University of Thessaloniki

Thessaloniki
GREECE
Chapter 6. Aggregator: A Knowledge-Based Comparison Chart Builder for eShopping

Xuan F. Zha
Design and Process Group
Manufacturing Systems Integration Division
National Institute of Standards and Technology
Gaithersburg, Maryland
USA
Chapter 1. Platform-Based Product Design and Development: Knowledge Support Strategy and Implementation

VOLUME 2: INFORMATION TECHNOLOGY

Aleš Brezovar
Faculty of Mechanical Engineering
University of Ljubljana
Ljubljana
SLOVENIA
Chapter 4. Techniques and Analysis of Sequential and Concurrent Product Development Processes

Chris R. Chatwin
School of Engineering and Information Technology
University of Sussex
Brighton
UNITED KINGDOM
Chapter 3. Modeling Techniques in Integrated Operations and Information Systems in Manufacturing

Ke-Zhang Chen
Department of Mechanical Engineering
The University of Hong Kong
HONG KONG
Chapter 5. Design and Modeling Methods for Components Made of Multi-Heterogeneous Materials in High-Tech Applications

Adrian E. Coronado
Management School
The University of Liverpool
Liverpool
UNITED KINGDOM
Chapter 2. Information Systems Frameworks and Their Applications in Manufacturing Systems

Xin-An Feng
School of Mechanical Engineering
Dalian University of Technology
Dalian
CHINA
Chapter 5. Design and Modeling Methods for Components Made of Multi-Heterogeneous Materials in High-Tech Applications

Janez Grum
Faculty of Mechanical Engineering
University of Ljubljana
Ljubljana
SLOVENIA
Chapter 4. Techniques and Analysis of Sequential and Concurrent Product Development Processes

George Hadjinicola
Department of Public and Business Administration
School of Economics and Management
University of Cyprus
Nicosia
CYPRUS
Chapter 9. Product Design and Pricing in Response to Competitor Entry: A Marketing-Production Perspective

Jared Jackson
IBM Almaden Research Center
San Jose, California
USA
Chapter 7. Web Data Extraction Techniques and Applications Using the Extensible Markup Language (XML)

D. F. Kehoe
Management School
The University of Liverpool
Liverpool
UNITED KINGDOM
Chapter 2. Information Systems Frameworks and Their Applications in Manufacturing Systems

Andreas Koeller
Department of Computer Science
Montclair State University
Upper Montclair, New Jersey
USA
Chapter 6. Quality and Cost of Data Warehouse Views

K. Ravi Kumar
Department of Information and Operations Management
Marshall School of Business
University of Southern California
Los Angeles, California
USA
Chapter 9. Product Redesign and Pricing in Response to Competitor Entry: A Marketing-Production Perspective

Janez Kušar
Faculty of Mechanical Engineering
University of Ljubljana
Ljubljana
SLOVENIA
Chapter 4. Techniques and Analyses of Sequential and Concurrent Product Development Processes

Henry C. W. Lau
Department of Industrial and Systems Engineering
The Hong Kong Polytechnic University
Hunghom
HONG KONG
Chapter 10. Knowledge Discovery by Means of Intelligent Information Infrastructure Methods and Their Applications

Amy Lee
The Ohio State University
Columbus, Ohio
USA
Chapter 6. Quality and Cost of Data Warehouse Views

Choon Seong Leem
School of Computer and Industrial Engineering
Yonsei University
Seoul
KOREA
Chapter 1. Techniques in Integrated Development and Implementation of Enterprise Information Systems

A. C. Lyons
Management School
The University of Liverpool
Liverpool
UNITED KINGDOM
Chapter 2. Information Systems Frameworks and Their Applications in Manufacturing Systems

Jussi Myllymaki
IBM Almaden Research Center
San Jose, California
USA
Chapter 7. Web Data Extraction Techniques and Applications Using the Extensible Markup Language (XML)

Anisoara Nica
Sybase Incorporated
Waterloo, Ontario
Canada
Chapter 6. Quality and Cost of Data Warehouse Views

Jörg Niemann
IFF University of Stuttgart
Fraunhofer IPA
Stuttgart
GERMANY
Chapter 8. Product Life Cycle Management in the Digital Age

Andrew Ning
Department of Industrial and Systems Engineering
The Hong Kong Polytechnic University
Hunghom
HONG KONG
Chapter 10. Knowledge Discovery by Means of Intelligent Information Infrastructure Methods and Their Applications

Elke A. Rundensteiner
Department of Computer Science
Worcester Polytechnic Institute
Worcester Massachusetts
USA
Chapter 6. Quality and Cost of Data Warehouse Views

Marko Starbek
Faculty of Mechanical Engineering
University of Ljubljana
Ljubljana
SLOVENIA
Chapter 4. Techniques and Analyses of Sequential and Concurrent Product Development Processes

Jong Wook Suh
School of Computer and Industrial Engineering
Yonsei University

Seoul
KOREA
Chapter 1. Techniques in Integrated Development and Implementation of Enterprise Information Systems

Qian Wang
School of Engineering and Information Technology
University of Sussex
Brighton
and
Department of Mechanical Engineering
University of Bath
Bath
UNITED KINGDOM
Chapter 3. Modeling Techniques in Integrated Operations and Information Systems in Manufacturing Systems

Engelbert Westkämper
IFF University of Stuttgart
Fraunhofer IPA
Stuttgart
GERMANY
Chapter 8. Product Life Cycle Management in the Digital Age

Christina W. Y. Wong
Department of Industrial and Systems Engineering
The Hong Kong Polytechnic University
Hunghom
HONG KONG
Chapter 10. Knowledge Discovery by Means of Intelligent Information Infrastructure Methods and Their Applications

R. C. D. Young
School of Engineering and Information Technology
University of Sussex
Brighton
UNITED KINGDOM
Chapter 3. Modeling Techniques in Integrated Operations and Information Systems in Manufacturing Systems

VOLUME 3: EXPERT AND AGENT SYSTEMS

Dimitris Askounis
Institute of Communications & Computer Systems
National Technical University of Athems

Athens
GREECE
Chapter 2. Expert Systems Technology in Production Planning and Scheduling

G. A. Britton
Design Research Center
School Of Mechanical and Production Engineering
Nanyang Technological University
SINGAPORE
Chapter 1. Techniques in Knowledge-Based Expert Systems for the Design of Engineering Systems

Jing Dai
School of Computing
National University of Singapore
SINGAPORE
Chapter 9. Finding Patterns in Image Databases

Robert Gay
Institute of Communication and Information Systems
School of Electrical and Electronic Engineering
Nanyang Technological University
SINGAPORE
Chapter 6. Agent-Based eLearning Systems: A Goal-Based Approach

Angela Goh
School of Computer Engineering
Nanyang Technological University
SINGAPORE
Chapter 4. The Knowledge Base of a B2B eCommerce Multi-Agent System

Ivan Romero Hernandez
Technological University of Grenoble
LCIS Research Laboratory
Valence
FRANCE
Chapter 5. From Roles to Agents: Considerations on Formal Agent Modeling and Implementation

Tu Bao Ho
Japan Advanced Institute of Science and Technology
Ishikawa
JAPAN
Chapter 7. Combining Temporal Abstraction and Data-Mining Methods in Medical Data Analysis

Wynne Hsu
School of Computing
National University of Singapore
SINGAPORE
Chapter 9. Finding Patterns in Image Databases

Chun-Che Huang
Department of Information Management
National Chi Nan University
Taiwan
REPUBLIC OF CHINA
Chapter 3. Applying Intelligent Agent-Based Support Systems in Agile Business Processes

K. Karibasappa
Department of Electronics and Telecommunication Engineering
University College of Engineering, Burla
Sambalpur, Orissa
INDIA
Chapter 10. Cognition Techniques and Their Applications

Nelly Kasim
Singapore-MIT Alliance
National University of Singapore
SINGAPORE
Chapter 4. The Knowledge Base of a B2B eCommerce Multi-Agent System

Saori Kawasaki
Japan Advanced Institute of Science and Technology
Ishikawa
JAPAN
Chapter 7. Combining Temporal Abstraction and Data-Mining Methods in Medical Data Analysis

Jean-Luc Koning
Technological University of Grenoble
LCIS Research Laboratory
Valence
FRANCE
Chapter 5. From Roles to Agents: Considerations on Formal Agent Modeling and Implementation

Si Quang Le
Japan Advanced Institute of Science and Technology
Ishikawa

JAPAN
Chapter 7. Combining Temporal Abstraction and Data-Mining Methods in Medical Data Analysis

Mong Li Lee
School of Computing
National University of Singapore
SINGAPORE
Chapter 9. Finding Patterns in Image Databases

Antonio Liotta
Center for Communication Systems Research
University of Surrey
Guildford, Surrey
UNITED KINGDOM
Chapter 8. Distributed Monitoring: Methods, Means, and Technologies

Kostas Metaxiotis
Institute of Communications & Computer Systems
National Technical University of Athens
Athens
GREECE
Chapter 2. Expert Systems Technology in Production Planning and Scheduling

Chunyan Miao
School of Computer Engineering
Nanyang Technological University
SINGAPORE
Chapter 4. The Knowledge Base of a B2B eCommerce Multi-Agent System

Yuan Miao
Institute of Communication and Information Systems
Nanyang Technological University
SINGAPORE
Chapter 6. Agent-Based eLearning Systems: A Goal-Based Approach

Trong Dung Nguyen
Japan Advanced Institute of Science and Technology
Ishikawa
JAPAN
Chapter 7. Combining Temporal Abstraction and Data-Mining Methods in Medical Data Analysis

Srikanta Patnaik
Department of Electronics and Telecommunication Engineering
University College of Engineering, Burla

Sambalpur, Orissa
INDIA
Chapter 10. Cognition Techniques and Their Applications

John Psarras
Institute of Communications & Computer Systems
National Technical University of Athens
Athens
GREECE
Chapter 2. Expert Systems Technology in Production Planning and Scheduling

Zhiqi Shen
Institute of Communication and Information Systems
School of Electrical and Electronic Engineering
Nanyang Technological University
SINGAPORE
Chapter 6. Agent-Based eLearning Systems: A Goal-Based Approach

S. B. Tor
Singapore-MIT Alliance
Nanyang Technological University
SINGAPORE
Chapter 1. Techniques in Knowledge-Based Expert Systems for the Design of Engineering Systems

W. Y. Zhang
Design Research Center
School of Mechanical and Production Engineering
Nanyang Technological University
SINGAPORE
Chapter 1. Techniques in Knowledge-Based Expert Systems for the Design of Engineering Systems

VOLUME 4: INTELLIGENT SYSTEMS

Cheng-Leong Ang
Singapore Institute of Manufacturing Technology
SINGAPORE
Chapter 4. An Intelligent Hybrid System for Business Forecasting

Sistine A. Barretto
Advanced Computing Research Centre
The University of South Australia
Adelaide

AUSTRALIA
Chapter 6. Techniques in the Utilization of the Internet and Intranets in Facilitating the Development of Clinical Decision Support Systems in the Process of Patient Care

Billy Fenton
International Test Technologies
and
University of Ulster
Letterkenny, Donegal
IRELAND
Chapter 5. Intelligent Systems Technology in the Fault Diagnosis of Electronic Systems

Robert Gay
Institute of Communication and Information Systems
School of Electrical and Electronic Engineering
Nanyang Technological University
SINGAPORE
Chapter 4. An Intelligent Hybrid System for Business Forecasting

Victor Giurgiutiu
Mechanical Engineering Department
University of South Carolina
Columbia, South Carolina
USA
Chapter 8. Mechatronics and Smart Structures Design Techniques for Intelligent Products, Processes and Systems

Marc-Philippe Huget
Leibnitz Laboratory
Grenoble
France
Chapter 9. Engineering Interaction Protocols for Multiagent Systems

Richard W. Jones
School of Engineering
University of Northumbria
Newcastle upon Tyne
England
UNITED KINGDOM
Chapter 2. Intelligent Patient Monitoring in the Intensive Care Unit and the Operating Room

Jean-Luc Koning
Technological University of Grenoble
LCIS Research Laboratory

Valence
FRANCE
Chapter 9. Engineering Interaction Protocols for Multiagent Systems

Xiang Li
Singapore Institute of Manufacturing Technology
SINGAPORE
Chapter 4. An Intelligent Hybrid System for Business Forecasting

Liam Maguire
Department of Informatics
University of Ulster
Derry
NORTHERN IRELAND
Chapter 5. Intelligent Systems Technology in the Fault Diagnosis of Electronic Systems

T. M. McGinnity
Department of Informatics
University of Ulster
Derry
NORTHERN IRELAND
Chapter 5. Intelligent Systems Technology in the Fault Diagnosis of Electronic Systems

Tolety Siva Perraju
Verizon Communications
Waltham, Massachusetts
USA
Chapter 3. Mission Critical Intelligent Systems

Mauricio Sanchez–Silva
Department of Civil and Environmental Engineering
Universidad de los Andes
Bogotá
COLOMBIA
Chapter 7. Risk Analysis and the Decision-Making Process in Engineering

Garimella Uma
South Asia International Institute
Hyderabad
INDIA
Chapter 3. Mission Critical Intelligent Systems

James R. Warren
Advanced Computing Research Centre
The University of South Australia

Mawson Lakes
AUSTRALIA
Chapter 6. Techniques in the Utilization of the Internet and Intranets in Facilitating the Development of Clinical Decision Support Systems in the Process of Patient Care

Xuan F. Zha
Design and Process Group
Manufacturing Systems Integration Division
National Institute of Standards and Technology
Gaithersburg, Maryland
USA
Chapter 1. Artificial Intelligence and Integrated Intelligent Systems: Applications in Product Design and Development

VOLUME 5: NEURAL NETWORKS, FUZZY THEORY AND GENETIC ALGORITHM TECHNIQUES

Kazem Abhary
School of Advanced Manufacturing and Mechanical Engineering
University of South Australia
Mawson Lakes
AUSTRALIA
Chapter 8. Assembly Sequence Optimization Using Genetic Algorithms

F. Admiraal-Behloul
Division of Image Processing
Leiden University Medical Center
Leiden
THE NETHERLANDS
Chapter 4. Fuzzy Rule Extraction Using Radial Basis Function Neural Networks in High-Dimensional Data

Kemal Ahmet
Faculty of Creative Arts and Technologies
University of Luton
Luton
UNITED KINGDOM
Chapter 1. Neural Network Systems Technology and Applications in CAD/CAM Integration

Carl K. Chang
Department of Computer Science
Iowa State University
Ames, Iowa
USA
Chapter 7. Genetic Algorithm Techniques and Applications in Management Systems

Lian Ding
Faculty of Creative Arts and Technologies
University of Luton
Luton
UNITED KINGDOM
Chapter 1. Neural Network Systems Technology and Applications in CAD/CAM Integration

Shing-Hwang Doong
Department of Information Management
Shu-Te University
Yen Chau
TAIWAN
Chapter 10. Computational Intelligence for Facility Location Allocation Problems

Yujia Ge
Department of Computer Science
Iowa State University
Ames, Iowa
USA
Chapter 7. Genetic Algorithm Techniques and Applications in Management Systems

Andrew Kusiak
Department of Mechanical and Industrial Engineering
University of Iowa
Iowa City, Iowa
USA
Chapter 5. Fuzzy Decision Modeling of Product Development Processes

Chih-Chin Lai
Department of Information Management
Shu-Te University
Yen-Chau
TAIWAN
Chapter 10. Computational Intelligence for Facility Location Allocation Problems

Wen F. Lu
Product Design and Development Group
Singapore Institute of Manufacturing Technology
SINGAPORE
Chapter 6. Evaluation and Selection in Product Design for Mass Customization

Lee H. S. Luong
School of Advanced Manufacturing and Mechanical Engineering
University of South Australia

Mawson Lakes
AUSTRALIA
Chapter 8. Assembly Sequence Optimization Using Genetic Algorithms

Romeo Marin Marian
CSIRO Manufacturing & Infrastructure Technology
Woodville North, SA
AUSTRALIA
Chapter 8. Assembly Sequence Optimization Using Genetic Algorithms

Stergios Papadimitriou
Department of Information Management
Technological Education Institute of Kavala
Kavala
GREECE
Chapter 9. Kernel-Based Self-Organized Maps Trained with Supervised Bias for Gene Expression Data Mining

Johan H. C. Reiber
Division of Image Processing
Department of Radiology
Leiden University Medical Center
Leiden
THE NETHERLANDS
Chapter 4. Fuzzy-Rule Extraction Using Radial Basis Function Neural Networks in High-Dimensional Data

Kwang-Kyu Seo
Division of Computer, Information and Telecommunication Engineering
Sangmyung University
Chungnam
KOREA
Chapter 2. Neural Network Systems Technology and Applications in Product Life–Cycle Cost Estimates

Joaquin Sitte
Faculty of Information Technology
Queensland University of Technology
Brisbane
AUSTRALIA
Chapter 3. Neural Network Systems Technology in the Analysis of Financial Time Series

Renate Sitte
Faculty of Engineering and Information and Technology
Griffith University
Queensland
AUSTRALIA
Chapter 3. Neural Network Systems Technology in the Analysis of Financial Time Series

Ram D. Sriram
Design and Process Group
Manufacturing Systems Integration Divison
National Institute of Standards and Technology
Gaithersburg, Maryland
USA
Chapter 6. Evaluation and Selection in Product Design for Mass Customization

Fu J. Wang
Design and Process Group
Manufacturing Systems Integration Division
National Institute of Standards and Technology
Gaithersburg, Maryland
USA
Chapter 6. Evaluation and Selection in Product Design for Mass Customization

Juite Wang
Department of Industrial Engineering
Feng Chia University
Taichung, Taiwan
REPUBLIC OF CHINA
Chapter 5. Fuzzy Decision Modeling of Product Development Processes

Chih-Hung Wu
Department of Information Management
Shu-Te University
Yen Chau
TAIWAN
Chapter 10. Computational Intelligence for Facility Location Allocation Problems

Yong Yue
Faculty of Creative Arts and Technologies
University of Luton
Luton
UNITED KINGDOM
Chapter 1. Neural Network Systems Technology and Applications in CAD/CAM Integration

Xuan F. Zha
Design and Process Group
Manufacturing Systems Integration Divison
National Institute of Standards and Technology
Gaithersburg, Maryland
USA
Chapter 6. Evaluation and Selection in Product Design for Mass Customization

VOLUME III. EXPERT AND AGENT SYSTEMS

TECHNIQUES IN KNOWLEDGE-BASED EXPERT SYSTEMS FOR THE DESIGN OF ENGINEERING SYSTEMS

G. A. BRITTON, S. B. TOR AND W. Y. ZHANG

QUOTATION

EXPERT: Somebody who knows more than anybody else.

NON-EXPERT: Anybody else

EXPERT SYSTEM: A computer system whose logic complies with the following syllogism.

   n experts (somebodies) input their knowledge into the system,

   the system outputs its inputs to a non-expert (anybody else),

   a non-expert (anybody else) knows more than n-1 experts (somebodies).

   In short, an expert system helps many somebodies turn anybody into a somebody.

1. INTRODUCTION

Engineering design is a process of inventing new physical products and systems to fulfill human needs. It is one of the most important and challenging phases in the development lifecycle of a product (Figure 1). Note that the figure depicts the feedback loops for design only; the other feedback loops have been omitted for clarity.

Design is usually considered to consist of two phases. The first is a conceptual design phase during which the functionality and overall form (architecture) of a product are defined. This is followed by a detail design phase that produces a detailed physical description of the product, which is a model that is used as template for replicating the product as many times as is required [1]. Verification activities are carried out during the design process to ensure the design will achieve user needs and to reduce design uncertainty. These activities include engineering analysis, simulation, building

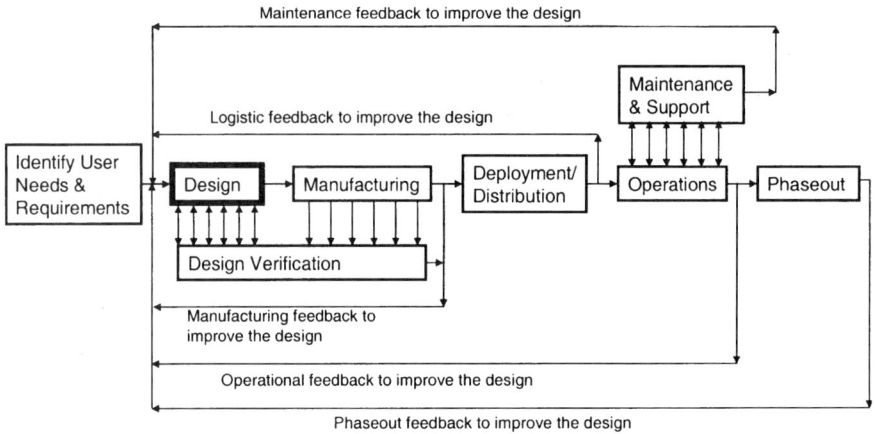

Figure 1. Design process and the product lifecycle.

demonstration prototypes, and engineering tests. Typically all designs go through a 'design-build-test' cycle, in which physical prototypes are built and tested to confirm design margins and product reliability. After verification the design is used as a template to manufacture components and to assemble them to create the final product. The design is also used to support maintenance and repair activities.

Computer Aided Design (CAD) software helps designers create designs more productively, with fewer design changes and errors compared to manual design methods. This software is evolving along three axes of development: communication, modeling and knowledge. Figure 2 shows evolution along the communication axis. Initially CAD was performed on stand-alone, individual workstations. This situation has changed dramatically today as CAD workstations are connected to the internet, facilitating global, concurrent engineering.

Evolution along the modeling axis is shown in Figure 3. Initially CAD software was simply a 2D drafting tool. Today, however, CAD software is capable of representing the complete geometric shape of a product in a 3D solid model [2, 3] and supports design by features and variational modeling [4]. Within the research community, functional design software has been developed [5–7].

A recent development in commercial CAD systems is 'process threading' (EDS, http://www.eds.com/products/plm/teamcenter/) or 'process-centric design' (Dassault Systemes, http://www.3ds.com/en/brands/enovia-ipf.asp). The purpose of process threading is to link together a set of 3D solid modeling software tools, using a common CAD platform, to undertake all phases of product development in a particular domain of business; this is the process thread. Existing tools are used where possible, and new software is written to fill in the "gaps". For example, EDS Corp. has developed *MoldWizard* to complement its CAD and CAM (Computer Aided Manufacturing) software for mold design and manufacture. Process threads are available for

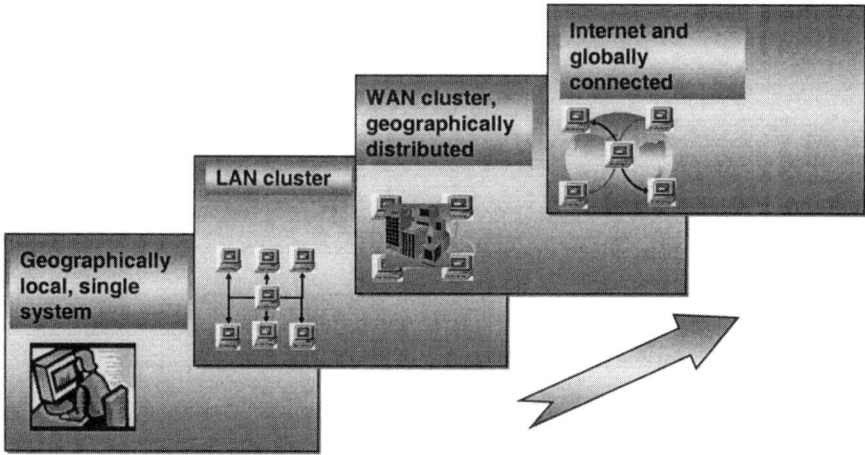

Figure 2. CAD evolution along the communication axis.

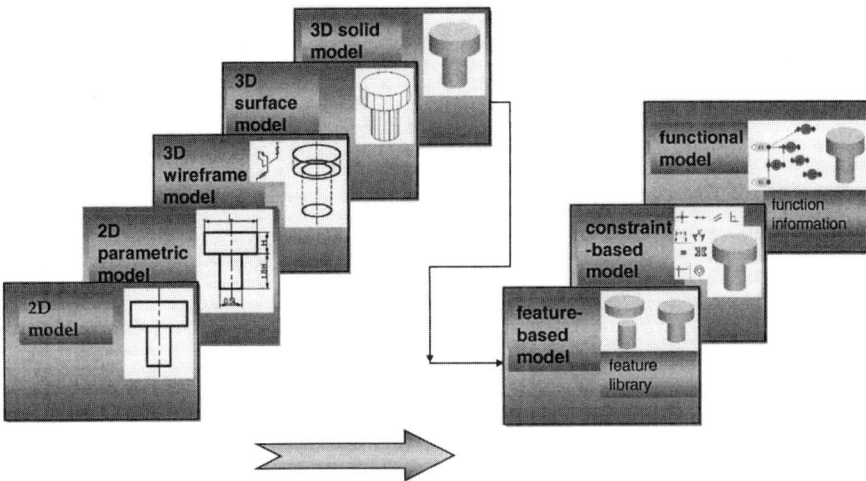

Figure 3. CAD evolution along the modeling axis.

the following domains: automotive, aerospace, electrical/electronic, machine tool and consumer products (especially plastic products). Process thread software is primarily aimed at automating routine design and other tasks, but it also includes expert knowledge specific to each domain, e.g., rules for determining the location of parting lines in plastic injection molds.

Evolution along the engineering knowledge axis has proceeded from single data files to knowledge-based databases distributed over intranets and the internet (Figure 4).

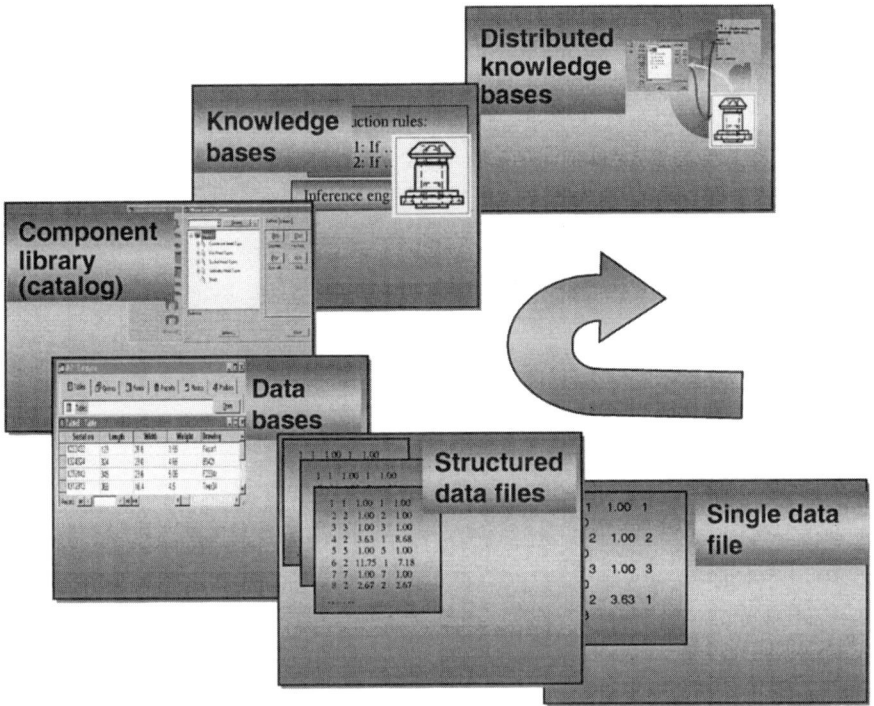

Figure 4. CAD evolution along the knowledge axis.

Commercial, intelligent CAD software extends the capability of traditional CAD systems by employing heuristic knowledge on top of geometric models. *ICAD* [8] from Knowledge Technologies Inc. is capable of modeling and automating the engineering design process, by incorporating not only geometry, but also non-geometric logic such as product structures, development processes, standard engineering methods, and manufacturing rules.

In *Unigraphics* V18 [9], EDS Corp. incorporated a new engineering expert system featuring a fully integrated knowledge-based engineering language, *Intent!* [10] from Heide Corp. The software provides facilities for capturing and reusing a wide variety of technical rules that define design objects and assemblies, their relationships and their interdependencies. As a result it can automatically track design parameters and constraints between design objects.

Expert knowledge is applied as guidelines or rules for design, 'design for X' knowledge, e.g., design for manufacturing, design for test, and design for maintenance. The knowledge is gained through experience and lessons learned from the other phases in the product lifecycle, refer to the feedback loops in Figure 1. The authors expect more of this kind of knowledge to be incorporated into intelligent CAD software in the future.

The discussion thus far has considered computer-based expert knowledge in design. Brief reference has been made to design verification, an activity closely coupled with design. Verification is the phase that probably requires more expert knowledge than any other in the product lifecycle. It is performed by engineering experts. Some verification is achieved by analyses and simulations using specialist Computer-Aided Engineering (CAE) software. It is also possible to perform computer-based (virtual) tests on CAD models. Virtual testing reduces the amount of effort required for physical testing, resulting in shorter development times, improved productivity, and fewer late design changes. CAD and CAE software suppliers are working together to provide better integration between their software, in order to provide better support to designers. The result is 'design-centric' CAE software, which can be used effectively by designers without expert help. Such software does not replace experts, but it does significantly reduce design lead times. It also allows designers to explore and evaluate many more design options than would otherwise be possible using a conventional design-verification approach.

This brief introduction has shown that commercial CAD systems have become smarter through embedding expert knowledge in CAD software and linking CAD software with specialist engineering software. This trend will continue as new, more powerful, expert systems are developed for engineering design and verification. The major challenge is to develop a 'design-centric' expert system that incorporates knowledge from all phases of the product lifecycle and supports global, concurrent design and engineering.

The purpose of this chapter is to describe knowledge-based techniques and explain how they can be applied to engineering design. Section 2 introduces the reader to knowledge-based expert systems and discusses the conceptual foundations of knowledge-based organization and reasoning. Section 3 describes the different knowledge-based techniques and explains how they can be applied to engineering design. Section 4 discusses the specific application of the techniques using an approach known as functional design.

2. CHARACTERISTICS OF KNOWLEDGE-BASED EXPERT SYSTEMS

Knowledge-based Experts Systems (KBES's) derive from the Artificial Intelligence (AI) discipline, a branch of computer science concerned with the design and implementation of programs capable of performing actions that emulate human cognitive skills, such as understanding, reasoning, and learning. KBES's capture the specific knowledge of a particular domain and mimic the problem-solving strategies of human experts. That is, they simulate human reasoning, not the application domain being modeled.

The development of a KBES requires knowledge about both human reasoning and computer techniques. Analysis of these aspects is known as knowledge engineering [11]. Knowledge engineering can be divided into two levels as shown in Figure 5. The *knowledge level* deals with the conceptual models underlying human reasoning [12]. The *computational level* deals with the representation of this knowledge and reasoning in computer systems [13].

Domain knowledge	Inferential knowledge
Ontology	Inferential strategies
Domain models	Problem solving methods

Knowledge Level

••

Computational Level

Implementation-specific knowledge-based techniques	Generic knowledge-based techniques
Rule-based representation	Control strategies
Semantic networks	Search strategies
Frame-based representation	Constraint processing
Object-oriented representation	Case-based reasoning
Logic-based representation	Blackboard architecture
Fuzzy logic	

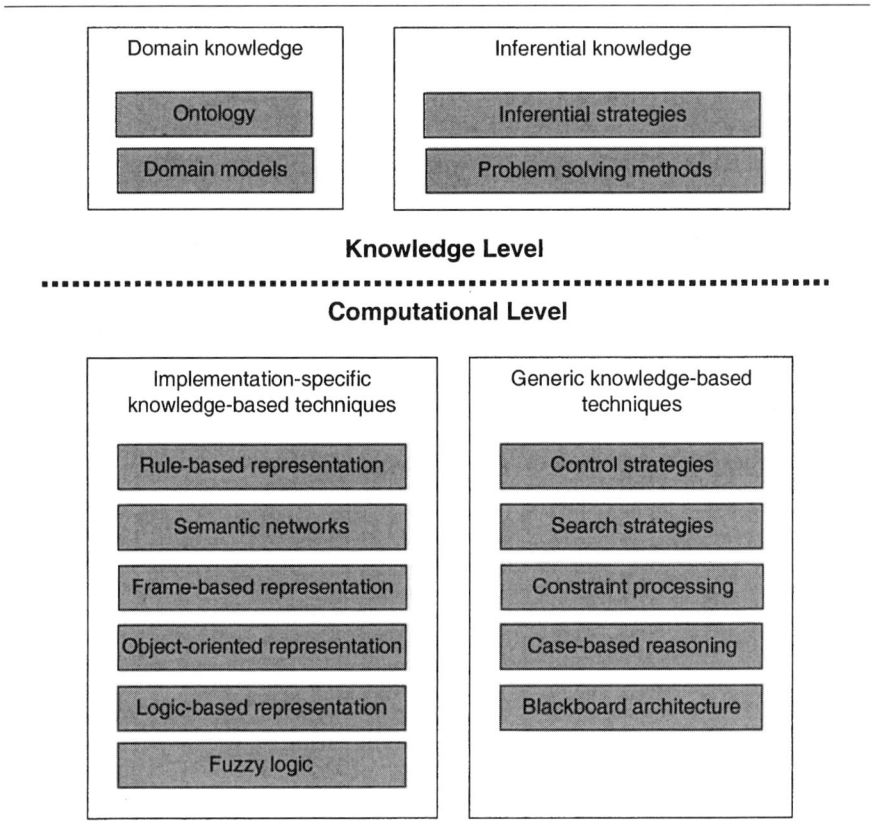

Figure 5. Knowledge engineering.

The knowledge level consists of conceptual models for representing the world, domain knowledge, and reasoning models, inferential knowledge. These models are abstract so they can be used irrespective of the formal language encoding the knowledge. The knowledge level is discussed below. The computational level deals with implementation-specific knowledge-based techniques, which are associated with specific computer-based knowledge representation schemes, and generic techniques that are applicable to most, if not all, of the representation schemes. The computational level is discussed in Section 3.

2.1. Domain knowledge

Domain knowledge refers to knowledge about the application domain. It deals with the way humans view and model the world. The conceptual models here can be divided into those that are generic, ontological models, and those that are application specific, domain models.

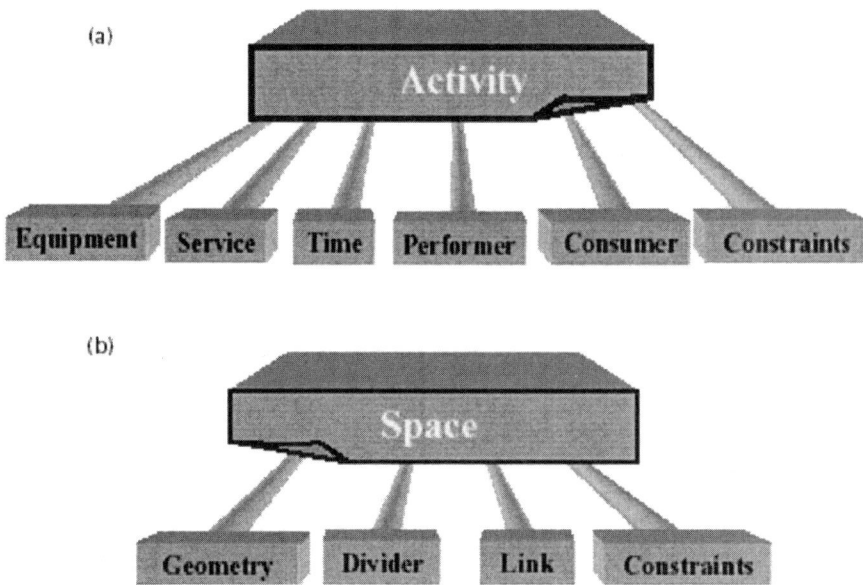

Figure 6. A/S design ontology [17].

Ontology is a branch of philosophy dealing with the nature of existence of things such as materials, objects, mind, people, etc. A particular theory about what exists, or a list of things that are considered to exist, can be called an ontology [14]. Ontology is important because it determines what is modeled and how it is modeled, and perhaps more importantly, what is not modeled. In short, it provides the conceptual foundation for inference and computation. We will adopt Gruber's [15] definition of ontology as *a formal, explicit specification of a shared conceptualization*. Here the term *conceptualization* refers to an abstract model defining relevant and key concepts of some aspect of the real world, the application domain [16].

Two examples will illustrate the meaning of ontology in the context of engineering design. The first example is an ontology for the design of buildings, called A/S (*Activity/Space*) design ontology by Simoff & Maher [17]. The A/S ontology includes a description of a building's design requirement, a description of building design solutions, and the relationship between design requirements and design solutions. It serves as a knowledge source to develop and evolve a new design. Building design knowledge is classified as *Activity* and *Space* (Figure 6). Activity connotes the functionality of the design and denotes the activities taking place in a given space. Space denotes the geometry of areas within the building, and the links between geometry and constraints imposed on them. Hence this knowledge model not only represents the geometrical description of the building, but also the functionality of the spaces in the building.

The second example illustrates the idea of a list of 'things taken to exist'. In design ontologies these 'things' are conceptual primitives, such as *concepts, attributes, states,*

Table 1 Examples of ontological primitives

Ontological primitive	CML primitive	Design example
Concept	Component	Car Buffer, car guide rail
Attribute	Attribute-slot	Weight, height, width
Expression	Attribute-slot-expression	Height = 28.75
Relation	Has-attribute	Car buffer has height

actions, causes, expressions, entities and *relations*, that are used to model the application domain. CommonKADS is a conceptual modeling language (CML) for knowledge modeling [18]. It has been used to develop an ontology for elevator design [19] by providing a set of representational primitives. Some of these primitives are shown in Table 1. The actual knowledge base can be viewed as a pure *instantiation* of the ontology. Figure 7 shows some example 'fragments' from the knowledge base.

A domain model is an ontology applied to a specific engineering design problem or domain. It can be used as communication medium between experts and knowledge engineers to acquire expert knowledge and to aid in structuring the knowledge in a way that will be useful for the users. For example, using *concepts* such as *function, behavior, structure* and *environment*, the authors have proposed a constructive approach of two-level knowledge modeling for mechanical engineering design [20]. The approach develops two domain models: a functional model and an object model. The functional model serves as a basis for communication between domain experts and knowledge engineers, while the object model is used to bridge the gap between the functional model and an executable knowledge base (the implemented expert system). Together they constitute the performance specification for an expert system, and are valuable because they provide a rich description of domain-specific, functional design knowledge independent of the implementation.

2.2. Inferential knowledge

Inferential knowledge refers to domain-independent knowledge that describes the reasoning steps needed to achieve a particular goal. This can be generic knowledge, inferential strategies, or knowledge aimed specifically at solving particular problems, problem solving methods (PSM's).

Inferential strategies describe the underlying logic of reasoning in general. They are used to define the generic control for executing inferences, i.e., they determine how task specific PSM's are selected and applied. A given strategy may also be applicable to several PSM's. The study of inference is very important because it determines the capability of expert systems. For this reason we will discuss the topic in some detail in order to clearly illustrate the difficulty in developing an expert system and the limitations of current systems.

The study of inference and reasoning has been extensively studied by philosophers. One influential philosopher in this area is the pragmatist Charles Peirce. For Peirce [21] there are three types of inference: abduction, induction and deduction. Abduction suggests hypotheses and theories. Deduction proves that these theories must be true in a logical sense. Induction relates the hypotheses and theories to facts in the real world.

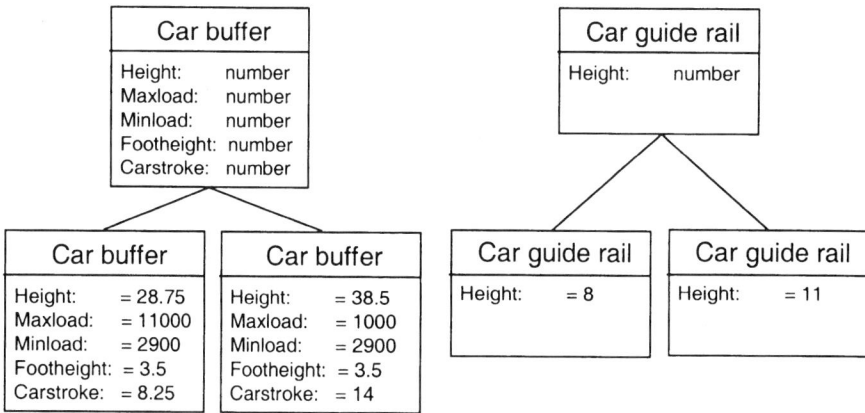

Figure 7. Example of knowledge base 'fragments' for elevator design [17]. (Springer-Verlag, FUTURE KNOWLEDGE ACQUISITION: PROCEEDINGS OF EKAW '94, G. Schreiber, B. Wielinga, H. Akkermans, W. Van e Velde and A. Anjewierden, pp. 1–25, figure 5, 1994, copyright notice of Springer-Verlag.)

"Abduction is the process of forming an explanatory hypothesis. It is the only logical operation which introduces any new idea . . . " [21, p. 230], and "All the ideas of science come to it by the way of abduction. Abduction consists in studying facts and devising a theory to explain them." [21, p. 218]. For Peirce, abduction is a creative act by which new ideas are generated. These ideas are uncertain and must be tested using deduction and induction.

Induction involves experimental investigation. Its aim is to validate a theory proposed by abduction and verified by deduction. Inductive reasoning generalizes from specific instances or facts. The experimental method of inference must be capable of demonstrating that it will generate future instances in the same manner as past instances. The following quote from Peirce illustrates clearly his notion of induction.

"Induction consists in starting from a theory, deducing from it predictions of phenomena and observing those phenomena in order to see *how nearly* they agree with theory. The justification for believing an experiential theory which has been subjected to a number of experimental tests will be in the near future sustained about as well by further such tests as it has hitherto been, is that by steadily pursuing that method we must in the long run find out how the matter really stands. . . . Thus the validity of induction depends upon the necessary relation between the general and the singular." [21, p. 229–230].

As for deduction, Peirce states: "In deduction, or necessary reasoning, we set out from a hypothetical state of things which we define in certain abstracted respects. Among the characteristics to which we pay no attention in this mode of argument is whether or not the hypothesis of our premises conforms more or less to the state of things in the outward world. We consider this hypothetical state of things and are led to conclude that, however it may be with the universe in other respects, wherever and whenever the hypothesis may be realized, something else not explicitly supposed in that hypothesis will be true invariably." [21, p. 225]. In short, the conclusion of a deductive argument is already contained in the starting premises and the method of deduction. Given these, the conclusion must necessarily follow.

There is one further interesting point made by Peirce that is relevant to current expert systems. He notes the following: "One of these (opinions) is that although Abductive and Inductive reasoning are distinctly not reducible to Deductive reasoning, nor to the other, nor Deductive reasoning to either, yet the *rationale* of Abduction and Induction must itself be Deductive." [21, p. 277]. What this means is that in order to show that an abduction or induction is sound we must use a deductive type of argument. It is important to note that this occurs after the inductive or abductive act.

With the three definitions clearly stated we are now in a position to state the types of inference current expert systems can perform. First, let us consider abduction. Abduction is a creative act. No current expert system can perform abduction because the creative process is not well understood or defined. We can't specify what we don't know. It is possible, however, for expert systems to 'explain' the rationale of abductions that have been performed by human experts. The explanations are generated by deduction.

Induction, according to Peirce, relates to experimental investigation of the real world. It is very difficult to develop an expert system that meets the logical requirements of inductive reasoning. There have been attempts to develop inductive expert systems, either partially or wholly. Two good examples, Leibnizian and Lockean inquirers, are discussed by Churchman [22, Chapters 4 & 5].

Most expert systems deduce. Deduction allows an expert system to derive *facts* (such as *goal states*, *intermediate states* and *solutions*), given some *general laws* (such as *rules*, *algorithms* and *constraints*) and some *initial facts* (such as *initial states*, *intermediate states* and *causes*) [23]. Deductive expert systems cannot create knowledge. All facts generated by these systems are already implicitly contained in the facts and theories in their knowledge bases and the rules of inference. New knowledge has to be input by human experts.

A Problem Solving Method (PSM) refers to a task-specific reusable inference pattern that describes the inferential actions to perform a particular task. The rationale underlying PSM's is to make the inferential knowledge explicit and reusable, and to represent it in an implementation- and domain-independent manner.

PSM's have been widely recognized as valuable components in current knowledge engineering frameworks, e.g., *heuristic classification* [24], *generic task* [25], *role-limiting methods* [26], *CommonKADS* [18], *MIKE* [27]. The aim of *Heuristic classification* [24] was to characterize the problem solving behavior of a large number of KBES's performing tasks such as diagnosis and data interpretation. A common inference pattern was found comprised of three basic inferential actions - *data abstraction*, *heuristic match* and *solution refinement*, and four knowledge roles - *data, data abstractions, solution abstractions* and *solutions* (Figure 8). It is worth noting that the generality of heuristic classification allows it to be used in a wide range of KBES's in different domains such as SOPHIE [28] for electronic circuits troubleshooting and COMPASS [29] for electronic components diagnosis.

In contrast to heuristic classification for classification problem solving, where solutions can be selected from some fixed set, Jackson [30] describes several PSM's for

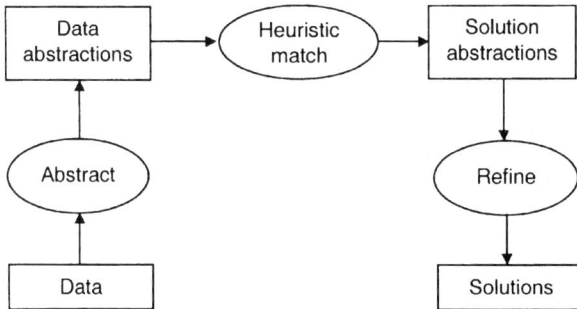

Figure 8. The inference structure of heuristic classification [24]. (Reprinted from ARTIFICIAL INTELLIGENCE, 27, W. J. Clancy, "Heuristic classification," 289–350, 1985, with permission from Elsevier.)

constructive problem solving. These include *propose-and-apply* and *propose-and-revise*, which build solutions out of primitive components. The PSM *Propose-and-apply* has been identified by Bachant [31] in R1 program [32] for computer systems configuration design. Its basic inferential actions are *initialize-goal, propose-operator, prune-operator, eliminate-operator, select-one-operator, apply-operator* and *evaluate-goal*. A major problem with this PSM is its inefficiency because it has to propose and apply all possible design alternatives. The PSM*propose-and-revise* used for the VT elevator design problem [19] is more efficient.

A number of other PSM's have also been proposed by other researchers [33, 34] for design and configuration problem solving, including *select-and-verify, match-modify-and-test, generate-and-test, propose-and-backtrack,* and *hierarchical-hypothesis-and-test*. A structured development of PSM's can be found in Fensel & Motta [35].

3. KNOWLEDGE-BASED TECHNIQUES AND THEIR APPLICATION IN ENGINEERING DESIGN

Like all problem solving, design can be formulated as a goal-directed search in a problem space [36]. In most cases, the design search space is very large due to the diversity and large amount of information that must be handled, such as functional requirements, constraints, designer expertise, design guidelines, design history, standards, tools, costs, etc. Engineering design problems are said to be ill-structured because there is no simple, linear method for solving them [37, 38]. Even the simpler task of configuring products is difficult to solve [39]. Knowledge-based techniques offer a feasible approach to solve these ill-structured design problems by empowering traditional CAD techniques with human-like reasoning. Computational level design methods are often described in terms of various knowledge-based techniques: either implementation-specific or generic.

3.1. Implementation-specific knowledge-based techniques

The implementation-specific knowledge-based techniques are often characterized by specific knowledge representation languages or environments, e.g., the rule-based language *Prolog* and object-oriented shell *CLIPS*. Sometimes the design know-how and knowledge is modeled in multiple forms, requiring multiple representation and implementation techniques.

3.1.1. Rule-based representation

The most straightforward technique for representing knowledge in KBES's today is in the form of rules. Systems using rule-based architecture are often called production systems, as the rules "produce" a result [40]. Rules have the general form:

IF (*Condition$_1$*, *Condition$_2$*, ..., *Condition$_m$*) → THEN (*Action$_1$*, *Action$_2$*, ..., *Action$_n$*)

which can be read as:

IF *Condition$_1$*, *Condition$_2$*, ..., and *Condition$_m$* are true, THEN perform *Action$_1$*, *Action$_2$*, ..., and *Action$_n$*.

Rule-based systems work in a match, select and act cycle. During matching, the rules whose conditions are totally satisfied by the facts are executed. If more than one rule has its conditions satisfied at the same time then a global conflict resolution mechanism or a local conflict resolution mechanism will be used to determine the order of execution [30].

Two examples of rules to determine the bending radius of a steel, sheet metal part in progressive die design are shown below:

Rule 1:
    IF   *Material type = Steel* 1008
    AND   *Bending operation no.* ≤ 2
    THEN *Bending radius* = 1.5 × *Material thickness*

Rule 2:
    IF   *Bending angle* = 90° ∼ 135°,
    THEN *Bending operation no.* = 2

To illustrate rule operation, assume there are two facts in working memory: *Bending angle* = 120°, and *Material type = Steel* 1008. With its condition satisfied, *Rule 2* is executed first, resulting in a new fact, i.e., *Bending operation no.* = 2. With both of its conditions satisfied, *Rule 1* is then executed, resulting in the value of required bending radius, i.e., 1.5 × *Stock thickness*. As this example shows, the data flow in a rule-based system differs greatly from a procedural program where the data flow is fixed and rigid. Instead, in rule-based systems, the rules-to-be-executed and the sequence are determined by the available data or facts in the working memory.

In general, rule-based representation is uniform, simple and modular, thus highly comprehensible to the system developer. As a result, many rule-based systems have been developed for engineering design; for example, Li et al. [41] for mechanism design, Moulianitis et al. [42] for the conceptual design of grippers for handling fabrics, Kim

& Im [43] for the design of roll pass and profile sequences for the shape rolling of round and square bars, and Masood & Soo [44] for the selection of various rapid prototyping systems suitable for different industry requirements. Commercial rule-based intelligent CAD systems have also been developed, two well-known examples being *ICAD* [8] and *Unigraphics* [9].

3.1.2. Semantic networks

The systematic use of semantic networks for knowledge representation began with Quillian's [45] work on language understanding, a study of the relationship between words and phrases and their intended meaning. A semantic network is a directed, labeled graph, in which the nodes represent entities, concepts, or events, and the links between the nodes represent inheritance relationships between entities, concepts, or events. These relationships include, but are not restricted to, *is-a, has-a, is-an-instance-of*, and *is-a-kind-of*.

Semantic networks are suitable for domains where reasoning is based on inheritance. Suppose that we would like to develop a representation capable of accurately detailing all of the feature-based relationships in a sheet metal part for stamping process planning. Figure 9 shows a partial graph of this semantic network. A class represented by *Flat* is a sub-class of the class represented by *Positive feature* by means of *is-a-kind-of* relationship. *Hole* is a sub-class of *Negative feature* by means of *is-a-kind-of* relationship. Both *Positive feature* and *Negative feature* are sub-classes of a generic class *Stamping feature*. *Hole7 is-an-instance-of Hole* class. *Hole7* will inherit the properties from *Hole*: *has-a Feature ID, Coordinate of base point, Internal precision, Depth* and *Diameter* attributes, and *is-in Flat* associated with *Hole*.

Semantic networks provide a form of structured representation that is easy to develop and understand. Thus they are very appropriate for engineering design. Fujimoto & Yamamoto [46] developed a decision support system to assist production line design using a semantic network. Cherneff et al. [47] presented a knowledge-based system called "Builder" for automating the task of generating and maintaining construction schedules from architectural drawings. Its main feature is a semantic network for representing and communicating the architecture-engineering-construction (AEC) problem state. Rogers et al. [48] used a semantic network to support concurrent engineering in the design of semiconductor devices. The network retains knowledge of a product in a central repository as various engineers contribute to the product's development. In order to address the critical research issues in life-cycle engineering: design representation and measures for life-cycle evaluation, Ishii [49] adopted a design representation scheme based on a semantic network that is effective for evaluating structural layouts. Bullinger et al. [50] represented knowledge from various experts by means of an active semantic network to integrate interdisciplinary teams for rapid product development.

3.1.3. Frame-based representation

The capabilities of semantic networks can be extended by further clustering and grouping related concepts and attributes into a frame structure. Frames were first introduced

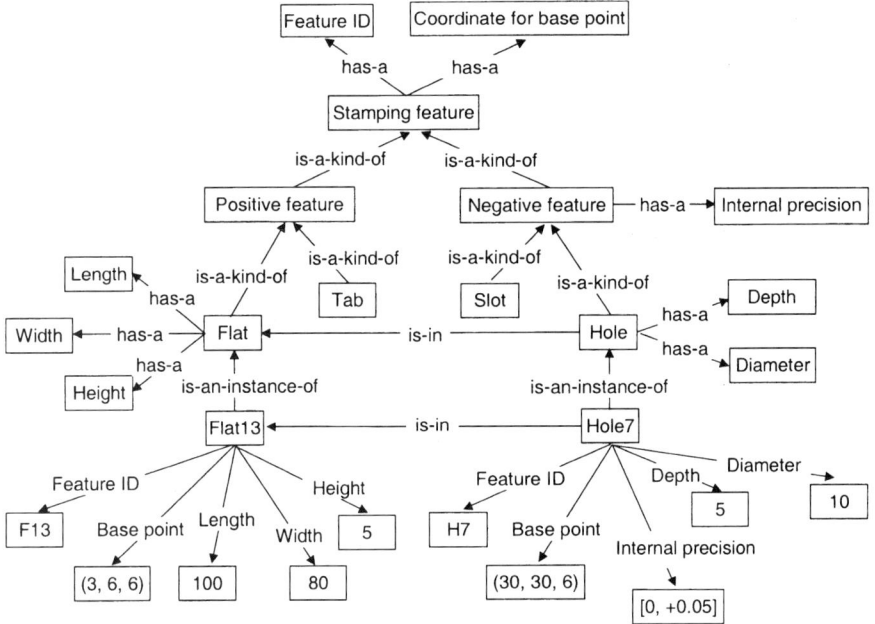

Figure 9. A semantic network representation of sheet metal part.

by Minsky to represent stereotypical situations [51]. Frames may associate both data and methods with objects or classes of objects by incorporating a set of attribute descriptions, called *slots*. Frames are more effective in representing declarative and procedural knowledge than semantic networks because the latter cannot group data into associated clusters. Frames are typically linked in an inheritance-based hierarchical structure. Frames lower down the network can inherit information from broader classes of frames higher up the network. The main link types in a frame system indicate class membership between instances and classes, and between classes and super classes.

A frame representation of the semantic network (Figure 9) is shown below. It can be seen that this representation is simpler.

Generic frame *Stamping feature*:

   Feature ID:
   Coordinate position for base point:

Frame *Negative feature*:

   Inherit: *Stamping feature*
   Precision:

Frame *Hole*:
   Inherit: *Negative feature*
   Depth:
   Diameter:
   In:

Instance *Hole 7*:
   Instance of: *Hole*
   Feature ID = *H7*
   Coordinate for base point = *(30, 30, 6)*
   Internal precision = *[0, +0.05]*
   Depth = *5*
   Diameter = *10*
   In = *F13*

Frames are very powerful at inheritance-based inference due to their structured representation, and they perform adequately at analogical reasoning and reasoning about events and procedures [52]. Roschke [53] used frame-based representation to model traffic barriers, such as roadside barriers, median barriers, bridge rails and crash cushions, for a design advisory system of highway safety structures. Yau et al. [54] described an architectural floor plan design expert system that assists architects in checking their residential building floor plans against government building codes by employing a frame-based data structure that contains descriptions of the drawing objects, including their inter-relationships. Glass et al. [55] explored the suitability of frames for modeling design artifacts in the structural design domain. The representation facilitates the computation of design values and default values, integrity maintenance, and supporting explanation. Wang et al. [56] adopted a frame-based hierarchical structure to partition a complicated, conceptual, process design problem into sub-problems, which are handled by a set of knowledge units closely attached to the slots in frames.

3.1.4. Object-oriented representation

Object-oriented technology has become increasingly popular in the recent years as an extension to semantic networks and frame-based representations because it includes both language features and a design methodology [57]. The technology is based on objects, which are abstractions of real world entities or concepts. An object has the following characteristics [57]:

- identity: it is distinct from other objects,
- state: its internal conditions at a given moment of time, and
- behavior: operations that can change the state of the object and communicate with other objects.

In other words, an object contains both declarative and procedural knowledge.

An object-oriented system consists of objects that interact. Each object performs one or more tasks and invokes other objects to act by passing messages. A message is a request from one object to another asking it to perform one or more of its behaviors. In an object-oriented system there is no concept of a program in the traditional sense, instead objects collaborate to perform tasks and achieve goals. Objects can be related in three ways: *inheritance, aggregation* and *co-operation*. Inheritance involves *is-a* or *is-a-kind-of* relationships, e.g., *this* particular progressive die *is-a-kind-of* machine tool, the latter being the class. *Aggregation* involves *has* or *contains* relationships, e.g., *this* particular progressive die *contains (has)* four stations. *Co-operation* involves *uses* or *depends-on* relationships. *This* progressive die *depends-on* the de-coiler, which precedes it. All three relationships are needed to describe engineering systems.

The key characteristics of object-oriented representation are: *abstraction (classification), encapsulation, polymorphism* and *inheritance* [58]. *Classification* is a way to organize data and knowledge from specific facts to general facts. This is achieved in object technology through a set of definitions that specify the type of behavior and attributes of an object class. Specific instances of objects are created from this class through *inheritance*. *Classes* are factories for creating *objects*. *Inheritance* is the ability of an object (the child) to acquire the attributes and behavior of another object (the parent). Objects (children) can over-ride (re-define) the inherited characteristics of their parents. Thus inheritance permits both reusability (of code) and extendibility.

Encapsulation means the combining of attributes (data) and behavior into a single object in such a way that the implementation details are hidden from the other objects. Thus other objects do not need to know how to implement the behavior, they simply need to know how to invoke the behavior. This low level modularity greatly simplifies the design, coding and testing of software.

Polymorphism is the ability of different objects to perform the appropriate behavior in response to the same message. It enhances reuse of software by allowing generic software to be built. Polymorphism is automatically provided by inheritance.

Figure 10 illustrates these concepts. A *Hole* class is defined with attributes *Depth*, *Diameter*, and *In*. An instance of *Hole*, *Hole 7*, is created by instantiating the attribute slots with initial values. This isn't very different from the way an instance of *Hole* frame is created. However, the *Hole* class also defines a procedure (or method) for the object to carry out. Let it be *Perimeter ( ) = 3.1416 × (Diameter)^2/4*, to calculate the perimeter of the holes. The code for executing the method is contained at the class level (Figure 10). The method is invoked by a message sent to *Hole 7* to calculate its perimeter. *Hole 7* then looks to the class *Hole* for the method, which is performed using parameter values specified by *Hole 7*.

An example of a class-inheritance hierarchy is contained within Figure 9. It consists of all the features or entities joined by *is-a-kind-of* and *is-an-instance-of* relationships.

Since modeling of engineering systems can be performed very naturally with object-oriented representation, object-oriented programming (OOP) languages are now widely used, providing software modularity, reusability and scalability.

Akagi & Fujita [59] used an object-oriented architecture to support ship design. Tong & Gomory [60] provided a knowledge-based computer environment for electromechanical conceptual design using an object-oriented structure to model parts of standard electromechanical appliances. Part interactions are modeled using messages.

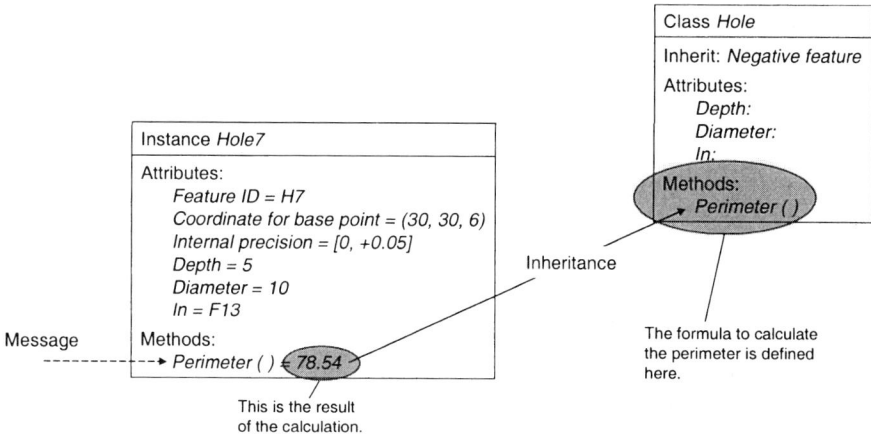

Figure 10. Object-oriented manipulation through messages and inheritance.

Gorti & Sriram [61] developed a conceptual product design support system over a layered, knowledge architecture, following the object-oriented principles of encapsulation and inheritance. In the field of building design, Clayton et al. [62] employed the concept of virtual components for automated reasoning to evaluate the emerging design. Using object-oriented classes, virtual components describe the parts of the building in terms of forms, functions and behaviors. Michalek & Papalambros [63] presented an interactive design optimization method for conceptual design of architectural floor plan layouts. During optimization an object-oriented representation allows the designer to interact with physically relevant building objects.

3.1.5. Logic-based representation

Logic programming is a technique for expressing knowledge in mathematical calculus with syntactic rules of deduction. Its two main components are propositional and predicate logic. Propositional logic is the study of the form of propositions, ignoring their content. It is therefore relevant in determining valid rules of inference. On its own it cannot represent knowledge efficiently because it does not contain any semantics.

On the other hand, predicate logic enables ideas about rules, objects, classes, propositions, properties, and other relationships to be expressed. It includes a deductive proof theory to generate valid inferences, using syntactic rules of deduction and semantic rules to interpret expressions. A statement in predicate logic takes the following form:

$$F(x_1, x_2, \ldots x_n)$$

where $x_1, x_2, \ldots x_n$ (the arguments) are the subjects (objects and events in the real world), F is the predicate, and n is the degree of the predicate.

Statements with $n = 1$ are called predicational statements. Essentially statements of this kind assign properties to objects and events. For example, the statement *Hole7 is round* would be expressed as *is round(Hole7)*, or in symbolic form $F_1(x_1)$, where F_1 denotes *is round* and x_1 denotes *Hole7*. More than one property can be assigned to an object or event by using a compound predicational statement $[F_1(x_1), F_2(x_1) \ldots F_n(x_1)]$. For example, the statement *Hole7 is round, has a diameter of 5 mm, and a depth of 14 mm* could be expressed as $[F_1(x_1), F_2(x_1), F_3(x_1)]$, where F_1 and x_1 are defined as before, F2 denotes *has a diameter of 5mm*, and F3 denotes *has a depth of 14 mm*.

Predicational statements are used to *identify* objects and events. This is achieved by specifying a set of properties necessary and sufficient to distinguish this particular object (event) from all other objects (events). They are also used to *classify* objects (events). In this case, a common property of the objects (events) is specified in the predicate and x represents the set of objects (events) that have this property.

Statements with $n > 2$ are called relational statements. For example, the statement *Hole7 lies between Hole6 and Hole9* can be expressed as $F_1(x_1, x_2, x_3)$, where F denotes *lies between*, x_1 denotes *Hole7*, x_2 denotes *Hole6*, x_3 denotes *Hole9*. The arguments of relational statements can be either constants (features in a design model), variables (unknown features), or functions (mapping of features).

Note that predicates with $n = 1$ are not very flexible for knowledge representation, but they can be combined using *connectives* such as 'And', 'Not', 'Equivalent', 'Or' and 'Implies', and quantifiers such as 'Universal' and 'Existential' to increase the expressional power substantially.

Use of predicate logic in engineering design involves more than just forming statements. The statements usually need to be evaluated to determine whether they are true or not. In addition, some statements may be conditional on other statements. So there needs to be means to check that the conditions have been met before proceeding.

As a final example, consider a stamping part with a *Flat2* that is adjacent to a feature *Bend3*. It might be necessary to determine all the features that *Flat2* is adjacent to. This can be achieved in predicate logic using the expression $F_1(x_1, x_2)$, where F_1 denotes *adjacent to*, x_1 denotes *Flat2*, and x_2 is a variable representing any other feature on the part. If the variable x_2 takes the value of *Bend3* then the evaluation of the statement is TRUE. This kind of evaluation is useful to determine whether design constraints and performance requirements have been met.

A formal theory using predicate logic has been formulated by Lakmazaheri & Rasdorf [64] to capture engineering design knowledge associated with the physical behavior of structural systems. A robust resolution theorem proving strategy is employed to support accurate analysis and synthesis. Rasdorf & Lakmazaheri [65] also used predicate logic and its resolution theorem proving strategy for representing and reasoning about the organization of design standards. Hoare [66] developed a systematic engineering design methodology using predicate logic to represent basic design concepts such as components, behaviors, assemblies and interactions.

Predicate logic can be integrated into a frame-based or object-oriented paradigm to improve its knowledge representation capabilities. For example, to provide formal computational support to an intelligent CAD process, Feijo et al. [67] proposed a hybrid agent architecture in which the symbolic automated reasoning is carried out by the first-order predicate logic. The reactive behavior of the agents is achieved through an object-oriented environment [68].

3.1.6. Fuzzy logic

Predicate logic is based on all or none membership. An object either has the properties specified or it does not, and a statement is either true or false. This is quite a severe limitation for design, because a designer may be uncertain about many aspects of the design in the early stages of design. There is no way to express this uncertainty using predicate logic. Fuzzy logic, a generalization of fuzzy set theory formalized by Zadeh [69], is a scientific approach for reasoning with imprecision or uncertainty.

In fuzzy logic, statements are made using qualitative properties, e.g., "low", "medium", "fairly high", or "very high". These are converted into mathematical statements, in a precise way. Uncertainty relates to membership of the sets defined by the qualitative properties. Thus, in a universe of discourse U, a fuzzy set A of U is defined by a membership function $\mu_A : U \rightarrow [0, 1]$. The membership function $\mu_A(x)$ expresses the degree of membership of each element x in the fuzzy set A, with 0 denoting no membership, 1 denoting full membership, and any other value between 0 and 1 denoting partial membership. Fuzzy inference rules define the way mathematical operations are applied to these fuzzy sets.

As an example, consider a stamping die for which an important property is cycle time. The cycle time will vary depending on the design of the die and the material. It is convenient to represent the feasible range of values for the cycle time using fuzzy logic. In the early design stages this range could be represented by three qualitative variables: *slow*, *normal* and *fast*. A fuzzy set defining the *Normal cycle time* might take the membership function:

$$\mu(x) = 1 - (x/10 - 1)^2,$$

as shown in Figure 11.

The interpretation of this figure is as follows. If the cycle time has a value of 10 seconds then the likelihood of it being denoted as *normal* is 1. On the other hand, if the cycle time is 2 seconds then the likelihood of it being denoted as *normal* is 0.35. Furthermore, a cycle time of 2 seconds will have a high probability, say 0.8, of being denoted as *fast*. Thus it can be seen that a quantitative property is associated with one or more qualitative properties through fuzzy set membership that is expressed as probabilities.

Fuzzy logic potentially has many successful applications in knowledge-based engineering design because the domain knowledge is usually imprecise, especially in the early design stage. Jones & Hua [70] proposed a fuzzy knowledge base to support routine engineering design, in which fuzzy logic is used to represent the range of variants on the available mechanisms in the knowledge base. Shragowitz et al. [71] adopted a fuzzy logic structure in conjunction with constructive and iterative algorithms for selection of design solutions for different stages of the design process, including utilization

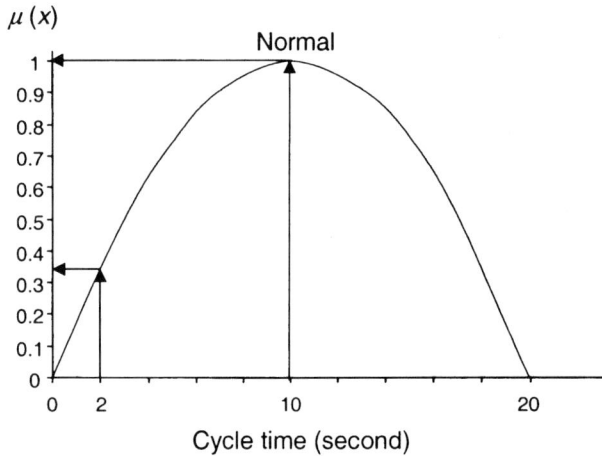

Figure 11. Membership function of cycle time.

of domain knowledge, interpretation of uncertainties in design data, and adaptation of design algorithms. Wang [72] proposed a fuzzy outranking preference model to evaluate alternative design concepts. Qin et al. [73] developed a real-time and fuzzy logic based sketch tool for mechanical conceptual design. The fuzzy knowledge is applied to capture the user's drawing intention in terms of sketching position, direction, speed and acceleration.

Fuzzy logic can be easily incorporated into other knowledge-based representations, such as rule-based or object-oriented representation. Shehab & Abdalla [74] presented an object-oriented and rule-based system for product cost modeling and design for automation at an early design stage. Fuzzy logic is incorporated to handle the uncertainty in the cost estimation model, which could not be easily addressed by traditional analytical methods.

3.2. Generic knowledge-based techniques

This section discusses generic knowledge-based techniques: control strategies, search strategies, constraint processing, case-based reasoning, and blackboard architecture.

3.2.1. Control strategies

Control strategies are used to generate conclusions from facts, *forward-chaining*, or to prove a conclusion against facts, *backward-chaining*. Forward-chaining starts from specified facts and knowledge. Using these facts and rules of inference it moves in a connected sequence (chain) to a final conclusion. Backward-chaining starts from a conclusion, the hypothesis, and moves backward in a chain to prove this hypothesis against the existing facts. Although both strategies can be used independently, it is more common for them to be used in combination, especially if the knowledge database is large.

The chaining concepts will be illustrated by a simple example of a partial rule-based system to troubleshoot an automatic film feeding unit for packaging pharmaceuticals. This knowledge might consist of the following set of rules:

Rule 1:
  IF   the film gang-track device is working
  AND   the film doesn't move
  THEN the film transmission system is faulty

Rule 2:
  IF   the film transmission system is faulty
  AND   the gear pair is working
  THEN the film wheel-feeding device is faulty

Rule 3:
  IF   the film wheel-feeding device is faulty
  AND   the driving wheel is working
  AND   the driven wheel is not working
  THEN adjust the distance between both wheels

Assume the working memory contains the following facts:

F1. The film gang-track device is working
F2. The film doesn't move
F3. The gear pair is working
F4. The driving wheel is working
F5. The driven wheel is not working

These rules may be used in a causal chain of forward reasoning to deduce the troubleshooting method. In forward-chaining, a rule is selected for execution when its conditions are satisfied. Facts *F1* and *F2* exist therefore *Rule 1* is executed first, resulting in a new fact "the film transmission system is faulty". With this new fact and fact *F3*, *Rule 2* is executed resulting in a new fact "the film wheel-feeding device is faulty". Finally because of the existence of this new fact and facts *F4* and *F5*, *Rule 3* is executed to determine the troubleshooting method as "adjust the distance between both wheels".

Backward-chaining is the reverse control strategy. Suppose we want to prove the troubleshooting method is "adjust the distance between both wheels"; this is the hypothesis. The aim is to find a chain of facts and rules linking the existing facts to the hypothesis. The hypothesis matches the action side of *Rule 3*, whose condition parts are *F4*, *F5* and "the film wheel-feeding device is faulty". *F4* and *F5* exist, so the new hypothesis becomes "the film wheel-feeding device is faulty". This matches the action side of *Rule 2*, whose condition parts are *F3* and "the film transmission system is faulty". *F3* exists so the new hypothesis becomes "the film transmission system is faulty". This matches against the action side of *Rule 1*, whose condition parts are *F1* and *F2*, which exist. Therefore the verification procedure terminates with success, and the troubleshooting method "adjust the distance between both wheels" is supported by the facts.

Akagi & Fujita [59] developed an object-oriented architecture for ship design. Both forward- and backward-chaining approaches are employed to implement the message passing. The selection of chaining approach depends on the search requirements. The former is used to recognize how the original values of the assigned variables should be changed so as to satisfy the design requirement, while the latter is used to determine the appropriate values of the variables starting from the design requirement. Tong & Gomory [60] employed a backward-chaining control strategy to search for standard electromechanical parts represented in an object-oriented structure. Melli & Sciubba [75] employed a backward-chaining control strategy across equipment and resource object libraries to support an automatic procedure for selecting the most convenient process configuration for a given set of design goals. In the conceptual design application of grippers for handling fabrics, Moulianitis et al. [42] use a forward-chaining approach to determine the type of the grippers, the general characteristics of the grippers and the auxiliary equipment from the requirements for the handling process. In the design of roll pass and profile sequences for shape rolling of round and square bars, Kim & Im [43] employed a backward-chaining control strategy for the inference engine to determine the manufacturing sequences in reverse order, based on design rules extracted from the literature.

3.2.2. Search strategies

Search strategies are used to locate knowledge and facts in a knowledge database. Two kinds of search strategies are widely used: *uninformed* and *informed search*. An uninformed search has no information about the path from the current state to the goal state, and explores all possible alternatives blindly. Uninformed search strategies include *depth-first search* and *breadth-first search*.

With depth-first search, the state space is searched by exploring all possible paths to the desired goal state. When a state is examined, all of its descendant states are examined until it either reaches the goal state or a dead end. Consider the search tree represented in Figure 12, in which, the starting state is labeled as *S*, the goal state is labeled as *G*, and the intermediate states are labeled as *A1, A2, B1, B2, B3*, etc. Depth-first search examines the states in the order of *S, A1, B1, B2, D1, D2, B3, A2, C1, F1, F2, C2, H1, K1, K2, H2* and *G*. Note that when a dead end, e.g., state *B1*, is encountered, the depth-first search backtracks to the nearest ancestor state *A1*, to see whether it has any unexplored alternatives. In this case, the procedure move forwards, via the state *B2*, and eventually reaches the goal state *G*. The memory requirements of depth-first search vary linearly with the number of levels of depth, and thus are very modest. A drawback of depth-first search is that it may become trapped in an infinite loop, never finding a goal state.

Hart & Rodriguez [76] employed a depth-first search for preliminary shape synthesis of structural and mechanical elements in the conceptual design.

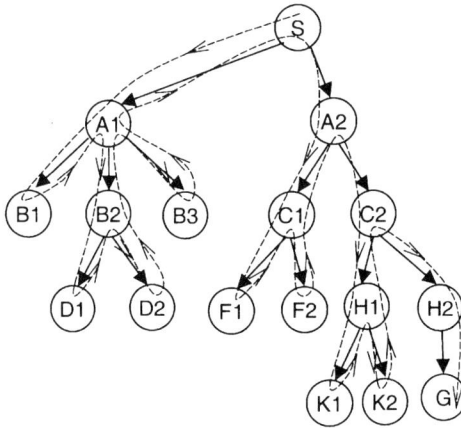

Figure 12. Search tree for depth-first search example.

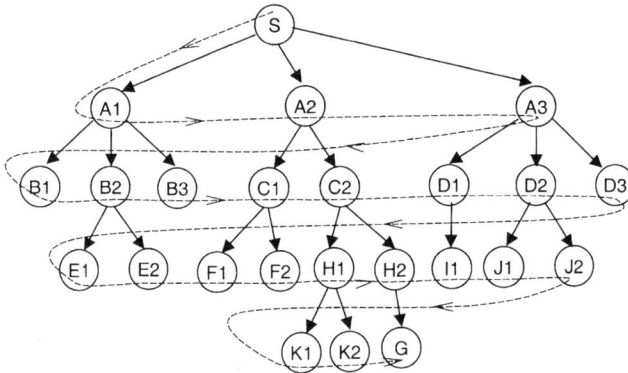

Figure 13. Search tree for breadth-first search example.

In contrast, breadth-first search is a very systematic strategy because the state space is examined one level at a time before going to the next deeper level. Figure 13 depicts the breadth-first search procedures in the order of S, A1, A2, A3, B1, B2, B3, C1, C2, D1, D2, D3, E1, E2, F1, F2, H1, H2, I1, J1, J2, K1, K2 and G. Unlike depth-first search, breadth-first search will not be trapped in infinite loops, but it can be less efficient as it explores more possible paths.

Melli & Sciubba [75] used a breadth-first search in the equipment and resource object libraries to develop all technically feasible combinations of components.

Research in AI has resulted in advances in informed search strategies that employ rules of thumb to reduce the size of the search space, instead of blindly exploring all possible alternatives. The strategies include *hill climbing search*—simple hill climbing,

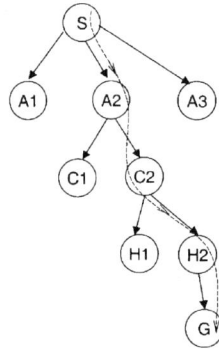

Figure 14. Search tree for hill climbing search example.

generalized hill climbing, ordinal hill climbing and steepest-ascent hill climbing algorithms [77, 78], and *best-first heuristic search* - A*, IDA* (iterative deepening A*) and
SMA* (simplified memory-bounded A*) algorithms [79].

A hill climbing search applies a local, heuristic, evaluation function at each step in
the path to determine the direction of the next step. Figure 14 depicts a hill climbing
search procedure resulting in the order S, A2, C2, H2 and G. Starting at S, state A2
is closest to the goal state G compared to its sibling states A1 and A3, so it is chosen.
A2 is expanded to give descendent states C1 and C2. Next state C2 is chosen rather
than state C1. C2 is expanded to give states H1 and H2. H2 is selected and the goal
state G is achieved. Note that one of the drawbacks of hill climbing search is that it
makes irrevocable decisions based on local information. This may result in a local best
solution but not a global best solution.

Sullivan & Jacobson [78] employed ordinal hill climbing algorithms to solve discrete
manufacturing process design optimization problems. Their method combines the
search space reduction feature of ordinal optimization with the global search feature
of generalized hill climbing algorithms.

As in hill climbing, a best-first heuristic search process applies a heuristic evaluation
function at each step to move to the next step. However it differs from a hill climbing
search in one important aspect. Previous states, which were rejected, are re-evaluated
at each step and so this method can find a global best solution. Figure 15 depicts a best-
first search procedure resulting in the order S, A2, C2, A3, C1, H1, H2 and G. Starting
at S, state A2 is best compared to its sibling states A1 and A3, so it is selected. State A2
is expanded to give descendent states C1 and C2. State C2 is best compared to other
unexplored states, including A1, A3 and C1, so it is selected. State C2 is expanded
to give states H1 and H2. Now, unexplored state A3 is best compared to other states,
including A1, C1, H1 and H2. State A3 is expanded to give states D1, D2 and D3.
The next best state is C1, which is expanded to F1 and F2. Finally state H2 is selected
and results in the goal state G. A best-first search can find a global optimum because
it re-evaluates previous states, but is computationally more expensive due to this.

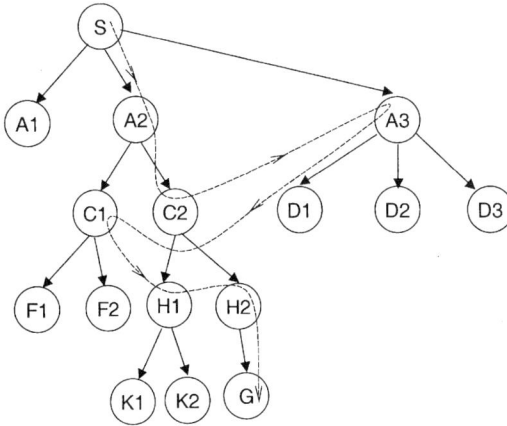

Figure 15. Search tree for best-first heuristic search example.

Moulianitis et al. [42] employed a combination of depth-first and best-first heuristic search strategies in rule-based reasoning for the conceptual design of grippers for handling fabrics. The best-first search strategy finds a final solution from a set of feasible solutions produced by an initial depth-first search process, and can synthesize new solutions to accomplish the required specifications.

3.2.3. Constraint processing

Constraints are fundamental to design problems. They are used to restrict the range of values of design variables and the allowable relationships between two or more attributes or variables. There are two types of constraints in the design domain: *hard* and *soft* [80]. The former can only be either wholly satisfied or violated, while the latter can be met by degree. The main aim of using constraints in engineering design is to minimize the search space, by evaluating the current assignment of values to design variables against the allowable values, and propagating the constraint information through the constraint network, circumscribing the design, to remove violating search branches. This is known as the *Constraint Satisfaction Problem* (CSP) [81], which is solved using constraint processing techniques.

Figure 16 shows an illustrative constraint network for bolt, nut and washer objects. Each bolt, nut, or washer object has instances as follows: *bolt1*, *bolt2*, *bolt3*, *nut1*, *nut2*, *washer1* and *washer2*. Table 2 shows some of their attributes including *thread_diameter*, *internal_diameter*, and *head_width*. The constraints are represented by the expressions:

C1: *bolt.thread_diameter* = *nut.thread_diameter*
C2: *bolt.thread_diameter* < *washer.internal_diameter* < *bolt.head_width*

In Figure 16, configuration design starts from the selection of the first component, e.g., bolt, with three alternatives, *bolt1*, *bolt2* and *bolt3*. They are further expanded to

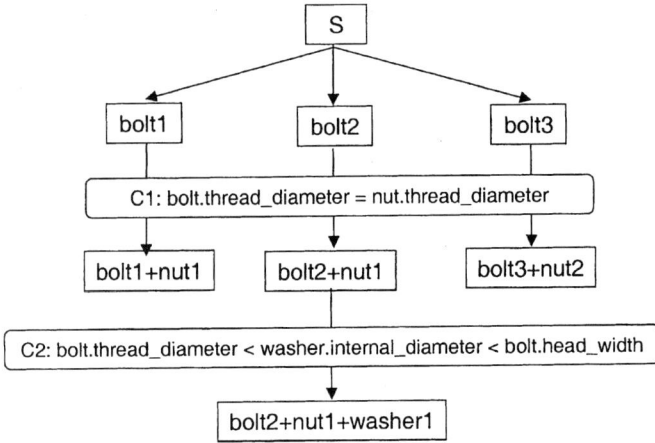

Figure 16. Example of constraint network for configuration design.

produce three new alternatives, *bolt1* + *nut1*, *bolt2* + *nut1*, and *bolt3* + *nut2*, subject to the imposed constraint *C1*. Note that the other alternatives don't work, e.g., *bolt1* cannot be connected to *nut2* because the constraint *C1* would be violated (evaluate to False). Finally only *bolt2* + *nut1* + *washer1* is developed as a design solution subject to the imposed constraint *C2*. The other two alternatives are discarded because no washer can be found to satisfy the constraint *C2*.

Constraints may be handled flexibly by means of a variety of formalisms including rules, semantic networks, frames, objects, predicate logic, fuzzy logic, etc., thus allowing them to be easily integrated into any type of engineering design or any stage of a design process. Takanori [82] proposed an object-oriented and constraint-based knowledge representation system for design object modeling. Constraints are described in declarative form and added to objects dynamically, thus facilitating constraint propagation among objects. Guan & Gerhard [83] applied fuzzy control to the *constraint satisfaction problem* (CSP) for structural design. Allowing constraints to be fuzzy helps to optimize the design by reasoning about the degree to which they are satisfied, which avoids the static classification of constraints into hard and soft. Wu et al. [84] presented a mechanical system constraint model for design change propagation and change management, by formally defining entity relationships using first order predicate logic, and modeling assembly related geometry constraints using predicates. Hassan [85] proposed the use of constraint networks to model knowledge for concurrent product and process design. In the proposed constraint networks, a number of design constraints are formulated and modeled using rule-based representation. To support the conceptual design process, O'Sullivan & Bowen [86] modeled design entities as frames in a constraint programming language, and then developed a frame-based constraint network to assist designers in reasoning out design concepts that are consistent with restrictions imposed on the design. Finally, it should be noted that a number

Table 2 Attributes of components' instances

Component name	Attributes		
	Thread_Diameter	Internal_Diameter	Head_Width
Bolt1	10		14
Bolt2	10		18
Bolt3	20		28
Nut1	10		
Nut2	20		
Washer1		15	
Washer2		30	

of commercial CAD systems allow constraint based processing. This is usually coupled with design-by-features capability.

3.2.4. Case-based reasoning

Case-based reasoning (CBR) is based on the recall and reuse of past experiences. The foundation of CBR lies in the psychological theory of human recognition [87]. CBR usually involves the following steps: representation of cases, indexing of cases, retrieval of cases through similarity analysis, adaptation of the retrieved cases, and storing of new cases in the case library for future usage.

It is widely accepted that common design practices rely heavily on searching and reusing past design experiences to solve new problems, instead of designing everything ab initio. The design experiences may be encoded symbolically and manipulated using the previously discussed representation schemes. Figure 17 shows a high-level framework of CBR for the design of engineering systems.

CBR has been successfully applied to design problems where experience is strong and data is rich, but the domain model is weak or design theory is poor. Goel & Chandrasekaran [88] developed a case-based design system for mechanical devices using structure-behavior-function models. Behaviors express how the devices' structural elements achieve their functions. The cases are indexed and retrieved based on the functions associated with the designs in the case library. Falting [89] represented architectural design cases as existing floor plans using networks of geometric constraints, and implemented case adaptation using algorithms for constraint satisfaction problem solving. Rivard & Fenves [90] applied CBR in conceptual building design with a case library implemented in an object-oriented database management system. Kwong [91] adopted CBR for process design of injection molding. The case library is organized as a combination of a linear list and a hierarchy of classes of cases. Stefania & Sara [92] used CBR, combined with fuzzy indexing and fuzzy retrieval, to design compounds for tire treads.

Note that other knowledge-based techniques are frequently used with CBR, not only to represent design cases intelligently, but also to produce design cases to populate the initial case library.

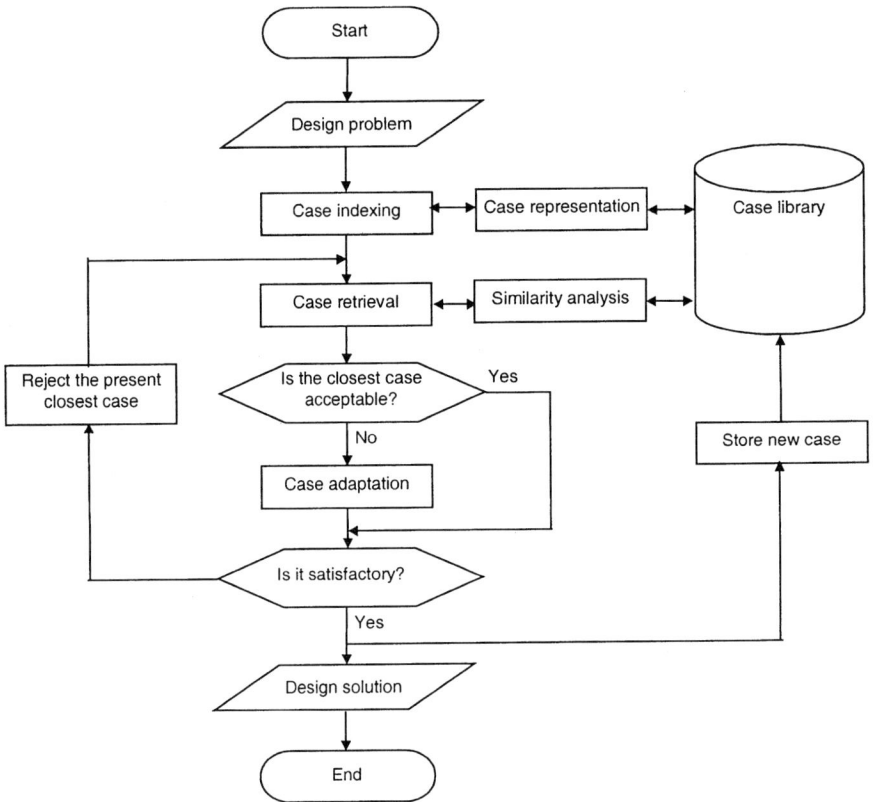

Figure 17. High-level framework of CBR for the design of engineering systems.

3.2.5. Blackboard architecture

Blackboard problem solving involves cooperative decision-making between software programs that contain different kinds of expert knowledge. These are referred to as knowledge sources (KS's). Each KS develops a partial solution of a design problem based on its expertise. The partial solutions are posted in a common area, called the blackboard. The KS's revise their solutions on the basis of the other KS solutions. The final solution is achieved when all the partial solutions meet their requirements and constraints.

The basic structure of a blackboard architecture contains partitioned KS's, the blackboard, and a control module (Figure 18). KS's may be expressed using any of the representation techniques described previously. Partitioning of the knowledge, and hence the KS's, is domain specific. The blackboard is a globally accessible database containing relevant data and partial solutions. It is shared by the cooperating KS's. The control module is used to monitor the changes on the blackboard and control the interactions to ensure a solution is achieved.

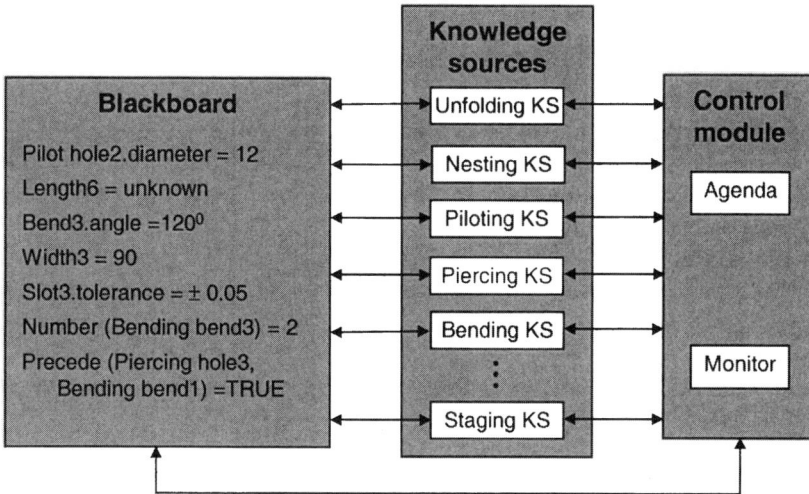

Figure 18. An illustrative blackboard architecture for stamping process planning.

Figure 18 shows an illustrative, blackboard architecture for stamping process planning. In this case the blackboard might contain input data, stamping features, stamping operations, and the evolving stamping process plan.

A blackboard architecture is well suited for constructive problem solving where the problem space is large and knowledge from many different sources must be integrated to achieve a solution. Thompson & Lu [93] used a blackboard architecture for concurrent product and process design. Urban et al. [94] described an object-oriented database system with blackboard architecture to support integration and communication between different CAD tools. Kwong et al. [95] employed a blackboard-based approach for concurrent process design of injection molding. Different areas of production knowledge are represented by KS's that are composed using rules, frames, objects and procedures. Roy & Liao [96] developed an automated fixture design system using a blackboard architecture. The KS's are represented as procedures, collections of rules, algorithms or geometric reasoning methods. Chau & Albermani [97] developed a prototype KBES for the preliminary design of liquid retaining structures using a blackboard architecture combined with hybrid knowledge representation techniques, including production rule and object-oriented approaches.

4. KNOWLEDGE-BASED APPLICATION IN FUNCTIONAL DESIGN

In engineering design, products are designed with some purpose in mind. The design intent can be described as the product's function [98]. Functional design [7] is a relatively new perspective in design research. It is especially applicable to the early stages of design when the physical structure of the product is not known or defined. Its objective is to provide computer tools to link design functions with the structural (physical)

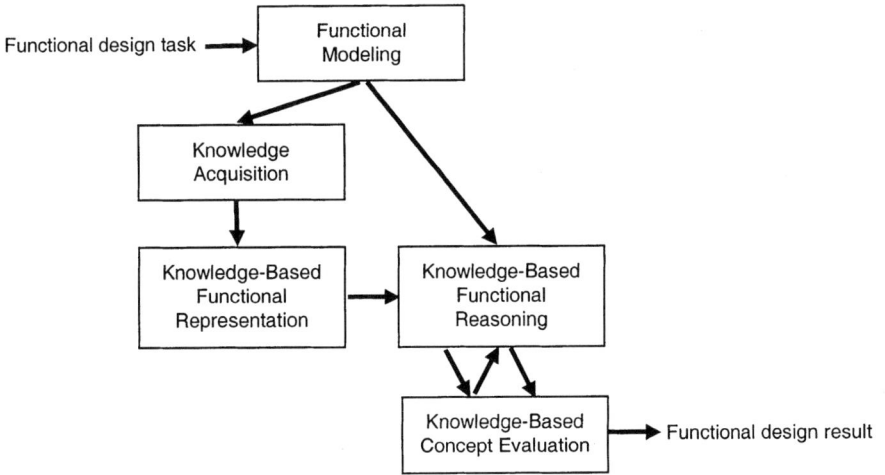

Figure 19. Activity flow in integrated knowledge-based functional design framework.

embodiments used to realize the functions. Considerable research advances have been made in functional modeling [5, 6, 99, 100] over the last two decades. This section presents an integrated knowledge-based system for functional design automation of mechanical products, which was developed by the authors at the Design Research Center, Nanyang Technological University, Singapore. It demonstrates clearly how a number of different techniques can be combined to provide a powerful, yet effective, expert system for design.

The proposed functional design paradigm (Figure 19) covers five design activities: functional modeling, knowledge acquisition, knowledge-based functional representation, knowledge-based functional reasoning, and knowledge-based concept evaluation. Functional modeling models a design and requirements from their functional aspects and permits reasoning about design functions. The acquisition of functional design knowledge plays an important role in the development of a knowledge-based system for functional design. The acquired functional design knowledge should be represented in an executable knowledge base properly, so as to allow knowledge-based functional reasoning and man–machine communication. Due to the large design space for behavioral configurations, a powerful search method is used to narrow the search during knowledge-based functional reasoning. The method evaluates design alternatives during functional reasoning and uses the results to guide reasoning.

4.1. B-FES functional modeling framework

The Behavior-driven Function-Environment-Structure (B-FES) functional modeling framework [101] is the latest of a family of evolving, functional modeling frameworks that have been developed by our research group since 1998 [7, 101, 102]. It defines the ontology underlying our expert system.

Figure 20 shows the main features of the B-FES functional modeling framework. It consists of three layers: function, behavior and environment. The function layer defines relations among functions. For example a function may be supported by supportive functions or it may be decomposed into sub-functions. The behavior layer describes how a desired function is achieved by a set of interacting behaviors. The environment layer describes the working environment within which the design object operates. Though the functional modeling framework is not characterized by structures explicitly, a structure is implicitly involved in a behavior in the behavior layer, because the structural configuration is determined once the behavioral schema is fixed.

Three salient features of this functional modeling framework are Functional Supportive Synthesis (FSS), Causal Behavioral Inference (CBI) and functional decomposition. FSS is used to develop supporting functions. Functional decomposition is used to decompose functions into sub-functions. To prevent the domain problem being decomposed "too fine", a behavior-driven modeling strategy has been implemented to ensure that a desired function will not be decomposed unless a matching behavior can not be found to achieve the desired function. Here, behavior is represented as input-output flow-of-action in terms of driving input (a kind of functional requirement), behavior actor (structure), and functional output (intended output action) [102].

In the behavior layer, behaviors are interconnected to each other, with one's functional output matching the other's driving input to form a causal behavioral process (CBP) network [102]. The behavior-driven reasoning process on the CBP network is defined as Causal Behavioral Inference (CBI). The reasoning process is terminated when all the newly generated functional requirements during FSS, CBI and functional decomposition process can be satisfied by the environment.

Generally, a desired function (overall functional requirement, sub-function, driving input of a retrieved behavior, or supportive function) can be accomplished using one of the following generalized B-FES path types:

• B-FES path type I: achieved by a set of interconnected behaviors through CBI.
• B-FES path type II: supported by supportive functions through FSS, which are then achieved by a set of interconnected behaviors through CBI.
• B-FES path type III: decomposed into sub-functions through functional decomposition, which are then achieved by a set of interconnected behaviors through CBI.

In practice, several path types are used to define a particular design configuration.

4.2. Acquisition of functional design knowledge through two-level knowledge modeling

The acquisition of functional design knowledge has been a significant hurdle in the use of knowledge-based techniques for functional design, mainly because different experts use different frameworks to organize their knowledge. The B-FES framework provides a common framework for acquiring design knowledge. In our approach the acquisition of functional design knowledge is a cyclic and collaborative modeling process between domain experts and knowledge engineers, rather than a prototyping process. New

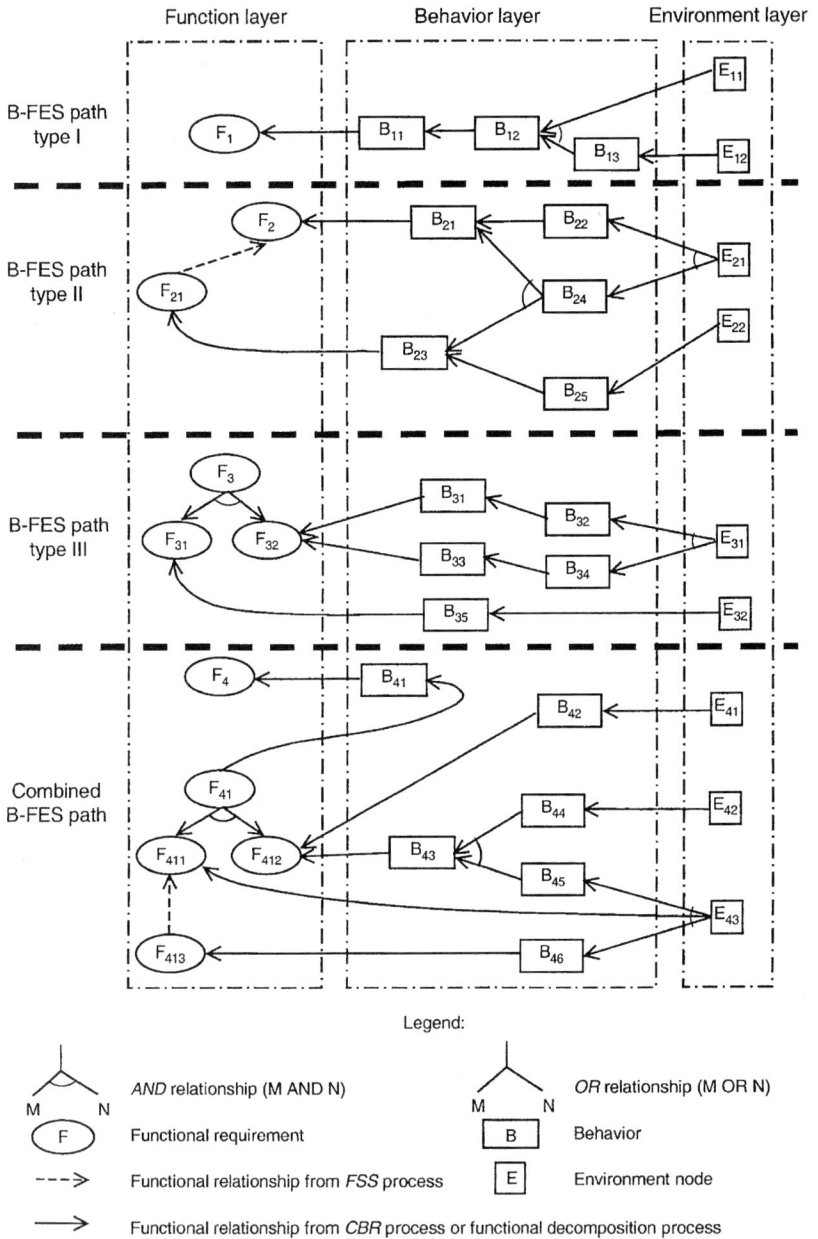

Figure 20. Features of B-FES functional modeling framework [101]. (From INTERNATIONAL JOURNAL OF PRODUCTION RESEARCH, "Guiding functional design through rule-based casual behavioural reasoning," S. B. Tor, G. A. Britton and W. Y. Zhang, 40, pp. 667–682, copyright notice of Taylor & Francis, http://www.tandf.co.uk.)

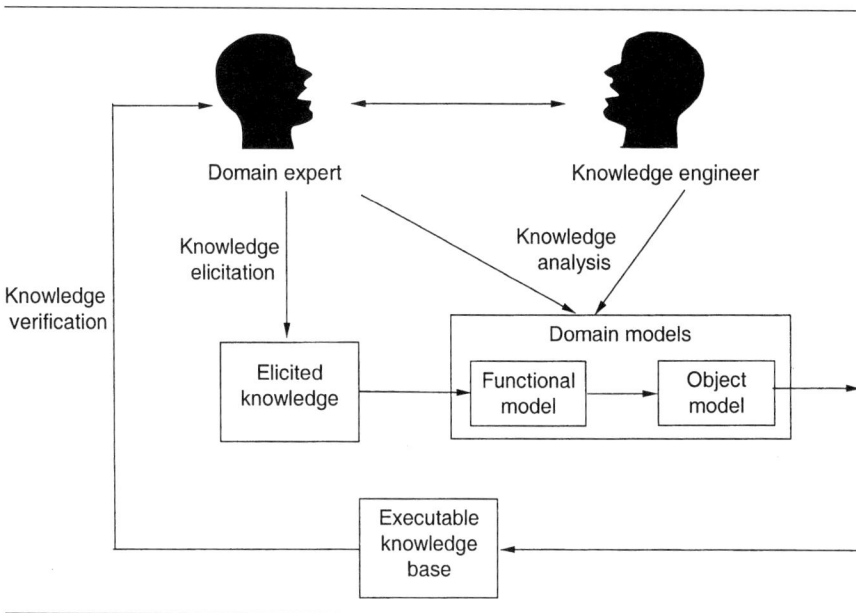

Figure 21. Acquistion of functional design knowledge through knowledge modeling [20]. (Springer-Verlag, INTERNATIONAL JOURNAL OF ADVANCED MANUFACTURING TECHNOLOGY, "A two-level modelling approach to acquire functional design knowledge in mechanical engineering systems," W. Y. Zhang, S. B. Tor and G. A. Britton, 19, pp. 454–460, figure 2, 2002, copyright notice of Springer-Verlag.)

observations may lead to a refinement or modification of existing models, and the models can guide further knowledge acquisition. The acquisition process is shown in Figure 21. It consists of knowledge elicitation, knowledge analysis and knowledge verification activities.

Knowledge elicitation covers the interactions with domain experts through a series of knowledge acquisition sessions in order to elicit knowledge about the domain. The elicited knowledge is analyzed in the knowledge analysis activity in order to structure it and develop models of the domain. The domain models are used as a communication medium between domain experts and knowledge engineers, to aid in structuring and describing the domain independently of the implementation. A two-level approach is used to create the domain models: the functional and the object models [20]. The functional model serves as a basis for communication between domain experts and knowledge engineers, while the object model is used to bridge the gap between the functional model and an executable knowledge base. The formalized representation of functional design knowledge is presented to domain experts for knowledge verification.

As described earlier, the B-FES functional modeling framework was originally developed to guide functional design through functional reasoning steps including functional supportive synthesis (FSS), causal behavioral inference (CBI) and functional decomposition. However it can also facilitate the knowledge modeling process by providing a medium for experts to model their valuable, but difficult-to-articulate, knowledge in terms with which they are familiar. Hence the B-FES functional model can improve the knowledge acquisition process by developing and improving representational devices available to the experts and knowledge engineer.

Compared to the functional model, the object model is a more comprehensive model of the domain describing each design characteristic (e.g., function, behavior, structure) as a design object. The proposed formalism for the design object is an object-oriented functional representation scheme [103]. The object model provides a description of the domain that is as complete as possible, and facilitates representing causal knowledge modularly as well. This is achieved by representing functional design knowledge in classes of objects (e.g., function objects, behavior objects and structure objects) including their design attributes, and about how objects interact with each other.

4.3. Knowledge-based functional representation scheme

This sub-section will show how functional design knowledge is represented in an executable knowledge base by integrating several knowledge-based representation techniques; the main ones being rule-based representation, fuzzy logic and object-oriented representation. The application of the techniques will be illustrated using an example of a knowledge base for the design of a film feeding unit for pharmaceutical products.

4.3.1. Rule-based representation in rule base

Two kinds of production rules are presented here: general rules and domain-specific rules. General rules refer to a set of rules that are used to solve general problems. Domain-specific rules are a set of rules used to solve domain dependent problems.

One example of a general production rule is formulated as follows (in pseudo code):

Rule *General_CBI*:
    IF   a desired function is matched with a behavior in the behavior base
    THEN retrieve this behavior object to develop the design alternative
    AND   continue this searching branch

This general rule is used to search for a matching behavior with functional output matching a desired function. The rule is applied every time a design alternative is updated.

Examples of the domain-specific rules for a film feeding unit are:

Rule *Specific_Decompose1*
    IF   a desired function is *Provide low speed rotational motion within a certain range*
    AND   it needs to be decomposed
    THEN decompose it into *Provide low speed rotational motion*
    AND   *Control moving range*

This is a functional decomposition rule. It will be executed when a function cannot be matched directly by a behavior in the knowledge database. This kind of rule is used to facilitate the subsequent causal behavior inference.

Rule *Specific_FSS1*

    IF   a desired function is *Feed film*

    AND   it has not been supported

    THEN a supportive function *Guide film through track* needs to be synthesized

This rule generates a supportive function for a function. It is only invoked if no support is provided to a desired function, but needed.

4.3.2. *Fuzzy logic in FMCDM model base*

A Fuzzy Multi-Criteria Decision-Making (FMCDM) evaluation model has been incorporated to evaluate alternative design configurations. The universe of discourse is a finite set of fuzzy numbers used to express an imprecise level of performance rating (of the behaviors) and the weights of the different criteria used for evaluation. For example, *speed* is defined by a range of imprecise levels with the following linguistic values: *extremely low, very low, low to very low, low, fairly low, medium, fairly high, high, high to very high, very high, extremely high*. A conversion scale for numerical approximation is used to transform a linguistic value into a triangular or trapezoidal fuzzy number, following the approach of Chen et al. [104]. Each of the linguistic values is associated with at least one fuzzy set. There are eight different scales of the converted linguistic values, ranging from the smallest scale (scale no. 1), which has only two linguistic values ("medium" and "high"), to the largest scale (scale no. 8), which has all the linguistic values (from "extremely low" to "extremely high"). The designer selects the scale according to the precision requirements.

Figure 22 depicts the first and fifth scales. Scale 1 contains only two linguistic values and scale 5 contains seven. The scales are not only dissimilar in that the number of linguistic values are different, but also the shape and location of the fuzzy sets for the same value vary. This reflects the fact that the same linguistic value, e.g., *medium*, may possess different meanings on different occasions.

The different conversion scales take into account the user's ability in classifying the performance rating and weight of each criterion. For instance, if a designer selects the performance rating criterion *manufacturability* and the linguistic values "very low", "fairly high" and "high", then scale 5 is adequate and would be selected. If the designer selects *assemblability* and the linguistic values "medium" and "high" then, although all scales contain these values, only the simplest scale (scale 1) would be chosen.

Once a designer has assigned each linguistic variable (performance rating and weight of each criterion) design alternatives can be evaluated by the FMCDM model, as will be illustrated later on.

4.3.3. *Knowledge-based functional representation in an object-oriented behavior base*

With knowledge-based functional representation scheme, behaviors are defined as intelligent design objects encapsulating functional design knowledge. The most generic behaviors are represented as the top-most generic class object. This class of object is defined as follows:

a) Scale no. 1

b) Scale no. 5

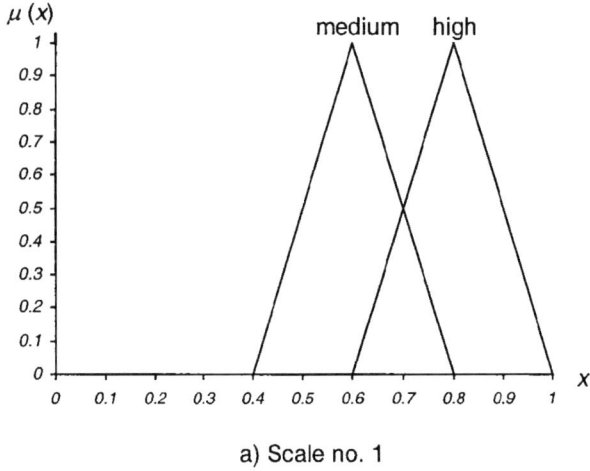

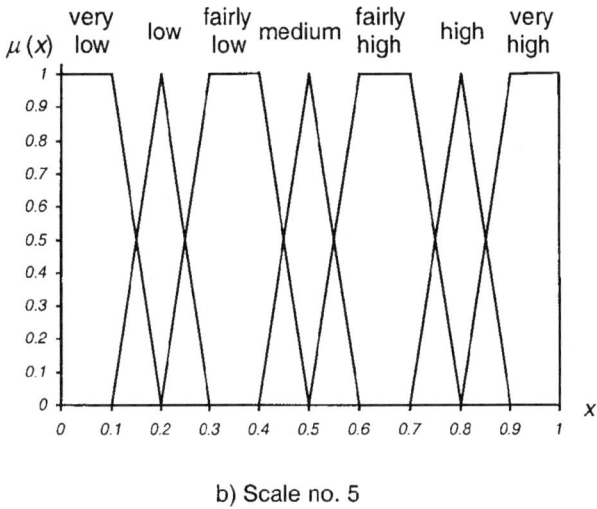

Figure 22. Linguistic conversion scales for numerical approximation [104]. (Springer-Verlag, FUZZY MULTIPLE ATTRIBUTE DECISION MAKING: METHODS AND APPLICATIONS, S.-J. Chen, C.-L. Hwang and F. P. Hwang, figure 5.45, 1992, copyright notice of Springer-Verlag.)

Class Behavior {
    Basic design attributes:
        Name:
        Behavior_Type:
        Behavior_Actor (Structure):
        Driving_Inputs:
        Functional_Outputs:
        ....

(Fuzzy) Design constraints satisfaction attributes:
    Precision:
    ....
(Fuzzy) Performance ratings of design criteria:
    Manufacturability:
    Assemblability:
    ....
General rule subset:
    General_CBI;
    General_FSS;
    General_Decomposition;
    ....
Methods:
    Input_Data ( );
    FMCDM_Method ( );
    ....
}

As shown in the above pseudo codes, the generic class *Behavior* integrates declarative knowledge (basic design attributes), fuzzy knowledge (design constraints satisfaction attributes and performance ratings of design criteria), heuristic knowledge (rule subset) and procedural knowledge (methods). The general rule subset includes some attached general rules such as *General_CBI*, *General_FSS* and *General_Decomposition*. The attached rule subset can control the relevant design procedures related to this behavior object. The methods such as *Input_Data ( )* and *FMCDM_Method ( )* allow the behavior objects to be defined without repetition of the basic procedural programs. For example, *FMCDM_Method ( )* is used to calculate the weighted performance rating aggregation of the retrieved device behavior.

With the inheritance mechanism from object-oriented technology, any other lower-level behavior class can be represented as the child class object of the generic class *Behavior*. It can inherit the latter's slots, and also add specific slots pertinent to itself. The behavior classes can be instantiated with concrete design values to result in instances of behaviors. Some domain-specific rule subset may also be included in the behavior instances. Thus the object-oriented representation is very convenient for maintenance and modification of the behavior base.

4.4. Knowledge-based functional reasoning strategy

Figure 23 is a flow diagram of the proposed knowledge-based functional reasoning strategy [105] in a backward-chaining control structure, that includes three functional reasoning steps: knowledge-based Functional Supportive Synthesis (FSS) process, knowledge-based Causal Behavioral Inference (CBI) process and knowledge-based functional decomposition process.

The system begins *FSS* by firstly deciding whether a functional requirement requires supportive functions. This is achieved by means of relevant domain-specific FSS

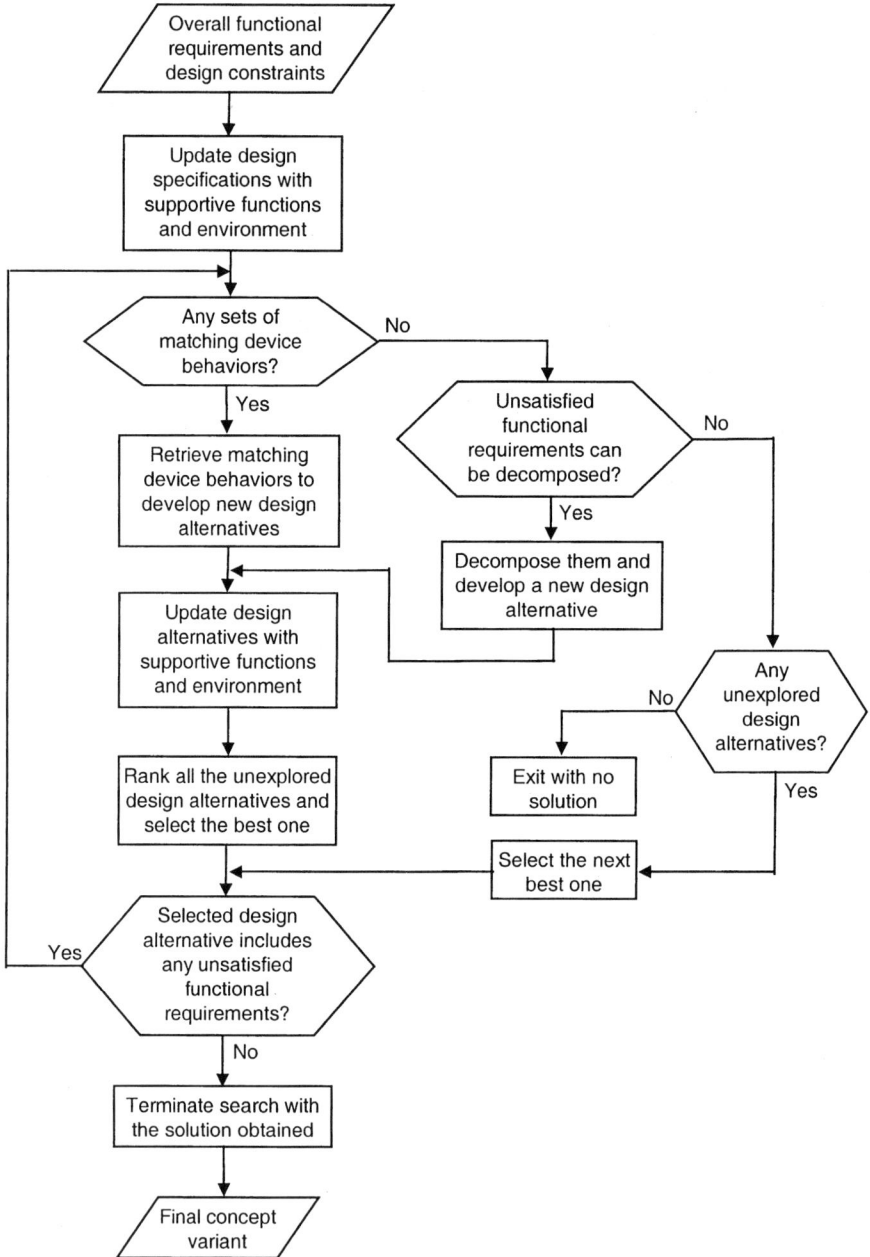

Figure 23. Knowledge-based functional reasoning strategy [105]. (Springer-Verlag, INTERNATIONAL JOURNAL OF ADVANCED MANUFACTURING TECHNOLOGY, "A heuristic state-space approach to the functional design of mechanical systems," W. Y. Zhang, S. B. Tor and G. A. Britton, 19, pp. 235–244, figure 3, 2002, copyright notice of Springer-Verlag.)

rules. If applicable, the relevant functions are created as supportive functions, which in turn become new functional requirements. The system will then check whether some or all functional requirements are satisfied by the environment (matched by the environmental outputs), and match the corresponding ones to update the design specification.

The system then searches the object-oriented behavior base for device behaviors whose functional outputs match some or all of the functional requirements, using CBI. The search criteria include design constraints and function integration (if applicable). A single physical mechanical device often implements several functional requirements simultaneously [41, 106]. Thus it is preferable to create a behavioral schema of mechanical devices that maximize function integration. This usually results in a more compact and less costly design.

If there are several sets of device behaviors that achieve all functional requirements, they will be retrieved to form a group of new design alternatives, with their driving inputs becoming new functional requirements. If there is no device behavior to match the functional requirements the function will be decomposed to generate new sub-functions. These sub-functions will then processed in the manner described above.

When there are two or more design alternatives, the system will rank all the un-explored design alternatives according to their evaluation indexes and select the one that it is best. Evaluation is performed using the best-first heuristic search method. If the selected design alternative consists of only physical specifications (a set of retrieved device behaviors) that satisfy all functional requirements, it is adopted as the design solution and the process terminates. Otherwise, the system repeats, using the unsatisfied functional requirements of the selected design alternative as the starting point for a new FSS and CBI process.

The proposed knowledge-based FSS and CBI methodology can reason out device behaviors from a set of desired functions automatically. Interconnection of these behaviors is possible when there is compatibility between the functional outputs of one device and the corresponding functional requirements of a following one.

4.5. Best-first heuristic search in functional reasoning

The design space for behavioral configuration during functional reasoning is huge, so a best-first heuristic search method, the A* algorithm [107], is used to ensure a near optimum solution is obtained in a reasonable amount of time. The algorithm guides the functioning reasoning process. The system calculates the weighted performance rating aggregation of each retrieved mechanical device by analyzing the trade-offs among the design criteria. It then calculates the dynamic evaluation index of each design alternative by summing the weighted performance ratings of its constituent mechanical devices and the estimated optimum ratings of its possible succeeding mechanical devices.

4.5.1. Weighted performance rating aggregation of a mechanical device

A weighted performance rating aggregation of a retrieved mechanical device contains two components: the partial performance ratings and the weights of the design criteria.

Using the linguistic conversion scales in FMCDM model base introduced earlier, the linguistic values of partial performance ratings R_{ij} and weights W_j of the criteria can be transformed into triangular or trapezoidal fuzzy numbers defined in the interval $[0, 1]$.

The aggregation of fuzzy numbers in an analytic form requires a complex arithmetic process. Thus a centroid-based defuzzification method [108] is used to defuzzify the fuzzy numbers to the crisp values early on, then the defuzzified results can be aggregated easily and the execution is very fast.

For example, if a fuzzy set is represented as a triangular fuzzy number (4.5.2a), then it can be parameterized by a triplet (a, b, c) and its membership function is as follows [109]:

$$\mu(x) = \begin{cases} 0, & x < a \\ (x - a)/(b - a), & a \leq x \leq b \\ (c - x)/(c - b), & b \leq x \leq c \\ 0, & x \geq c \end{cases} \tag{1}$$

The crisp defuzzied value (centroid) of this triangular fuzzy number is:

$$\frac{\int x\mu(x)dx}{\int \mu(x)dx} = \frac{a + b + c}{3} \tag{2}$$

Similarly the crisp defuzzied value (approximate centroid) for a trapezoidal fuzzy number (Figure 24b) is parameterized by a quadruple (a, b, c, d), is $(a + b + c + d)/4$ [110].

With the approximate centroid-based defuzzification method, the fuzzy linguistic performance rating R_{ij} and fuzzy linguistic weight W_j can be respectively transformed into the crisp performance rating $r_{ij} \in (0, 1)$ and crisp weight $w_j \in (0, 1)$.

Now the numerical weighted performance rating $\overline{r}_i \in (0, 1)$ of a retrieved mechanical device D_i can be simply calculated according to the classic weighted average aggregation formula [111] shown below. For each retrieved mechanical device, the higher $\overline{r}_i$ is, the better its aggregated performance is.

$$\overline{r}_i = \frac{\sum_{j=1}^{n} w_j \cdot r_{ij}}{\sum_{j=1}^{n} w_j}, \quad i = 1, 2, \ldots, m \tag{3}$$

Where $i = 1, 2, \ldots, m$, and $j = 1, 2, \ldots, n$;

R_{ij}: denotes the linguistic performance rating with respect to a criterion C_j for a retrieved mechanical device D_i;

W_j: denotes the linguistic weight of a criterion C_j.

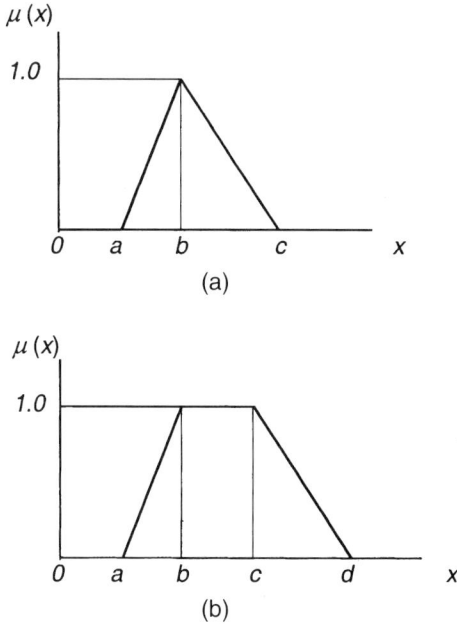

Figure 24. Representation of fuzzy numbers.

4.5.2. Dynamic evaluation index of a design alternative

After calculating the numerical weighted performance ratings of all the retrieved mechanical devices in a design alternative, the dynamic evaluation index (used as heuristic evaluation function $\hat{h}$) can be calculated by summing the weighted performance ratings $\overline{r}_i$ ($i = 1, 2, \ldots, m$) of its constituent mechanical devices and estimated optimum ratings of its possible succeeding mechanical devices. This is given by the following formula:

$$\hat{h} = \sum_{i=1}^{m} (1/\overline{r}_i) + \frac{\sum_{i=1}^{m} (1/\overline{r}_i)}{m} \times k \tag{4}$$

Where $\overline{r}_i \in (0, 1)$ is the numerical weighted performance rating of mechanical device D_i;

$(1/\overline{r}_i) \in (1, +\infty)$ is defined as the performance cost of mechanical device D_i (the higher weighted performance rating of a mechanical device corresponds to lower performance cost);

$\sum_{i=1}^{m} (1/\overline{r_i})$ represents the accumulated performance cost of a design alternative along the search path so far;

$\dfrac{\sum_{i=1}^{m} (1/\overline{r_i})}{m} \times k$ represents a heuristic estimate of the minimal remaining performance cost of a design alternative along all the possible succeeding search paths;

$\hat{h}$ represents the estimate of the total performance cost of a design alternative, and is called evaluation index or heuristic evaluation function.

The best design alternative is the one with the lowest value of dynamic evaluation index $\hat{h}$. A bigger $\overline{r_i}$ (better aggregated performance of each retrieved device D_i) and smaller m or k (higher compactness of a design alternative) usually result in a smaller $\hat{h}$ (lower evaluation index of a design alternative).

4.6. Case study

This section presents a design case study demonstrating the application of our knowledge-based expert system in the design of a film feeding unit for packaging pharmaceutical products.

4.6.1. Problem description and user input

Assume the following functional design and environment specifications are given:

(1) To design a film feeding unit with an overall functional requirement: *Feed film*.
(2) An applied design constraint: *High precision*.
(3) The environment can provide the following:
　　a. *Provide pneumatic air*;
　　b. *Provide electric power*;
　　c. Secure device.

4.6.2. Automated functional design process and system output

The automated functional design process is illustrated by a heuristic search tree (Figure 25). The steps are described below.

(1) The initial design alternative node A_0 consists of the overall functional requirement $F_1 - A_0$: {FUNC: F_1}. The system begins FSS first. A relevant FSS rule is executed to synthesize a supportive function F_{11} for the functional requirement F_1. The initial design alternative is subsequently updated to A_0: {FUNC: F_1, F_{11}} with F_{11} becoming a new functional requirement.
Where:

　　F_1 : *Feed film*;
　　F_{11} : *Guide film through track*.

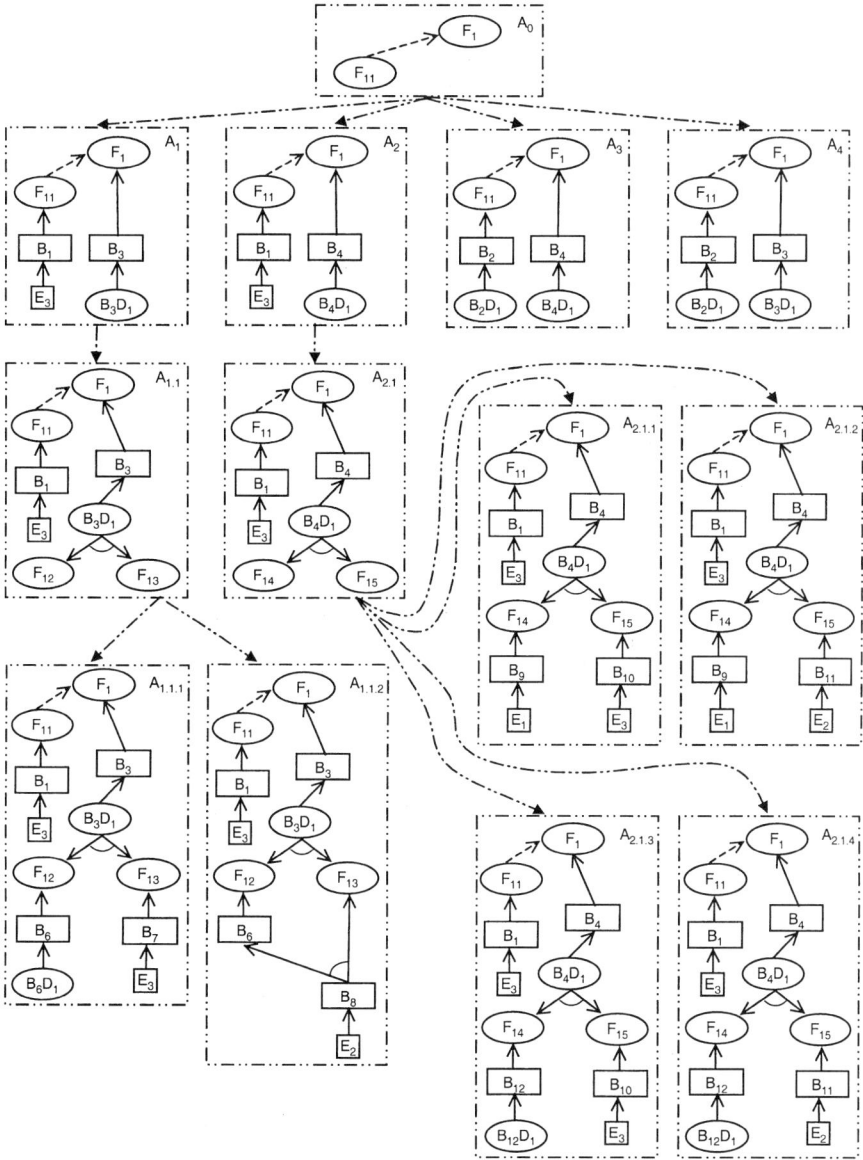

Figure 25. Heuristic search tree in automated functional design process.

(2) The system then starts to search the object–oriented behavior base for device behaviors whose functional outputs match one or both of functional requirements. All retrieved device behaviors must satisfy the imposed design constraint: *High precision*. It is found that device behaviors B_1 or B_2 can achieve F_{11} and device behaviors B_3 or B_4 can achieve F_1. Though the device behavior B_5 can also achieve F_{11}, it is rejected because it doesn't meet the constraint requirement: *High precision*. Together B_1 and B_3 can achieve all the functional requirements of A_0, so they are retrieved to develop a new design alternative A_1: $\{(\text{PHY: } B_1, B_3\}, (\text{FUNC: } B_1D_1, B_3D_1)\}$ with B_1D_1 (i.e., first driving input of B_1) and B_3D_1 becoming the new functional requirements. The environment E_3 can satisfy B_1D_1, so design alternative A_1 is updated to A_1: $\{(\text{PHY: } B_1, B_3), (\text{FUNC: } B_3D_1)\}$. Similarly, B_1 and B_4 are retrieved to develop a new design alternative A_2: $\{(\text{PHY: } B_1, B_4), (\text{FUNC: } B_4D_1)\}$ with B_4D_1 becoming the new functional requirement. Another two more design alternatives A_3: $\{(\text{PHY: } B_2, B_4), (\text{FUNC: } B_2D_1, B_4D_1)\}$ and A_4: $\{(\text{PHY: } B_2, B_3), (\text{FUNC: } B_2D_1, B_3D_1)\}$ are developed from A_0. Thus design alternative A_0 is expanded into four design alternatives A_1, A_2, A_3 and A_4.
Where:

> B_1: *Film gang-track device*;
> B_1D_1: *Secure device*;
> B_2: *Film stitch-track device*;
> B_2D_1: *Provide intermittent motion*;
> B_3: *Film wheel-feeding device*;
> B_3D_1: *Provide low speed rotational motion within a certain range*;
> B_4: *Film finger-feeding device*;
> B_4D_1: *Provide translational motion within a certain range*;
> B_5: *Film side-track device*;
> E_3's environmental output: *Secure device*.

(3) There are now four unexpanded design alternatives A_1, A_2, A_3 and A_4. The system ranks these in the order of their evaluation indexes, i.e., values of heuristic evaluation functions, respectively, $\hat{h}_1$, $\hat{h}_2$, $\hat{h}_3$ and $\hat{h}_4$. Because $\hat{h}_1 < \hat{h}_2 < \hat{h}_4 < \hat{h}_3$, design alternative A_1 is ranked first and is selected as the best one for further CBI.

(4) Next the system scans the behavior base to search for device behaviors whose functional outputs match B_3D_1 of A_1. Assume no matching is found after scanning the whole behavior base. Therefore, one domain-specific functional decomposition rule is executed to decompose B_3D_1 into less complex sub-functions F_{12} and F_{13}. Now design alternative A_1 is expanded into a new design alternative $A_{1.1}$: $\{(\text{PHY: } B_1, B_3), (\text{FUNC: } F_{12}, F_{13})\}$ with F_{12} and F_{13} becoming new functional requirements.
Where:

> F_{12}: *Provide low speed rotational motion*;
> F_{13}: *Control moving range*.

(5) There are now four unexpanded design alternatives A_2, A_3, A_4 and $A_{1.1}$. The system ranks these in order of their evaluation indexes and selects design alternative A_2 as the best one for further CBI.

(6) In a similar manner, design alternative A_2 is expanded into a new design alternative $A_{2.1}$: $\{(\text{PHY: } B_1, B_4), (\text{FUNC: } F_{14}, F_{15})\}$ with F_{14} and F_{15} becoming new functional requirements.
Where:

F_{14}: *Provide translational motion*;

F_{15}: *Control moving range*.

(7) There are four unexpanded design alternatives A_3, A_4, $A_{1.1}$ and $A_{2.1}$. The system ranks these in order of their evaluation indexes and selects design alternative $A_{1.1}$ as the best one for further *CBI*.

(8) Design alternative $A_{1.1}$ is developed into two new design alternatives $A_{1.1.1}$: $\{(\text{PHY: } B_1, B_3, B_6, B_7), (\text{FUNC: } B_6 D_1)\}$ and $A_{1.1.2}$: $\{\text{PHY: } B_1, B_3, B_6, B_7\}$.
Where:

B_6: *Reduction gear pair*;

$B_6 D_1$: *Provide high speed rotational motion*;

B_7: *Limit control switch*;

$B_7 D_1$: *Secure device*;

B_8: *Step motor device*;

$B_8 D_1$: *Provide electric power*;

E_2's environmental output: *Provide electric power*.

(9) There are five unexpanded design alternatives A_3, A_4, $A_{2.1}$, $A_{1.1.1}$ and $A_{1.1.2}$. The system ranks these in order of their evaluation indexes and selects design alternative $A_{2.1}$ as the best one for further CBI.

(10) Design alternative $A_{2.1}$ is developed into four new design alternatives $A_{2.1.1}$: $\{\text{PHY: } B_1, B_4, B_9, B_{10}\}$, $A_{2.1.2}$: $\{\text{PHY: } B_1, B_4, B_9, B_{11}\}$, $A_{2.1.3}$: $\{(\text{PHY: } B_1, B_4, B_{12}, B_{10}), (\text{FUNC: } B_{12} D_1)\}$ and $A_{2.1.4}$: $\{(\text{PHY: } B_1, B_4, B_{12}, B_{11}), (\text{FUNC: } B_{12} D_1)\}$.
Where:

B_9: *Cylinder device*;

$B_9 D_1$: *Provide pneumatic air*;

B_{10}: *Limit control switch*;

$B_{10} D_1$: *Secure device*;

B_{11}: *Step motor device*;

$B_{11} D_1$: *Provide electric power*;

B_{12}: *Rotation-to-translation cam device*;

$B_{12} D_1$: *Provide low speed rotational motion*;

E_1's environmental output: *Provide pneumatic air*.

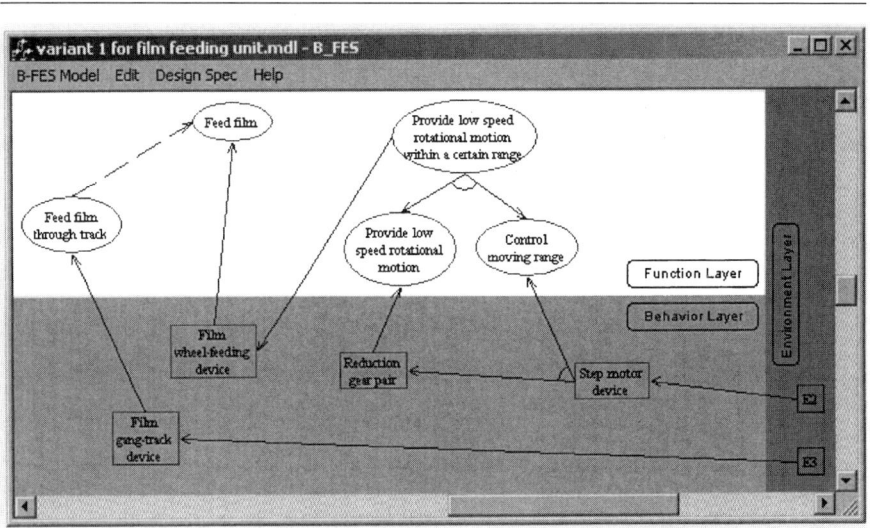

Figure 26. Behavioral schema of the best concept variant.

(11) There are now eight unexpanded design alternatives A_3, A_4, $A_{1.1.1}$, $A_{1.1.2}$, $A_{2.1.1}$, $A_{2.1.2}$, $A_{2.1.3}$ and $A_{2.1.4}$. The system ranks these in order of their evaluation indexes and selects design alternative $A_{1.1.2}$ as the best one for further consideration. $A_{1.1.2}$ consists of physical specifications that satisfy all functional requirements, therefore it is selected as the best design solution, and the search process is terminated. The interconnections of the retrieved device behaviors for the design solution $A_{1.1.2}$ are used to configure a best concept variant as follows:

Best Concept Variant: *Film gang-track device* + *Film wheel-feeding device*
                        + *Reduction gear pair* + *Step motor device*

Figure 26 and Figure 27 respectively show the behavioral schema and graphical representation of the best concept variant.

5. CONCLUSION

Knowledge engineering is an approach for developing knowledge-based systems for engineering design. It can be divided into two levels as shown in Figure 28. The knowledge level deals with the conceptual models underlying human reasoning. The computational level deals with the representation of this knowledge and reasoning in computer systems.

The knowledge level consists of conceptual models for representing the world, domain knowledge, and reasoning models, inferential knowledge. These models are

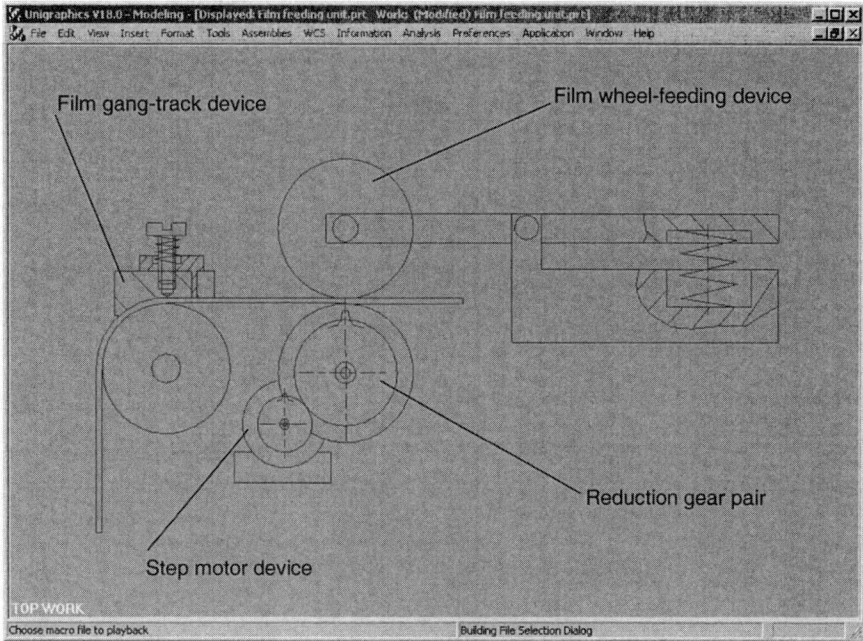

Figure 27. Graphical representation of the best concept variant.

abstract so they can be used irrespective of the formal language encoding the knowledge. Domain knowledge refers to knowledge about the application domain. It deals with the way humans view and model the world. These conceptual models can be divided into those that are generic, ontological models, and those that are application specific, domain models. Inferential knowledge refers to domain-independent knowledge that describes the reasoning steps needed to achieve a particular goal. This can be generic knowledge, inferential strategies, or knowledge aimed specifically at solving particular problems, problem solving methods (PSM's).

Section 3 described the computational techniques listed in Figure 28, as well as their application to engineering design. It was seen in this section that techniques are often combined together. Section 4 described a knowledge-based expert system for mechanical design. It is based on a functional design framework and is implemented by combining several computational techniques: rule-based representation, object-oriented representation, fuzzy logic, backward-chaining control strategy and best-first heuristic search strategy. Operation of the expert system was demonstrated by a case study.

Expert systems are making an impact in industry. Commercial CAD systems are becoming smarter through embedding expert knowledge in CAD software and linking

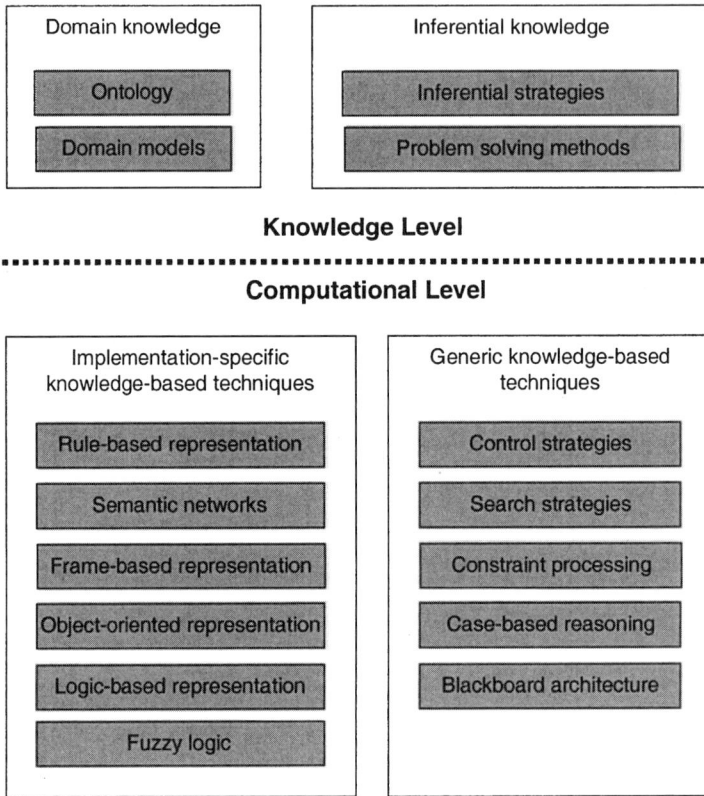

Figure 28. Knowledge engineering.

CAD software with specialist engineering software. This trend will continue as new, more powerful, expert systems are developed for engineering design and verification.

REFERENCES

[1] Asimow, M. 1962. *An Introduction to Design*. Englewood Cliffs, NJ: Prentice-Hall.
[2] Mantyla, M. 1988. *An Introduction to Solid Modelling*. Rockville, MD: Computer Science Press.
[3] Zeid, I. 1991. *CAD/CAM Theory and Practice*. New York: McGraw-Hill.
[4] Shah, J. J. and Mantyla, M. 1995. *Parametric and Feature-Based CAD/CAM*. New York: Wiley.
[5] Chandrasekaran, B. 1994. Functional representation: a brief historical perspective. *Applied Artificial Intelligence*, 8 (2), pp. 173–197.
[6] Chakrabati, A. and Blessing, L. 1996. Special issue: representing functionality in design. *Artificial Intelligence for Engineering Design, Analysis and Manufacturing*, 10 (4), pp. 251–253.
[7] Tor, S. B., Britton, G. A., Chandrashekar, M. and Ng, K. W. 1998. Functional Design. In: Usher, J. M. et al. (eds.), Chapter 2 of *Integrated Product and Process Development: Methods, Tools and Technologies*. New York: Wiley, pp. 29–58.
[8] *The ICAD System User's Manual*, Release 7.0. 1999. Luxembourg: Knowledge Technologies International Inc.

[9] *Unigraphics User's Manual, Version 18.0.* 2001. Maryland Heights, MO: Unigraphics Solutions Inc.

[10] *The Intent! User's Manual,* Version 4.0. 1999. Medfield, Massachusetts: Heide Corp.

[11] Shaw, M. L. G. and Gaines, B. R. 1992. The synthesis of knowledge engineering and software engineering. In: Loucopoulos, P. (ed.), *Advanced Information Systems Engineering.* Manchester: Spring-Verlag.

[12] Newell, A. 1982. The knowledge level. *Artificial Intelligence,* 18 (1), pp. 87–127.

[13] Ramoni, M., Stefanelli, M., Magnani, L. and Barosi, G. 1992. An epistemological framework for medical knowledge-based systems. *IEEE Transactions on Systems, Man, and Cybernetics,* 22 (6), pp. 1361–1375.

[14] Lacey, A. R. 1986. *A Dictionary of Philosophy.* London: Roultedge & Kegan Paul.

[15] Gruber, T. R. 1993. A translation approach to portable ontology specifications. *Knowledge Acquisition,* 5 (2), pp. 199–221.

[16] Studer, R., Benjamins, V. R. and Fensel, D. 1998. Knowledge engineering: principles and methods. *Data & Knowledge Engineering,* 25, pp. 161–197.

[17] Simoff, S. J. and Maher, M. L. 1998. Designing with the activity/space ontology. In: Gero, J. S. and Sudweeks, F. (eds.), *Artificial Intelligence in Design' 98.* London : Kluwer Academic, pp. 23–44.

[18] Schreiber, G., Wielinga, B., Akkermans, H., Van e Velde, W. and Anjewierden, A. 1994. CML: the CommonKADS conceptual modeling language. In: Steels, L., Schreiber, A. T. and Van de Velde, W. (eds.), *Future for Knowledge Acquisition: Proceedings of EKAW'' 94.* Berlin: Springer-Verlag, pp. 1–25.

[19] Marcus, S., Stout, J. and McDermott, J. 1988. VT: an expert elevator configurer that uses knowledge-based backtracking. *AI Magazine,* 9 (1), pp. 95–112.

[20] Zhang, W. Y., Tor, S. B. and Britton, G. A. 2002. A two-level modeling approach to acquire functional design knowledge in mechanical engineering systems. *International Journal of Advanced Manufacturing Technology,* 19 (6), pp. 454–460.

[21] Peirce, C. S. 1997. *Pragmatism as a Principle and Method of Right Thinking: The 1903 Harvard Lectures on Pragmatism.* Edited and Introduced by Turrisi, P. Albany: State University of New York Press.

[22] Churchman, C. West. 1971. *The Design of Inquiring Systems.* New York: Basic Books.

[23] Kiritsis, D. 1995. A review of knowledge-based expert systems for process planning, methods and problems. *International Journal of Advanced Manufacturing Technology,* 10, pp. 240–262.

[24] Clancey, W. J. 1985. Heuristic classification. *Artificial Intelligence,* 27, pp. 289–350.

[25] Chandrasekaran, B. 1986. Generic tasks in knowledge-based reasoning: high-level building blocks for expert system design. *IEEE Expert,* 1, pp. 23–30.

[26] Marcus, S. (ed.). 1988. *Automating Knowledge Acquisition for Expert Systems.* Boston: Kluwer.

[27] Angele, J., Fensel, D. and Studer, R. 1996. Domain and task modeling in MIKE. In: Sutcliffe, A., et al. (eds.), *Domain Knowledge for Interactive System Design.* New York: Chapman & Hall.

[28] Brown, J. S., Burton, R. R. and De Kleer, J. 1982. Pedagogical, natural language and knowledge engineering techniques in SOPHIE I, II, III. In: Sleeman, D. and Brown, J. S. (eds.), *Intelligent Tutoring Systems.* London: Academic Press, Chapter 11.

[29] Prerau, D. S. 1990. *Developing and Managing Expert Systems.* MA: Addison-Wesley.

[30] Jackson, P. 1999. *Introduction to Expert Systems,* 3rd ed. Harlow, HK: Addison-Wesley.

[31] Bachant, J. 1988. RIME: preliminary work towards a knowledge acquisition tool. In: Marcus, S. (ed.), *Automating Knowledge Acquisition for Expert System.* Boston: Kluiver Academic, Chapter 7.

[32] McDermott, J. 1982. R1: a rule-based configurer of computer systems. *Artificial Intelligence,* 19, pp. 39–88.

[33] Chandrasekaran, B. 1990. Design problem solving: a task analysis. *AI Magazine,* 11 (4), pp. 59–71.

[34] Wielinga, B. and Schreiber, G. 1997. Configuration design problem solving. *IEEE Expert Intelligent Systems & Their Applications,* 12, pp. 49–56.

[35] Fensel, D. and Motta, E. 2001. Structured development of problem solving methods. *IEEE Transactions on Knowledge and Data Engineering,* 13 (6), pp. 913–932.

[36] Nillson, N. 1971. *Problem-Solving Methods in Artificial Intelligence,* New York: McGraw Hill.

[37] Coyne, R. D., Rosenman, M. A., Radford, A. D., Balachandran, M. and Gero, J. S. 1990. *Knowledge-Based Design Systems.* New York: Addison-Wesley.

[38] Chan, Y. W. and Sim, S. K. 1994. A knowledge-based expert system for gearing design application using Prolog and C. *Advances in Engineering Software,* 19, pp. 149–159.

[39] Brown, D. C. and Birmingham, W. P. 1997. Understanding the nature of design. *IEEE Expert Intelligent Systems and Their Application,* 12 (2), pp. 14–16.

[40] Newell, A. and Simon, H. A. 1972. *Human Problem Solving.* Englewood Cliffs, NJ: Prentice-Hall.

[41] Li, C. L., Tan, S. T. and Chan, K. W. 1996. A qualitative and heuristic approach to the conceptual design of mechanisms. *Engineering Application of Artificial Intelligence*, 9 (1), pp. 17–31.

[42] Moulianitis, V. C., Dentsoras, A. J., and Aspragathos, N. A. 1999. A knowledge-based system for the conceptual design of grippers for handling fabrics. *Artificial Intelligence for Engineering Design, Analysis and Manufacturing*, 13, pp. 13–25.

[43] Kim, S.-H. and Im, Y.-T. 1999. Knowledge-based expert system for roll pass and profile design for shape rolling of round and square bars. *Journal of Materials Processing Technology*, 89, pp. 145–151.

[44] Masood, S. H. and Soo, A. 2002. A rule based expert system for rapid prototyping system selection. *Robotics and Computer-Integrated Manufacturing*, 18, pp. 267–274.

[45] Quillian, M. R. 1968. Semantic memory. In: Minksy, M. L. (ed.), *Semantic Information Processing*. Cambridge, MA: MIT Press, pp. 227–270.

[46] Fujimoto, H. and Yamoto, H. 1990. Development of design support system with new reasoning and its applications to production line design. In: *Proceedings of the 1990 ASME International Computers in Engineering Conference and Exposition*. Boston, MA, USA, pp. 17–24.

[47] Cherneff, J., Logcher, R. and Sriram. D. 1991. Integrating CAD with construction-schedule generation. *Journal of Computing in Civil Engineering*, 5 (1), pp. 65–84.

[48] Rogers, K. J., Priest, J. W. and Haddock, G. 1995. Use of semantic networks to support concurrent engineering in semiconductor product development. *Journal of Intelligent Manufacturing*, 6 (5), pp. 311–319.

[49] Ishii, K. 1995. Life-cycle engineering design. *Journal of Mechanical Design, Transactions of the ASME*, 117B, pp. 42–47.

[50] Bullinger, H.-J., Warschat, J. and Fischer, D. 2000. Rapid product development—an overview. *Computers in Industry*, 42 (2), pp. 99–108.

[51] Minsky, M. L. 1975. A framework for representing knowledge. In: *The Psychology of Computer Vision*. New York: McGraw-Hill, pp. 211–277.

[52] Forbus, K. D. 1984. Qualitative process theory. *Artificial Intelligence*, 24, pp. 85–168.

[53] Roschke, P. N. 1991. Advisory system for design of highway safety structures. *Journal of Transportation Engineering*, 117 (4), pp. 418–434.

[54] Yau, M. Y., Lai, E. M. -K. and Chun, H. W. 1994. FPDX: A knowledge-based system for architectural floor plan design. In: *Proceedings of the IEEE International Conference on Expert Systems for Development*. Bangkok, Thailand, pp. 309–314.

[55] Glass, A., Holtz, N. and Rasdorf, W. J. 1994. System for describing design artifacts using the knowledge representation technique of frames. *Engineering with Computers*, 10 (4), pp. 197–211.

[56] Wang, Q., Zhu, J. Y., Shu, Y. Q., Rao, M. and Chuang, K. T. 1995. An intelligent design environment for conceptual process design. *Engineering Application of Artificial Intelligence*, 8 (2), pp. 15–127.

[57] Meyer, B. 1988. *Object-Oriented Software Construction*. New York: Prentice-Hall.

[58] Hsu, W. and Woon, I. M. Y. 1998. Current research in the conceptual design of mechanical products. *Computer-Aided Design*, 30 (5), pp. 377–389.

[59] Akagi, S. and Fujita, K. 1990. Building an expert system for engineering design based on the object-oriented knowledge representation concept. *Journal of Mechanical Design*, 112, pp. 215–222.

[60] Tong, C. and Gomory, A. 1993. A knowledge based computer environment for the conceptual design of small electromechanical appliances. *Computers*, 26 (1), pp. 69–71.

[61] Gorti, S. R. and Sriram, R. D. 1996. From symbol to form: a framework for conceptual design. *Computer-Aided Design*, 28 (11), pp. 853–870.

[62] Clayton, M. J., Teicholz, P., Fischer, M. and Kunz, J. 1999. Virtual components consisting of form, function and behavior. *Automation in Construction*, 8 (3), pp. 351–367.

[63] Michalek, J. J. and Papalambros, P. Y. 2002. Interactive design optimization of architectural layouts. *Engineering Optimization*, 34 (5), pp. 485–501.

[64] Lakmazaheri, S. and Rasdorf, W. J. 1990. Formal approach to structural design automation. In: *Design Theory and Methodology—Proceedings of DTM' 90*. American Society of Mechanical Engineers, Design Engineering Division (Publication) DE, Chicago, USA, Vol. 27, pp. 259–266.

[65] Rasdorf, W. J. and Lakmazaheri, S. 1990. Logic-based approach for modeling organization of design standards. *Journal of Computing in Civil Engineering*, 4 (2), pp. 102–123.

[66] Hoare, C. A. R. 1996. Logic of engineering design. *Microprocessing and Microprogramming*, 41, pp. 525–539.

[67] Feijo, B. and Bento, J., 1998. Logic-based environment for reactive agents in intelligent CAD systems. *Advances in Engineering Software*, 29 (10), pp. 825–832.

[68] Bento, J., Feijo, B. and Smith, D. L. 1997. Engineering design knowledge representation based on logic and objects. *Computers & Structures*, 63 (5), pp. 1015–1032.

[69] Zadeh, L. A. 1965. Fuzzy sets. *Information and Control*, 8, pp. 338–353.

[70] Jones, J. D. and Hua, Y. 1998. A fuzzy knowledge base to support routine engineering design. *Fuzzy Sets and Systems*, 98, pp. 267–278.

[71] Shragowitz, E., Lee, J.-Y. and Kang, E. Q. 1998. Application of fuzzy logic in computer-aided VLSI design. *IEEE Transactions on Fuzzy Systems*, 6 (1), pp. 163–172.

[72] Wang, J. 2001. Ranking engineering design concepts using a fuzzy outranking preference model. *Fuzzy Sets and Systems*, 119, pp. 161–170.

[73] Qin, S. -F., Wright, D. K. and Jordanov, I. N. 2001. A conceptual design tool: a sketch and fuzzy logic based system. In: *Proceedings of the Institution of Mechanical Engineers, Part B: Journal of Engineering Manufacture*, 215 (1), pp. 111–116.

[74] Shehab, E. M. and Abdalla, H. S. 2002. A design to cost system for innovative product development. In: *Proceedings of the Institution of Mechanical Engineers, Part B: Journal of Engineering Manufacture*, 216 (7), pp. 999–1019.

[75] Melli, R. and Sciubba, E. 1997. A prototype expert system for the conceptual synthesis of thermal processes. *Energy Conversion and Management*, 38 (17), pp. 1737–1749.

[76] Hart, P. K. and Rodriguez, J. 1989. Hybrid knowledge-based expert system for design of structural elements. In: *Proceedings of the International Computers in Engineering Conference and Exhibition*, pp. 287–292.

[77] Rich, E. and Knight, K. 1991. *Artificial Intelligence*, 2nd edn. New York: McGraw-Hill.

[78] Sullivan, K. A. and Jacobson, S. H. 2000. Ordinal hill climbing algorithms for discrete manufacturing process design optimization problems. *Discrete Event Dynamic Systems: Theory and Applications*, 10 (4), pp. 307–324.

[79] Russell, S. J. and Norvig, P. 1995. *Artificial Intelligence: A Modern Approach*. Englewood Cliffs, NJ: Prentice-Hall.

[80] Sriram, D. 1987. ALL-RISE: a case study in constraint-based design. *Artificial Intelligence in Design*, 2, pp. 186–203.

[81] Mackworth, A. K. 1977. Consistency in networks of relations. *Artificial Intelligence*, 8, pp. 99–118.

[82] Takanori, Y. 1990. An object-oriented and constraint-based knowledge representation system for design object modeling. In: *Proceedings of the Conference on Artificial Intelligence Applications*. Santa Barbara, CA, USA, pp. 146–152.

[83] Guan, Q. and Gerhard, F. 1993. Fuzzy control over constraint satisfaction problem solving in structural design. *1993 IEEE International Conference on Fuzzy Systems*, pp. 1316–1320.

[84] Wu, J. K., Wang, J. H., Feng, C. X. and Liu, T. H. 1995. Logic-based mechanical system constraint model. *Engineering with Computers*, 11 (3), pp. 157–166.

[85] Hassan, S. A. 1998. Concurrent engineering constraint-based system. *Computers & Industrial Engineering*, 35, pp. 459–462.

[86] O'Sullivan, B. and Bowen, J. 1998. A constraint-based approach to supporting conceptual design. In: Gero, J. S. and Sudweeks, F. (eds.), *Artificial Intelligence in Design'98*, pp. 291–308.

[87] Schank, R. C. and Riesbeck, C. K. 1989. *Inside Case Based Reasoning*. Hillsdale, NJ: Lawrence Erlbaum.

[88] Goel, A. K. and Chandrasekaran, B. 1992. Case-based design: a task analysis. In: *Artificial Intelligence in Engineering Design*, Vol. 2. Boston: Academic Press.

[89] Falting, B. 1997. Case reuse by model-based interpretation. In: Mary, L. M. and Pu, P. (eds.), *Issues and Applications of Case-Based Reasoning in Design*. Mahwah, NJ: Lawrence Erlbaum Associates, pp. 39–60.

[90] Rivard, H. and Fenves, S. J. 2000. SEED-Config: a case-based reasoning system for conceptual building design. *Artificial Intelligence for Engineering Design, Analysis and Manufacturing: AIEDAM*, 14 (5), pp. 415–430.

[91] Kwong, C. K. 2001. A case-based system for process design of injection molding. *International Journal of Computer Applications in Technology*, 14 (1), pp. 40–50.

[92] Stefania, B. and Sara, M. 2002. Improving CBR for compound design with fuzzy indexing and retrieval. *International Journal of Engineering Intelligent Systems for Electrical Engineering and Communications*, 10 (3), pp. 125–130.

[93] Thompson, J. B. and Lu, S. C.-Y. 1989. Representing and using design rationale in concurrent product and process design. *Concurrent Product and Process Design*. ASME Winter Annual Meeting, pp. 109–115.

[94] Urban, S. D., Shah, J. J., Liu, H. and Rogers, M. 1996. Shared design manager: interoperability in engineering design. *Integrated Computer-Aided Engineering*, 3 (3), pp. 158–176.

[95] Kwong, C. K., Smith, G. F. and Lau, W. S. 1997. A blackboard-based approach to concurrent process design of injection molding. *Journal of Materials Processing Technology*, 70, pp. 258–263.

[96] Roy, U. and Liao, J.-M. 1998. Application of a blackboard framework to a cooperative fixture design system. *Computers in Industry*, 37, pp. 67–81.

[97] Chau, K. W. and Albermani, F. 2002. Expert system application on preliminary design of water retaining structures. *Expert Systems with Applications*, 22 (2), pp. 169–178.

[98] Hirtz, J., Stone, R., McAdams, D., Szykman, S. and Wood, K. 2002. A functional basis for engineering design: reconciling and evolving previous efforts. *Journal of Research in Engineering Design*, 13 (2), pp. 65–82.

[99] Umeda, Y., Ishii, M., Yoshioka, M., Shimomura, Y. and Tomiyama, T. 1996. Supporting conceptual design based on the function–behavior–state modeler. *Artificial Intelligence for Engineering Design, Analysis and Manufacturing: Aiedam*, 10, pp. 275–288.

[100] Otto K. and Wood, K. 2001. *Product Design: Techniques in Reverse Engineering and New Product Development*. Upper Saddle River, NJ: Prentice-Hall.

[101] Tor, S. B., Britton, G. A., Zhang, W. Y. and Deng, Y.-M. 2002. Guiding functional design of mechanical products through rule-based causal behavioral reasoning. *International Journal of Production Research*, 40, pp. 667–682.

[102] Deng, Y. -M., Tor, S. B. and Britton, G. A. 2000. Abstracting and exploring functional design information for conceptual product design. *Engineering with Computers*, 16, pp. 36–52.

[103] Deng, Y. -M., Britton, G. A. and Tor, S. B. 1998. A design perspective of mechanical function and its object-oriented representation scheme. *Engineering with Computers*, 14, pp. 309–320.

[104] Chen, S.-J., Hwang, C.-L. and Hwang, F. P. 1992. *Fuzzy Multiple Attribute Decision Making: Methods and Applications*. Berlin: Springer-Verlag.

[105] Zhang, W. Y., Tor, S. B. and Britton, G. A. 2002. A heuristic state-space approach to the functional design of mechanical systems. *International Journal of Advanced Manufacturing Technology*. 19 (4), pp. 235–244.

[106] Hoover, S. P. and Rinderle, J. R. 1989. A synthesis strategy for mechanical devices. *Research in Engineering Design*, 1, pp. 87–103.

[107] Nilsson, N. J. 1998. *Artificial Intelligence: A New Synthesis*. San Francisco, Calif.: Morgan Kaufmann.

[108] Tseng, T. Y. and Klein, C. M. 1992. A new algorithm for fuzzy multicriteria decision making. *International Journal of Approximate Reasoning*, 6, pp. 45–66.

[109] Zimmermann, H.-J. 1991. *Fuzzy Set Theory and Its Applications*. Boston, USA: Kluwer.

[110] Chen, S. M. 1996. Evaluating weapon systems using fuzzy arithmetic operations. *Fuzzy Sets and Systems*, 77, pp. 265–276.

[111] Pahl, G. and Beitz, W. 1996. *Engineering Design—A Systematic Approach*. London: Springer-Verlag.

EXPERT SYSTEMS TECHNOLOGY IN PRODUCTION PLANNING AND SCHEDULING

KOSTAS METAXIOTIS, DIMITRIS ASKOUNIS AND JOHN PSARRAS

1. INTRODUCTION

In recent years the growing complexity of industrial manufacturing and the need for higher efficiency, shortened product life cycle, greater flexibility, better product quality, greater satisfaction of customer's expectations and lower cost have changed the face of manufacturing practice. A great challenge for today's companies is not only how to adapt to this changing business environment but also how to draw a competitive advantage from the way in which they choose to do so. As a basis to achieve such advantages, companies have started to seek to optimize the operation of their manufacturing systems. Since traditional, centralized manufacturing planning, scheduling and control mechanisms were found insufficiently flexible to respond to this new situation, many manufacturing companies decided to adopt intelligent solutions. Expert systems technology provides a natural way to overcome such problems, and to design and implement distributed intelligent manufacturing environments.

In the past decade there has been a virtual explosion of interest in the field known as expert systems (or, alternatively, as knowledge-based systems). Expert systems provide powerful and flexible means for obtaining solutions to a variety of problems that often can not be dealt with by other, more orthodox methods. One relative study reported an investment of over $100 million in AI research by large American manufacturing companies, some of which have already achieved impressive results [1]. Typical examples are Digital Equipment Corporation's XCON, Boeing and Lockheed-Georgia Corporation's GenPlan.

On the other hand, many researchers and authors have strongly supported the view that expert systems can make a significant contribution to improving control and manufacturing systems [2–3]. This chapter aims to review the use of expert systems in the area of production planning and scheduling. It firstly provides, for the benefit of the readers who may be unfamiliar with this technology, an introduction to the main features of expert systems and a systematic methodology for their development. Concepts and characteristics of well-known expert systems in this area are then described and benefits gained through their utilization are analyzed. A case study related to the expert system GENESYS is presented and speculations on future trends are finally discussed.

2. THE EXPERT SYSTEMS TECHNOLOGY

Human thought is undoubtedly one of the most complex and least understood processes in nature. Thinking about the world is the purview of art and science. In computer science, attempts to describe, capture and apply knowledge are generally grouped into that branch called Artificial Intelligence, or AI for short.

One of the most mature and commercially successful sub-branch of Artificial Intelligence is Expert Systems (ES). Welbank [4] defines an expert system as follows:

> *An expert system is a program, which has a wide base of knowledge in a restricted domain, and uses complex inferential reasoning to perform tasks which a human expert could do.*

In other words, an expert system is a computer system containing a well-organized body of knowledge, which emulates expert problem solving skills in a bounded domain of expertise. The system is able to achieve expert levels of problem solving performance, which would normally be achieved by a skilled human when confronted with significant problems in the domain (BCS, Expert Systems Specialist Group). It may also be said that an expert system exhibits or mimics the cognitive behavior of a human expert. The characteristics of human expert behavior include the ability to reason through the manipulation of concepts and rules-of-thumb acquired over many years of experience; the ability to cope with uncertain or incomplete evidence; the ability to explain the need for more information; the ability to justify conclusions; the ability to satisfy a variety of lines of enquiry during the course of a dialogue. As illustrated in Figure 1, expert systems are generally considered to consist of three essential components, which include the knowledge base, the inference engine and the user interface.

The user interacts with the system through a *user interface*, which may use menus, natural language or any other style of interaction. Then an *inference engine* is used to reason with both the expert knowledge and data related to the particular problem being solved. The *knowledge base* is the heart of the system and contains the knowledge needed for solving the specific problem. Knowledge may be in the form of facts, heuristics (e.g. experiences, opinions, judgements, predictions, algorithms) and relationships usually gleaned from the mind of experts in the relevant domain. Knowledge can be represented using a variety of representation techniques (e.g. semantic nets,

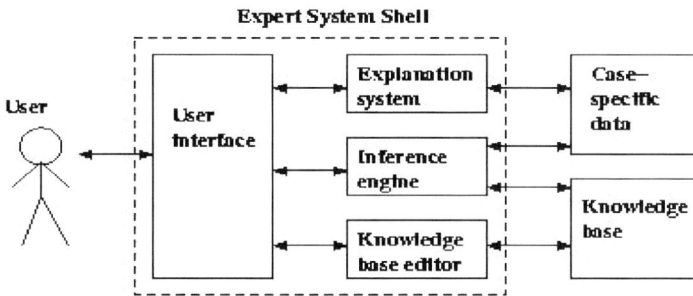

Figure 1. Expert systems' anatomy.

frames, predicate logic) [5–7], but the most commonly used technique is "If-Then" rules, also known as production rules.

Almost all expert systems also have an *explanation subsystem*, which allows the program to explain its reasoning to the user. Some systems also have a *knowledge base editor*, which help the expert or knowledge engineer to easily update and check the knowledge base. The *case specific data* includes both data provided by the user and partial conclusions (along with certainty measures) based on this data.

Expert systems have some significant advantages in comparison with the traditional computer systems. These advantages are presented in the following Table 1.

A successful ES development needs a well-planned course of activities, as shown in Figure 2. It is important that a systematic approach is adopted from the identification of the problem domain, through the construction of the knowledge base and eventually to the implementation and validation of the system. Concerning the implementation of expert systems, there are mainly two groups of development tools [8–10].

• High level programming languages (C++, PROLOG, LISP, etc.). Using these languages, the system designer has a great deal of freedom in his choice of knowledge representation techniques and control strategies. However, use of these languages requires a high degree of expertise and skill.
• Expert system shells. They combine the flexibility of AI languages with the cost-effectiveness and provide more general development facilities. There are a number of commercial shells available in the market with varying features (Nexpert Object, XpertRule, KnowledgePro, CLIPS, ReSolver, EXSYS, VP-Expert, ACQUIRE, etc.). Most of them are relatively low priced and provide a rule-based knowledge representation mechanism.

It is common knowledge that the knowledge acquisition stage is the major bottleneck in the development of expert systems, regardless of the domain. In few words, the success of an ES depends on how much knowledge it has and how qualitative that knowledge is.

Table 1 Expert systems' advantages

☑ **Availability**

Experts are not born. They have to be trained and then practiced. It generally takes over five years for someone to acquire expertise in a particular area. In contrast to the human, expert system has all the expertise inside, it never gets tired or dies. The included knowledge is often more readily available to trainee experts or users.

☑ **Consistency**

Even the best experts can make mistakes or may forget an important point. Once an expert system is programmed to ask for and use certain inputs, it is not prone to forgetfulness. If a line of reasoning is acceptable, it will remain so in different consultations.

☑ **Comprehensiveness**

An expert can only draw upon his own knowledge and experience. In some domains an expert systems could encapsulate the knowledge of more than one expert and consequently offer several options.

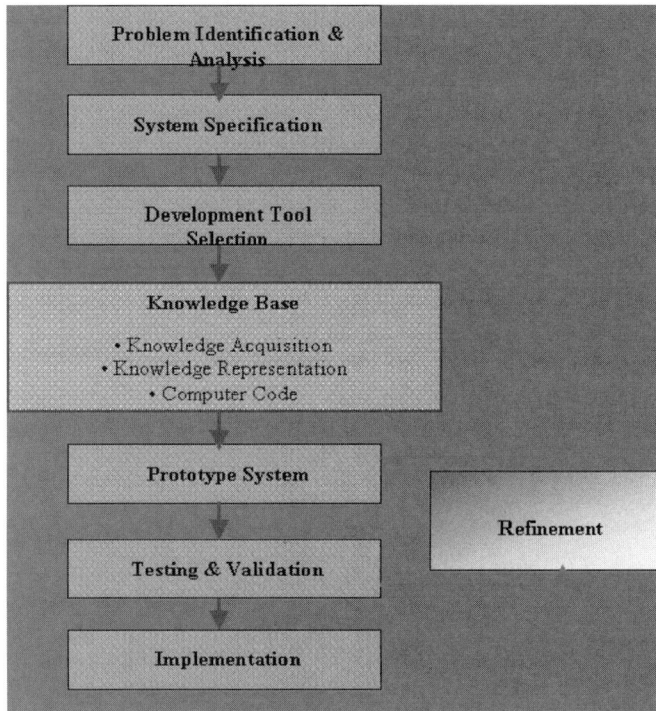

Figure 2. Expert system development approach.

3. EXPERT SYSTEMS IN PRODUCTION PLANNING & SCHEDULING

Planning and scheduling are forms of decision-making, which play a crucial role in manufacturing as well as in service industries. Planning is the process of selecting and sequencing activities such that they achieve one or more goals and satisfy a set of domain constraints. Scheduling is the process of selecting among alternative plans and assigning resources and times to the set of activities in the plan. These assignments

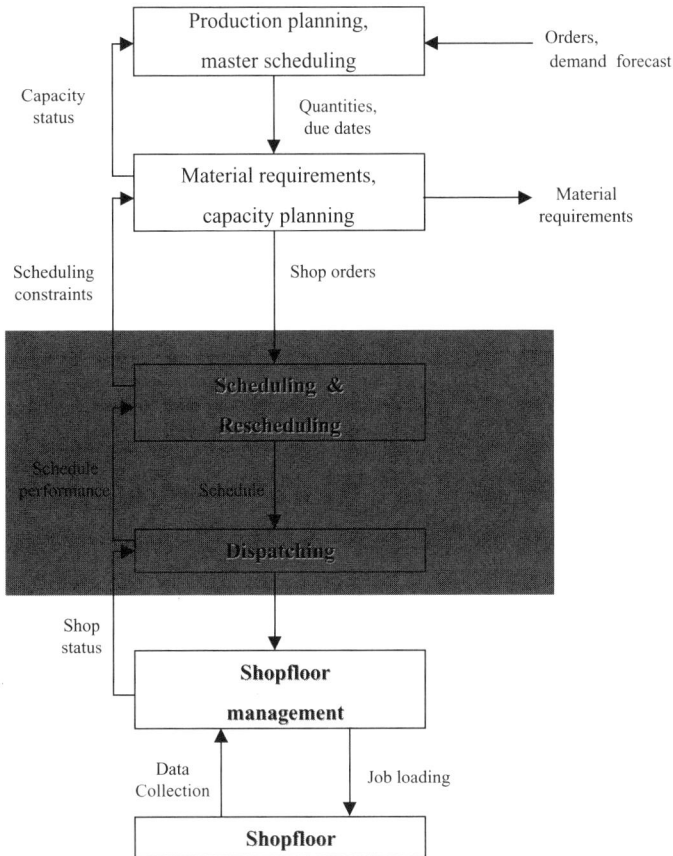

Figure 3. Information flow diagram in a manufacturing system.

must obey a set of rules or constraints that reflect the temporal relationships between activities and the capacity limitations of a set of shared resources [11–13].

In general, in a manufacturing system orders should be released and have to be translated into specific jobs with associated due dates. The jobs often have to be processed by the machines in a workcenter in a given order or sequence. Jobs may have to wait for processing on machines that are busy, and preemptions may occur when high-priority jobs arrive at machines and have to proceed at once. Also, unexpected events, such as machine breakdowns, or foreseen events, such as standard maintenance activities, have always to be taken into consideration because they may have major impact on the schedules. The Figure 3 presents a typical diagram of the information flow in a manufacturing / production system.

Table 2 Areas of ES applications—Survey of Wong, Chong & Park (1994)

System domain	Frequency	Percentage[1]
Scheduling	18	35.3
Process Design	16	31.4
Maintenance and repair	15	29.4
Process selection	13	25.5
Facility layout	11	21.6
Material selection	6	11.8
Production planning & control	4	7.8
Capacity planning	4	7.8
Facility location	3	5.9
Project management	3	5.9
Tool selection	2	3.9
Data selection	2	3.9
Quality control	2	3.9
Forecasting	2	3.9
Storeroom design	1	2.0
Vendor selection	1	2.0

[1] Percentages do not add up 100 because the respondents could choose more than one area of application.

In the current competitive environment, effective planning and scheduling has become a necessity for survival in the marketplace. Companies have to meet shipping dates committed to the customers, as failure to do so may result in a significant loss of good will and reliability. They also should schedule activities in such a way as to use the resources available in an efficient way. Research [14] has shown that a company with an effective production scheduling can achieve the following:

➢ Reduction by 10–15% to production cost, which is able to lead to the doubling of the profit margin of the company.
➢ Reduction by 8–10% to inventory costs.
➢ Increase by 30% to "on time" deliveries to the customers.

On the other hand, the scheduling function interacts with the other functions of a company. It is affected by the middle-range planning, which examines the stock levels, the demand forecasting and the requirements plan, in order to achieve the optimization of the combination "Production—Allocation of Resources". In this context, the construction of a feasible, optimized (as far as possible) production schedule from the Production Manager, without the support of an advanced Decision Support System, is a very difficult and time-consuming procedure that requires not only deep knowledge of all data and parameters of the production system at any time but also specific knowledge in the particular field. In addition, many times the Production Manager, without a decision support tool, is not in the position to achieve a multi-criteria scheduling objective, because these criteria may conflict each other. For instance, satisfying the most significant customers may be in conflict with the criterion of meeting the due dates and that result in a further delay to several customers who are for some reasons less significant to the manufacturing company.

Table 3 Total number of ES used and being developed—Stud of Byrd (1995)

Status	Number of ESs
Currently used	
0	1
1–5	15
6–10	6
11–40	3
>40	2
Being developed	
0	0
1–5	13
6–10	7
11–40	1
>40	4

In this framework, during the last decade a lot of manufacturing companies decided to adopt intelligent solutions, since the traditional manufacturing planning and scheduling mechanisms were found insufficiently flexible to respond to changing production styles and highly dynamic variations in product requirements [15–16]. A mid 1990s survey reported by Durkin [17] has revealed manufacturing industry to be one of the most widely applied area for expert systems.

In addition, another study [18] examined the current utilization of ES and their benefits in manufacturing among the 500 largest industrial companies in the USA. They invited all Fortune 500 industrial corporations (based on the 1990 ranking) to participate in a mail survey. The mailing procedure produced 98 usable responses in total, which meant a usable response rate of 19.6%. Among the 98 responding companies, the mean number of employees was 19,000, while gross annual sales averaged 6.2 billion dollars. In this study, production scheduling emerged as the most common application area of ES.

In an other study implemented by Byrd [19], who interviewed 74 Knowledge 1 Engineers (KEs) of 28 organisations, production scheduling appeared to be the second most common type of ES in general, the first being diagnosis. The Table 3 gives an indication of how many expert systems—related to production management—were in use and being developed in the 28 organisations of the KEs. Concerning the benefits reported from the use of this technology by the KEs, the interviewees said they received from their expert systems :

➢ Better customer service
➢ Reduction in time to complete tasks
➢ Organisational learning
➢ Increases in production
➢ More effective use of resources
➢ Reduction in staff

Moreover, many researchers have regularly written about the use of expert systems in production planning and scheduling and their potential benefits [20–29]. According to these researchers, expert systems can help organizations to cut costs by reducing the need for some personnel, preserve and disseminate scarce expertise throughout the organization, give better consistency to decision making, improve quality of products.

4. EXPERT SYSTEMS RESEARCH IN PRODUCTION PLANNING & SCHEDULING

A number of applications of ESs to the area of production planning and scheduling have been developed and documented. The intelligent scheduling and information system **ISIS** was the first application of ES to job-shop scheduling [30]. ISIS used hierarchical planning to decompose complex problems into manageable pieces. The research with ISIS led to work on the development of the opportunistic scheduler **OPIS** [31], a knowledge-based factory scheduling system which uses problem decompositions to generate constraint-satisfying shop schedules.

The Prototype Expert Priority Scheduler **PEPS** [32] is a rule-based ES which solves problems at the shopfloor control level, although its drawback is the fact that it is not able to recognize uncertainty and downstream data dependency.

PATRIARCH [33] is a multilevel planning, scheduling and control system that was developed at Carnegie Mellon University for manufacturing. The four levels of the PATRIARCH system include: 1) strategic planning, 2) capacity planning, 3) scheduling, 4) dispatching. The **OPT** scheduling system was reported by D.R. Jacobs [34] in 1983.

A hybrid expert system **HESS** [35] was developed at the University of Houston in support of product scheduling at a major petrochemical firm's refinery. The knowledge base in HESS was developed to determine what products to produce at what time, and through which processors. HESS was developed using the EXSYS expert system shell and consists of approximately 400 production rules.

A management analysis resource scheduler **MARS** [36] has been developed to schedule resources for the space transportation system. In 1980, Chiodini developed an expert system for dynamic manufacturing rescheduling [37], while Biegel & Wink proposed an expert system for industrial job-shop scheduling in 1989 [38].

In 1992 a knowledge-based simulation system for manufacturing scheduling was proposed by Palaniswami & Jenicke [39], while Alexander [40] developed an expert system for the selection of scheduling rules in a job shop.

A knowledge-based simulation model for job shop scheduling was also proposed by Abdallah (1995). The knowledge base of the model was built using the simulation technique by studying the effect of different technological factors on the selection of scheduling decisions [41].

De Toni et al. [42] proposed an intelligence-based production scheduler, which utilizes a hybrid push/pull approach to schedule. This scheduler uses some blackboard techniques of the type hypothesized by Hayes-Roth [43]. The production scheduling blackboard consists of frames, lists and production rules, plus a blackboard controller with a shopfloor control system interface and codes/routings archives.

Custodio et al. [44] discussed the issue of production planning and scheduling using a fuzzy decision system, while several outlines concerning the development of a rule-base for the specification of manufacturing planning and control systems were recently made by Howard et al. [45].

A fuzzy rule-based scheduler was proposed by Subramaniam at al. [46] in 2000, which dynamically selects, from several candidate dispatching rules, the most appropriate dispatching rule to employ, based on the prevailing job shop conditions. An expert system named **KDPAG** was built by Chen et al. [47] applied to materials design and manufacture.

In addition, particular attention is also dedicated to the issue of effective rescheduling [48–50]. Yamamoto and Nof [51] suggested a Regeneration Method when they exploited production schedule expert system. Driscoll [52] studied a knowledge-based rescheduling expert system, which was adapted to the flexible manufacturing environment, while Tayanlthi et al. proposed a knowledge-based simulation system to analyze and handle the disturbances (including machine breakdowns and rush orders) in a flexible manufacturing environment [53].

Recently a production rescheduling expert simulation system was also proposed by Li et al. [54]. This system integrates different techniques and methods, including simulation techniques, artificial neural networks, expert knowledge and dispatching rules and deals with four sources of production disturbances: a) incorrect work, b) machine breakdowns, c) rework due to quality problems; and d) rush orders.

Several companies in Japan have given a strong emphasis on the development of expert systems for production planning and scheduling during the last decade. Using corporate estimates, somewhere between 30–40 % of knowledge-based systems in Japan focus on planning or scheduling, with a significant recent trend toward more applications. Examples include:

❑ Crew scheduling time at JAL was reduced from 20 to 15 days
❑ Scheduling time for a Toshiba paper mill was reduced from three days to two hours
❑ A Fujitsu printed circuit board assembly and test planner reduced the scheduling task by a man-year each calendar year.

Approximately 500 expert systems have been developed at Toshiba for both internal and external use, with about 10% in routine use. Design and planning/scheduling are the major growth application areas. The most successful expert system is a paper production scheduling system for the Tomakomai mill of Ohji Paper Co., Ltd. The system uses 25 kinds of pulp, which are combined in 10 papermaking machines to produce 200 different paper products. There are hundreds of constraints to be satisfied. The system employs a top-down hierarchical scheduling strategy, starting with scheduling product groups, then individual products, and then line balancing. This application has reduced the time required to produce a monthly schedule from three days to two hours.

Fujitsu Laboratories reported that it has built about 240 expert systems for internal use. The company also has knowledge of about 250 expert systems built by its

Table 4 Summary list of projects using expert systems technology

Project	Group	Domain
MASCOT	Parunak 1993 ITI	Manufacturing Scheduling & Control
DAS	Burke & Prosser 1991 U. of Strathclyde	Manufacturing Scheduling
ABACUS	McEleney et al. 1998 UCB, UMIST	Manufacturing Scheduling
MetaMorph II	Shen et al 1998 U. of Calgary	Intelligent Manufacturing Production
SFA	Parunak 1996 NCMS	Manufacturing Scheduling & Control
A Case Based Expert System For Generative Computer-Aided Process Planning With Manufacturing Uncertainty	Wong 1997 MSERC	Manufacturing Planning
IAO	Kwok & Norrie 1994 U. of Calgary	Intelligent Manufacturing

customers, but can not categorize any of them in terms of operationality. Because of the experience base it now has, Fujitsu is better able to select problems which are solvable by this technology and the success rate is now somewhere between 75–90 %.

During this survey's literature research, we found also some research projects using expert systems technology for manufacturing planning, scheduling and execution control. Table 4 presents a summary of these projects.

5. GENESYS: A QUICK CASE STUDY

This section focuses upon the process of designing and developing an expert system prototype for production planning and scheduling. It describes in detail the operational characteristics of the prototype constructed and indicates some ways in which this prototype could be developed into an integrated information system.

5.1. Introduction

Following step by step the development approach described in the section 2, a complete prototype expert system called "GENESYS" (GENeric Expert SYstem for Scheduling) has been developed with the aim to schedule the production of small and medium sized manufacturing companies in the most effective way, taking into consideration the prevailing conditions (production characteristics, constraints, performance criteria, etc.) in the industrial environment.

Since the scheduling problem becomes extremely complex very often, even for simple problems, when dynamic uncertainties such as machine breakdowns, tool failures, order cancellation, due date changes and uncertain arrival of jobs appear, we should always keep in mind that looking for an optimized solution (when possible) for realistic applications can be very expensive and time consuming. In scheduling one should be

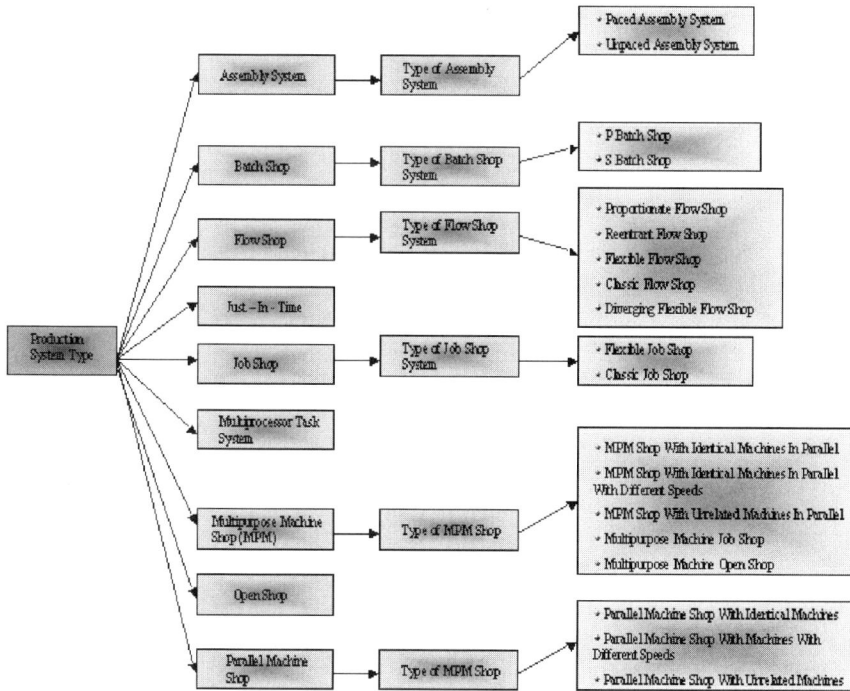

Figure 4. Various types of production systems.

mainly interested in a feasible, good solution and this "attitude" is reflected to the proposed expert system.

5.2. Problem analysis

Production scheduling is a decision–making process that exists in most manufacturing systems and its role is strategic. In few words, scheduling is the process of allocating limited resources to tasks over time in order to produce the desired outputs at the desired times, while a large number of time and relationship constraints among the activities and the resources is being satisfied [55]. A proper allocation of resources enables the company to optimize its objectives and achieve its goals. In modern industries there are many different combinations of machine configurations and consequently of production systems, as presented in Figure 4.

➢ *Flow shop*: Jobs have to undergo multiple operations on a different number of machines. They have the same routing and the same job sequence is maintained throughout the system. An other version of this shop is the flexible flow shop.
➢ *Job shop*: It is a manufacturing environment that produces a wide variety of products. Each order many be individually routed to its unique combination of work centers.

➤ *Batch shop*: In a production system of this type, the production of identical finished or unfinished products is massive and it is preferable to have a batch processing in order to achieve large economies of scale. Flow of jobs in these systems is not totally linear, but it is less complicated than in open shops.

➤ *Flexible assembly systems*: Here we have a limited number of different product types and a given quantity of each product type must be produced by the system. A material handling system is responsible for the movement of jobs in a flexible assembly system.

➤ *Multiprocessor task systems*: In these systems, tasks require processing by one or more machines at a time.

➤ *Multipurpose machine shop*: In this case there are a number of multipurpose machines, capable of processing different jobs.

➤ *Just – in – time*: The basis for JIT concept was the production system of Toyota after the Second World War. A definition of this system is:

> *The JIT is simple: Produce and deliver finished goods just in time to be sold, sub – assemblies just in time to be assembled to finished goods, fabricated parts just in time to go into sub – assemblies, and purchased materials just in time to be transformed into fabricated parts (Schonberger, 1982).*

Job processing has many distinctive characteristics and is often subject to constraints that are peculiar. For example, sometimes a job can start only after a given set of jobs has been completed. Such constraints are referred to as precedence constraints. In other cases, it is not necessary to keep a job on a machine until completion, so preemption is allowed. If the order in which the jobs go through the first machine is maintained throughout the system, then permutation is confirmed. Recirculation may occur in some shops, when a job may visit a machine more than once. If some jobs are more important than others, then we attribute to them a priority factor known as weight.

Machines often have to be reconfigured or cleaned between jobs. This process is known as setup. If the length of the setup depends on the sequence of jobs, then the setup times are sequence–dependent. Machine breakdowns imply that machines are not continuously available. Blocking is another phenomenon that may occur. If a shop has a limited buffer in between two successive machines, it may happen that when the buffer is full the upstream machine is not allowed to release a completed job.

Many different types of objectives are important in production scheduling. Meeting due dates, as a reflection of customer satisfaction, is one of the scheduling criteria that is frequently encountered in practical problems. The natural quantification of this qualitative goal involves the tardiness measure. Such measures may be the minimization of the flow time of jobs, the total tardiness of jobs, their total completion time, and the number of tardy jobs or of the WIP inventory costs and others [56–57].

5.3. The knowledge base

Having analyzed the production scheduling problem domain, the next crucial step was the acquisition of the necessary knowledge concerning the different techniques that are used for its solution. This knowledge was acquired from various sources available. Such sources included production scheduling textbooks, papers, specific company literature, and in some cases direct interviews with senior experts in the field of production scheduling. Some knowledge refinement was necessary as differences in knowledge prevailed from different sources of knowledge.

In GENESYS, the knowledge base is structured as following: there are five classes that operate like libraries containing information about the general scheduling problem. These classes contain sub-classes, objects and sub-objects. The first class is called "Production System Type" and contains the majority of production systems that are used in practice, as well as their variations. The class "Production System Objectives" contains the possible objectives of the scheduling process, such as the Minimization of Total Completion Time or the Minimization of Maximum Tardiness. The user has the possibility to choose an objective from a list that the system presents to him/her. The content of this list is not static but it changes according to the previous answers of the user. In some cases, he/she is able to choose two objectives at the same time (bicriteria problem).

The class "Actions" contains eight sub-classes that correspond to the eight basic types of production system. For each sub-class there are respective approaches that can be proposed to the user. The approach proposed by the system may be either a dispatching rule either an algorithm [58–63]. A dispatching rule is a rule that prioritizes all the jobs that are waiting for processing on a machine. The prioritization scheme may take into account the jobs' and the machines' attributes, as well as the current time. Whenever a machine is free, a dispatching rule inspects the waiting jobs and selects the job with the highest priority. Dispatching rules are used for the minimization of various performance measures such as mean, maximum and variance of flow time and tardiness in dynamic shops (i.e. with a dynamic arrival of jobs during the scheduling period). The knowledge base contains some classic but, in some cases, particularly efficient dispatching rules while new, "state-of-the art", rules have also been included.

The use of algorithms is mostly resorted to in the case of static scheduling problems. In the proposed expert system, we tried to incorporate a wide range of algorithms of different types in order to satisfy the requirements of a generic ERP module. There are optimization algorithms that try to provide an optimal solution (where possible), heuristics, approximation algorithms, which are useful for difficult (NP-hard) problems, and algorithms that try to improve existing solutions (improvement type algorithms).

We must note that the dispatching rules are more popular in real-life manufacturing systems than algorithms, mainly because they are simple to implement and use in any shopfloor and most real-life systems have dynamic job arrivals. In total, 75 dispatching rules and sequencing algorithms (26 dispatching rules and 49 sequencing algorithms) are integrated into the system.

The class "Production Characteristics" contains some special production characteristics (e.g. preemption, blocking, precedence constraints, etc.). The last class of the system is called "Achievements" and contains some specific benefits that can exist (e.g. decrease of the inventory costs, low buffers, etc.) if a particular objective for production scheduling is chosen. It is stressed that this information plays only consulting role for the user.

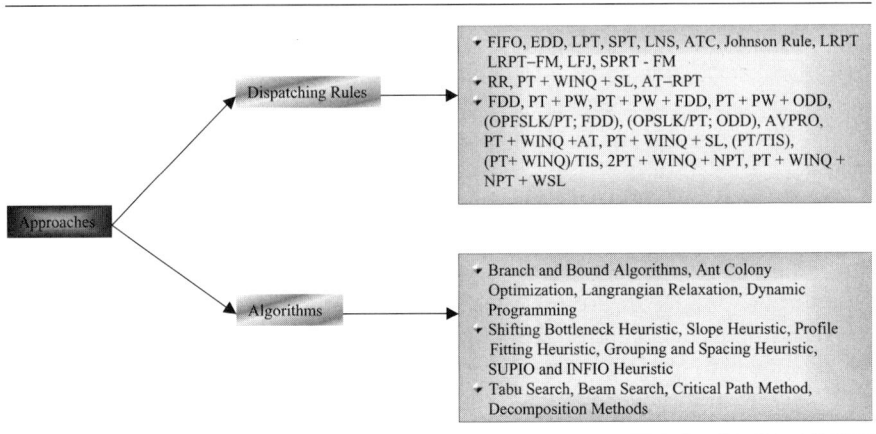

Figure 5. Dispatching rules and algorithms.

5.4. Construction & features

Having acquired the required knowledge, the next step was to represent this knowledge in a computer usable form. A PC-based expert system shell (NEXPERT OBJECT™ by Neuron Data®) was chosen as the development tool. In this system, the knowledge is represented by production rules in IF-THEN format. Specifically, the system consists of 300 production rules. The NEXPERT architecture is event-driven. It is able to use *backward* (deductive) or *forward* (evocative) *reasoning*. These inference mechanisms are completely interdependent. The operation of the current prototype system comprises three stages. In the first stage, as presented in Figure 6, the user is required to respond to the questions and provide data for the parameters concerning the structure of the production system, so that its basic nature (e.g. flexible flow shop or paced assembly system) can be identified.

In the second stage, the user defines the objective to be minimized (e.g. total completion time). This objective may be a single objective or a combination of two others, where it is possible (Figure 7). Finally, in the third stage the system collects information about the particular characteristics of the production (e.g. precedence constraints or permutation).

In the following example we give a rule used by the system:

IF   the production system is of type flow shop
AND   production goal is minimization of mean tardiness
AND   number of machines is between 5 and 15
AND   number of jobs is between 1 and 500
THEN use PT + WINQ + SL dispatching rule

In Figure 8, a typical screenshot of the operation of GENESYS is presented.

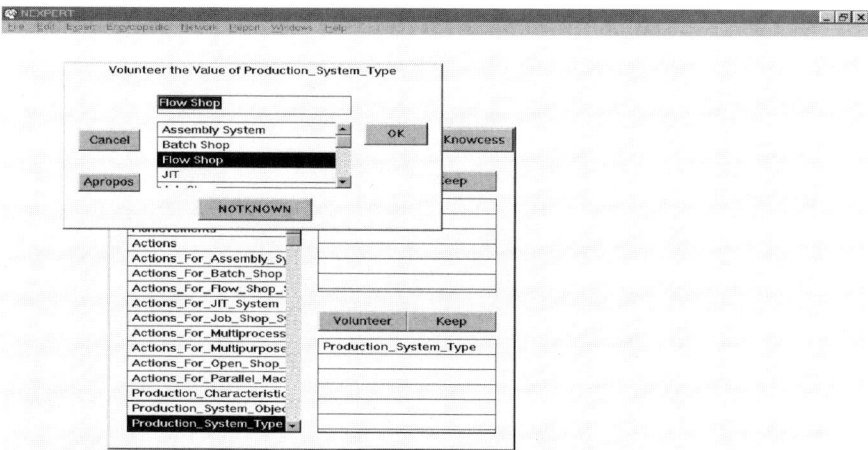

Figure 6. Identification of production system.

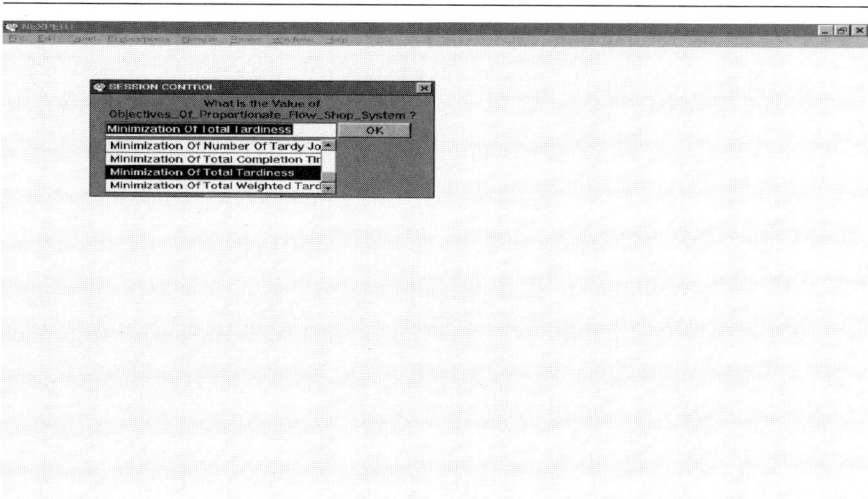

Figure 7. Definition of scheduling objective.

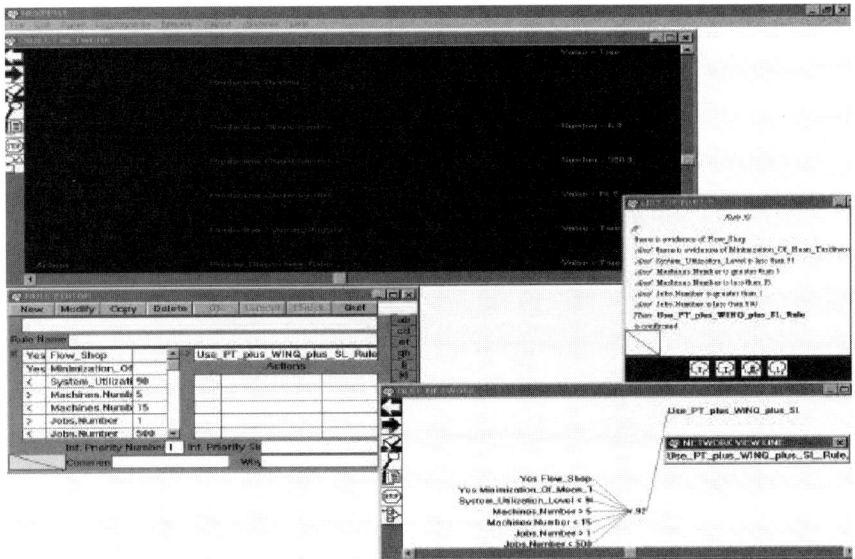

Figure 8. Operation of GENESYS.

5.5. Performance evaluation

In order to validate and test GENESYS towards the quality and reliability of the produced schedules, we used a real data set, which concerned the small-medium Greek company "Papoutsanis S.A." specialized in the production of cosmetics, perfumes, etc. The Table 5 presents the basic characteristics of the production system of this company in which the pilot application of the module took place. It is stressed that in any case the company wanted as an output from the system a monthly production schedule with details per week.

For this specific data set, we, in co-operation with the Production Manager of the company, made a comparison between the results produced by the real application of the proposed schedule and the results produced by the potential application of the Production Manager's schedule.

The detailed study of this comparison resulted to the following quantitative and qualitative conclusions:

√ Reduction of the total number of late production orders by 18%
√ Reduction of the total number of early production orders by 6%
√ Increase in the average machine utilization rate by 7%
√ Increased flexibility by using various (or multiple) scheduling criteria (e.g. minimization of makespan, minimization of tardiness, etc.)
√ Facility for the Production Manager's dynamic intervention in the proposed production schedule in order to make potential modifications (through a Gantt chart).

Table 5 Basic characteristics of the production system of "Papoutsanis S.A."

Shop floor configuration	Data
Production system	Job-shop
	No pre-emption
	Each machine can perform only one operation at a time on any job
Number of work centres (machines)	9
Number of job-orders	500
Number of operations	4–11
Machine utilization levels	85, 90, 95%
Breakdown	Gamma Distribution
Customer design changes	Frequency = 1.00%
Planned set-up time exceeded	Frequency = 4.00%. Magnitude = 25 mins

6. CONCLUSIONS/RECOMMENDATIONS

In this chapter, a state-of-the-art study related to the use of expert systems technology in the production planning and scheduling has been presented. The authors, conceiving that the specific field is an active research area in which many research attempts have been taking place, and believing that expert systems will be one of the main competitive focuses of enterprises in future, proceeded to the implementation of this survey in order to "push" researchers and practitioners to further explore this field and intensify their research activities.

This survey presented recent developments in the relative area—supported by an extensive and updated literature—and showed some new and interesting possibilities. The findings of this survey show that expert systems are generally perceived to be very useful in production planning and scheduling [64–65]. Expert systems are becoming more and more common decision-making tools in many organizations. The benefits reported from the use of ESs in this area include more accurate decisions, time gains, improved quality and more efficient use of resources. It is our belief that the usefulness of ESs in production planning and scheduling will gain more recognition, if they are properly integrated with Operations Research (OR) techniques, especially simulation. Major benefits provided by expert simulation systems have been observed by Sabuncuoglu and Hommertzheim [66].

Most of the expert systems that have been discussed and developed are essentially stand-alone systems. However, it is very likely that in the near future a large portion of the ESs developed will be embedded systems, that is, systems which form a part of the overall software package. Hybrid expert systems are one example of such an approach. Since most operations management problems—in general—are not isolated problems by their nature, isolated expert systems can not solve exactly the problem of the manufacturing manager.

On the other hand, taking into consideration the need for the development of new managerial approaches as a result of the competitive pressure in today's global economy and of the availability of new information technologies, integration will be the main task facing manufacturing systems in the future. Living in the Enterprise

Reason	SD	D	U	A	SA	Mean	SD
			Frequency				
Nobody proposes to use ES in the company	5	10	8	17	7	3.23	1.24
There are no artificial intelligence experts in the company	1	10	4	24	8	3.60	1.07
Integration of ES technology into our current manufacturing system is not possible	9	16	18	0	4	2.45	1.07
Top management do not have any knowledge about ES	1	2	6	28	10	3.94	0.84
Investment is too expensive	0	4	30	13	0	3.19	0.57
Benefits of ES are unknown	0	4	6	25	12	3.96	0.85

Value of coding: SD (Strongly disagree) = 1, D (Disagree) = 2, U (Undecided) = 3, A (Agree) = 4, SA (Strongly agree) = 5

Figure 9. Reasons for not using ES.

Resource Planning (ERP) era, the authors have started dealing with the development of a scheduling expert system and its interconnection to a commercial ERP package. Actually, it is an extended version of the system GENESYS which was presented in this chapter as a case study for successful development of an expert system for production planning and scheduling.

Finally, it must be pointed out that top management play a pivotal role in the productive implementation of expert systems. One study [67] reported that some executives have never even heard of the term "expert system", while others have different perceptions of what an expert system is or does and to what extent their expectations can be realized. These findings are also verified by the survey of Wong et al. [18], as presented in Figure 9. There is no doubt that lack of knowledge about ESs often results in a lack of interest in utilization. In some cases top management do not support ES projects because they see the computer as a tool solely for financial and accounting applications. So, in order to ensure success, top management should show a genuine interest in exploring the applications of ESs in manufacturing planning and scheduling.

REFERENCES

[1] Dornan, B. (1987), "A Status Report: Artificial Intelligence", *Production*, pp. 46–50.
[2] Wilson, J. (1985) "Expert Systems Capture Manufacturing Brainpower", *Production*, Vol. 96, No. 5, pp. 60–64.
[3] Shaw, P. and Whinston, B. (1986), "Application of Artificial Intelligence to Planning and Scheduling in Flexible Manufacturing", in Kusiak, A. (Ed.), *Flexible Manufacturing Systems: Methods and Studies*, North-Holland, pp. 223–42.
[4] Welbank, M. (1983), "*A Review of Knowledge Acquisition Techniques for Expert Systems*", British Telecommunications Research Laboratories Technical Report, Ipswich, England.
[5] Badiru, A. B. (1992), "Expert Systems Applications in Engineering and Manufacturing", Prentice Hall, New Jersey.
[6] Mital, A. and Anand, S. (1994), "Handbook of Expert Systems", Chapman & Hall.
[7] Ignizio, J. P. (1991), "Introduction to Expert Systems", McGraw-Hill Inc., USA.
[8] Jackson, P. (1986), "Introduction to Expert Systems", Addison-Wesley, Wokingham, England

[9] Baker, S. (1988), "Nexpert Object: Mainstreaming AI applications", *IEEE Expert*, Winter 1988, pp. 82.

[10] Huntington, D. (1985), "*EXSYS Expert Systems Development Package*", EXSYS Manual, Albuquerque, New Mexico.

[11] Pinedo, M. (1995), "Scheduling: Theory, Algorithms and Systems", Prentice Hall.

[12] Brucker, P. (1998), "Scheduling Algorithms", Springer Verlag.

[13] Artiba, A. (1997), "Planning and Scheduling of Production Systems—Methodologies and Applications", Chapman & Hall.

[14] Advanced Manufacturing Research, Inc. (1996), "*Advanced planning and scheduling systems: just a fad or a breakthrough in manufacturing and supply chain management?*", The Report on Manufacturing, December 1996.

[15] Kusiak, A. (1990), "Intelligent Manufacturing Systems", Englewood Cliffs, NJ: Prentice-Hall.

[16] Meredith, J. R., McCutcheon, D. M., and Hartley, J. (1994), "Enhancing competitiveness through the new market value equation", *International Journal of Operations & Production Management*, Vol. 14, No. 11, pp. 7–22.

[17] Durkin, J. (1996), "Expert Systems: A view of the Field" in *IEE: Expert, Intelligent Systems with Applications*, April, pp. 56–63.

[18] Wong, B. K., Chong, J. K. S., and Park, J. (1994), "Utilization and Benefits of Expert Systems in Manufacturing: A Study of Large American Industrial Corporations", *International Journal of Operations & Production Management*, Vol. 14, No. 1, pp. 38–49.

[19] Byrd, T. A. (1995), "Expert systems implementation: interviews with knowledge engineers", *Industrial Management & Data Systems*, Vol. 95, No. 10, pp. 3–7.

[20] Coursey, D. H. & Shangraw, R. F. (1989), "Expert system technology for managerial applications: a typology", *Public Productivity Review*, Vol. 12, No. 3, pp. 237–62.

[21] Kusiak, A. & Chen, M. (1988), "Expert Systems for Planning and Scheduling Manufacturing Systems", *European Journal of Operational Research*, Vol. 34, No. 2, pp. 113–130.

[22] Mertens, P. and Kanet, J. (1986), "Expert Systems in Production Management: An Assessment", *Journal of Operations Management*, Vol. 6, No. 4, pp. 393–404.

[23] Jayaraman, V. and Srivastava, R. (1996), "Expert systems in production and operations management", *International Journal of Operations & Production Management*, Vol. 16, No. 12, pp. 27–44.

[24] Meziane, F., Vadera, S., Kobbacy, K., & Proudlove, N. (2000), "Intelligent systems in manufacturing: current developments and future prospects", *Integrated Manufacturing Systems*, Vol. 11, No. 4, pp. 218–238.

[25] Pham, D. T. & Pham, P. T. N. (1999), "Artificial Intelligence in engineering", *International Journal of Machine Tools & Manufacture*, Vol. 39, pp. 937–949.

[26] Zhang, Y. and Chen, H. (1999), "A knowledge-based dynamic job-scheduling in low-volume/high-variety manufacturing", *Artificial Intelligence in Engineering*, Vol. 13, No. 3, pp. 241–9.

[27] Ehner, W., & Bax, F. R. (1983), "Factory of the Future—A Manufacturing Viewpoint", *Production*, Vol. 91, No. 4, pp. 38–48.

[28] Pereira, M. G. (1996), "Expert systems—aspects we must consider for use in production programming", *Computers & Industrial Engineering*, Vol. 31 (1–2), pp. 413–425.

[29] Kanet, J. J. & Adelsberger, H. H. (1987), "Expert systems in production scheduling", *European Journal of Operational Research*, Vol. 29, pp. 51–59.

[30] Fox, M. S. and Smith, S. F. (1984), "ISIS: a knowledge-based system for factory scheduling", *Expert Systems*, Vol. 1, No. 1, pp. 25–49.

[31] Ow, P. S. & Smith, S. F. (1986), "Viewing scheduling as an opportunistic problem-solving process", Working paper, Carnegie-Mellon University, Pittsburg, PA.

[32] Robbins, J. H. (1985), "*PEPS: The Prototype Expert Priority Scheduler*", Technical paper MM-1093, Society of Manufacturing Engineers, Dearborn, MI.

[33] Morton, T. E., Fox, M., & Sathi, A. (1984), "PATRIARCH: A multilevel system for cost accounting, planning, scheduling", partial working document Graduate School of Industrial Administration, Carnegie Mellon University.

[34] Jacobs, R. D. (1983), "The OPT Scheduling System: A Review of a New Production Scheduling System", *Production and Inventory Management*, Vol. 24, No. 3.

[35] Deal, D. E., Chen, J. G., Ignizio, J. P., & Jayakamer, V. (1992), "An expert system scheduler: some reflections on expert system development", *Journal of Computers and Operations Research*.

[36] Marsh, C. A. (1985), "MARS—an expert system using the automated reasoning reasoning tool to schedule resources", *Robotics and Expert Systems—Proceedings of Robex 85, Instrument Society of America*, pp. 123–125.

[37] Chiodini, V. (1980),"An Expert System for Dynamic Manufacturing Rescheduling", *Symposium on Real Time Optimisation in Automated Manufacturing Facilities*, National Bureau of Standards, Gaithersburg, MD.

[38] Biegel, J. E. & Wink, L. J. (1989), "Expert systems can do job shop scheduling: an exploration and a proposal", *Computers & Industrial Engineering*, Vol. 17, No. 1, pp. 347–52.

[39] Palaniswami, S. & Jenicke, L. (1992), "A knowledge-based simulation system for manufacturing scheduling", *International Journal of Operations & Production Management*, Vol. 12, No. 11, pp. 4–14.

[40] Alexander, S. M. (1987), "An expert system for the selection of scheduling rules in a job shop", *Computers & Industrial Engineering*, Vol. 12, No. 3, pp. 167–171.

[41] Abdallah, M. (1995), "A knowledge-based simulation model for job shop scheduling", *International Journal of Operations & Production Management*, Vol. 15, No. 10, pp. 89–102.

[42] De Toni, A., Nassimbeni, G., & Tonchia, S. (1996), "An artificial, intelligent-based production scheduler", *Integrated Manufacturing Systems*, Vol. 7, No. 3, pp. 17–25.

[43] Hayes-Roth, B. (1985), "A blackboard architecture for control", *Artificial Intelligence*, Vol. 26, pp. 251–321.

[44] Custodio, L. M. M., Sentieiro, J. J. S., & Bispo, C. F. G. (1994), "Production planning and scheduling using a fuzzy decision system", *IEEE Transactions on Robotics and Automation*, Vol. 10, No. 2, pp. 160–168.

[45] Howard, A., Kochhar, A., & Dilworth, J. (2000), "Case studies based development of a rule-base for the specification of manufacturing planning and control systems", *International Journal of Production Research*, Vol. 38, No. 12, pp. 2591–2606.

[46] Subramaniam, V., Ramesh, T., Lee, G. K., Wong, Y. S., & Hong, G. S. (2000), "Job Shop Scheduling with Dynamic Fuzzy Selection of Dispatching Rules", *International Journal of Advanced Manufacturing Technology*, Vol. 16, pp. 759–764.

[47] Chen, N., Li, C., & Qin, P. (1998), "KDPAG expert system applied to materials design and manufacture", *Engineering Applications of Artificial Intelligence*, Vol. 11, pp. 669–674.

[48] Szelke, E. & Kerr, R. M. (1994), "Knowledge-based reactive scheduling", *Production Planning & Control*, Vol. 5, No. 2, pp. 124–45.

[49] Sarin, S. C. & Salgame, R. (1989), "A knowledge-based system approach to dynamic scheduling", in Kusiak, A. (Ed.), *Knowledge-based Systems in Manufacturing*, Taylor & Francis, Philadelphia, PA.

[50] Brown, M. C. (1989), "The dynamic reproduction scheduler: conquering the changing production environment", in Pau, L. F., Motiwalla, J., Pao, Y. H. and Theh, H. H. (ed.), *Expert Systems in Economics, Banking and Management*, North-Holland, Amsterdam.

[51] Yamamoto, M. & Nof, S. (1985), "Scheduling/rescheduling in the manufacturing operating system environment", *International Journal of Production Research*, Vol. 23, No. 4, pp. 705–722.

[52] Driscoll, W. C. (1993), "A microcomputer-based scheduling assist system", *Computers and Industrial Engineering*, Vol. 25, No. 4, pp. 223–226.

[53] Tayanlthi, P., Manivannan, S., & Banks, J. (1992), "A knowledge-based simulation architecture to analyze interruptions in a flexible manufacturing system", *Journal of Manufacturing Systems*, Vol. 11, No. 3, pp. 195–214.

[54] Li, H., Li, Z., Li, L., & Hu, B. (2000), "A production rescheduling expert simulation system", *European Journal of Operational Research*, No. 124, pp. 283–293.

[55] Morton, T. and Pentico, D. (1993), *"Heuristic Scheduling Systems"*, John Wiley & Sons.

[56] Pinedo, M. (1995), *"Scheduling: Theory, Algorithms and Applications"*, Prentice-Hall, Englewood Cliffs, pp. 9–14.

[57] Pinedo, M. and Chao, X. (1999), *"Operations scheduling with applications in manufacturing and services"*, McGraw-Hill Inc., USA, pp. 15–23.

[58] Brucker, P. (1998), *"Scheduling Algorithms"*, Springer Verlag.

[59] Holthaus, O. and Rajendran, C. (2000), "Efficient jobshop scheduling dispatching rules: further developments", *Production Planning & Control*, Vol. 11, No. 2, pp. 171–178.

[60] Rajendran, C. and Holthaus, O. (1999), "A comparative study of dispatching rules in dynamic flowshops and jobshops", *European Journal Of Operational Research*, Vol. 116, pp. 156–170.

[61] Armentano, A. and Ronconi, D. (1999), "Tabu search for total tardiness minimization in flowshop scheduling problems", *Computers & Operations Research*, Vol. 26, pp. 219–235.

[62] Kaskavelis, C. and Caramanis, M. (1998) "Efficient Langrangian relaxation algorithms for industry size job-shop scheduling problems", *IIE Transactions*, Vol. 30, pp. 1085–1097.

[63] Armentano, A. and Scrich, C. (2000) "Tabu search for minimizing total tardiness in a job shop", *International Journal Production Economics*, Vol. 63, pp. 131–140.

[64] Liebowitz, J. & Lightfoot, P. (1987), "Expert systems for scheduling: a survey and preliminary design concepts", *Applied Artificial Intelligence Journal*, Vol. 1, No. 3.

[65] Kumura, S., Joshi, S., Kashyap, R., Moodie, C., & Chang, T. (1986), "Expert systems in industrial engineering", *International Journal of Production Research,* Vol. 24, pp. 1107–25.

[66] Sabuncuoglu, I. & Hommertzheim, L. (1989), "Expert Simulation Systems—Recent Developments and Applications in Flexible Manufacturing Systems", *Computers & Industrial Engineering*, Vol. 16, No. 4, pp. 575–85.

[67] Grindley, K. (1988), "End Users Are Key To Success". *Datamation*, Vol. 34, No. 7, pp. 100–111.

APPLYING INTELLIGENT AGENT-BASED SUPPORT SYSTEMS IN AGILE BUSINESS PROCESSES

CHUN-CHE HUANG

1. INTRODUCTION

Business is undergoing a major paradigm shift, moving from traditional management into a world of agile organizations and processes. An agile corporation should be able to rapidly respond to market changes. Corporation managers make informed decisions based upon a combination of judgments and information from marketing, sales, research, development, manufacturing, and finance departments. Ideally, all relevant information should be brought together before a judgment is exercised. However obtaining pertinent, consistent and up-to-date information across a large company is a complex and time-consuming process. For this reason, corporations have been seeking to develop a number of information technology (IT) systems to assist with the information management of their business processes. Such systems aim to improve the way that information is gathered, managed, distributed, and presented to people in key business functions and operations.

The notion of an intelligent agent (IA) is one of the most important concepts to emerge in IT systems in the 1990s, as Guilfoyle [1] noted:

"in 10 years time most new IT development will be affected, and many business processes will contain embedded agent-based systems."

Nwana [2] views *intelligent agents* as "software components and/or hardware that are capable of acting exactingly to accomplish tasks on behalf of its user and learn as they react and/or interact with their external environment." The partial view of an

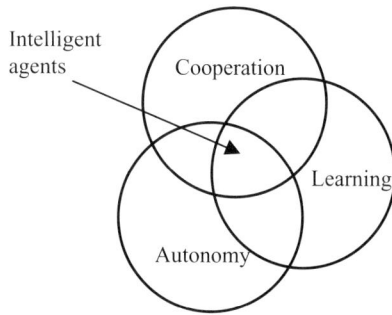

Figure 1. A partial view of an agent typology.

agent typology is presented in Figure 1. Three are main components: Cooperation, autonomy, and learning [3].

Agent technology is set to radically alter not only the way in which computers interact, but also the way complex systems are conceptualized and built. An important part of the agent approach is the principle that agents (like humans) can function more effectively in groups that are characterized by cooperation and division of labor. Agent programs are designed to autonomously collaborate with each other in order to satisfy both their internal goals and the shared external demands generated by virtue of their participation in agent societies. Widely range application domains in which agent solution are being applied or investigated including workflow management [4], telecommunications network management [5], air-traffic control [6], business process re-engineering [7], information retrieval/management [8], personal digital assistants and e-mail filtering [9], digital libraries [10], health-care provisioning and monitoring [11], smart databases [4], and scheduling/diary management [12], electronic commerce [13, 14], supply chain management [15–18], simulation techniques [19, 20], software engineering [21, 22], interface [23, 24], product design and planning [25–27], managing business processes [28–30]. Knowledge-based multi-agent systems have been found useful in many applications related to manufacturing including scheduling, vehicle routing and enterprise modeling [31–35].

"Multi-agent" systems work through the interaction with other agents, cooperating or competing to achieve their goals. The importance of automated intelligent agents in the organizations comes from their natural distribution, their ability to pre-process information for users, their continuous presence and availability and the interactions with other agents and users [36]. Agents blend many of the traditional properties of Artificial Intelligent (AI) programs-knowledge-level reasoning, flexibility, pro-activeness, goal-directedness, and so forth—with insights gained from distributed software engineering, machine learning, negotiation and teamwork theory, and the social sciences. The agent metaphor, due to its suitability for open environments, has recently become popular with distributed, large-scale, and dynamic nature applications such as e-commerce and virtual enterprises. The key aspects of agents are their autonomy, their abilities to perceive, reason, and act in their surrounding environments, as well as the capability to cooperate with other agents to solve complex problems. These reasons why to use intelligent agents are illustrated as the following [37, 38]:

- Decision support: There is a need for increased support for tasks performed by knowledge workers, especially in the decision-making area. Timely and knowledge-able decisions made by these professionals greatly increase their effectiveness and the success of their businesses in the marketplace.
- Repetitive office activity: There is a pressing need to automate performed by ad-ministrative and clerical personnel in functions such as sales or customer support to reduce labor costs and increase office productivity. Today labor costs are estimated to be as much as 60 percent of the total cost of information delivery.
- Mundane personal activity: In a fast-paced society, time-strapped people need new ways to minimize the time spent on routine personal tasks such as booking airline tickets so that they can devote more time to professional activities. One specific form of smart agents is the voice-activated interface agent that reduces the burden on the user of having to explicitly command the computer. Another is that of a personal assistant, which learns your work patterns and replicates them on typical but mundane tasks suck as appointments, meal reservations, and e-mail processing.
- Search and retrieval: It is not possible to directly manipulate a distributed database system in an electronic commerce setting with millions of data objects. Users will have to relegate the task of searching and cost comparison to agents. These agents perform the tedious, time-consuming, and repetitive tasks of searching database, retrieving and filtering information, and delivering it back to the user.
- Domain experts: It is advisable to model costly expertise and make it widely available. Examples of expert software agents could be models of real-world agents such as translators, lawyers, diplomats, union negotiators, stockbrokers, and even clergy.

In addition, a major value of intelligent agents is that they are able to assist in processing and searching through all the data. They save time by making decisions about what is relevant to the user. They are able to access through the Internet and the various databases effortlessly and with unswerving attention to detail to extract the best data. They are not limited to hard (quantitative) data, but can also be useful in obtaining soft data about new trends that may cause unanticipated changes (and opportunities) in local or even global markets. With the agent at work, the competent user's decision making ability is enhanced with information rather than paralyzed by too much input.

The potential of agent technology has been hailed in a 1994 report by Ovum [39], a UK-based market research company, titled "Intelligent agents: the new evolution in software." The choice of agents as a solution technology is motivated by the following observations [40]:

- the domain involves an inherent distribution of data, problem solving capabilities, and responsibilities

- the integrity of the existing organizational structure and the autonomy of its sub-parts must be maintained
- interactions are fairly sophisticated, including negotiation, information sharing, and coordination
- the problem solution cannot be prescribed entirely from start to finish

When taken together, the following set of requirements leaves agents as the strongest solution candidate—(i) distributed object systems have the necessary encapsulation, but not the sophisticated reasoning required for social interaction or proactive behavior; (ii) distributed processing systems deal with the distributed aspect of the domain but not with the autonomous nature of the components. Specifically, the sets of requirements must be satisfied in agile business processes.

To date, the need for agile industry to deliver high quality products at low cost has long been recognized. What is also becoming clear is that the further requirements of high variety and rapid business processes, e.g., design process, are gradually being superimposed on these older requirements, so that, for example:

"The complex product markets of the twenty-first century will demand the ability to quickly and globally deliver a high variety of customized products."
Earl Hall quoted in Davidow and Malone [41].

The agent-based system shows a great promise for agility and satisfying these requirements. The remainder of this chapter describes the work undertaken to conceptualize business process and product development through a collection of intelligent agents. Section 2 proposes an intelligent framework. The framework is applied to object-oriented design process in Section 3, processes of supply chain in Section 4, and knowledge management in Section 5. Section 6 concludes this chapter and issues further researches.

2. INTELLIGENT AGENT FRAMEWORK

In this section, an intelligent agent-based system is designed to enhance the agility of existing business processes, rather than to modify or replace these processes. The intelligent agent (IA) researches both the technology and the methods that are needed to improve the way information is gathered, managed, distributed and utilized to decision-makers in key business functions and operations. The system characteristics [42]:

- Intelligent: The agent automatically customizes itself to the preferences of its client (or customer), based on previous experience and imprecise information from interaction with customers. The agent also automatically adapts to changes in its environment.
- Autonomous: An agent is able to take the initiative and exercise a non-trivial degree of control over its own actions through service agreements.
- Cooperative: An agent does not blindly obey commands, but makes suggestions to modify requests or ask clarification questions. It also cooperates with other agents to query the information needed.

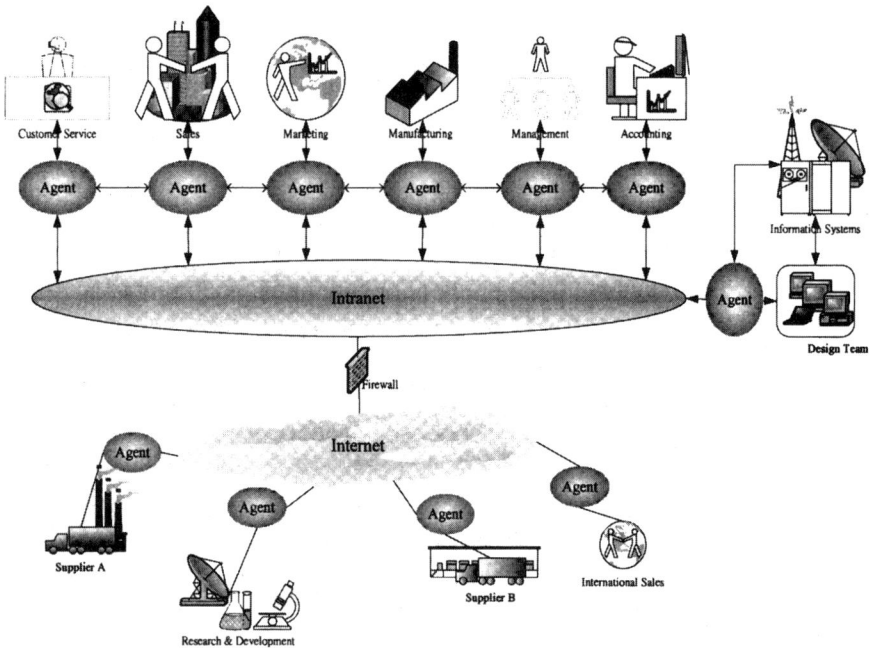

Figure 2. The environment of the agent-based system.

2.1. Intelligent agent system environment

In the agent-based system, each IA is able to perform one or more *services* (Figure 2). A service corresponds to some problem solving activities in business. The simplest service (called a *elemental job*) represents a problem solving atomic activity endeavor in the IA system, e.g., combining two modules into a higher-level module in product design. These atomic activities can be combined to form *complex services*, e.g., creation of a PC including a terminal, a motherboard, a keyboard modules, etc., by adding ordering constraints (e.g. two tasks can run in parallel, must run in parallel, or must run in sequence). The nesting of services can be arbitrarily complex and at the topmost level the entire business process ultimately can be viewed as a service.

Service requirements are issued either from other department, e.g., market teams through an Intranet, or from external customers through the Internet. Services are associated with one or more agents that are responsible for the management and execution of those services. Each service is managed by one agent, although the execution of it's sub-services may involve a number of other agents. Since agents are autonomous, there are no control dependencies between them. Therefore, if an agent requires a service, which is managed by another agent, it cannot simply instruct that agent to start the service. Rather, the agents must come to a mutually acceptable agreement about the terms and conditions under which the desired service will be performed. The mechanism for making agreements is *negotiation*—a joint decision making process in which the parties verbalize their (possibly contradictory) demands and then move towards agreement by a process of concession or search for new alternatives.

To negotiate with one another, a *protocol* is required to specify the role of the current message interchange, e.g., whether the agent is providing a service, responding with a counter-solution, or accepting or rejecting a service [42, 43]. Additionally, agents need a means of describing and referring to the domain terms involved in the negotiation. For example, both agents need to be sure that they are describing the same service even though they may both have a different (local) name for it and represent it in a different manner. This heterogeneity is inherent in most organizations because each department typically models its own information and resources in its own way. Thus when agents interact, a number of semantic mappings and transformations may need to be performed to create a mutually comprehensible semantic map that can be used as an *information sharing language* [44].

Agents communicate with other agents in two ways: loosely coupled and tightly coupled. In a loosely coupled interaction each agent has an equal status, and nobody dominates the other. In a tightly coupled mode, one agent is a controlling agent and the other agents have restricted access from agents outside the agency [28]. However, these agents still have a large degree of autonomy. In this organizational model, servant agents reside in an agency. These servant agents are loosely coupled to each other but tightly coupled to the dominating agent. The dominating agent provides access to the world outside its agency. Agents within an agency may only negotiate with the external agents and a servant agent. A dominating agent will normally be a loosely coupled agent in a higher-level agency. Agents in an agency will usually be the dominating agents of lower level agencies. This leads to a hierarchical organization of agencies reflecting the logical structure.

To extend this model further, the agent requesting the services is designated as the dominating agent and then a set of agents from different agencies can be selected to form a *virtual agency* [45]. This model reflects the principle of a virtual corporation in [46] whereby agents from different parts of a logical organization may cooperate in providing some specific service. Figure 3 shows the virtual agency involved in two services and a dominating agent with two other agents.

There are three distinct phases to the service lifecycle in the agent-based systems (Figure 4). First, the agent has to describe the service and how it is realized. This is carried out using a *service description diagram* (SDD) template [47]. A SDD template is described by a name, input and output fields of the services. The name uniquely identifies the service provided by that agent. The input and output field specifies what related information is needed by the service, who is to provide or receive it, and if it is mandatory (must be provided before the service can start) or optional (if available it will be used, but if it is unavailable the service can still proceed).

2.2. Architecture of an IA

All agents have the same basic architecture (Figure 5). This involves an *agent body* that is responsible for managing the agent's activities and interacting with peers, and an *agency*

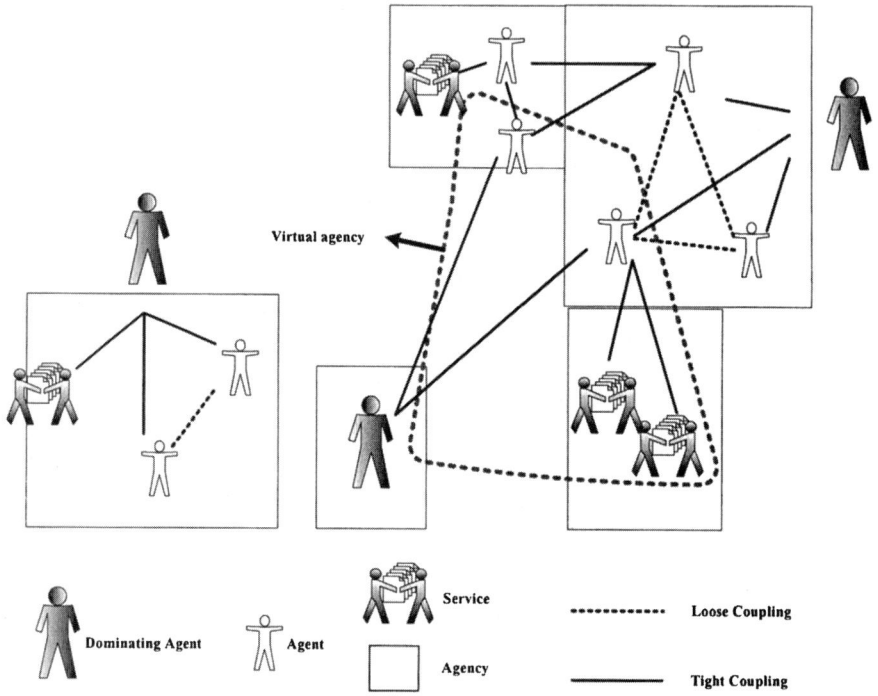

Figure 3. A virtual agency.

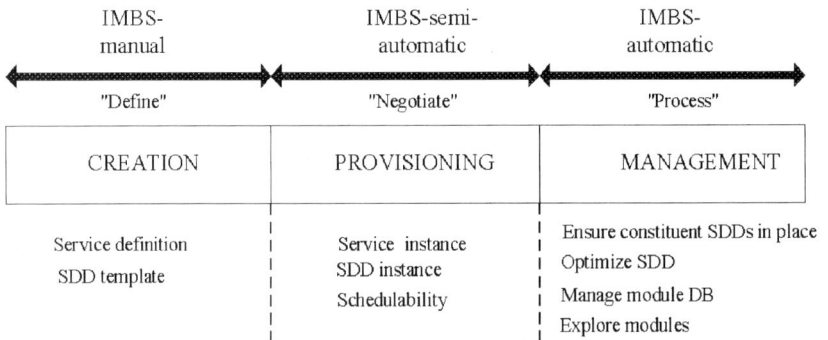

Figure 4. The service lifecycle.

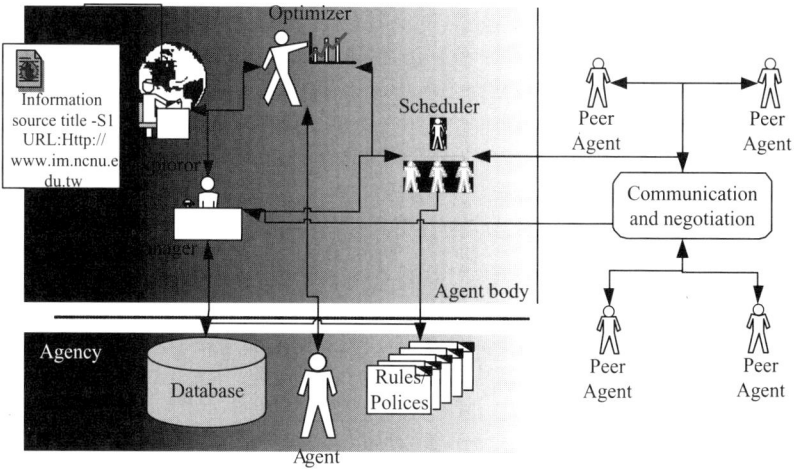

Figure 5. The agent architecture.

that represents the solution resources for the problems of business processes. The body has a number of functional components responsible for each of it's main activities—scheduling jobs, searching available resources, optimizing process of problem-solving, and managing the databases. This internal architecture is broadly based on the ADEPT [28, 45] and ARCHON [44] agent models.

The domain resources include not only databases and jobs, but also other agents. The latter case allows a *nested (hierarchical) agent system* to be constructed in which higher-level agents realize their functionality through lower level-agents (the lower-level agents have the same structure as the higher-level agents and, can, therefore, have sub-agents as well as the jobs in their agency). For example, the higher-level agent may represent a product development department whose work is carried out by a number of design teams (the lower-level agents). This structure enables flat, hierarchical, and hybrid organizations to be modeled in a single framework.

The differences between an agent in an agency and a peer agent relate to the levels of autonomy and helpfulness. In both cases, the agents negotiate to reach agreements—however in the former case: (i) the agent cannot reject the proposal outright (although it can counter-propose until an acceptable agreement is reached); and (ii) the agent must negotiate in a cooperative (rather than a competitive) manner (since there is some degree of commonality of purpose).

The agent plays four basic roles in the system:

Scheduler: Responsible for assessing and monitoring the agent's ability to meet: (i) The SDD agreement that is already agreed upon and (ii) the potential SDD agreement that it may agree to in the future. This involves two main roles: scheduling and exception handling. The former involves maintaining a record of the availability of the agent's resources, which can then be used to determine whether SDDs can be met or new SDDs can be accepted. The exception handler receives exception reports from the optimizer during service execution (e.g. "service may fail", "service has failed", or "no SDD in place") and decides upon the appropriate response. For example, if a service is delayed then the scheduler may decide to locally reschedule it, to renegotiate its SDD, or to terminate it altogether.

Optimizer: Responsible for optimizing the service results throughout the execution. Three main roles involve: service execution management (optimizing executed services as specified by the agent's SDDs), solution presentation (routing solutions between servers, clients and other agents), and exception handling (monitor the execution of jobs and services for unexpected events and then react appropriately).

Manager:
1. Maintains and provides access to (i) the SDDs agreed upon with other agents and a list of peers which can provide services of interest, and (ii) database.
2. Delivers the status messages of active services
   (i) between the optimizer and the clients
   (ii) between an agent and its agency
   • between the optimizer and agents within the agency during service execution
   • between the scheduler and agents within the agency during negotiation; and
   (iii) between peer agents
   • between the optimizer and peer agents during service execution
   • between the scheduler and peer agents during negotiation.
3. (i) Communicates between the optimizer and clients within the agency relating to job management activities (e.g. activate, suspend, or resume a job), and (ii) communicates between agents within that agency or peer agents relating to service execution management (e.g. an instruction to start service, service finished, service results). The scheduler's communications with both agency agents and peer agents relates to service negotiation.

Explorer: perform the role of managing, querying or collating information from many distributed sources. It is able to traverse the WWW, gather information and report what it retrieves to a home location. Figure 6 depicts how the typical static explorer works. It shows how an explorer is associated with some particular search engines. A search engine is able to search the WWW, depth-first, and store the topology of the WWW in a database management system (DBMS) and the full index of URLs in the WAIS [48]. Public search/indexing engines such as Lycos or Webcrawler can be used similarly to build up the index. The explorer, which has been requested to collate information, issues various search requests to one or several URL search engines. The information is collated and sent back to the IMBS agent.

Due to nature of the diverse processes in business, different optional roles are required in different problem domains and will be consider later.

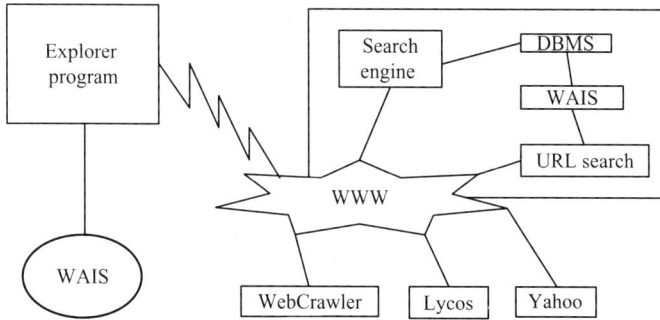

Figure 6. A view of how an explorer works.

2.3. The agent communication

The collaboration of agents is necessary and becomes an important issue. To solve this problem, this section presents the communication language and conversation policy of agents.

2.3.1. The agent communication language

In order to cooperate and share information/knowledge, agents interact and communicate with other agents. It is required that agents have a common or inter-translatable representation language to interpret the exchanged messages. An agent communication language (ACL) is the language in which communicative acts can be expressed [49]. There are two kinds of ACL in which to represent information and queries are universally accepted and used commonly: FIPA (Foundation for Intelligent Physical Agents) and KQML (Knowledge Query and Manipulation Language). In this paper, FIPA is used because FIPA is designed to remedy some of the perceived weaknesses of various versions of KQML, and is accepted as a suitable language for the agents' community to get standardized [50].

An FIPA ACL message contains a set of one or more message elements. The elements that are needed for effective agent communication will vary according to the communication situation [49]; the only element that is mandatory in all ACL messages is the performative. The performative is the type of communicative acts such as "Agree", "Confirm", "Request" and etc. The FIPA Performative and FIPA ACL Message Elements of the agent-based system are referred in [51].

FIPA defines encoding-representation is a way of representing a message in a particular transport encoding. Examples of possible representations are XML, Bit-efficient encoding and serialized Java objects [49]. XML is chosen as the representation method in this chapter because XML makes ACL more WWW friendly. FIPA defines an XML document type definition (DTD) according to the FIPA ACL Message Structure and FIPA Performative. The original FIPA message can become a well-defined XML document according to the DTD. Figure 7 is a simple FIPA-ACL message for agent 1 to

```
(Reply
:sender agent1
:receiver agent2
:content (CPU Pentium IV 1.3 micrometer manufacturing capacity)
:ontology laptop
:language KIF)
```

Figure 7. A simple FIPA-ACL message.

```
<?xml version "1.0"?>
<!DOCTYPE FIPA_ACL_DTD "fipa.acl.xml.std">
<fipa-message>reply</fipa-message>
<sender>Agent1<sender>
<receiver>Agent2</receiver>
<content>
CPU .13 micrometer Pentium IV
</content>
<ontology>laptop</ontology>
<language>KIF</language>
```

Figure 8. The FIPA-ACL message encoded with XML.

reply "CPU Pentium IV 1.3 micrometer manufacturing capacity" to agent 2 for agent 1's question, "Which CPU manufacturing capacity saves more power?" Figure 8 is the XML representation of this message.

2.3.2. The content language

A content language is a language used to express the content of a communication between agents [49]. In the agent-based system, the information is transferred using the content language. The ACL packs the message using a content language; that is, the content of the message is expressed in a content language.

FIPA allows considerable flexibility in the selection, form, and encoding of a content language [49]. There are many content languages, such as FIPA-SL (Semantic Language), FIPA-RDF (Resource Description Framework), FIPA-KIF (Knowledge Interchange Format) and FIPA-CCL (Collaborative Coaching & Learning) available for far. In the proposed system, FIPA-RDF is used because it is in the XML format. The XML document can make the knowledge or information exchange more easily through the World Wide Web.

Figure 9 illustrates the relationship between agents, ACL, and content language. Agents communicate using ACL; and content language, where the information/knowledge is contained is packed inside the ACL.

For example, an *AA (analysis agent)* requests a *CA (collection agent)* to collect the desired data, and then a *IA (integration agent)* sends the collective results to the AA.

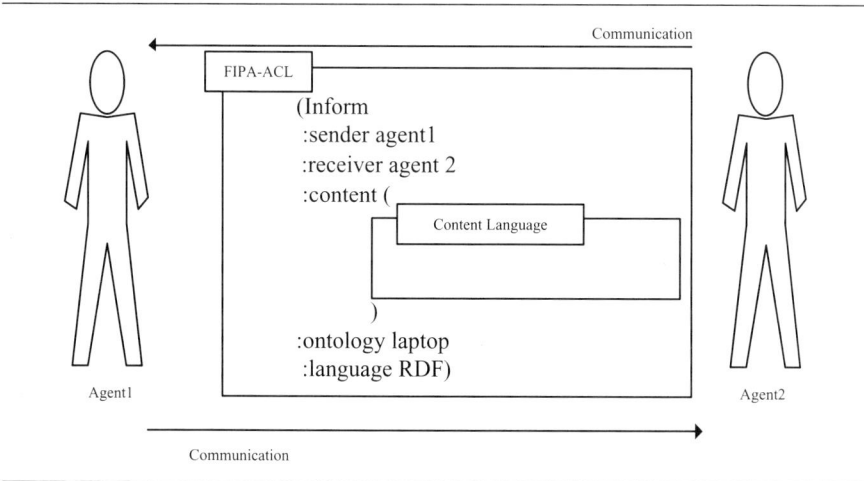

Figure 9. The Relationship between agent, ACL and content language.

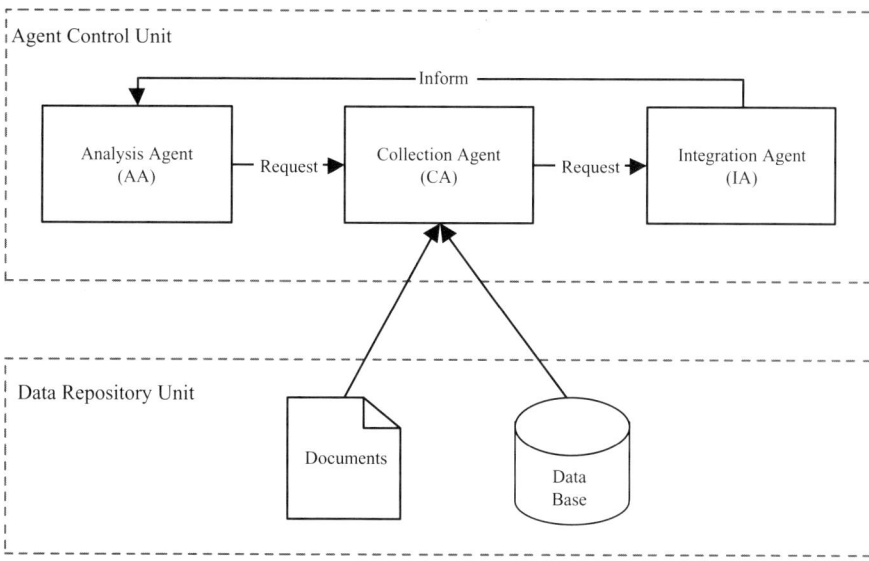

Figure 10. Conversation process of data analysis.

Figure 10 illustrates the flowchart. A set of communication messages is defined to support information/knowledge exchange.

A complete message has two parts: "ACL" and "Content." In the ACL part, the value in "fipa–message" tag corresponds to the "FIPA Performative." In this message, the performative is a "request." The value in "sender" tag corresponds to the "sender agent" in the FIPA ACL. In this message, the sender is "*AA*." The value in "receiver" tag corresponds to the "receiver agent" in FIPA ACL. In this message, the receiver is "*CA*." The value in "language" tag corresponds to the "language element" in FIPA ACL. In this message language is FIPA-RDF.

In the content part, the values of tags in the "fipa:argument" tag correspond to the parameters carried by message, which contains four types of parameters. The "DBkind" parameter represents the database name in which the *CA* collects data. In this message, the database name is "Transaction." The "timeBegin" and "timeEnd" tags illustrate the time period when the data is collected by the *CA* from "timeBegin" to "timeEnd." In this illustrated example, the data *AA* extends from 1997/7/1 to 1998/1/1. The final parameter in this message is "analysisMethod." It informs the *CA* how the data is analyzed. However, the CA does not use it. The *CA* will send this parameter to the *IA*. This also tells the *IA* how to organize data, because different analysis techniques have different data formats. The "language" in content describes the programming language that the agent uses to perform the task. In this example "Java Language" is used. The "code-uri" tag shows the physical location, where the agent performs a task. In this example, the agent runs the program located in the [52] to perform the acquisition task:

```
<?xml version "1.0"?>
<!DOCTYPE FIPA_ACL_DTD "fipa.acl.xml.std">
<fipa-message>request</fipa-message>
 <sender>AA</sender>
 <receiver>CA</receiver>
 <content>
 <?xml version "1.0"?>
 <rdf:RDF>
  <fipa:Action rdf:ID="AARequestData">
   <fipa:actor>CA</fiap:actor>
   <fipa:act>CollectData</fipa:act>
   <fipa:argument>
    <argument:timeBegin>1997/7/1</argument:timeBegin>
    <argument:timeEnd>1998/1/1</argument:timeEnd>
    <argument:analysisMethod>Association</argument:analysisMethod>
    <argument:DBkind>Transaction<argument:DBkind>
    <fipa:implementedby>
<fipa:Code>
<fipa:language>Java</fipa:language>
 <fipa:code-uri>
  https://iskmlab.im.ncnu.edu.tw/DataClooect.jsp
</fipa:code-uri>
</fipa:Code>
   <fipa:implementedby>
  </fipa:argument>
 </fipa:Action>
 </rdf:RDF>
</content>
  <language>fipa-rdf0</language>
```

2.3.3. *The agent conversation policy*

In most agent-based systems, communication between agents takes through the use of messages. A message consists of a packet of information, usually sent asynchronously.

The message type is represented by a verb corresponding to some kind of illocutionary act (e.g., request, inform). Agents in the context of conversations exchange messages. A conversation is a sequence of message between two agents, taking place over a period of time that may be arbitrarily long, yet is bounded by certain termination conditions for any given occurrence. Conversations may give rise to other conversations as appropriate. Each message is part of an extensible protocol—consisting of both message names and conversation policies (CPs) (also called pattern or rules) common to the agents participating in the conversation. The content portion of a message encapsulates any semantic or procedural elements independent of the conversation policy itself [53]. Based on the notion of patterns, a conversation schema (schema, for short) -based method for specifying CPs is presented. A conversation schema is defined as a pattern of conversation interactions specifying CPs centered on one or more conversation *topics*. Topics are extracted from application domain at the domain analysis stage. A goal-directed schema is a schema in which the pattern of interaction is directed towards achieving a specified goal of participating agent(s) [54]. According to [54], there are four advantages in using scheme-based conversation policy:

(1) It ensures consistency and effectiveness of the agent conversation by considering sub-task constraints.
(2) It reduces communication transaction by incorporating with CM(s) (Conversation Managers) that can quickly determine for the participating agents what to do instead of resorting to lengthy reasoning by them.
(3) It decreases the complexity of implementation by constructing CM(s) that separate the description of common agents' functionality from that of communication and synchronization, to ensure local and global coherency.
(4) It enhances the reusability of software components. Domain-independent and domain-specific conversation knowledge are organized and formulated into hierarchies of conversation schema classes using object-oriented methodologies.

For these reasons, a schema-based approach is used to specify conversation policies in the agent-based system. The five steps of the schema-based conversation processes are presented in Figure 11 based on the work of Lin and Norrie [54]:

Step 1. Define the conversation topics.
Step 2. Define the conversation schemata
Step 3. Use Coloured Petri Nets (CPNs) to check if there is deadlock or livelock. If deadlock occurs, identify it.
Step 4. Create "If-then" rules based on CPNs.
Step 5. Generate java thread classes based on the "If-then" rules

Step 1:
The main target of the first step is to identify conversation topics. A conversation typically focuses on one or more "topics" each associated with task-related information. A topic can be described by a set of variables, which have values to be agreed upon by the agents involved and have constraints to be satisfied by other agents

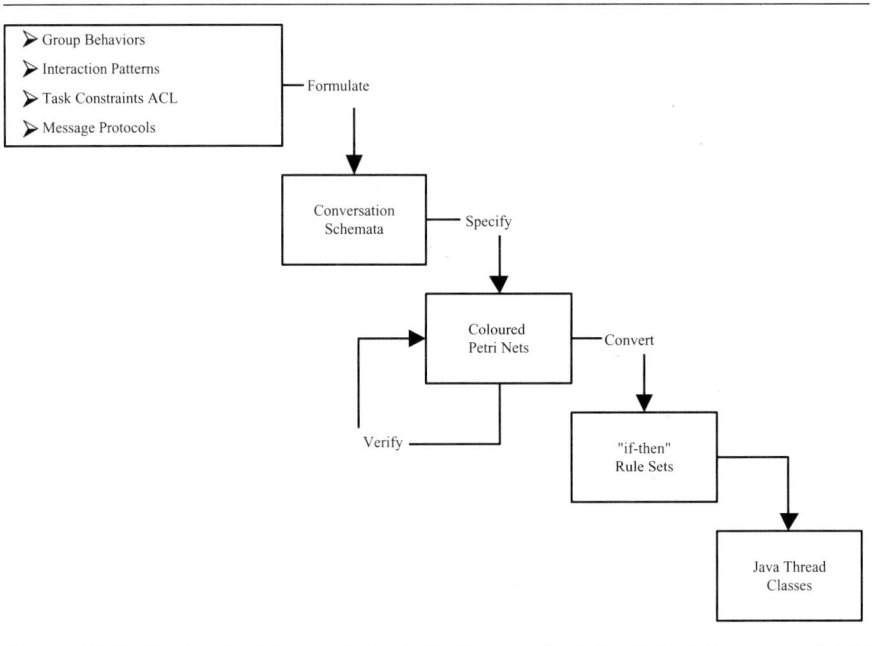

Figure 11. The steps of the schema-based conversation processes.

or users. Conversation topics, denoted by TP, can be described by TP = (TP_ID, ARGUMENTS), where TP_ID is the identification of a conversation topics and ARGUMENT lists all arguments of the topics. Table 1 illustrates the TP of the agent-based system.

Step 2:
The second step identifies the schema. Figure 10 and 12 present the process and schema, respectively.

In Figure 12, "Name" represents the schema's name and "Task" describes the purpose of this conversation. In this example, the purpose of this conversation is to analyze the data from various data sources. The "Agent_type" corresponds to the agents involved in this conversation. In the example, three agents, *AA*, *CA* and *IA* involve in the conversation. The "Status" describes the status, which occurs in this conversation.

Step 3:
After defining the schema, it is described by CPNs (Coloured Petri Nets). The CPNs provide a framework for the design, specification, validation, and verification of agent-based systems [55]. The advantages of this approach is that it not only represents the information being exchanged among agents, but also describes their internal states, thus describing the conversation process in much more detail [53]. In this section, CPNs

Table 1 The TP in the agent-based system

Topics	Description	Arguments
Analysis_Process	The process of analyzing data.	Analysis_method, Time_beg, Time_end
Get_Uprofile	Getting information form User Profile	DBName, Analysis_Method
Get_Dprofile	Getting information form Domain Expert Profile	DBName, Analysis_Method
Get_Kprofile	Getting information form Knowledge Store Profile	DBName, Analysis_Method
Knowledge	Getting expert knowledge	Query_String, Knowledge
Get_Comment	Getting comment from domain expert	DEID (Domain Expert ID)
Send_Uknowledge	Sending expert knowledge to user	UID (User ID)
Submit_Query	Submitting query operation	Query_String
. . .	. . .	. . .

Schema
  Name: Analysis_Data
  Task: Analyze the data from various data source
  Topic: Analysis
  Agent_types: *AA*, *CA*, *IA*
  Acts: Request by *AA*, request by *CA*, inform by *IA*
  Status: READY A, READY B, READY C, Request, Inform, WAITING A, WATTING B
&

Figure 12. The schema corresponding to the process of data analysis.

are used to check if there are deadlock or livelock in the agent-based system. The sub-schemata of schema are represented as transitions of CPN. Its states are described by places with tokens holding structured messages. Relation Flows are represented as preconditions and post-conditions in the forms of arc expressions.

The following steps present the construction process of schemata [20]:

Step 3.1. Identify agent types, attributes and state variables of the schema according to the topics.

Step 3.2. For every agent type, add the transitions for communicative acts or sub-schemata, and represent the actions performed by the same agent, which are aligned horizontally.

Step 3.3. Add the places and flow expressions between the transitions and connect them.

Step 3.4. Add the information exchange represented by collective state places that occur among the agents for the topics.

Step 3.5. Establish an external interface.

Figure 13 illustrates the CPN, colors, and variables used in the "Analysis_Data" schema. The derived CPN representation of schemata allows the verification for logical consistency, completeness, and absence of deadlock and livelock. The simulation technique can be used for verification [56].

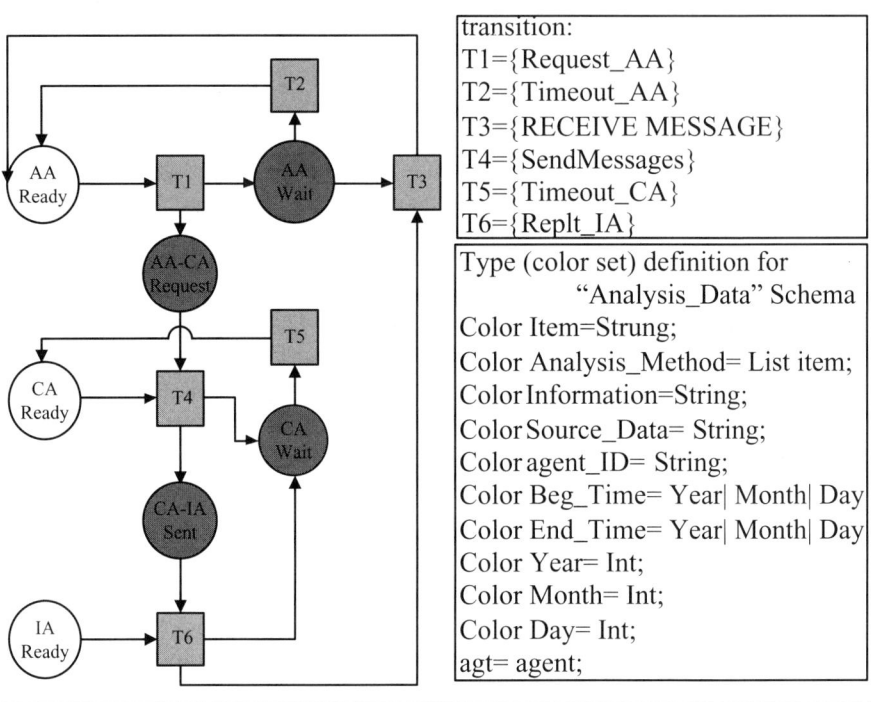

| transition: |
| T1={Request_AA} |
| T2={Timeout_AA} |
| T3={RECEIVE MESSAGE} |
| T4={SendMessages} |
| T5={Timeout_CA} |
| T6={Replt_IA} |

Type (color set) definition for "Analysis_Data" Schema
Color Item=Strung;
Color Analysis_Method= List item;
Color Information=String;
Color Source_Data= String;
Color agent_ID= String;
Color Beg_Time= Year| Month| Day
Color End_Time= Year| Month| Day
Color Year= Int;
Color Month= Int;
Color Day= Int;
agt= agent;

Figure 13. The CPN, colors, and variables.

Step 4:

After verification, each conversation schema is converted to a set of rules. Each 'place(s)-> transition' of individual agents participating in the conversation in a CPN corresponds to the "condition" part of a rule. Every 'transition -> place(s)' in a CPN corresponds to the "action" part of a rule [54]. Figure 14 is an example of rule creation, where the rules initiate agents CA and IA to process their jobs while agent AA is ready.

Step 5:

A set of java classes can be implemented based on these rules created in Step 4. When a set of java classes are created, the Conversation Manager (CM) can be formed based on these classes.

A conversation manager, in a traditional agent communication approach, is "point-to-point", "multi-cast" or "broadcast" manager. Each of them communicates directly with each other. Lin and Norrie [54] proposed an agent conversation architecture called "conversation manager." In this architecture, a group of agents work together in a cooperation area. Each agent in a cooperation area routes all its outgoing messages through a local CM (Conversation Manager). All incoming messages are received from CM as well. The architecture is used in the ABKM system.

```
Rule 1 (for Request in A)
 If (Color(Ready_A,agt) = AA) then
  begin
   setValue(waiting, time) =5;
   setValue (requisted)=getValue(Ready_A);
   sendMessage (CA,Analysis_Method,Beg_Time,End_Time);
  end

Rule 2 (for Request in B)
 If (Color (Requested_AB,agt)=AA) then
   begin
    setValue(waiting, time) =5;
    Source_Data=getData (Analysis_Method,Beg_Time,End_Time);
    sendMessage (IA,Analysis_Method,Beg_Time,End_Time,Source_Data);
   end
```

Figure 14. The rule creation.

The Components of CM are defined as the following [54]:

• IE (Inference Engine): It utilizes a load balancing mechanism, which allows a message to be forwarded to a new conversation.
• ANS (Agent Naming Sub-system): It is used to recognize the process from agent class to agent instance, for the registered agent stored in a yellow page (YP).
• ASP (Active Schema Pool): It stores all acting schemata. It has a particular size called "threshold," which is set for performance based on certain criteria.
• EE (CPN Execution Engine): The schema is executed by EE.
• Schemata Library: It consists of a set of schema thread classes, which comprise the template to construct schema instance.
• I/O: Message input/output module

Figure 15 describes the structure of conversation manager based on Lin and Norrie [54].

In the CM architecture, the incoming messages come from other CM(s). When the I/O module receives messages, it sends them to IE. IE detects the message if the size of ASP reaches its threshold. If it is below the threshold, the CM selects an appropriate schema class from the schema library and creates an instance of the class and adds it to the ASP. The EE analyzes messages, recognizes current situation and states, creates the rules based on schema, and sends an instruction to appropriate agents about the topics. The topics rely on the current state.

3. AGENT-BASED OBJECT-ORIENTED DESIGN PROCESSES

A complex design is often carried out through collaborative works. Multi-agent systems are particularly suitable for supporting collaborative work. To achieve the goals of product development, each service required by a customer is carried out with a *design process*. Such design process considers five functions: planning, producing, distributing,

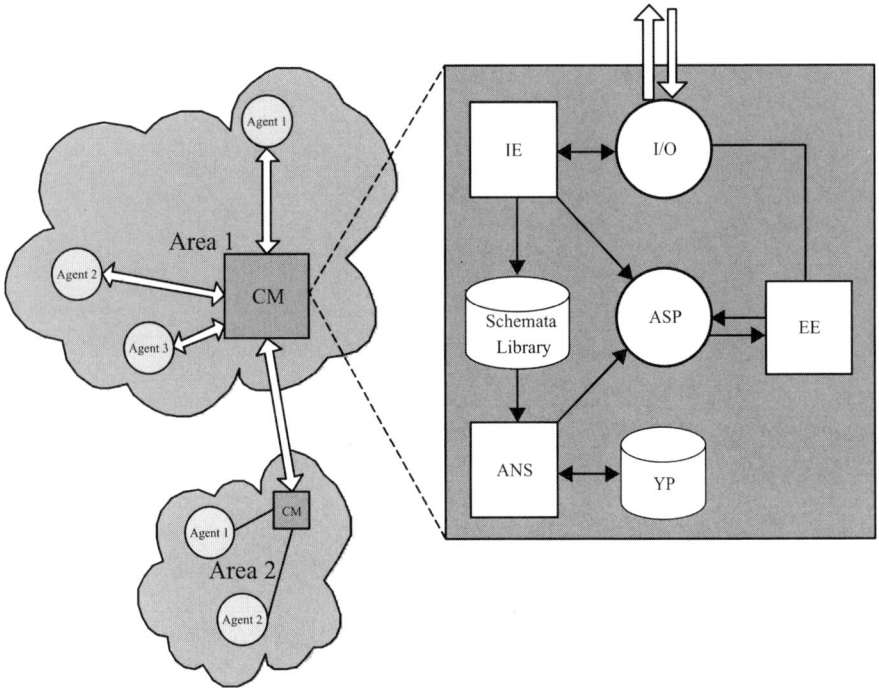

Figure 15. The conversation manager.

displaying, and acquiring of objects related to the customer service. The design process (DP) requires the following basic features (adapted from [57] and [58]):

- The process is essentially of a *non-hierarchical control* in character.
- The process is highly *decentralized*, with each element of the process operating quasi-independently.
- The process is *self-managing*, in that each element of the process will adjust dynamically.
- The process is *scaleable*, in that elements of the process can be added to the network without changing essential characteristics.
- The process is *efficient*, in that the element of the model is handled in a systematic way in coding or computing.

Paramount among the challenges of future decision-making in the DP is the development and delivery of decision support technologies that are responsive and portable to ever changing and distributive decision-making situations [59]. One promising approach is that of *object-oriented design* based on *agent technology*—via the World Wide Web (WWW):

In this section, an Object-Oriented (OO) approach, Design with Objects (DwO) is used in the agent body that solves the problems of design process. The DwO approach is implemented in the intelligent object-oriented agent (IOOA) package.

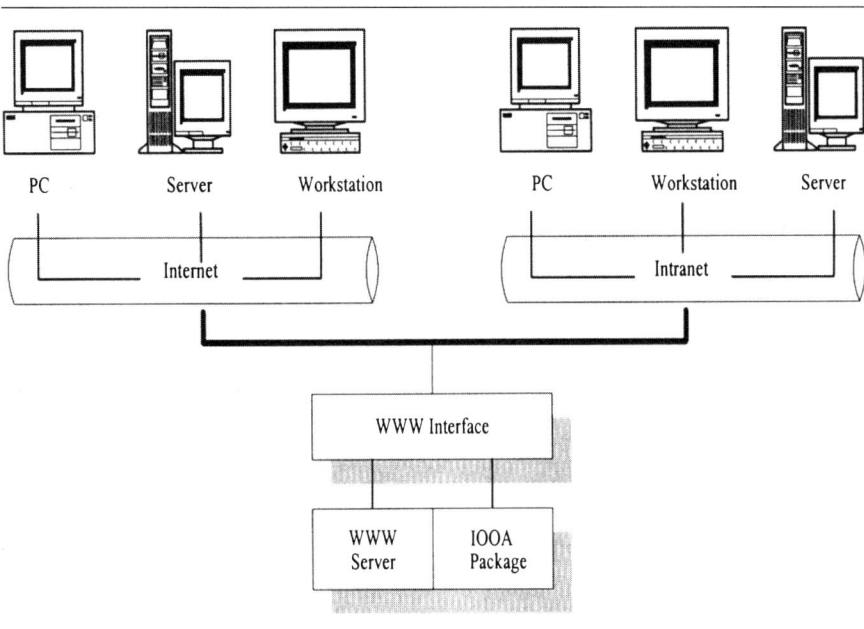

Figure 16. Overall architecture of an OO approach via the WWW.

Decision-makers or clients use the browsers to input their requirements and run the IOOA package through the World Wide Web (WWW), regardless of what platforms are used (Figure 16). The WWW is potentially useful for remote decision making because it allows the disparate functions that are involved in remote decision making to share data relatively easily.

3.1. An object-oriented approach

Sub-section 3.1.1 describes the concept of the DwO approach. This approach is then briefly presented in Sub-section 3.1.2. This approach can be extended to apply to modular software, which is presented in Sub-sections 3.1.3 and 3.1.4.

3.1.1. The concept of a design object

The DwO approach views design objects as being objects that represent not only *physical* entities, such as parts or components, but also *non-physical* entities, such as the design history or vendor information. Objects can have the following features: *Methods, Data, and Interface.* Stipulating the above view of a design object, the relationship between design objects can be established by using the following object operators: *Inheritance, Import and Message passing.*

Regardless of the above, before the DwO becomes more widespread, there are still, as yet, several research issues that must be addressed. The main research issues associated with DwO can be divided into two segments: those associated with the *identification of objects* and the *design of objects.*

The area of *identification of objects* is concerned with identifying the object elements with the granularity of the objects being an important consideration. There are several research issues concerned with the management of objects. The first is concerned with the object taxonomy and with the content of the object library. As the size of an object library is limited by various factors, selecting an appropriate set of objects is a research issue. A second research issue is associated with the organization of the objects to allow for their efficient use. An additional research issue is associated with the user-defined objects. User-defined objects would allow for a more flexible framework but present problems regarding validation and links with other objects.

The area of *design of objects* is concerned with the design of individual object to best satisfy the requirements such as cost, size, reliability, and quality. As indicated above, one main advantage of the DwO approach is that the design of individual object can be carried out in a relatively autonomous manner.

The remainder of this section is focused on the area of design with objects (DwO), which is centered on the need to use a combination of standard objects in order to satisfy functional requirements. Such requirements are the "demands" and "wishes" that clarify the design task in the space of needs [60]. They provide an abstraction of the design task from the most general demand (the overall requirement) to more specific demands (sub-requirements). Requirements and functions are domain specific and represent part of the knowledge base of the design system. In theory, it is possible to decompose functions so that the lowest level of the function structure consists exclusively of functions that cannot be sub-divided further, whilst remaining generally applicable. Each function may then be satisfied by one object and each function may correspond to one requirement.

3.1.2. A design process model formalism for DwO

This section describes a Design with Objects (DwO) approach that can lead to develop a process model for the design process problem. The model aims to show how design processes can be carried out using IOOA framework. The central design process inherent in DwO can be represented as the architecture shown diagrammatically in Figure 17, with five main types of objects involved: namely design models (DS), design objects (DO), design algorithms (DA), requirements and constraints (RC), and the evaluation schema (ES). Three object operators—*inherit, import,* and *message passing* express the relationship between these objects. The architecture in Figure 17 exhibits how the particular instance of a design model, ds, is obtained from the design algorithm, evaluation schema, requirements, constraints and the design model object. In this model, DwO views the design model (DS) as a central element of design. DS is the representation of an artifact to be designed and represents a model that consists of one or more design objects, do_i, that can be physical or non-physical objects. From a DwO perspective:

$$DS = [do_{i..}(z)]$$

Where z is the location of the item and is a variable of the form of a numeric, symbolic and/or Boolean data type.

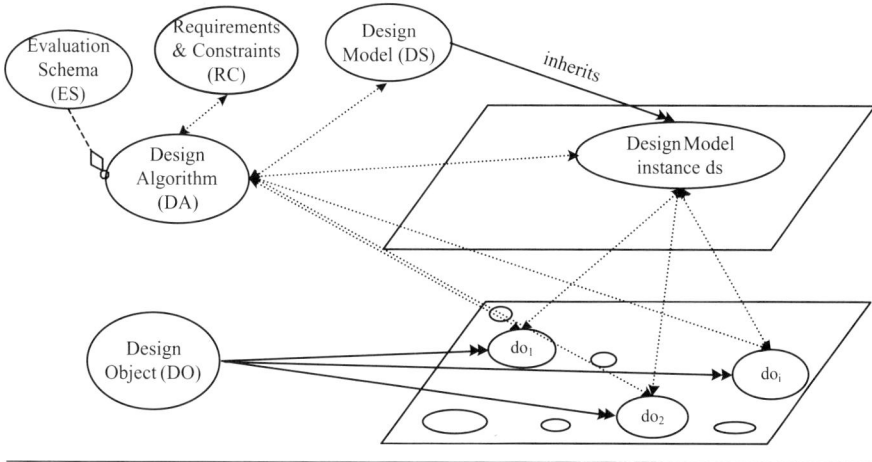

Figure 17. Overall Architecture of DwO.

The exact form of DS will vary with the design process model and with the artifact being designed. For example, for evolutionary design where the design goes through a number of generations and where there may be several design models at each generation, then

$$DS_1^k = [do_1^l.(z)]^k = [do_{1,}^l.(z), do_{2,}^l.(z), do_{3,}^l.(z)........do_{n,}^l.(z)]^k$$

Where DS_1^k represents the design model l at generation k, and $do_1^l.(z)$ represents a design object from location z included in design model l at generation k, while n represents the number of design objects in the design model. Note: the design objects may come from differing locations, z.

For pure formulation design (or creative design), a new design model object DS is defined and describes the form of the model. A specific instance, ds, of this design model can then be created. For pure parametric design then the design model object DS has already been defined and the design process therefore only involves the determination of a specific instance, ds, of this design model. A specific instance, ds, can be obtained by the following DwO design process model (Note: this is just one example process, a variety of design processes are possible), which consists of three steps:

Step 1 (refinement):
Refine the set of initial design specification into an equivalent set of functional requirements, such that each requirement is ready to be mapped into a subset of design objects. This step is described in details in [61].

Step 2 (Design Initialization):
Design algorithm (DA) *imports* evaluation schema (ES)
Design algorithm (DA) *gets data (message passing)* from requirements and constraints (RC)

Instance of design model ds$_i$ *inherits* from design model (DS)
Instance of design object do$_{i,}$ *inherits* from design object (DO)

Step 3 (function–object transformation):

In this step, each functional requirement is mapped into a set of design objects and the design objects are added to the instance of the design model by applying object design methods. This step involves selecting a functional requirement followed by selecting a design object that satisfies the requirement. When all functional requirements have been satisfied the main design stage has been completed. In this step, a variety of selection procedures are possible. One particular selection procedure is described as below.

Step 3.1 If the set of unsatisfied requirement is empty, stop since the design is finished. Subsequently, arbitrarily select one requirement from R

Step 3.2 Find a set of design object $\{do_i\}$ that satisfies the selected functional requirement of each attribute.

Step 3.3 If the set of design object $\{do_i\}$ is empty, stop. In this case there are no design objects that will satisfy the selected functional requirement and the design process can only proceed if either, the selected functional requirement is relaxed or, if alternative design objects can be made available.

Step 3.4 Ranking the set of design object $\{do_i\}$ into an ordered set according to the evaluation scheme ES, such that the do$_i$ with higher ranking comes first. This ranking is based on the objective function. Select the highest ranked do$_i$ and then add the selected do$_i$ into the current instance of the design model ds$_i$.

Step 3.5 Check that none of the set of constraints from C is violated when the method is applied. This procedure is called validity-preservation.

Step 3.6 If the model violates any of the constraints C, undo Step 3.4 and delete do$_i$ from the ordered set of design objects. Then Repeat from Step 3.4 and choose do$_i$ with the next rank. Otherwise, Go to Step 3.7

Step 3.7 Delete this functional requirement from the set of functional requirements. Go to Step 3.1.

This design process could be applied in the lower-level objects (as in object-oriented design/programming) or applications. However, the example in next sub-section is used to illustrate the operations on middle-ware.

3.1.3. Modular software components

As computers have evolved with increasing processor speed and memory, correspondingly so has the level of programming. The nascent of computers and the relatively limited computational capabilities meant that much of the programming was performed at the very detailed machine level. Such detailed machine level programming, for example assembly level programming, was required to utilize the power of the processor in the most efficient manner. As processor power has increased, the need for such fine-tuning has diminished. Thus, decision-makers have become more concerned with programmer efficiency. As a result decision-makers are more concerned with writing a program as quickly as possible and not necessarily on the efficiency of the resultant code.

This has meant those languages and tools that help in the development process have become increasing popular. The use of reusable code in object oriented programming languages such as Java or C++ is perhaps the most visible example. What can also be discerned is that this trend is not diminishing—rather there is now beginning the development of what might be termed modular software components. Such modular software components can be grouped together quickly to produce a finished program. We can think of this as using Lego™ blocks of code which when put together, with some additional programming where necessary, results in a final program that can be developed very quickly with an efficient use of programmer resources.

There are some important potential advantages to the use of such modular software components for program development:

- Faster development time—which should arise, due to the fact that modules have already been developed and the programmers can now place them into their code.
- A more efficient process—since the modules can be shared across several programs increasing the overall efficiency of the programming operation, and this should reduce the overall cost of software development.
- Increased functionality—since it is the aim that modules will be used in many different programs, the developers of the modules can afford to put increased functionality into each module.
- Increased reliability of modules which should arise as a consequence of the modules being used on a number of applications, with a resultant large scale testing
- Autonomous development. The modules are developed using different teams in different locations. This results in program development being decentralized with each module being developed in a relatively autonomous environment.
- Software upgrading and maintenance is more straightforward. This result is due to the modular nature of the software in that a module upgrade can easily replace an existing module.
- However, there are several potential disadvantages to modular software components:
- There is a need to develop clearly defined interfaces. The modules are only defined in terms of their interfaces, so the issue of what should be the interface is important and needs to be carefully designed. Ideally, each module should be used in as large a number of applications as possible in order to maximize any potential benefits
- Need to build and test modules. Having designed the interfaces, the modules now have to be developed. They will also have to be tested thoroughly, since the modules may be used on a wide variety of applications.
- Modules may be less efficient that specific code. This arises from the fact that the modules have to be developed to meet a more general need and may therefore, contain some portions that are redundant in a particular application. This may mean that the modules are less efficient in operation than if a developer had directly written the code for that application. Against this must be weighed the development time saved by using modular software components

Several modular software component architectures have been proposed and some of these have been implemented. Of concern to our Internet interest is the work on COM components and JavaBeans.

3.1.4. *Object-oriented approach in modular software components*

An important characteristic of large computer networks such as the Internet, the World Wide Web (WWW), and corporate Intranets is that they are *heterogeneous* [62]. Ideally, heterogeneity and open systems enable us to use the best combination of hardware and software components for each portion of an enterprise. Unfortunately, dealing with heterogeneity in distributed computing enterprise is rarely easy. In particular, the development of software applications and components that support and make efficient use of heterogeneous networked system is very challenging. Many programming interfaces and packaging currently exist to curtail the burden of developing software for a single homogenous platform. However, few help to deal with the integration of separately developed systems in a distributed heterogeneous environment.

In recognition of this problem, two architectures have been proposed to deal with this kind of problem using the object-oriented approach. They are CORBA and DCOM. We will discuss each in the following:

- CORBA (Common Object Request Broker Architecture): is a standard for distributed objects being developed by the Object Management Group (OMG) [63]. The OMG is a consortium of software vendors and end users. Many OMG member companies are developing commercial products that support these standards. The aims of the architecture and specifications described in the Common Object Request Broker, is to allow the software designers and developers who wish to produce applications that comply with OMG standards for the Object Request Broker (ORB) [64]. The benefit of compliance is, in general, to be able to produce interoperable applications that are based on distributed, inter-operating objects.

- The Distributed Component Object Model (DCOM): is a protocol that enables software components to communicate directly over a network in a reliable, secure, and efficient manner [65]. There is a natural tendency in a networked environment to create entirely new application-level protocols as each new or seemingly unique combination of client, user agent, and server requirement arises. A design goal of the DCOM protocol is the inherent support of standard features required by any distributed application communication protocol. Correspondingly, to act as a framework to facilitate the construction of task-specific communication paths between distributed applications. Several companies have implemented this technology to commercial product, which includes The SAP DCOM Component Connector, John Deere Health Care: Development of Client/Server Enterprise Solution, and DCOM Cariplo Home-Banking.

Both CORBA and DCOM are a single step on the pathway to object-oriented standardization and interoperability. COM and CORBA are not the only two object technologies that can be usefully combined. It is also reasonably useful to combine both

COM and CORBA with Java. Given the popularity of both distributed computing and object technology, it is not surprising that distributed objects will be formed in a future main frame.

3.2. Agent-based system in design process

In this section, an agent-based framework designated Intelligent Object-Oriented Agent (IOOA) system is developed to support the design process, enabling the services requested from clients or customers to be completed.

All IOOAs have the same basic architecture (Figure 18) and involve an *agent body* that is responsible for managing the agent's activities and interaction with peers and an *agency* that represents solution resources for problems of design processes. The body has a number of functional components each responsible for its primary activities— scheduling object combination operations, searching desired objects, optimizing object combination, and managing the object databases.

The domain resources include not only object databases and object combination jobs, but also other IOOAs. The latter example allows a nested (hierarchical) agent system to be constructed, in which higher-level agents realize their functionality through lower-level agents (the-lower level agents have the same structure as the higher level agents and therefore, have sub-agents as well as object combination jobs in their agency). This structure enables flat, hierarchical, and hybrid organizations to be modeled in a single framework [44, 66].

The IOOA operates four roles in the design processes: see below for symbols and notations, followed by the operations of four roles.

S	a scheduler
O	an optimizer
M	a manager
E	an explorer
H	exception handler
C	engineering constraints
CA	customer agreement
OCB	object combination job
Ap	peer agent
R	resource
SE	service execution
P	solution presentation
Db_o	object databases

A *scheduler* is an agent, which schedules the object combination operations and is responsible for assessing and monitoring the agent's ability to meet: (i) the customer agreement that is already in place (ii) the potential customer agreement that it may be agreed to in the future. This scheduler involves two main roles: scheduling and exception handling. The former involves maintaining a record of the availability of the agent's resources, which can then be used to determine whether customer agreement

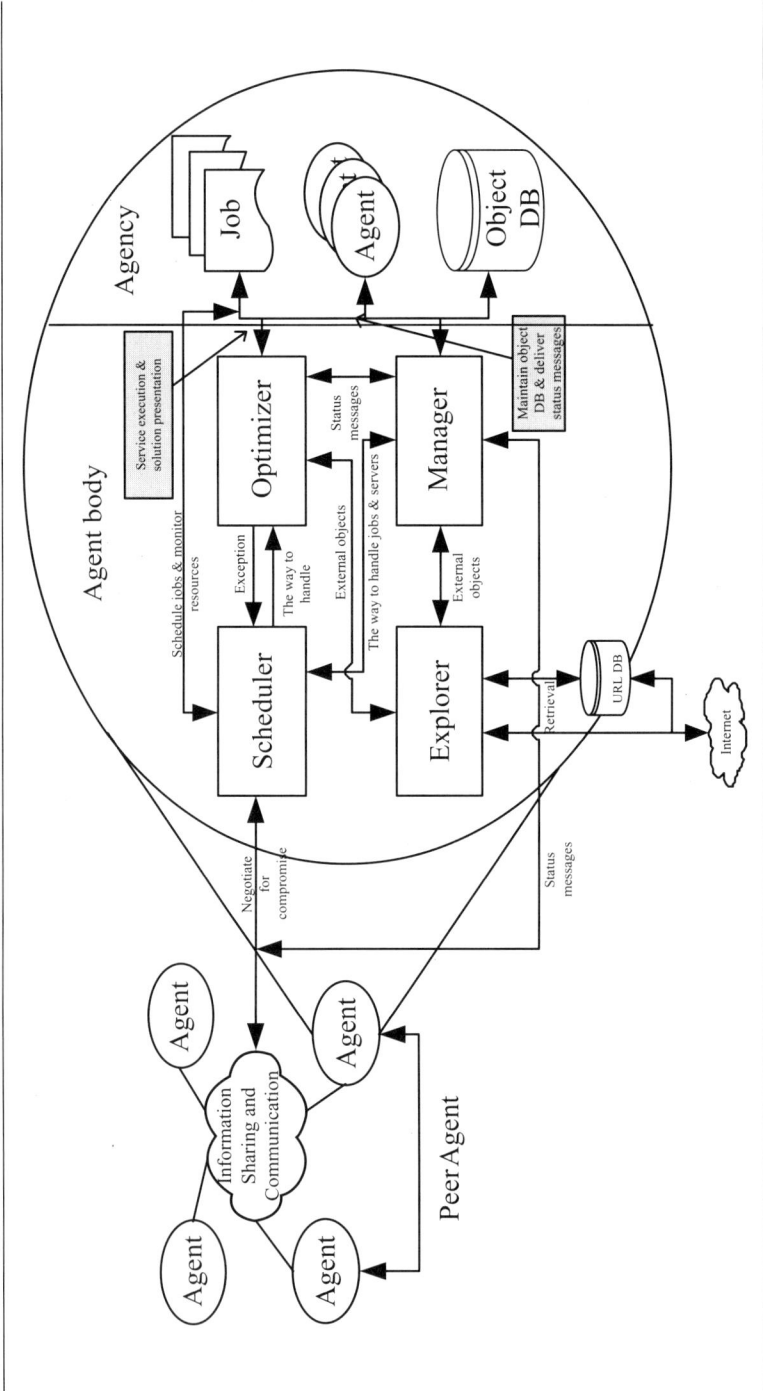

Figure 18. IOOA architecture.

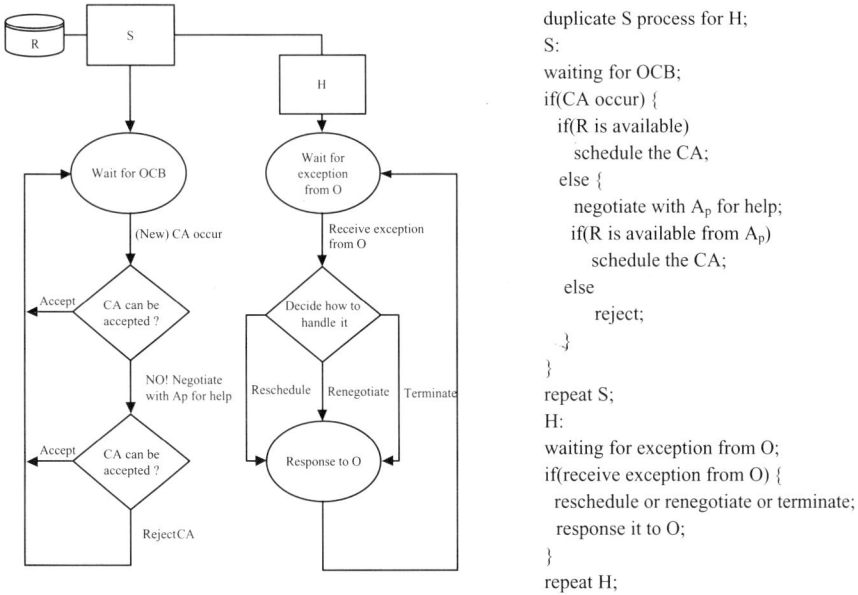

The figure contains the following pseudocode on the right side:

```
duplicate S process for H;
S:
waiting for OCB;
if(CA occur) {
    if(R is available)
        schedule the CA;
    else {
        negotiate with Ap for help;
        if(R is available from Ap)
            schedule the CA;
        else
            reject;
    }
}
repeat S;
H:
waiting for exception from O;
if(receive exception from O) {
    reschedule or renegotiate or terminate;
    response it to O;
}
repeat H;
```

Figure 19. Scheduler Role.

can be met or a new customer agreement needs to be formulated. The exception handler receives exception reports from the optimizer during service execution (e.g. "service may fail", "service has failed", or "no customer agreement in place") and decides upon the appropriate response. For example, if a service is delayed then the scheduler may decide to locally reschedule it, to renegotiate its customer agreement, or to terminate it completely (Figure 19).

An *optimizer* is an agent, which optimizes the object combination based upon the requirements from customers and engineering constraints (Figure 20) [67]. Three primary roles involve: service execution management (optimizing executed services, as specified by the agent's customer agreements), solution presentation (routing solutions between servers, clients and other agents), and exception handling (monitor the execution of jobs and services for unexpected events and react appropriately).

A *manager* is an agent, which (Figure 21):

• maintains the object database where object information is stored.
• delivers the status messages of active services between optimizer and clients, between an agent and its agency, and between peer agents.
• communicates
  (i) between the optimizer and clients within the agency relating to job management activities (e.g. activate, suspend, or resume a job), and
  (ii) between agents within that agency or peer agents relating to service execution management (e.g. an instruction to start service, service finished, service results).

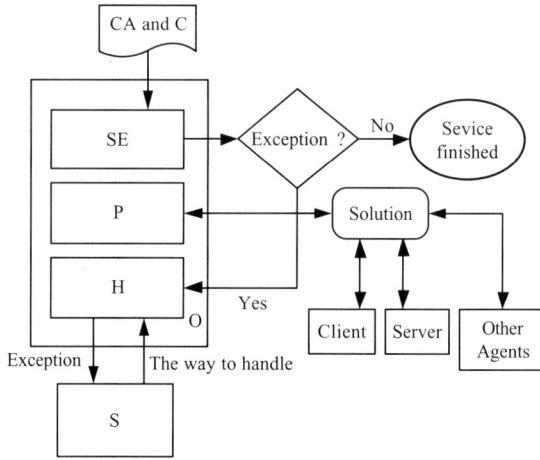

Figure 20. Optimizer role.

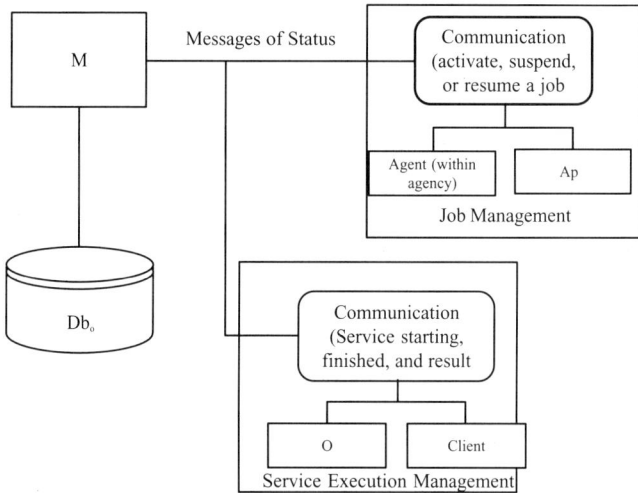

Figure 21. Manager role.

An explorer is an agent that searches the objects that are located in other distributed databases and performs the role of managing, querying or collating object information from many distributed sources. It is able to traverse the WWW, gather information and report retrievals to a home location. Figure 22 depicts how a typical static explorer works.

In this section, the object-oriented approach used by the IOOA aims to obtain the necessary insights to develop design process models and acts as the base for improving

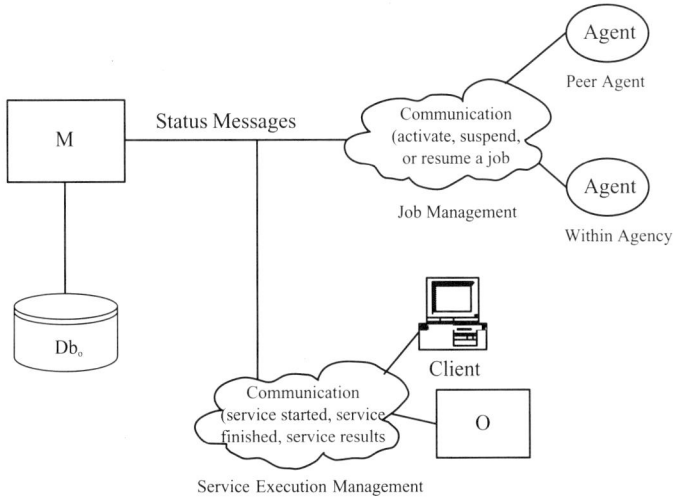

Figure 22. View of how an explorer works.

or computerizing the process. The IOOA framework is successfully used to design a distributed design team for a large geographically distributed organization. The implementation of the IOOA system is a computable model with reusable objects and that it allows for the ready exchange of objects, although care should be exercised in extrapolating from a particular example to the general case. This solution approach is agile because, by combining various objects, different types of design process problems are able to be resolved with the same agent-based framework. It aims at quick decision making in the design process, and supports the solutions through the World Wide Web (WWW) to the decision makers who may be geographically separated and operate on differing computer platforms. The implementation described uses the Internet as a vehicle but the proposed approach should also be applicable to any other computer network. This application is a first attempt to integrate the agent and OO technologies within the design process in terms of computability, re-usability, exchangeability, autonomy, concurrency, and social ability. As such, independently developed agents can communicate seamlessly and contact each other automatically; thereby reducing the load of the design process.

4. AGENT-BASED SUPPLY CHAIN PROCESSES

In this section, supply chain is viewed as a distributed network of entities interacting to deliver products or service to the end customer, linking flows from raw material supply to final delivery [68, 69]. There are only very few ITs available to support distributed asynchronous collaboration except the distributed artificial intelligence [70]. Distributed artificial intelligence, which is commonly implemented in the form of intelligent agents, offers considerable potential for the development of such ITs.

The approach proposed in this section utilizes multi-agents, called intelligent supply chain agent (ISCA) system for modeling and analyzing the supply chains. The agile interaction is focused and formulated to increase the collaboration of supply chain entities and to avoid the nature of fragment. Different types of agents are defined and each agent has the ability to utilize a set of control elements. The control elements help in decision making for structural problems by utilizing various policies (derived from analytical models such as inventory policies, just-in-time release, sales, and routing algorithms) for demand, supply, information and materials control among the supply chains. To deal with the non-structural problems, problem-solving agents using the resources in the agency are developed.

4.1. Classification of intelligent supply chain agents

Supply chain dynamics is too complicated to be modeled due to the heterogeneity of entities, multiple performance measures and complex interaction effects. The variety of supply chains poses a limitation on reusability of processes across them. For example, a supply chain could be highly centralized and have most of the entities belonging to the same organization (like IBM integrated supply chain) or could be highly decentralized with all the entities being separate organizations (like a grocery supply chain) [71]. As a result, it is a difficult task to develop a set of generic processes that captures the dynamics of supply chains across a wide spectrum. In this section, a classification of agents is presented.

Swaminathan et al. [72] classify the agents in supply chains into two broad categories: structural agents and control agents. *Structural agents* involve in actual production and transportation of products, whereas *control agents* coordinate the flow of products in an efficient manner with the use of messages. Structural agents are further played into two basic sets of agents, namely, the production and transportation agents. Control agents are played into inventory control, demand control, supply control, flow control, and information control agents.

In this section, based on the classification of [72], ISC agents, which enable the modeling and analysis of a large variety of SC activities, e.g., planning, monitor, control, and problem-solving, are classified into three types of agents: *Structural agents*, *control agents*, and *problem-solving agents*. Structural agents and control agents are same as the ones in [72] (Figure 23). Problem-solving agents deal with the semi-structural or non-structural problems for decision-making. Despite the three types of agents, *information and interface agents* are used as an information center to integrate and transfer all information.

Information and interface agents: the agents are essential for coordination within the supply chain. The two types of information flow are controlled:

• Directly accessible: Directly accessible information transfer refers to the instantaneous propagation of information.
• Periodic: Periodic information updates may be sent by different production and transportation agents to indicate changes in business strategy, price increase, introduction of new services or features in the products, and introduction of new production agents etc.

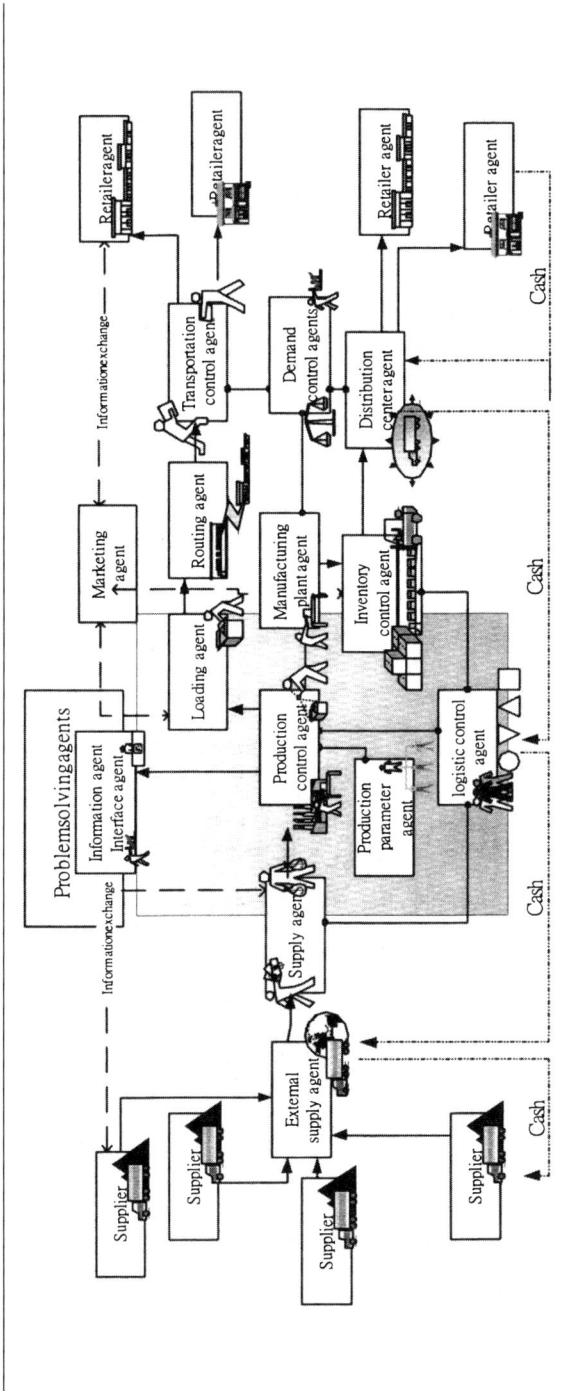

Figure 23. Structural agents and control agents.

Structural agents

Manufacturing plant agent: A manufacturing plant agent is where components are assembled and a product is manufactured. In general, orders come from the distribution center but they could also come from the retailer agent (when there is a cross-dock or the supply chain does not have a distribution center). The main focus here is on optimal procurement of components (particularly common components) and on efficient management of inventory and manufacturing processes.

Distribution center agent: A distribution center agent is involved in receiving products from the manufacturing plant and storing or sending them right away (cross-dock) to the retailer. The main focus here is to reduce the inventory carried and maximize throughput. In a standard distribution center, products come in from the manufacturing or supplier plants.

Retailer agent: A retailer agent is where customers buy products. The main focus here is on reducing the cycle time for the delivery of a customer order and minimizing stock-outs [73].

Transportation agent: A transportation agent consists of transportation vehicles, which move products from one production agent to another.

Marketing agent: A marketing agent interacts with retailers and consumers through Internet and provides a mechanism that can trigger additional demand for products in seasonal, random or permanent by numerous ways including advertisements, discounts, coupons and seasonal sales.

Production parameter agent: A production parameter agent is not only where components are assembled and a product is manufactured, but also where an agent monitors low level operations of shop floor including the use of resources, solving breakdown problems of production machines and production resource deployment. In general, orders come from the distribution center but they could also come from the retailer agent (when there is a cross-dock or the supply chain does not have a distribution center). The main focus here is on optimal procurement of components (particularly common components) and on efficient management of inventory and manufacturing processes.

Supply agents: Supply agents dictate terms and conditions for delivery of the material once orders have been placed.

External supplier agent: An external supplier agent models external suppliers. These suppliers could be a manufacturing plant or assembly plant, or could have their own supply chain for production. However, all these situations are modeled through a single agent because the parent organization has no direct control on their internal operations. The supplier agents supply parts to the manufacturing plant agent. They focus on low turn-around time and inventory. Their operation is characterized by the supplier contracts which determines the lead-time, flexibility arrangements, cost-sharing and the information-sharing with customers.

Control agents

Production control agents: Production agents cooperate with inventory control agents to manage inventory and contracts from downstream entities to control supply, with flow control agents to load and unload products, with forecast agents to propagate demand forecasts to the downstream entity and may cooperate with information control agents to interact with other entities in the supply chain.

Inventory control agents: Inventory Control agents are an integral part of supply chain. They control the flow of materials within the supply chain.

Logistic control agent: A logistic agent is associated with the delivery of both raw materials and components to the company, and the delivery of finished goods to its customers. The main focus here is to adopt optimal strategies to make the supply chain more flexible and efficient and to provide customers with a wide variety of products that can be delivered quickly.

Demand control agents: The demand process within a supply chain is sustained through actual and forecasts (these are modeled as messages in our framework). Orders contain information on the types of products which are being ordered, the number of products that are required, the destination where the product has to be shipped, and the due date of the order. Two important demand control agents are:

• Product management agents: One of the important aspects of product management is how well the product is marketed to consumers [74].
• Forecast agents: Forecast agents determine how forecasts are generated within the supply chain and how they evolve over time.

Supply control agents: Supply control agents dictate terms and conditions for the delivery of the material once orders have been placed.

Flow control agents: Flow control agents coordinate the flow of products between production and transportation elements. The two types of flow control agents are:

• Loading agents: Loading agents control the manner in which the products are loaded and unloaded by the transportation agents. This control is different based on the type of the production agent where products are loaded or unloaded.
• Routing agents: Routing agents control the sequence in which products are delivered by the transportation agent.

Problem-solving agent

Problem-solving agents deal with the non-structured problems, which have no structured phases of intelligence, choice, and decision [38]. The non-structured problems must be solved with both standard solution procedures and human judgment (Figure 24).

• Data management agent:
  Manage all the data related to decision-making, information, materials and finance in the supply chain. According to all conditions in the supply chain, the agent updates the database in a real-time basis.

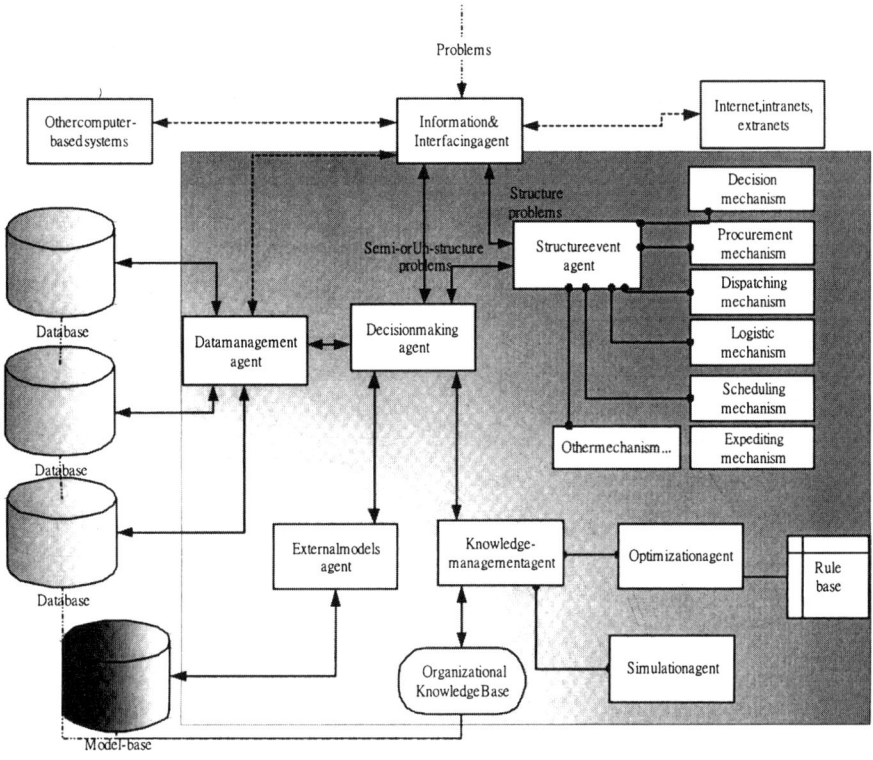

Figure 24. Problem-solving agents.

- External models agent:
  Modularize solution approaches and relevant information; provide flexible planning of resources for the decision-making agent in order to generate appropriate solution alternatives promptly.
- Structure event agent:
  Integrate any different kinds of decision making mechanisms which include

  Decision, procurement, dispatching, scheduling, logistic and expediting

  For off-line structural type of problems, prompt decisions can be anticipated through the defaulted mechanism.
- Knowledge management agent:
  Comprise, manage and update database; provide the decision-making agent the optimal decision through collaborating the simulation and the optimization agent.
- Simulation agent:
  The simulation agent has three objects:

(1) Incorporate the decision-making functions of manufacturing systems in a simulation in the form of intelligent agents;

(2) Represent the hierarchical structure (net) of supply chain systems within a simulation;

(3) Provide facilities for intelligent agents to receive information from the simulation at different levels of detail.

By using the concept of Intelligent Simulation Multi-agent tools (ISMAT) [75] the Simulation agent has the following modules:

(1) Intelligent-agent description module: The module defines a rule language to implement the decision-making rules for intelligent simulation agents.

(2) Hierarchical model module: This module defines classes to represent the structure of a manufacturing system in IMSAT simulations.

(3) Product-flow definition module and abstraction-mechanism: The product flow definition module implements a simulation kernel called the Object-oriented Manufacturing Simulation Language (OMSL). It provides the class definitions necessary to model machines, queues, stores, and manufacturing-process plans. The abstraction mechanism defined in this module provides a way of summarizing the process information for the use of intelligent agents.

(4) Simulation management module: The simulation management module maintains the simulation calendar. It also interacts with the knowledge management agent for running the simulation models.

• Optimization agent:

Optimization agents—a part of local decision making units—are associated with individual tasks of each agent. A rule-base model of interaction between agents is applied. Agents take part in an iterated rule to find the directions of solution in the system simulation, with the objective of minimizing the total execution time and cost of the program to solve problem in the supply chain in a given multiprocessor topology. Competitive co-evolutionary genetic algorithm, termed loosely coupled genetic algorithm, is used to implement the multi-agent system. The scheduling algorithm works with a global optimization function, which limits its efficiency. To make the algorithm truly distributed, decomposition of the global optimization criterion into local criteria is proposed. This decomposition is evolved with genetic programming. Results of successive experimental study of the proposed algorithm are presented [76].

• Decision-making agent:

1. (a) Retrieves relevant data from the data management agent. The agent cooperates with the external model agent and knowledge management agent in order to make right decisions for non-structural problems. (b) Transforms each sub-artifact solution as knowledge blueprint with the experience in the existing knowledge base; searches the solution approach incorporating with the data management agent and optimization agent to support the decisions.

2. Determines the desired solution module to fit in the solution from the external model agent with the assistance of the module-base.

3. Associates with the interface agent to allow the users to entry requirements.
4. Initializes the interface agent to retrieve the state–of–the–art IT, document the cases, and analyze the impacts, which can interact with other computer communication systems, e.g., Internet, Intranet and Extranet.
5. Interacts with the operation, scheduling and dispatching agent to model the optimal solutions.

The sets of agents defined above along with the customer agent that generates demand for the system constitute the proposed framework. The roles of agents are clearly defined, and their interaction processes are also clarified. The well-defined roles and standardized interaction processes can not only support the supply chain activities in organizations but also let the agents know which agent it should communicate with and what message it will receive or send. In this way, the agile collaboration of SC entities is enhanced.

4.2. Architecture of agents

Agent descriptions provide the ability to specify both static and dynamic characteristics of various supply chain entities. Each agent is specialized according to its intended role in the supply chain (e.g., production control agent, transportation agents, supplier agents, and so on). In this section, the architecture of agents is presented.

4.2.1. Message handling process

To handle the incoming message, part of the agent architecture and the handling process is illustrated in Figure 25.

The incoming message that is sent from an external source, (e.g., Web Application or Intranet application, or other agent), is accepted by the Message-Input Processor of the agent. The action is to be exercised only after the incoming message has been interpreted by the Services-Message Sense Processor and the contents of the message been recognized by the Knowledge Representation Mechanism incorporated with the Knowledge Base of the agent. Corresponding to each incoming message, the contents may have been transformed and described with the XML-based knowledge representation language, e.g., KQML (Knowledge Query Manipulation Language) or DAML + OIL (DARPA (Defence Advanced Research Projects Agency) Agent Markup Language + Ontology Inference Layer) [77] and consequently, the contents are recognized. In this case, they are stored to the Knowledge Base directly. In the other case, when the message contents are not in this format and can not be recognized, they are stored in the Knowledge Base and wait for being processed. Through (i) interaction with Internet Web Services, (ii) filtration by the Resource Gate, (iii) the inference of ontology and (iv) transformation of the message contents, the contents can be recognized later.

The Knowledge Base in each agent includes the Event-handling Knowledge Base and the Domain Knowledge Base. The Event-handling Knowledge Base stores the knowledge related to how this agent handle the incoming messages. The Domain Knowledge Base stores the knowledge related to how to interact with other

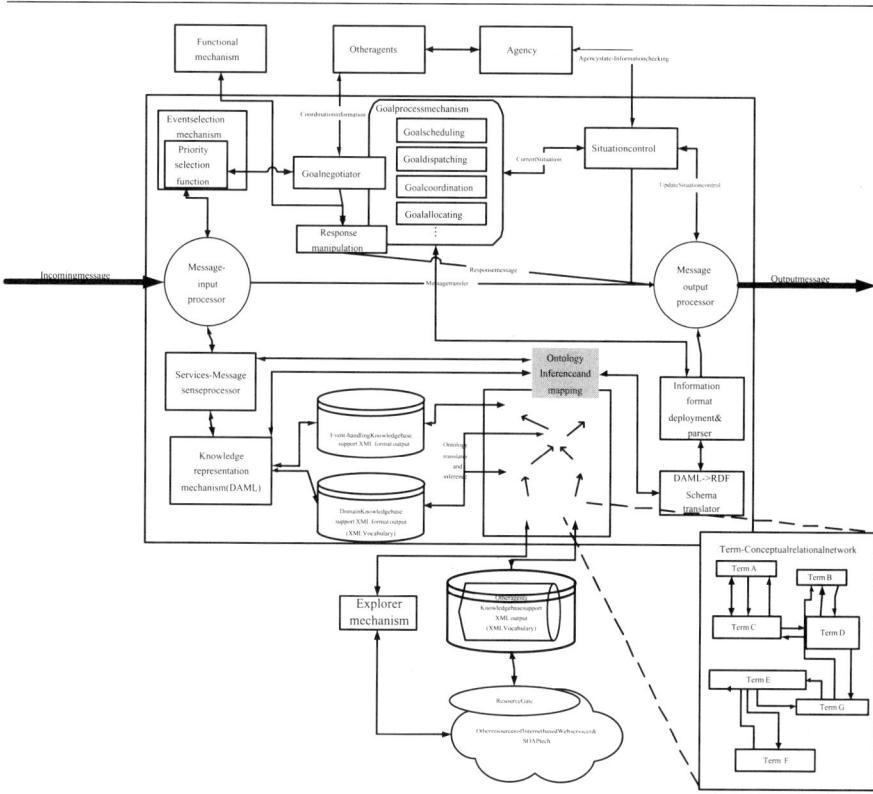

Figure 25. Part of agent architecture corresponding to message handling processing.

agents while handling incoming messages (e.g., pinpointing the operation schedule, interaction of firing sequence of agents, etc …). Both the knowledge bases support XML format output (XML Vocabulary) and are able to store numerous details of previous events.

While the new transformed XML-based incoming message is retrieved from the Knowledge Base and is processed, the agent retrieves relevant "knowledge resource" from the Event-handling Knowledge Base, and defines a common used set of vocabulary with the XML-based knowledge representation language. In this way, one can describe the incoming message, including statement, function, constant of the contained knowledge and the 5W1H framework [78]. Secondly, the collected knowledge resources are aggregated and the vocabulary is extended and widened; in this approach, a logic statement and axiom, which is accepted by all agents and relevant application resources are created. Thirdly, the knowledge base is updated and the ontology is formed while the domain knowledge is re-organized corresponding to each incoming massage. Fourthly, the inference of the contents in the new incoming message is made through the mapping and matching of the ontology, which is produced from various knowledge bases in various agents. Next, through the inferences, the facts and a solution approach to the problem that the agent needs to solve, are recognized and planned. At last, the plan is coordinated and disseminated through the Message output processor. Because of the functionality of Semantic Web, the incoming message can be interpreted and recognized clearly, agilely and efficiently.

In case that the incoming jobs are multiple, the required operations are processed as follows:

The selection of incoming messages corresponding to these jobs is made by the Priority Selection Function of the Event Selection Mechanism which will be discussed later. Then with the incorporation of Message-input Processor, the agent negotiator (the gate of Goal Process Mechanism) negotiates and communicates with other agents based on the results generated from the Goal Process Mechanism, for example the results of scheduling jobs, dispatching resources, or coordinating plans.

In this architecture, each agent operation and the global goal are optimized in the multi-agent environment since the designated agent architecture is able to: (i) negotiate with other agent, (ii) update the agency through the Explorer Mechanism and Situation Control Mechanism, (ii) prioritize the processing messages, (iv) map and match by the ontology operators to filter and retrieve relevant information and knowledge, and (v) recognize the facts and solution approach to solve the problems which the agent faces. Based on the command of Goal Process Mechanism, the Response Manipulation Mechanism informs the Functional Mechanism about the way to implement and send the output message to the Message Output Processor. The Message Output Processor formulates the output messages and then sends to the external resource or another agent. In the entire process, the agent updates the message and sends the updated (updated verification) massages to the external agency concurrently. In this way, the agent is able to respond and achieve the objectives in real time.

4.2.2. The XML-based contents of the message

The contents of message are represented with the six dimensions of the Zachman framework and coded with XML [79]. The content in each message is constructed by the six dimensions (5W1H) of the Zachman framework, including solution approach information, domain knowledge and know-how. The Zachman Framework provides a systematic approach to externalize unstructured contents in messages of agents, although not all contents can be represented in this format.

The Zachman Framework represents the perspectives and dimensions in the matrix form. The columns include: Entities (What? Interest or focus areas); Activities (How? Methods of problem-solving); Locations (Where? Places of interest or focus); People (Who? Individuals and organizations of interest or focus); Times (When? Activities occurring); Motivations (Why? Reasons for inspiration). The perspectives and goals of contents are classified in Table 2.

Designing the knowledge structure of messages is critical to achieve message interpretation and allows the messages to reside in a standard storage system. Through the exchange platform of ontology, the knowledge representation and inference language are used and incorporated with the RDF and RDFS to communicate and share the knowledge. The RDF and RDFS (RDF schema) language is based on XML. Therefore, the

Table 2 Dimensions of message contents

	ENTITIES (What)	ACTIVITIES (How)	LOCATIONS (Where)	PEOPLE (Who)	TIME (When)	MOTIVATION (Why)
Perspectives	Data, information, knowledge,	Capture, interpretation, measurement, accumulation, deployment, externalization, innovation, feedback	Organization, process	Users, administrators, developers	Time instance	Reason needed
Goal	Accuracy	Effectiveness/efficiency	Accuracy location	Accuracy location	Accurate timing	Motivated or not
Example	An association rule	Approach of discovering association rule	Marketing department	Marketing manager	2000–2001 year	Study the relationship between products A and B

```
<?xml version="1.0" encoding="big5" ?>
<SSK>
- <General_Information>
  - <Event>
      <Event_Name />           ]
      <Event_Description />    ]—  "What" dimension of this event.
      <Event_Observer />       ——▶  "Who" dimension of this event.
      <Event_When />           ——▶  "When" dimension of this event.
      <Event_Where />          ——▶  "Where" dimension of this event.
  </Event>
  </General_Information>
- <Process_Information>
  - <Subject>
      + <Subject_What>         ]
      + <Subject_Who>          ]   "How" dimension of this event.
      + <Subject_When>         ]
      + <Subject_Where>        }   Six dimensions of this subject.
      + <Subject_Why>          ]
      + <Subject_How>          ]
    </Subject>
  </Process_Information>
- <Feedback_Knowledge>
  - <Knowledge>
      + <Knowledge_Who>        ]
      <Knowledge_When />       ]
      <Knowledge_Where />      }   "Why" dimension of this event.
      <Reference_Id />         ]
      <Knowledge_Why />        ]
      <Suggest />              ]
    </Knowledge>
  </Feedback_Knowledge>
</SSK>
```

Figure 26. The example of an XML-based documentation representing knowledge.

representation language is transformed as XML-based format and knowledge can be easily presented. It also aims at offering quick transmission of the information communication and exchange. Moreover, XML shares many semi-structured features. For example: its structure can be irregular, is not always known in advance, and may change frequently and without any notice. Therefore, this chapter delineates the knowledge in each message using XML because XML-based documents are easy to store and manage. Figure 26 illustrates an XML-based documentation, where stores the contents of knowledge in each message. The document is constructed with the Zachman framework.

4.2.3. Basic agent architecture

All ISCAs have the same basic architecture (Figure 27). This involves an *agent body* that is responsible for managing the agent's activities and interacting with peers and an *agency* that represents the solution resources for the problems of supply chain, including (1) other agents, (2) services, and (3) agent repository: set of attributes, knowledge about other agents, interaction constraints, performance measures, control agents, message processing semantics, and selector with control policy. The body has four basic mechanisms responsible for each of its main activities: event selection mechanism, functional mechanism, negotiation mechanism, and explorer mechanism. This internal architecture is broadly based on the GRATE [66] and ARCHON [44] agent models.

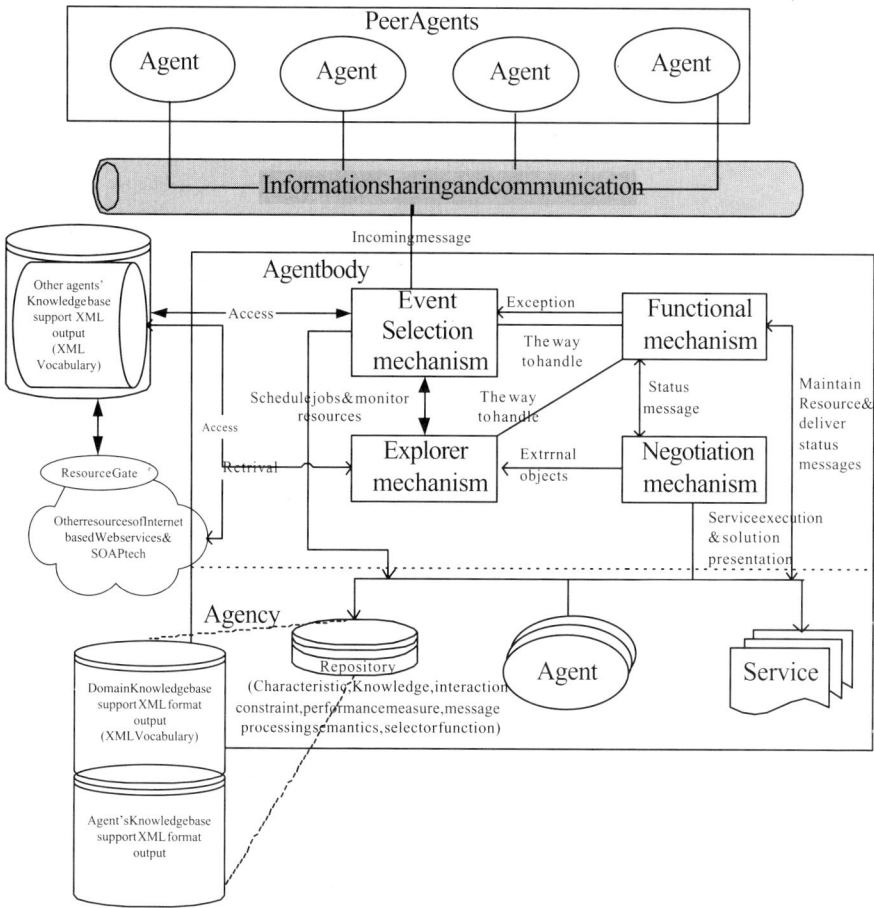

Figure 27. The ISCA Architecture.

The symbols and notation are listed below, and the operations of four mechanisms are then presented.

E   event selection mechanism,
F   functional mechanism,
N   negotiation mechanism,
S   a scheduler of event selection mechanism
E   an explorer
H   an exception handler of event selection mechanism
CA   customer agreement
SJ   selected job
Ap   peer agent

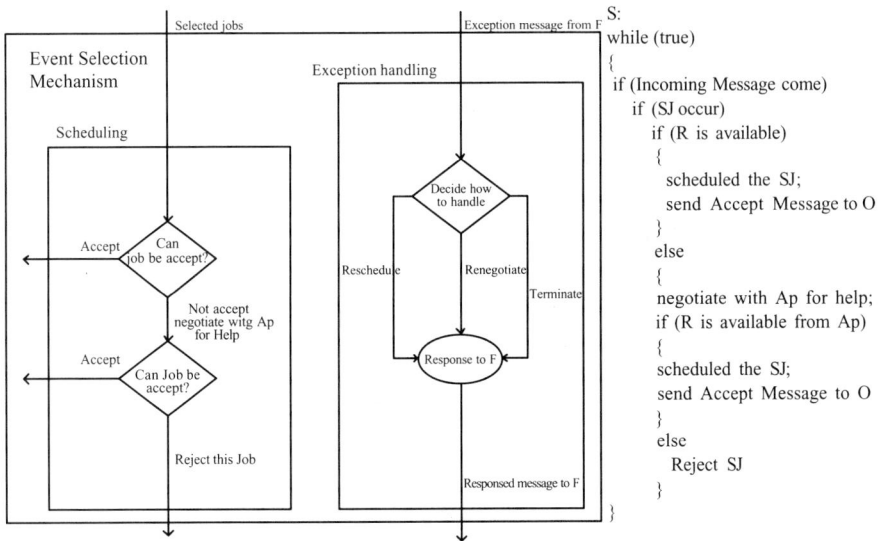

Figure 28. Event selection mechanism of ISCA.

R   resource
SE   service execution
P   solution presentation
Db$_o$ URL databases

Event selection mechanism: Based on the knowledge base, ontology, and message handling process, incoming messages are selected based on the rule of the event selection mechanism such as first priority first served (FPFS). Each message type has a message handler or a script that determines how the message will be processed. The message handler is parametrized according to the control policies that are used by the agent. Next, the mechanism schedules the selected job operations and responsible for assessing and monitoring the agent's ability to meet: (i) The service agreement that is already agreed upon and (ii) the potential service agreement that it may agree to in the future. This involves two main roles: scheduling and exception handling. The former involves in maintaining a record of the availability of the agent's resources, which can then be used to determine whether the service agreement can be met or new service agreement can be accepted. The exception handler receives exception reports from the functional mechanism during service execution (e.g. "service may fail", "service has failed", or "no customer agreement in place") and decides upon the appropriate response. For example, if a service is delayed, then the mechanism may decide to locally reschedule it, to renegotiate its service agreement, or to terminate it altogether (Figure 28).

Functional mechanism: Each type of agent has the specified functionality to complete the jobs (Table 3). For example, the marketing agent provides a mechanism that

Table 3 Function of each type of agents

Agent name	Objective function (OR function)
Structural agents	
Operation & Scheduling agent	Take charge in scheduling and resource distribution. According to the nature of the problems, the agent optimizes the operations and scheduling of the process.
Manufacturing plant agent	The main focus here is on optimal procurement of components (particularly common components) and on efficient management of inventory and manufacturing processes.
Supply agent	Update the orders and decide the delivery time corresponding to the current status of supply-demand relationship in the market. Update the orders of raw materials and determining the delivery time based on status of the raw material supply.
Distribution center agent	Reduces the inventory carried and maximizes throughput. In a standard distribution center products come in from the manufacturing or supplier plants.
Retailer agent	The main focus here is on reducing the cycle time for the delivery of a customer order and minimizing stock-outs
Transportation agent	Move products from one production agent to another.
Marketing agent	Interacts with retailers and consumers through Internet and provides a mechanism that can trigger additional demand for products in seasonal, random or permanent by numerous ways including advertisements, discounts, coupons and seasonal sales.
Production parameter agent	The main focus here is on optimal procurement of components (particularly common components) and on efficient management of inventory and manufacturing process.
External supply agent	They focus on low turn-around time and inventory. Their operation is characterized by the supplier contracts which determines the leadtime, flexibility arrangements, cost-sharing and information-sharing with customers. They are responsible to negotiate the reasonable price for raw materials.
Control agents	
Production control agent	Maximizes the production efficiency and minimizes the throughput and delay of order delivery incorporated with other agents. In addition to maximizing production efficiency, the agent cooperates different mechanisms from other agents. For example, the agent not only shortens the duration between placing order(s) and shipping product(s) but also controls over the delay time of the order(s) efficiently.
Loading agent	Loads the raw material, WIP or finished products
Routing agent	Determines the optimal routines to deliver materials. Searches the optimal path of product delivery.
Inventory control agent	Minimizes the inventory and response time of demand; respond the delivery time to customers. Controls over inventory as less as possible and minimizing the response time projected the purchase order. Determines the possibilities for prompt delivery if the inventory is sufficient; otherwise, determines the next available delivery time.
Transportation control agent	Controls the speed and number of transporter in a routine.
Logistic control agent	Adopts optimal strategies to make the supply chain more flexible and efficient that provide customers with a wide variety of products that can be delivered quickly.
Demand control agent	Optimizes the amount and types of information and presents the information of demands. Supports accurate information and presents the optimal information requirements. The demand process within a supply chain is sustained through actual and forecasts (these are modeled as messages in our framework).

(continue)

Table 3 (continued)

Agent name	Objective function (OR function)
Supply control agent	Supply control agents dictate terms and conditions for delivery of the material once orders have been placed. Supply control agent support the desired context of the orders and delivery time based on the determination of a particular order from Supply agent. Supply control agent provides the optimal terms and delivery time and condition based on the determination of a particular order from Supply agent.
Flow control agent	Coordinates flow of products between production and transportation elements.
Problem-solving agents	
Decision-making agent	Takes charge in non-structured problem-solving activities.
Data management agent	Updates the data, including material, cash, information flows and the data about the interaction among SC entities; supports the updated information to the Decision-making agent. Promptly updates all records from the Physical agents (e.g., material flows, cash flows, information flow and any records of interaction) in the supply chain. Instantly provides the latest information to Data management agent.
External models agent	Updates the mode base to support problem-solving. Updates the module base in a real time basis; provides the most updated and appropriate production modules.
Information & Interface agent	Manages the information and control the information flow; determines if a problem is structured or not: a non-structured problem will be sent to the interface agent where it is connects to problem-solving agents for solving it. Maximizes the efficiency of information communication and determines if it is required "decision making" for communication. If the "decision making" is necessary, Information agent should specify whether it is structured for information communication. At last, Interface Agent fetches information into the "Problem-Solution" system.

can trigger additional demand for products in seasonal, random or permanent by numerous ways including advertisements, discounts, coupons and seasonal sales. Three main roles such as service execution management (optimizing executed jobs as specified by the agent's service agreements), solution presentation (routing solutions between servers, clients and other agents), and exception handling (monitor the execution of jobs and services for unexpected events and then react appropriately) are involved (Figure 29).

Negotiation mechanism: An agent cannot simply instruct other agents to start the service. Rather, the agents must come to a mutually acceptable agreement about the terms and conditions under which the desired service will be performed. The negotiation mechanism makes agreements by a joint decision making process in which the parties verbalize their (possibly contradictory) demands and then move towards agreement by a process of concession or search for new alternatives. The mechanism (Figure 30):

(i)   maintains the agent repository where related information is stored,

(ii) delivers the status messages of active services between the functional mechanism and the clients, between an agent and its agency, and between peer agents, and

(iii) communicates

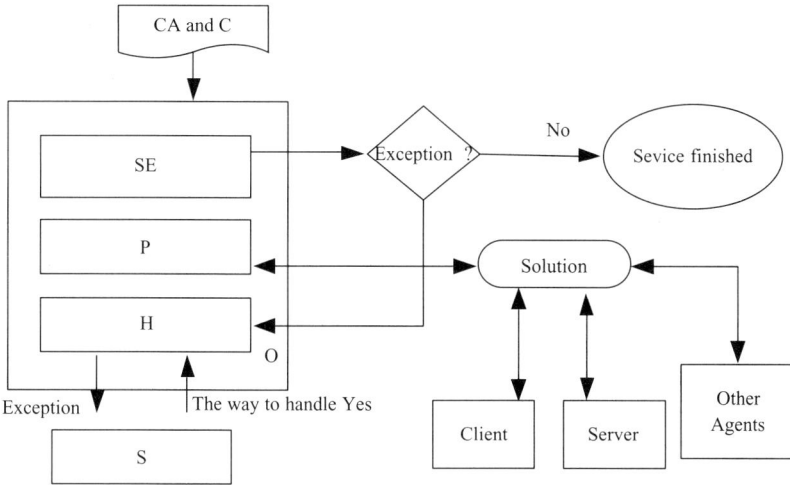

Figure 29. Functional mechanism of ISCA.

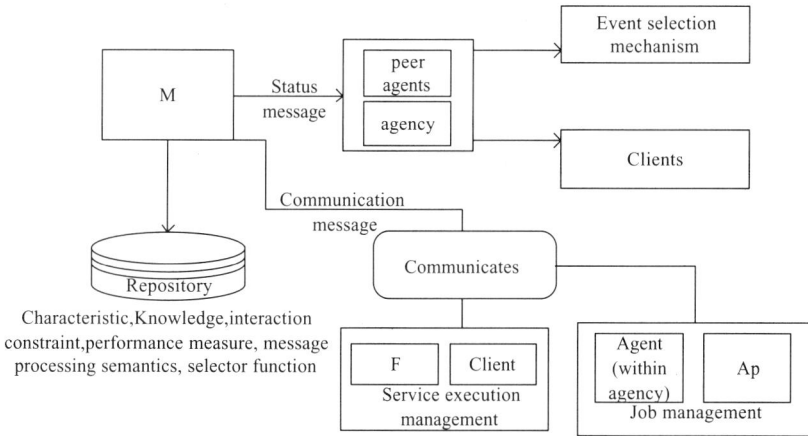

Figure 30. The Negotiation mechanism of ISCA.

- between the functional mechanism and clients within the agency related to job management activities (e.g. activate, suspend, or resume a job), and
- between agents within that agency or peer agents relating to service execution management (e.g. an instruction to start service, service finished, and service results).

Explorer mechanism: the mechanism searches the resources that are located in other distributed databases and performs the role of managing, querying or collating related information from many distributed sources. Based on the Web Services

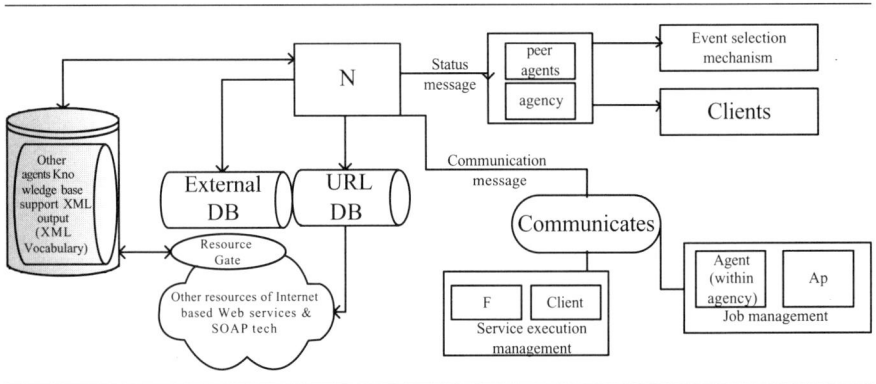

Figure 31. The working of a typical static explorer.

(http://www.w3.org/) and through the Universal Description Discovery Integration (UDDI) registry functionality (mechanism) and service description mechanism of Web Services Description Language (WSDL), relevant service and resources can be explored. The service and resource in need are retrieved through the resource gate and integrated into external knowledge base, in which all agents share the knowledge. Such explorer mechanism is able to traverse the WWW by using Web services, gather information and report what it retrieves to a home location. Figure 31 depicts the working of a typical static explorer.

The section describes the work undertaken to conceptualize the supply chain activities and interaction with a collection of intelligent agents. The agents in the system autonomously plan and pursue their actions and sub-goals, to cooperate, coordinate, and negotiate with others, and to respond flexibly and intelligently to dynamic and unpredictable situations. Agility is enhanced by using this virtual agency to exploit profitable changes in a volatile marketplace.

5. AGENT-BASED SYSTEMS OF KNOWLEDGE MANAGEMENT

In most organizations, knowledge is distributed among many individuals, departments and data stores. This is why many efforts for building centralized corporate memory or knowledge repositories of enterprises failed to be comprehensive or even useful [80]. A more suitable approach, naturally distributed, could come from research in "intelligent agents" [81–83]. In this section, an agent-based system, called Agent-based Knowledge Management (ABKM) system is developed to support the knowledge management activities, for example, acquiring, organizing, and distributing knowledge.

5.1. The definition of agents

In the Agent-based knowledge management (ABKM) system, agents are classified into three types based on the AOD model: "Acquire", "Organize", and "Distribute" [84]; and two interaction objects: "Profiles" and "External Entities."

1. Acquire
   a. Collection Agent (*CA*): Collecting data automatically from various data sources (e.g., database, data warehouse, documents).
   b. Integration Agent (*IA*): Organizing the data collected from the CA. The data could be in various formats depending on the type of analysis technique (e.g. data mining, statistic analysis, OLAP etc.).
   c. Analysis Agent (*AA*): Using desired analysis techniques to analyze data, which are organized from the *IA*, to obtain the analytic information.
2. Organize
   a. Knowledge Storage Agent (*KSA*): It is a kind of knowledge repository. All the knowledge from an organization is stored in it.
3. Distribute
   a. Delivery Agent (*DA*): This agent has three functions: (i) Deliver analytical information to a particular domain expert based on the information directed by Domain Expert Profile; (ii) Deliver knowledge to a particular user based on the information directed by User Profiles; (iii) Deliver knowledge to a particular *KSA* based on the information directed by Knowledge Storage Profile.
   b. Representation Agent (*RA*): The main function of this agent is to appropriately represent the knowledge resulting from the analysis technique.
   c. User Interface Agent (*UIA*): The main function of this agent is to provide a friendly interface and to allow a user or domain expert to entry data/knowledge.
4. Profiles
   a. User Profile: It stores the information about the relationship between end users and a particular knowledge (e.g., Peter is interested in knowledge engineering).
   b. Domain Expert Profile: It stores the information about the relationship between the domain expert and a particular knowledge (e.g., Peter's research area is IC design).
   c. Knowledge Storage Profile: It stores the information about the relationship between Knowledge Storage Agent and the knowledge; e.g., The knowledge about marketing is in the database, where ip = 163.22.22.123 and Database name = KM1)
5. External Entities
   a. User (*U*): users in the organization.
   b. Domain Expert (*DE*): experts in the organization.

5.2. The architecture of the agent-based system

Based on the agents and the interaction objects defined above, the agent-based system architecture as well as knowledge acquisition processes are illustrated in Figure 32.

There are two different types of knowledge acquisition processes: "Acquire Knowledge Actively" and "Acquire Knowledge Passively".

Process 1: Acquire knowledge actively

1. An *AA* sends a message to request *CA* to collect data and analyze the data. The message includes data that it needs and the analysis technique that is used.

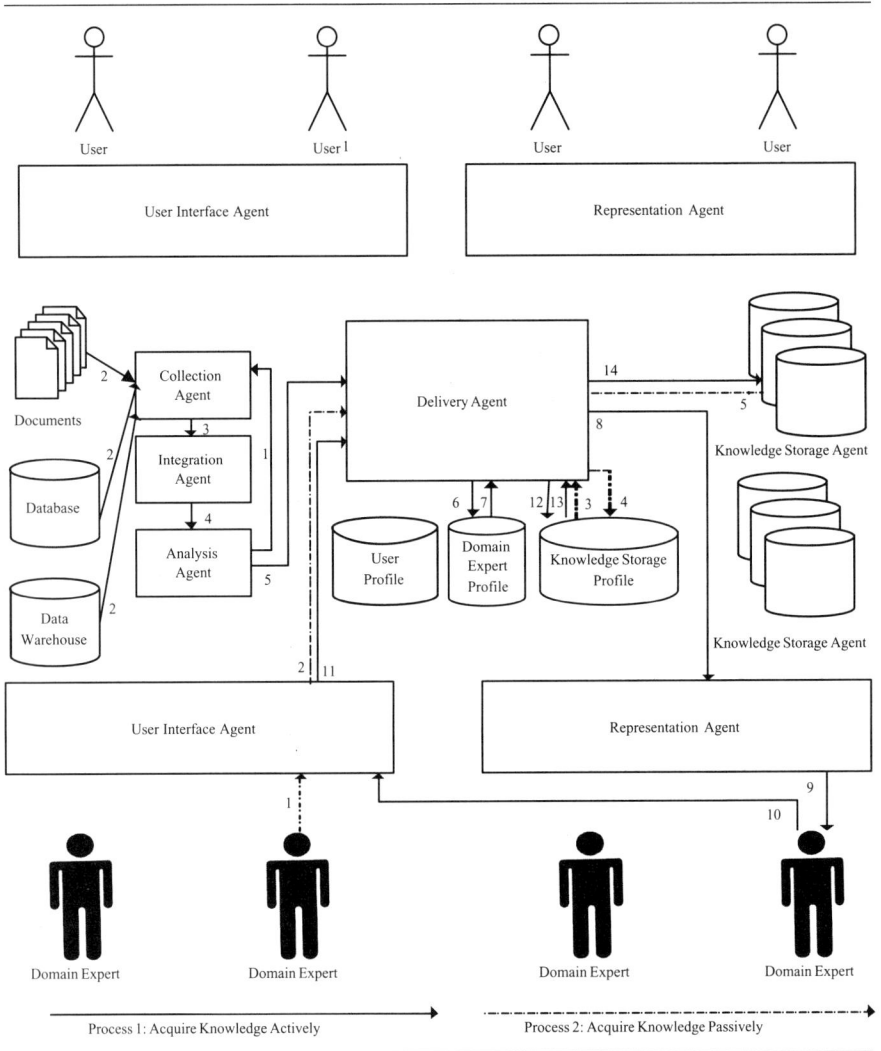

Figure 32. System architecture and knowledge acquisition processes.

2. The *CA* collects data from database, data warehouse, or documents.

3. The *CA* sends the collected data to *IA* and informs the *IA* type of analysis technique in use.

4. The *IA* organizes the collected data based on the analysis technique and then sends the organized data to the *AA*.

5. *AA* analyses the data and sends the results to *DA*.

6. The *DA* requests the Domain Expert Profile to get the information about the relationship between the knowledge and domain expert.

7. The Domain Expert Profile replies the information to the *DA*.

8. The *DA* sends the analytic information and the domain expert data to *RA*.
9. The *RA* sends the analytic information to the domain expert in an appropriate way of representation based on the analysis technique.
10. When the domain expert receives the information, some comments are added with expert knowledge. The domain expert submits the expert knowledge to *UIA*.
11. The *UIA* sends the expert knowledge to the *DA*.
12. The *DA* sends the expert knowledge to Knowledge Storage Profile and request Knowledge Storage Profile to obtain the information about the relationship between the knowledge storage and the expert knowledge.
13. The Knowledge Storage Profile replies the information to the *DA*.
14. The *DA* sends the expert knowledge to *KSA* based on the information sent by the Knowledge Storage Profile.

Process 2: Acquire knowledge passively

1. Expert knowledge is identified and submitted to *UIA* by the Domain Expert.
2. The *UIA* sends the expert knowledge to *DA*.
3. The *DA* sends the expert knowledge to Knowledge Storage Profile and requests for the information about the relationship between knowledge storage and expert knowledge.
4. The Knowledge Storage Profile replies the information to the *DA*.
5. The *DA* sends the expert knowledge to *KSA* based on the relation of knowledge and knowledge storage.

Figure 33 illustrates the two types of knowledge distribution processes: Distribute Knowledge Actively and Distribute Knowledge Passively.

Process 3: Distribute knowledge actively

1. After the 11th step in "Acquire Knowledge Actively," some expert knowledge are produced and stored. Then *DA* requests the User Profiles to get information about: users who needs or are interested in this knowledge.
2. The User Profile replies the information to the *DA*.
3. The *DA* sends the expert knowledge to *RA*.
4. The *RA* sends the expert knowledge to the user in an appropriate way based on the knowledge format and the relationship between knowledge and the user.

5.3. Process 4: Distribute knowledge passively

1. When a user needs a particular knowledge, he performs the query operation through *UIA*.
2. The *UIA* sends user data and query data to *DA*.
3. The *DA* sends the query data to Knowledge Storage Profile and requests the Knowledge Storage Profile to get information about the relationship between knowledge storage and knowledge.
4. The Knowledge Storage Profile replies the information to *DA*.

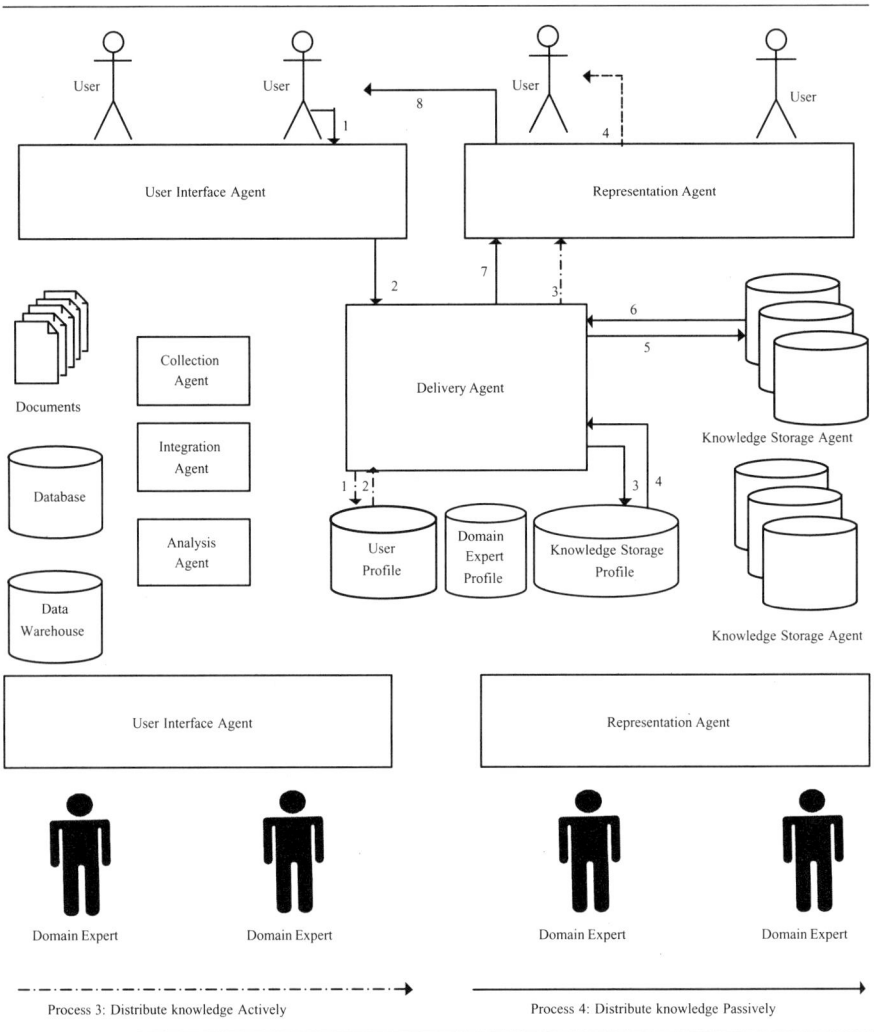

Figure 33. The two types of knowledge distribution processes.

5. The *DA* request *KSA* to get the desired expert knowledge.
6. The *KSA* sends the expert knowledge to *DA*.
7. The *DA* sends the expert knowledge to *RA*.
8. The *RA* sends the expert knowledge to the user in an appropriate way depending on the kind of knowledge.

In the ABKM system, the roles of agents are clearly defined, and their working processes are also clarified. The well-defined roles and standardized working processes of agents not only support the knowledge management activities in organizations, but also define the messages, which agents communicate with each other.

All the messages follow the FIPA ACL structure, and use XML representation and FIPA RDF content language to facilitate the knowledge or information exchange through the Internet (see Section 2.2). The schema-based agent conversation policy and conversation manager are used to decrease the communication transaction in the network. They provide a reliable and an effective agent communication mechanism.

The main contribution of this agent-based system in knowledge management is that (i) the complete agent framework is defined and constructed, rather than issued partially as in the previous literatures, (ii) conversation manager based on schema-based conversation policy is created to coordinate the activities, and (iii) the well-defined messages are defined to support four types of organizational memories completely. The ABKM system and the communication approach show a great promise for knowledge reuse and sharing through knowledge management activities in organizations.

6. CONCLUSIONS

This chapter described the work undertaken to conceptualize business processes through a collection of intelligent agents. The intelligent architecture and communication approach were proposed. The agent-based system was applied to object-oriented design process, supply chain processes, and knowledge management, respectively. The agents in the system autonomously plan and pursue their actions and sub-goals, to cooperate, coordinate, and negotiate with others, and to respond flexibly and intelligently to dynamic and unpredictable situations. Agility is enhanced by using this virtual agency to exploit profitable changes in a volatile marketplace.

The future researches are suggested as the following:

- Although the agent technologies are successful on the local network, they largely fail when transposed to a secure Internet environment. They are rather unwieldy, entail too tight a coupling between components, and above all, conflict with existing firewall technology.
- Extension and more rigorous specifications used in negotiation are required. There are few evaluative studies of negotiation, and most of these focus on the effects of different negotiation strategies upon the agent society [85].
- The approaches to enhancing this design process need to be explored in the future. One of them is to improve the searching procedure to make the system more effective and precise. Another possibility is to make this system to response to the designers' requirements immediately after each step.
- In the real-world, there is still a long way to go in order to universally implement the knowledge enriched in a supply chain. For example, [86] has stated that only about 7% of US retail supply chains operate effectively. He further argues that the main reason for this result is that supply chains are 20% technology problems, 80% people

or knowledge-sharing problems. The challenge of enriching the supply chain with knowledge sharing is on the way.
• Expansion to other business processes, e.g., the processes in electronic commerce (EC).

Acknowledgement

This work was partially supported by funding from the Nation Science Council of the Republic of China (NSC 90-2416-H-260-010).

REFERENCES

[1] Guilfoyle, C., "Ventors of agent technology," *UNICOM Seminar on Intelligent Agents and their Business Application*, London, 8-9, 1995, pp. 135–142.

[2] Nwana, H. S, "Software agents: An overview," *Knowledge Engineering Review*, 11(3), 1996, pp. 205–244.

[3] Etzioni, O., and Weld, D. S., "Intelligent agents on the internet: fact, fiction, and forecast," *IEEE Expert*, 10(4), 1995, 44–49.

[4] Huhns, M. N., and Singh, M. P., "Automating workflows for service procision provisioning integrating AI and database technologies," *Proc IEEE Conf. on Artificial intelligence for Applications (CAIA)*, 1994, pp. 405–411.

[5] Appleby, S., and Steward, S., "Mobile software agents for control in telecommunications networks," *BT Technol. J.*, 12 (2), 1994, pp. 104–113.

[6] Rao, A. S., and Georgeff, M. P., "BDI agents: from theory to practice," *Proc. 1st Int. Conf. On Multi-agent systems (ICMAS-95)*, San Francisco, USA, 1995, pp. 312–319

[7] Jennings, N. R., Faratin, P., Johnson, M. J., Norman, T. J., O'Brien, P., and Wiegand, M. E., "Agent-based business process management," *International Journal of Cooperative Information Systems*, 5(2-3), 1996, pp. 105–130.

[8] Davies, N. J., Weeks, R., and Revett, M., "JASPER: Communicating information agents," *Proc. 4th Int. Conf. on the World Wode Web*, Boston, USA, December, 1(1), 1995, pp. 473–482

[9] Maes, P., "Agents that reduce work and information overload," *Communications of the ACM*, 37(7), 1994, pp. 31–40.

[10] Durfee, E. H., Kiskis, D., and Birmingham, B., "The agent architecture of the university of michigan digital library," *IEEE Proceedings of Software engineering*, 144(1), 1997, pp. 61–71.

[11] Hayes-Roth, B., Brownston, L. and Van Gent, R. "An architecture for adaptive intelligent systems," *Artificial Intelligence*, 1-2, 1995, pp. 329–365.

[12] Mitchell, T., Caruana, R., Freitag, D., Mcdermott, J., and Zabowski, D., "Experience with a learning personal assistant," *Communications of the ACM*, 37(7), 1994, pp. 81–91.

[13] Karacapilidis, N., and Moraïtis, P., "Intelligent agents for an artificial market system, "*Proceedings of the fifth international conference on Autonomous agents*, Montreal, Quebec, Canada, 2001, pp. 592–599.

[14] Choi, S. P. M., Liu, J., and Chan, S. P., "A genetic agent-based negotiation system," *Computer Networks*, 37(2), 2001, pp. 195–204.

[15] Sandhom, T., and Lesser, V., "Issues in automated negotiation and electronic commerce: Extending the contract net framework", *Proc. 1st Int. Conf. On Multi-agent systems (ICAMS)*, San Franscisco, California, 1995, pp. 328–335.

[16] Swaminathan, J. M., Smith, S. F., and Sadeh, N. M., "Modeling supply chain dynamics: A multiagent approach," *Decision Sciences*, 29(3), 1998, pp. 607–632.

[17] Ito, T., and Salleh, M. R., "A blackboard-based negotiation for collaborative supply chain system," *Journal of Materials Processing Technology*, 107(1), 2000, pp. 398–403.

[18] Kaihara, T., "Supply chain management with market economics," *International Journal of Production Economics*, 73(1), 2001, pp. 5–14.

[19] Fischer, K., Chaib-draa, B., Muller, J. P., Pischel, M., and Gerber, C. "A simulation approach based on negotiation and cooperation between agents: A case study," *Systems, Man, and Cybernetics, Part C: Applications and Reviews, IEEE Transactions*, 29(4), 1999, pp. 531–545.

[20] Logan, B., and Theodoropoulos, G., "An approach to interest management and dynamic load balancing in distributed simulation," *Proceedings of the 2001 European Simulation Interoperability Workshop*

(ESIW'01), Simulation Interoperability Standards Organisation and Society for Computer Simulation, June 2001, pp. 565–571.

[21] Jennings, N., Sierra, R. C., and Faratin, P., "A service-oriented negotiation model between autonomous agents," in *Collaboration between Human and Artificial Societies—Coordination and Agent-Based Distributed Computing* (ed. J. Padget), Lecture Notes in Artificial Intelligence, 1624, 2000, Springer Verlag, pp. 201–220.

[22] Bresciani, P., Perini, A., Giorgini, P., and Giunchiglia, F., "A knowledge level software engineering methodology for agent oriented programming," *Proceedings of the Fifth International Conference on Autonomous Agents,* 2001, pp. 648–655.

[23] Akoumianakis, D., Savidis, A., and Stephanidis, C., "Encapsulating intelligent interactive behaviour in unified user interface artifacts," *Interacting with Computers,* 12(4), 2000, pp. 383–408.

[24] Descamps, S., and Ishizuka, M., "Bringing affective behavior to presentation agents," Proc. 3rd Int'l Workshop on Multimedia Network Systems (MNS2001) (IEEE Computer Soc.), Mesa, Arizona, 2001, pp. 332–336.

[25] Tan, G. W., Hayes, C. C., and Shaw, M., "An intelligent-agent framework for concurrent product design and planning," *Engineering Management, IEEE Transactions,* 43(3), 1996, pp. 297–306.

[26] Lewis, T., "Something for nothing [electronic commerce]," *Computer,* 32(5), 1999, pp. 118–119.

[27] Lazanský, J., Mayr, H. C., Quirchmayr, G., and Vogel, P., "Database and Expert Systems Applications," *12th International Conference, DEXA 2001,* Munich, Germany, September, 2001.

[28] Jennings, N. R., Faratin, P., Norman, T. J., O'Brien, P., Wiegand, M. E., Voudouris, C., Alty, J. L., Miah, T., and Mamdani, E. H., "Adept: Managing business processes using intelligent agents," *In Proceedings of BCS Expert Systems Conference (ISP Track),* Cambridge, UK, 1996, pp. 5–23.

[29] Tarumi, H., Matsuyama, T., and Kamabayashi, Y., "10 Evolution of business processes and a process simulation tool," *Software Engineering Conference, 1999. (APSEC '99) Proceedings.* Sixth Asia Pacific, 1999, pp. 180–187.

[30] Lin, F., and Pai, Y., "Using multi-agent simulation and learning to design new business processes," *Systems, Man and Cybernetics, Part A, IEEE Transactions,* 30(3), 2000 pp. 380–384.

[31] Kwok, A., and Norrie, D., "Intelligent agent systems for manufacturing applications," Journal of Intelligent Manufacturing, 4(4), 1993, pp. 285–293.

[32] Pan, J. Y. C., Tanenbaum, J. M., and Glicksman, J., "A framework for knowledge-based computer integrated manufacturing," *IEEE Transactions on Semi-conductor Manufacturing,* 2(2), 1989, pp. 87–100.

[33] Roboam, M., Sycara, K., and Fox, M. S., "Organization modeling as a plat-form for multi-agent manufacturing systems," *Proceedings of Computer Applications in Production and Engineering,* Bordeaux, France, 1991

[34] Sadeh, N., "Micro-opportunistic scheduling: The MICRO-BOSS factory scheduler," Technical Report, CMU-RI-TR-94-04, Carnegie Mellon University, Pittsburg, PA, 1994

[35] Smith, S. F., "The OPIS framework for modelling manufacturing systems," Technical Report, CMU-RI-TR-89-30, Carnegie Mellon University, Pittsburg, PA, 1989

[36] Aguirre, J. L., Brena, R., and Cantu, F. J., "Multiagent-based knowledge networks," *Expert Systems with Applications,* 20(1), 2001, pp. 65–75.

[37] Papazoglou, M. P., "Agent-oriented technology in support of e-business," *Communications of the ACM,* 44(4), 2001, pp. 71–77.

[38] Turban, E., Aronson, J. E., *Decision Support System and Intelligent System,* Prentice-Hall, New Jersey, 1998.

[39] Ovum, "Intelligent agents: The new revolution in software," *Ovum Report,* 1994.

[40] Muller, J. P., Wooldridge, M. J., and Jennings, N. R., "Proceedings of intelligent agent III: Agent theories, architectures, and languages," *ECAI '96 Workshop (ATAL),* Budapest, Hungry, 1996.

[41] Davidow, W., and Malone, M., *The Virtual Corporation,* Harper Collins, New York, 1992.

[42] Huang C. C., "Using intelligent agents to manage fuzzy business process," *IEEE Transactions on Systems, Man, and Cybernetics—Part A,* 31(6), 2001, pp. 508–523.

[43] Huang C. C., and Lai, G. H., "Concurrent engineering: Knowledge management of modular product design," *8TH ISPE International Conference on Concurrent Engineering: Research and Applications,* Los Angels, CA, 2001, pp. 85–106.

[44] Jennings, N. R., Corera, J., Laresgoiti, I, Mamdani, E. H., Perriolat, F., Skarek, P., and Varga, L. Z., "Using ARCHON to develop real-word DAI applications for electricity transportation management and particle accelerator control," *IEEE Expert,* 6(5), 1996, pp. 64–70.

[45] Alty, J. L., Griffiths, D., Jennings, N. R., Mamdani, E. H., Struthers, A., and Wiegand, M. E., "ADEPT-advanced decision environment for process tasks: Overview and architecture," *Proceedings of the BCS Expert Systems Conference*, Applications Track, Cambridge, UK, 1994, pp. 359–371.

[46] Naylor, B., Naim, M. M., and Berry, D., "Leagality: Integrating the lean and agile manufacturing paradigms in the total supply chain," *International Journal of Production Economics*, 62(1), 1999, pp. 107–118.

[47] Kusiak, A., and Szczerbicki, E., "A formal approach to specifications in conceptual design," *ASME Transactions: Journal of Mechanical Design*, 114(4), 1992, pp. 659–666.

[48] Indermaur, K., "Baby steps", *Byte,* March, 1995, pp. 97–104.

[49] FIPA, FIPA Abstract Architecture Specification (Refinements), 2001, http://www.fipa.org

[50] Dignum, F., and Greaves, M., "Agent communication: An introduction," in: Dignum, F. and Greaves, M., Eds, *Issues in Agent Communication*, Springer-Verlag, Berlin, 2000.

[51] Huang C. C., and Lai, G. H., 2001, " Agent-based knowledge management system and its effective communication approach," *Working Paper #02-12*, Department of Information Management, National Chi-Nan University, Taiwan.

[52] URL 1, NCNU-ISKM, https://iskmlab.im.ncnu.edu.tw/DataClooect.jsp

[53] Shen, Weiming, Norrie, Douglas H., and Barthes, Jean-Pual A., *Multi-Agent Systems for Concurrent Intelligent Design and Manufacturing,* Taylor & Francis, New York, 2001.

[54] Lin, F., and Norrie, D. H., "A schema-based conversation modeling for agent-oriented manufacturing systems," *Computer in Industry,* 46(3), 2001, pp. 259–274.

[55] Kristensen, L. M., Christensen, S., and Jensen, K., "The practitioner's guide to coloured Petri nets," *International Journal on Software Tools for Technology Transfer*, 2, 1998, pp. 99–132.

[56] Cost, R.S., Chen, Y., Finin, T., Labrou, Y., and Peng, Y., "Using colored petri nets for conversation modeling," in: Dignum, F. and Greaves, M., Eds, *Issues in Agent Communication*, Springer-Verlag, Berlin, 2000.

[57] O'Grady, P., *The Internet, Intranets and Extranets for Operations and Manufacturing*, Class Notes, University of Iowa, 1998.

[58] Panko, R., *Business Data Communications and Networking*, Prentice-Hall, London, 2001, pp. 2–14.

[59] Bui, T. X., "Decision support in the future tense," *Decision Support Systems,* 19(2), 1997, pp. 149–150.

[60] Pahl, G., and Beitz, W., *Engineering Design*, Springer-Verlag, New York, 1988.

[61] Liang, W. Y., and O'Grady, P., "Design with objects: an approach to object-oriented design," *Computer Aided Design*, 30(12), 1998, pp. 943–956.

[62] Vinoski, S., "CORBA: Integrating diverse applications within distributed heterogeneous environmenrs," *IEEE Communications Magazine*, 35(2), 1997, pp. 46–55.

[63] Schemidt, D., Levine, D., and Mungee, S., "Design of the TAO real-time object request broker," *Computer Communications*, 21(4), 1998, pp. 294–324.

[64] Tibbitts, F., "CORBA: A common touch for distributed applications," *Data Communications*, 24(7), 1995, pp. 77–75.

[65] Sessions, R., "COM and DCOM," *Microsoft's Vision for Distributed Objects*, John Wiley & Sons, 1997.

[66] Jennings, N. R., Mamdani, E. H., Laresgoiti, I., Perez J., and Corera, J., "GRATE: A general framework for cooperative problem solving" *IEE-BCS Journal of Intelligent Systems Engineering*, 1(2), 1992, pp. 102–114

[67] Kusiak, A., and Huang, C. C., "Design of modular digital circuits for testability," *IEEE Transactions on Components, Packaging, and Manufacturing Technology—Part C*, 20(1), 1997, pp. 48–57.

[68] Ellram, L. M., "Supply chain management: the industrial organization prospective," *International Journal of Physical Distribution and Logistics Management*, 21(1), 1991, pp. 13–22.

[69] Lee, H. L., and Ng, S. M., "Introduction to special issue on global supply chain management," *Production and Operation Management*, 6(3), 1997, pp. 191–192.

[70] Anumba, C. J., Ugwu, O. O., Newnham, L., and Thorpe, A., "Collaborative design of structures using intelligent agents," *Automation in Construction,* 11(1), 2002, pp. 89–103.

[71] Tan, G. W., Hayes, C. C., and Shaw, M., "An intelligent-agent framework for concurrent product design and planning," *Engineering Management, IEEE Transactions*, 43(3), 1996, pp. 297–306.

[72] Swaminathan, J., Smith, S., and Sadeh-Koniecpol, N., "Modeling supply chain dynamics: a multiagent approach," *Decision Sciences*, 29(3), 1998, pp. 607–632.

[73] Mason-Jones, R., and Towill, D. R., "Total cycle time compression and the agile supply chain," *International Journal of Production Economics*, 62(1), 1999, pp. 61–73.

[74] Lambert, D. M., and Cooper, M. C., "Issues in supply chain management—Don't automate, obliterate," *Industrial Marketing Management*, 29(1), 2000, pp. 65–83.

[75] Nadoli, G., and Biegel, J. E., "Intelligent manufacturing-simulation agents tool (IMSAT)," *TOMACS*, 3(1), 1993, pp. 42–65.

[76] Seredynski, F., Swiecicka, A., and Zomaya, A. Y., "Discovery of parallel scheduling algorithms in cellular automata-based systems," *Proceedings of the Workshop on Biologically Inspired Solutions to Parallel Processing Problems*, San Francisco, 2001.

[77] Hendler, J. and McGuinness, D. L., "The DARPA agent markup language," *IEEE Intelligent Systems*, 16(6), 2000, pp. 67–73.

[78] Inmon, W. H., Zachman, J. A., and Geiger, J. G., *Data stores, data warehousing, and the Zachman Framework: managing enterprise knowledge*, McGraw-Hill Companies, Inc. NY, U.S.A., 1997.

[79] Huang, C. C., and Kuo, C. M., "Transformation and searching of semi-structured knowledge in organizations," to appear in the *Journal of Knowledge management*, 2002.

[80] Breslin, J., and McGann, J., *The Business Knowledge Repository*, Quorum Books, Westport, Connecticut, 1988.

[81] Sycara, K., "Multiagent systems," *Artificial Intelligence,* 19(2), 1998, pp. 79–92.

[82] Weiss, G., *Multiagent Systems*, MIT Press, Boston, 1999.

[83] Wooldridge, M., and Jennings, N., "Intelligent agents—Theories, architectures and languages," *Lecture Notes in Artificial Intelligence*, Springer-Verlag, Berlin, 890, 1995.

[84] Schwartz, D. G., "On knowledge management in the internet age," in: D. G. Schwartz, Divitini, M. and Brasethvik, T., Eds., *Internet-Based Organizational Memory and Knowledge Management,* Idea Group Publishing, Hershey, USA, 2000.

[85] Kosoresow, A. P., "The efficiency of agents based systems", *Procedings of intelligent Autonomous Systems 3*, Groen, F. C. A., Hirose, S., and Thorpe, C. E. Eds., Washington: IOS Press, 1993, pp. 551–560.

[86] Andraski, J. C., "Foundations for a successful continuous replenishment programme," *International Journal Logistics Management*, 5(1), 1994, pp. 1–8.

THE KNOWLEDGE BASE OF A B2B eCOMMERCE MULTI-AGENT SYSTEM

CHUNYAN MIAO, NELLY KASIM AND ANGELA GOH

1. INTRODUCTION

Arising from economic globalisation, B2B e-commerce, which includes dynamic supply chain, business technology, and virtual organization, has grown considerably in the past few years. B2B E-Commerce is defined as *commerce between businesses* [1]. In order to stay competitive and to tap potential markets, it is necessary to enable consumers to customise their ever-changing demands. While most of the literature about software agents describes the use of agents to assist end users in B2C e-commerce, we propose the introduction of autonomous agents that can provide personalised information, undertake automated negotiations, and perform planning and scheduling functions [2, 3, 4] to support B2B e-commerce.

The term intelligent agent can be defined as an entity that is able to act rationally [5, 6]. It has abilities to monitor the environment, to perform inference (reasoning), and to act rationally. In the AI world, the concept of rationality in an agent is described by Russell and Norvig [7] as:

"For each possible percept sequence, an ideal rational agent should do whatever action is expected to maximize its performance measure, on the basis of the evidence provided by the percept sequence and whatever built-in knowledge the agent has."

The key aspect of the e-business world is that companies will inevitably move more and more into a customer-centric and knowledge-based paradigm in order to increase competitiveness in an ever-changing market [8, 9]. Intelligent agents support a natural merger of the customer-centric paradigm and knowledge-based technology. E-business agents can participate in high-level (task-oriented) dialogues through the use of interaction protocols in conjunction with built-in organizational knowledge. The opportunities for using intelligent agents in an e-business application are enormous. Papazoglou predicts the following four basic forms of e-business agents [8]:

- Application agents: An e-business application may comprise a large number of application agents. Each agent focuses on a single area of expertise and provides access to the available information and knowledge source in that domain.
- Personal agents: Personal agents work directly with users to help support the presentation, organisation and management of user profiles, and information collection.
- General business activity agents: General business activity agents perform a large number of general commerce support activities that can be customised to address the needs of a particular business organisation. Examples include marketing agents, negotiation/contracting agents and information brokering agents.
- System level agents: System level agents include workflow agents, business transaction agents, integration agents etc.

Agents that work together in a community form a multi-agent system (MAS) [10]. Within MAS, agents collaborate to achieve a common goal. To do so, each agent in the system normally has its specific task that contributes to the attainment of the final goal. In a multi-agent e-business environment, different types of e-business agents such as user interface agents, information gathering agents, broker agents, analyzer agents, scheduler agents etc. may live in the community. Agents that live in a multi-agent e-business community need to represent both domain knowledge and user's knowledge. Moreover, they need to share knowledge and coordinate their activities in order to be successful, both as an individual and collectively. To achieve this, the knowledge base of the multi-agent system plays an important role for both individual agents and the whole community.

The paper aims to describe the implementation of a multi-agent system with a specific focus on its knowledge base. The goal is to perform purchase recommendation. This is achieved by specifying a graph based knowledge base of the agent system. The following section reviews some related work. Section 3 introduces the agent inference model upon which the knowledge base is created. Section 4 describes the B2B application used to illustrate the system. Section 5 describes the details of the knowledge base. Section 6 gives a brief overview of the multi-agent system, with its ability to perform data gathering. Section 7 discusses some implementation issues. This is followed by a brief conclusion.

2. RELATED WORK

The review of related work will be focused on the knowledge base in support of intelligent agents, and multi-agent systems. Agents are classified by their knowledge representation and rational mechanisms as follows: 1) re-active agents which rely on a rule-based knowledge base to do inference [11]; 2) case based reasoning agents which use a case base to represent its knowledge, and infer by computing the similarity between the current situation and the past cases [12]; 3) practical reasoning agents, which are so called BDI (belief, desire, intension) agents [5]. As the name indicates, BDI agents employ human beings' "practical reasoning" philosophy which include belief, desire, and intention. Agents use BDI logic, which is an extension of first order logic to do inference. The knowledge base of BDI agents is also rule-based. Corresponding to the reflex agents, CBR agents, and BDI agents, there are reactive multi-agent systems, multi-agent case-based reasoning systems, and BDI based multi-agent systems. The following contains a comparison of rule-based knowledge base and case-based knowledge base to show how they enable the intelligent agents to represent knowledge and to act autonomously based on their knowledge.

The rule–based knowledge base has been around since the 1980's [13, 14]. To date, it remains widely used in various application systems including agent-based systems. In an agent system, the rule-based knowledge base usually includes a set of rules. These rules are represented as 'if <condition> then <conclusion>' statements. The 'if' portion represents the condition and the 'then' represents the action that will be taken if the condition is satisfied. Whenever an agent detects some changes, it searches for appropriate rules to fire. There are two kinds of such searches: *data driven* and *goal driven*. In the first case, agents have perceived some facts and want to reach a conclusion; in the other case, agents already have a conclusion but want to verify it. The first kind of search is also called 'forward chaining'. Forward chaining begins by matching known facts with the rules from the rule-based knowledge base. Once a rule has been found, the conclusion of that rule is added to the set of known facts. This new fact may be matched to another rule. The second type of search is called 'backward chaining'. Rule-based knowledge base has the following advantages [15]:

- The ability to use experimental knowledge acquired from human experts.
- Good performances in a small limited domain. If the domain is limited, small enough and well defined, it is possible to cover all the possibilities and foresee all the possible situations.
- Good explanation facilities. It is relatively easy for an agent to use the rule-based knowledge base to reach a conclusion

However, rule-based knowledge base also has some distinct weaknesses:

- Often, rules from a human expert are heuristic and it is difficult to capture a deeper knowledge of the domain. If the knowledge of the domain is not extremely precise, there is always a chance that an unexpected case occurs whereby the agents are unable to find a matching rule.
- Heuristic rules cannot handle missing information or unexpected data values. If a value is missing or a value is unexpected, the agent is not able to fire its rules.
- Rules are unable to adapt to new problems.
- The knowledge is very task dependent. Often, a set of rule is adapted to a particular problem and it is not possible to adapt it to another problem.

Unlike rule based knowledge base, a case-based knowledge base records previous experience as a case base. A case represents a situation that happened in the past. In general, it is represented as a pair, "problem, solution". The problem represents the description of the past situation and the solution is the description of the decision taken at that time. A case base consists of a set of cases. Agents reason and act based on the similarity of the current situation and past cases [16]:

The main advantages of case-based knowledge base include:

• Extensive analysis of domain knowledge is not required.
• It allows shortcuts for agents to reason and act. If an appropriate case is found, a solution can be found very fast (faster than generating a solution from scratch).
• It enables agents to avoid past errors and exploit past successes. In case-based knowledge base, the record of each situation that occurred is kept and used for new problems.

However, there are some pitfalls in a case based knowledge base:

• The search time (time complexity) in the retrieval process could increase due to poor library organization.
• The size of the case base (space complexity) could increase as the CBR agent learns new cases without an extensive improvement in the performance of the system. The agent has to repeat its search until it determines a partition of the cases by means of its similarity to previous cases.
• The implementation of case based knowledge base is very time consuming and complex.

Intelligent agent as an enabling technology of both B2C and B2B e-commerce has been applied to various e-commerce applications. Agents can assist in electronic commerce as mediators in a number of ways. Using given specifications, agents can "go shopping" for a user, and return with recommendations of purchases which meet those specifications. Agents as mediators in e-commerce can play roles such as monitoring and notification, product recommendation, merchant brokering, and negotiation [9, 11].

Instead of describing the use of agents to assist end users in B2C e-commerce, which can be found in much of the literature on software agents, a brief description is here on applications involving intelligent agents and multi-agent systems in B2B e-commerce. The IBM e-business research centre in Canada proposed computerized intelligent agents to facilitate decision support in e-business environment [17]. Agents perform tasks on behalf of the user. It uses knowledge and conditions in the environment to determine its actions. Two types of knowledge are used to determine the actions: (1) domain knowledge, and (2) user knowledge. Domain knowledge is needed to perform actions in a particular domain, and user knowledge is needed to adapt the actions to differences among individual users. Both types of knowledge are represented by case bases. An agent assists decision makers to describe new cases by recommending relevant descriptors. The agent presents the retrieved cases to the decision-maker by selecting the pertinent parts of previous cases and using these as a basis for recommending solutions. The agents use CBR to assist in decision making in a multi-agent e-business environment.

In addition, IBM T. J. Watson Research Center investigated a rule-based business process intelligent agent for e-commerce including business-to-business (B2B), to integrate supply chains; and business-to-consumer (B2C). The agents rely on the knowledge base that contains business rules, which are called *CommonRules* [18, 19]. The Multi-agent system for e-business process management developed by University of Technology Sydney also has a rule based knowledge base to represent the business rules [20]. Another example is the intelligent notification agent called Eyes developed by Amazon.com, which relies on both rule-based knowledge base and case based knowledge base [21].

Recently, Serenko et al. investigated 20 existing agent toolkits and found almost all 20 toolkits assessed lack support for some important eBusiness agent features, especially personalization (user centric) and knowledge-ability (both domain knowledge and user's knowledge) [22].

As a result, agent toolkits with its knowledge base specially designed for eBusiness have emerged. Tropos: Multi-agent framework for e-business developed by University of Toronto, uses a rule based knowledge base for storing the beliefs of e-business agents [23]. Open Multi-agent system for e-business proposed by MIT e-business Lab uses a rule-based knowledge base for handling exceptions in business activities [24]. In this chapter, we present the agent inference model from which a graph based knowledge base can be created. The proposed graph based knowledge base has the ability to facilitate both customer centric and knowledge-ability of e-business agents.

3. AGENT INFERENCE MODEL (AIM)

The Agent Inference Model, AIM, [25] captures knowledge as a collection of factors and impacts between the factors. It infers and makes decisions by manipulating factors and the impacts via a connected graph with one node representing a decision. Thus, AIM is a directed graph, which consists of two basic types of objects: *factor*, denoted by nodes, and *impact*, denoted by directed, signed and weighted arcs. A graphical representation of AIMs is illustrated in Figure 1.

Each factor represents a characteristic related to a real world problem that an agent deals with. In general a factor might be an event, property, action, goal etc. For instance, factors related to an airline-ticketing agent may include ticket price, flight transit, airline service, airline reputation, airplane type, flight length, time etc. Relationships between factors may be expressed either as a positive causal impact between two factors or negative causal impacts. A positive weight represents a causal increase impact and a negative weight represents a causal decrease impact.

In Figure 1, $factor_i$ has a negative impact on $factor_j$, $factor_j$ has a positive impact on $factor_k$, and $factor_k$ has a positive impact on $factor_i$, The three factors form a feedback loop. In rule based agent model and BDI model, feedback is not allowed as it is considered a knowledge conflict. However, feedback mechanisms are needed in real-world applications. AIM supports feedback to model real world complex problems.

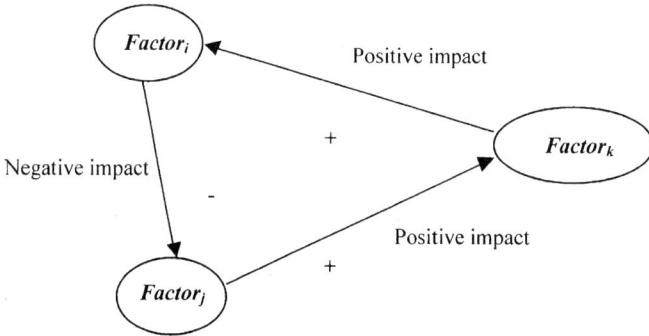

Figure 1. AIM graph.

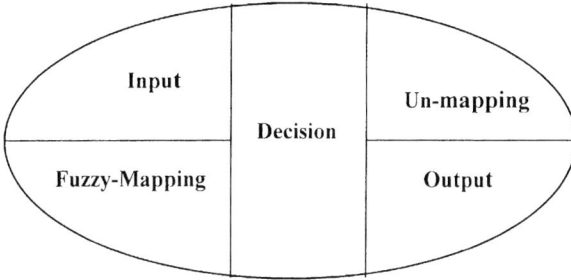

Figure 2. Behaviors of the factor.

Figure 2 shows the five main behaviors of the nodes/factor: obtain input from the environment, carry out fuzzy-mapping which transforms a state of a factor to a member of fuzzy set (fuzzy mapping), derive decision pertaining to the new state of the factor, unmapping (defuzzification) and output the un–mapped state of the factor.

The mapping is based on fuzzification. The fuzzification (mapping) function maps a real causal activation value to a fuzzy set. The decision function of a factor, which determines the state of *factor*, takes all impacts together into account, and works out a new state of the factor. Suppose the state of factor i is denoted by $x_i (i = 1, 2, \ldots, n)$; The impact from factors j to factor i is $y_{ij}(j = 1, 2, \ldots, n)$; The decision function of factor i, D_i is determined as:

$$x_i(t^+) = D_i(y_{i1}(t), y_{i2}(t), \ldots, y_{in}(t)), \text{ where } t^+ \text{ is the unit of time just after } t.$$

Each factor has a fuzzy state value from the transformation of the real value of the factor, in the interval $[-1, 1]$. Each causal impact (interconnections) between factors has a weight value in the interval $[-1, 1]$ showing the degree of the causality and an impact function describes how the impact takes effect. Assuming factor j has impact

y_{ij} over factor i. This is described by impact function w_{ij}.

$$y_{ij}(t) = w_{ij}(x_j(t))$$

Causal associations reflect the way the world is organized. It involves changes and is dynamic in nature. For instance, the rapid changing digital economy experiences markets changes, changes in business relationships, evolving business processes and so on. With AIM, agents perceive the changes of cause and causal relationships and infer the cause-effect dynamically and autonomously.

In AIM, the factors and impacts are application dependent. Each factor has its own state value set. The states of factors collectively represent the state of an AIM. With AIM, both domain knowledge and user's knowledge related to a problem are stored in the structure of nodes and interconnections of the map. Hence, each node represents one of the key-factors of the problem. AIM supports a knowledge visualization feature, which is not found in rule based agent models, case based agent model and BDI based agent model. The initialised AIM graph can be set up based on the knowledge from domain experts. After initialisation, different AIM models can be further derived. These adapt to different users by integrating the domain expert's knowledge with individuals user's knowledge.

AIM presents some desired customer-centric features,

• Ease of use: it is relatively easy to use AIM to do modeling and to represent both domain knowledge and user's knowledge. In the future, there will be more agents created by users and less agents created by software designers. AIM enables the agent users to specify the agent models by themselves easily;
• Knowledge visualization: using AIM, the represented knowledge is visualized by a easy-understood graph;
• Feedback: it allows the modeling of feedback.
• Dynamic knowledge: the changes of knowledge are updated dynamically

The next section describes an e-business application scenario. An agent inference model is specified to model the case scenario, upon which the knowledge base is created.

4. CASE STUDY SCENARIO

The scenario is based on transactions between suppliers and retailers. The latter acts as the 'customers' in a B2B context. As shown in Figure 3, a B2B transaction arises between the Suppliers and the Middle Distributors (A), and between the Middle Distributors and Retailers (B). Retailers are normally considered the middlemen (or distributors) in a complete business model in that they are not product consumers. However, in this chapter, they are referred to as the 'Customer'.

An Airlines Ticketing System (ATS) was selected as a case study in the Intelligent Multi-Agent System for B2B E-Commerce application, in order to demonstrate how a real world problem could be addressed. The customers are travel agencies or frequent flyers who wish to block-book tickets for single or multiple parties. The distribution

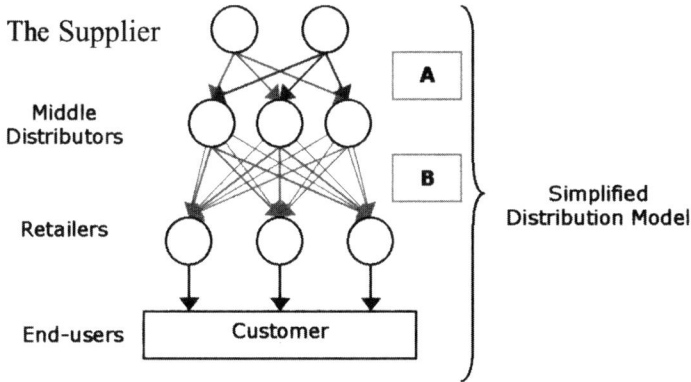

Figure 3. A distribution model.

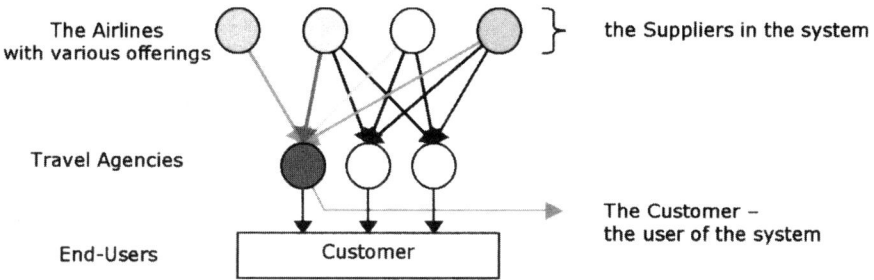

Figure 4. A B2B model of the airline ticketing system.

model of ATS is given in Figure 4 and can be seen as a simplified version of the general model in Figure 3. ATS assists customers to process flight information from international airlines with the objective of recommending a flight that suits the customers' needs and preferences. This scenario was selected for the following reasons:

• B2B e-commerce between parties in an Airlines Ticketing System is very commonplace. Most international airlines and travel agencies provide facilities for online reservation and booking. However, the use of multi-agent systems has not been utilized fully in this field.
• ATS has a straightforward distribution model that can be used to represent the commerce transactions. The line of distribution involves the Airlines (the supplier), Travel Agencies (the distributors) and Users (the customers).
• The information relating to ATS including schedules, prices and flight routes are readily available from various airlines' Internet sites or online travel agent. This fact facilitates information gathering and testing.

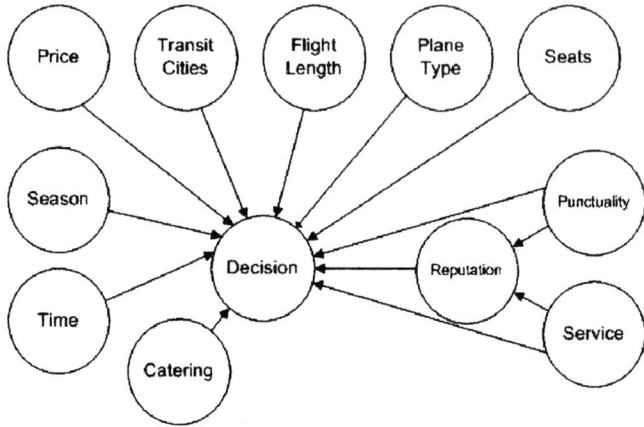

Figure 5. The knowledge base of the customer agent in the airline ticketing system.

- The airlines industry has the financial ability and economic rationale to support innovative e-commerce solutions. As a service industry, customisation of services and offerings to meet customer demands is crucial.
- The decision making process in ATS is determined by various factors that can be modelled in the knowledge graph. These factors are intuitive and are easily modified to suit different customers.

The *Airline Ticketing System* uses a knowledge graph to depict the factors involved in the decision making process as shown in Figure 4. These factors are typical of points of interest of the Customer (in this scenario, the travel agencies). Data gathering is performed by the system through queries to a number of airline systems. The queries include the origin and destination of the flights, number of seats requested, and the preferred date and time of the flight. This mechanism acquires information updates at regular intervals. A scheduling mechanism is incorporated into the system to initiate automatic data gathering cycles. The data analysis process then simulates a decision-making process that users normally carry out when presented with flight information. Through the data analysis process, each set of data is assigned a recommendation value. Based on these recommendation values, undesirable data (data with low recommendation values) are filtered out, and the final set of more-desirable data is presented to the user.

It should be highlighted that the factors shown in Figure 5 are used as illustration and that the customer may select any other factors that are deemed important:

- Price: The price of the tickets for the flight
- Plane type (comfort): The type of the plane used for the flight. This affects the comfort level associated with the flight.

- The length of the flight: This is the total time for the journey. The hours include time spent on the plane and in transit (if any).
- Number of transit cities during the flight: Some customers may prefer non-stop flights while others may prefer transits at specific cities.
- Number of seats available: Apart from availability, it should be noted that bulk purchases might affect the prices as well.
- The reputation of the airlines: This is affected by a combination of factors such as punctuality, security, cleanliness, and staff service. In our model, we simplify the situation by placing punctuality and service as those impacting reputation.
- The punctuality of the airlines.
- The catering service of the airlines.
- The on-board service of the airlines.
- Time of the flight: the flight may be in the morning, afternoon, evening, or night. The preferred time of the flight can be specified in the query.
- Season of the flight: the flight may be during certain holiday periods, or in certain months. The preferred date of the flight can be specified in the query

Though not illustrated, a corresponding knowledge base may be developed for the Supplier (the airlines). Just as a customer has a set of factors that determines an optimum decision, a supplier too may have its own constraints and issues to consider. This could be modelled and implemented as a knowledge base.

5. CREATING THE KNOWLEDGE-BASE

As mentioned in the above section, the data analysis process in the Agent System is carried out using a knowledge graph, which implements the AIM (Agent Inference Model). With the knowledge graph, all data, gathered as the result of a query can be analysed and assigned a preference value. The concepts of AIM, as described in section 3, were implemented as shown in Table 1.

As seen in Table 1, factors are represented in the graph as nodes. In addition to these 'Factor' nodes, there is a special node in the knowledge graph. This is the Decision node, which corresponds to the desirability of the current state of the graph. Thus the higher the value assigned to the decision node, the more desirable the state of the graph is.

Before any analysis is performed, the user must specify the knowledge graph that represents the purchase decision. The graph is created in the *graph creation phase*, where the factors that influence the purchase decision are added to the graph. There are different types of factors, each with its own characteristics and properties. For example, the *Airline Ticketing System* graph may have 12 factors, including the 'decision' factor. However, there may exist connections between two nodes. For example, a higher reputation of the airlines may imply a higher price. Thus, a connection is created between the Price node and the Reputation node. Connections are added after the nodes are specified. All these functions are made available through a simple-to-use interface shown in Figure 6.

Table 1 Implementation of AIM

Properties of AIM	Implementation
Nodes	Factors are represented as nodes and are divided into several categories for its practical use
Numerical representation	Quantitative representation is used internally and for computation of data analysis
Factor value set	Factors may have values ranging from 0 to the maximum weight value.
Fuzzy concepts	• Defuzzification of Factor values • Defuzzification of Importance value into importance value
Temporal concepts	The temporal concept is implemented by varying the value stored in the database very slightly in each cycle. As time passes, the varying value may have adjusted into a relatively different value
Dynamic causal relationship	Causal relationships are represented through the arcs from a node to another node.
Feedback	Feedback is implemented through arcs in the graph that allows connection to itself provided the arc must go through another node

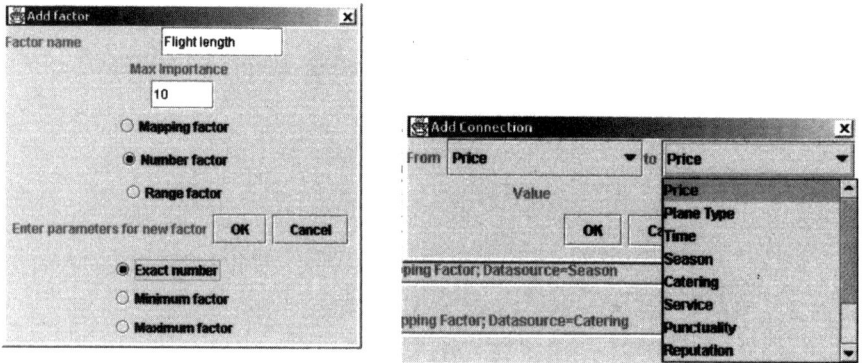

Figure 6. Adding factors and connections to the knowledge graph.

After the graph creation phase, the user specifies the way these factors influence the decisions. This phase is known as the *graph parameters specification phase*. In this phase, the importance of every factor in the graph is defined. The 'importance' value determines the extent to which the factor affects the decision. For example, if the user considers Price to be more important than Reputation in the purchase decision, the connection between Price and Decision nodes has a higher weight value than the connection between Reputation and Decision nodes. Figure 7 shows how the process is facilitated by an intuitive visual interface.

The Factors can roughly be divided into two categories: data and environmental. The former refers to values derived from the data gathered by Info-Gathering Agents. A value is assigned to a data factor from the information extracted from gathered data. For example, the number of seats available can be available directly from supplier sources. Other information such as the season of the flight requires intermediate processing

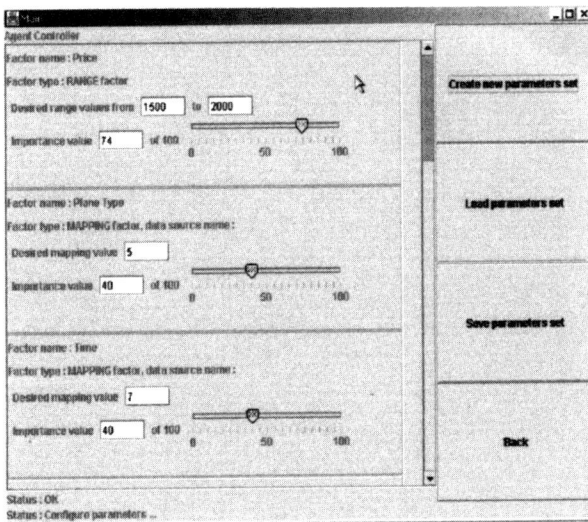

Figure 7. Snapshot of GUI graph parameter specification.

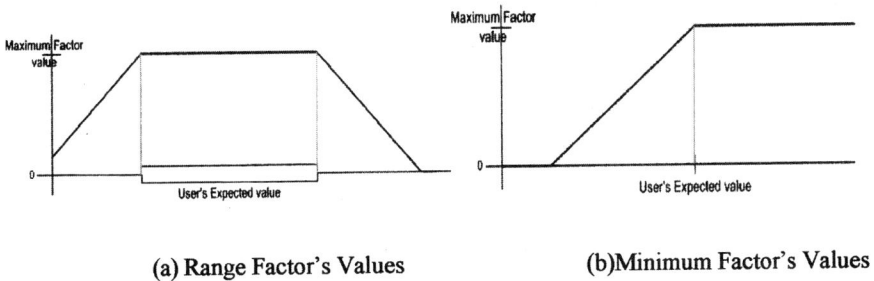

(a) Range Factor's Values   (b)Minimum Factor's Values

Figure 8. Mapping factors.

before the information can be translated into a factor value. The environmental factor, however, involves obtaining information that is beyond a specific query. These factors, such as the reputation of the airline, punctuality of the airline and quality of the on-board catering are gathered from external sources and require translation. The agent monitors and extracts information from trusted airlines watchdog websites, and uses the information as a reference. A factor such as "comfort" or "safety" may be derived from the type of plane used for the flight. This information has to be defuzzified before it can be used in the decision making process.

Range factors are factors where the user specifies a preferred range of values, for example, the preferred price is between $0 to $2,000. If the data returns a value that falls within the range, the factor is assigned a maximum value as illustrated in Figure 8(a).

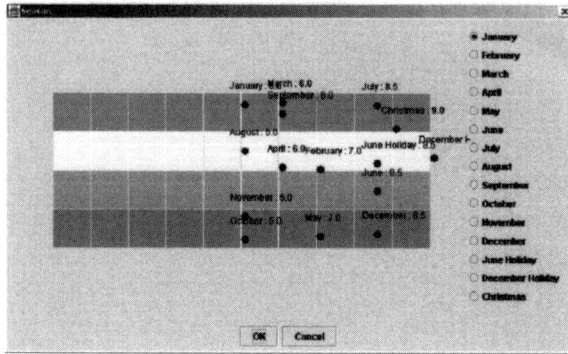

Figure 9. Graphical method of specifying requirements.

Everything that falls outside the range will have a factor value that decreases gradually as its value moves further away from the range.

Number factors are factors whose expected values are defined as an integer. This category is further divided into sub-categories: Exact factor; Minimum factor; Maximum factor. Taking the Minimum Factor as an example, if 'Seats' required is defined as 8, the user expects to have at least 8 available seats. Values with 8 or above will be assigned the maximum factor value while results below 8 will be mapped to decreasing factor values. Figure 8(b) shows an example of this minimum factor.

Mapping factors as a discrete quantity

An example of such a factor is Reputation. The reputation of an airline can be quantified and normalized to a scale ranging from minimum to maximum values. For example, the reputation of twelve admired airline companies in the Airlines industry were taken from the website of Fortune [26]. The values of the other factors such as Catering, Service, Punctuality were taken from Skytrax, the World Airline Site [27].

Mapping factors as a series of concepts

An example of such a factor is Season. As the factor value could refer to specific months or periods within a year, it requires intermediate processing before the information can be translated into a factor value. In order to make it convenient for the user, the system provides a number of simple-to-use input maps such as the one shown in Figure 9.

In the Graph Specification phase, the user specifies the importance of each factor to the purchasing decision using values 'Not Important', 'Somewhat Important', 'Important', 'Fairly Important', and 'Very Important'. These importance values are specified through a slide-bar similar to those in Figure 9.

The values must be defuzzified to determine the corresponding weight of the arc connecting the factor node to the decision node. When the user sets the factor to 'Not Important', the

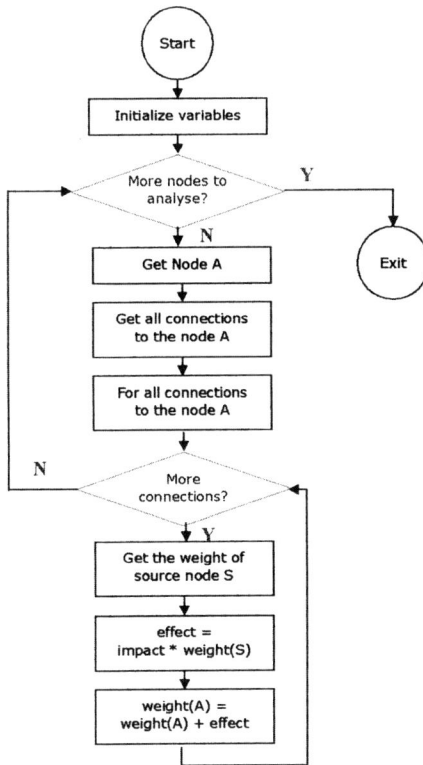

Figure 10. Computing the decision factor.

factor has no effect on the decision and the connection weight is set to zero. A graph GUI, as shown in Figure 7, provides a convenient means through which the user can customize his/her preferences without having to delve into lower-level details. The user would only go through this process when a new knowledge graph is created or when modifications are made to an existing knowledge graph. In summary, the derivation of the decision node is shown in Figure 10. After the data is analysed by the system, the recommendation value is accumulated as the value of the decision node. This recommendation value may range from 0.00 to 100.00 (a floating point number) after normalization. This decision may be fuzzified into a qualitative representation, for example, *Not Recommended, Recommended*, and *Highly Recommended*.

6. ARCHITECTURE

In this scenario, there are two independent multi-agent systems representing the customer and the supplier respectively. These MASs serve as the building blocks of the B2B system. It is the customer system that initiates contact, communication and requests. In order to interact with the environment, the customer system has information-gathering agents whose duty is to gather data in order to expand its knowledge base.

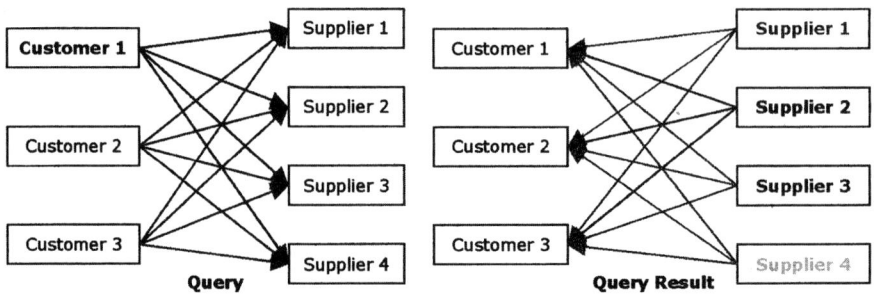

Figure 11. Interaction between customers and suppliers.

In this scenario, queries are sent to the supplier systems to gather information regarding flight schedules and so on. The supplier system, on the other hand, provides information. It serves query requests from customers. However, the supplier agents have the right not to respond to the customer agents' requests.

The relationship between the customers and suppliers is shown in Figure 11. The customer requests for data from the suppliers through queries, and the suppliers reply with results.

At first glance, the system architecture may resemble traditional client-server architecture. In reality, the architecture is not in the form of an N-tier system as each agent has an equal standing. Communication between agents is based solely on message passing.

The description that follows focuses on the design of the internal architecture of the customer agent system. The supplier system could be similarly modeled. In this prototype, it is assumed that the supplier simply provides requested information and no decision-making or analysis features are required. Hence, it is far less complex.

The agents involved in the customer agent architecture are as follows:

Information gathering agent (IGA) and its sub-agents (SIGAs)

The agent and its sub-agents will perform data gathering from the supplier's agents. Basically, the purpose is to extract the details from the suppliers' sites. As the volume of communication traffic can potentially be quite high, the agent is assisted by its sub-agents. The task of IGA is to manage these sub-agents. The other agents in this customer system will be unaware of the existence of these sub-agents.

Analyser agent

Its job is to analyse and perform computation on the data gathered by Info-Gathering Agent (IGA). The Analyser Agent is designed to be modular in relation to the knowledge base which is readily replaceable by other forms of knowledge representation in terms of its structure and/or its computational algorithm.

Scheduler agent

This agent performs schedule management and scheduling. It maintains the schedule that is initially drawn up by the user. As data is gathered and analysed, the schedule may be adjusted using an intelligent scheduling algorithm. This agent also provides schedule information to agents (the GUI Agent and the Info-Gathering Agent). Dynamic scheduling is permitted by adjusting the frequency of data gathering. Whenever a new recommendation value differs from the existing value by a specified amount, the data gathering frequency is reduced. In contrast, when the difference in values is higher, data is gathered more frequently. This enables the schedule to adjust itself in line with the rapidity (or otherwise) of data movements.

Global scheduling refers to a specific time when the Info-Gathering Agent (IGA) will dispatch its Sub-IGA to gather information from all suppliers. This was implemented because in the Airlines Ticketing System (ATS), changes in the industry are likely to affect all suppliers. Furthermore, changes in individual supplier are not of interest because analysis is not performed to observe the trend of the data movement. Rather, the analysis is concerned with the quality of data. It should be noted that due to its modular nature, alternative scheduling mechanisms are easily facilitated.

Master agent

The Master agent performs administrative role such as status check and synchronization. These tasks include: Handling status requests from the GUI Agent on behalf of the user; Tracking the progress of all other agents; Relaying the commands such as the initiating, dispatching orders from the GUI module to the Agent System; Filtering and relaying appropriate messages such as the status of the system that requires user's attention.

Graphical user interface (GUI) agent

This agent acts as the *gateway* between the user and the Master Agent. Its main task is to relay the commands instructed by the user to the Agent System. It is also responsible for relaying various states of the Agent System, especially notification about graph and schedule errors that require the user's action. The user is able to communicate with the agents through certain interfaces. The GUI is a wholly invoke-and-run module. Due to the different natures of the GUI and Agent System, the interface is a hybrid between one which communicates using message passing and one, which is under direct and complete control of GUIAgent. Whenever GUIAgent decides that it must inform the user about something (such as the status of the Agent System, warning, component request, and so on), it involves methods of the GUI module. On the other hand, synchronization between the GUIAgent and the user is carried out using an Event Dispatcher Thread mechanism. Thus, the GUI Module only has limited access and command over GUIA. These interfaces add appropriate behaviour to the GUIA response. When GUIAgent finishes its current task, the task submitted by the GUI Module will be picked up in the next round of scheduling. The agent can then select

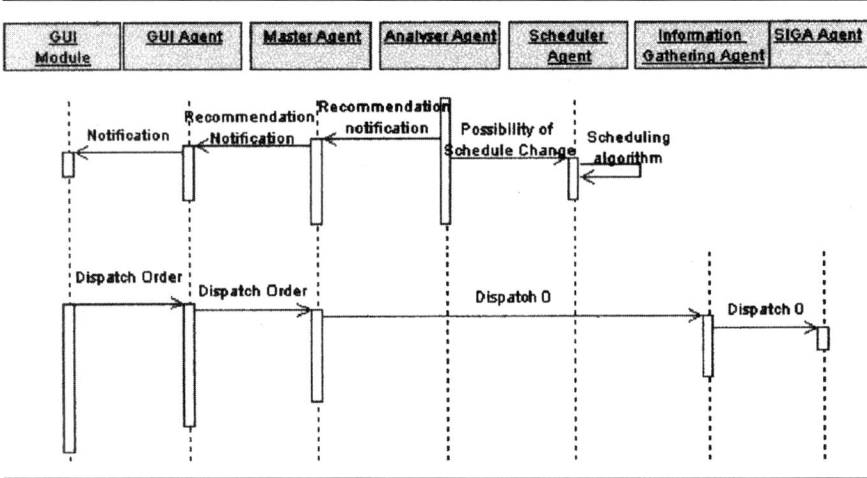

Figure 12. Examples of message passing between agents.

whether to execute the instructed tasks or defer the action. This way, the autonomous nature of GUIAgent is preserved while at the same time provides a way to interface the GUI module and Agent System.

We have assumed that all the businesses involved in the B2B e-Commerce transaction have agreed upon and will adhere to a certain communication protocol including

- The sequence of actions involved in communication (communication etiquette).
- The content and the format of the messages used in communication (the *vocabulary* and *the grammar*). In an agent system, the vocabulary corresponds to an ontology, and the grammar corresponds to the specific standard of communication protocol used.

By keeping each of these modules independent, the system improves on its ability to scale and evolve without impact on other functions. It should be noted that there are interdependencies between the agents as they access the knowledge graph and schedule as well as the knowledge base stored in a database. For example, the Scheduler Agent provides the Information Gathering Agents with the schedule to conduct its data gathering while the Analyser Agent sends schedule modification information to the Schedule where applicable. Hence, synchronization of access and modification of shared resources has to be controlled. An example of the message passing protocol is shown in Figure 12 in the form of a sequence diagram.

Two types of ontology were defined. The first, called *Common-Agent-Ontology*, is used for communication between the Customer Agents and the Supplier Agents. This ontology requires an agreement between the customer and supplier to facilitate communication. The other, called *Internal-Agent-Ontology*, is used for communication within the customer environment. This ontology could be viewed as proprietary with its implementation dependent on the preference of the customer. The use of different

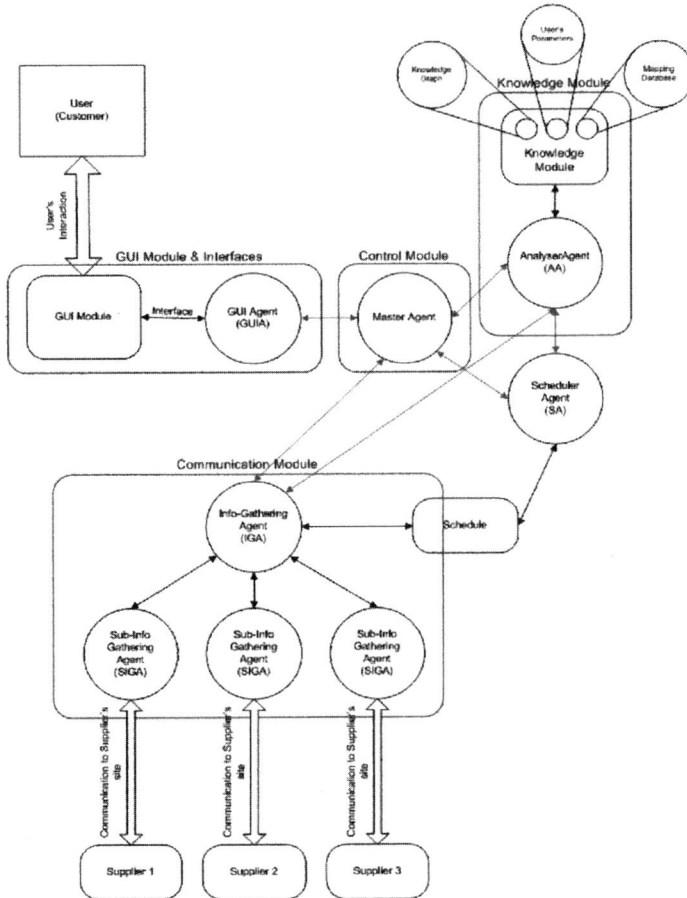

Figure 13. An overview of the customer-agent system.

Ontologies demonstrates the ability to distinguish between the ontology shared with external agents and the ontology used internally. It is equally possible to accommodate different ontologies for each supplier.

Figure 13 shows an overview of the customer agent system with the relationships between the sub-agents. It should be noted that the supplier agent system components are similar, though it would have its own knowledge base.

In order to promote interoperability with other agent systems, our system adheres to the FIPA Specification on the Agent Management Reference Model and ACL Message specification [28]. JADE API [29] was used to implement the Agent Management Reference Model as it provides a platform that is FIPA complaint. Furthermore, JADE provides support for AMS (Agent Management System), DF (Directory Facilitator), and MTS (Message Transport System).

7. IMPLEMENTATION & RESULT

It is well known that first generation multi-agent systems fall short of providing a rapid prototyping development environment for the systematic construction and deployment of agent applications [30]. Therefore the efforts of exploring standardization approaches for developing multi-agent systems have emerged which includes KQML-compliant Jackal, JATLite and FIPA-compliant JADE [31]. JADE (Java agent development platform) was chosen to implement our prototype as it provides a friendly agent development environment with a communication layer, a task scheduling layer and can be easily integrated with a user-defined reasoning layer. In addition, JADE as a multi-agent middleware offers a set of agent management, communication and interaction services. It has open source API, which are fully implemented in JAVA.

Based on the case scenarios and multi-agent architecture presented in earlier sections, a prototype multi-agent system for B2B e-Commerce has been successfully implemented using JADE. The system includes various types of B2B e-Commerce agents (such as IGA, SIGA, SA and MA) shown in Figure 13, common and internal agent ontology, and a knowledge base based on AIM. A reasoning layer has also been implemented based on the agent inference model (AIM).

As described in the case scenario in Section 4, the agents collaborate with each other to perform purchase recommendation. The twelve airlines used for the testing are the top 12 admired companies in the Airlines industry according to Fortune [26]. The reputation value of the airlines are collected from the website. The values of the other factors are taken from Skytrax, the World Airline Site [27]. The following graph (Figure 14) is used to test the data. The graph has been set with the importance (represented by the arcs from factor to the decision node) and other connections. The base graph is the default graph that is shown in Figure 5.

Data are collected from online web sites against the suppliers, which consist of twelve admired airline companies (SIA, CA, JAL, Delta etc.) in the Airlines industry. Figure 15 plots the various recommendation values of from different suppliers.

In this case study, *Airline A-L* is used to represent the twelve airline suppliers. Different suppliers contribute to different factor values for those mapping factors whose values are derived from the identity of the supplier. The factors are Catering, Service, Punctuality, and Reputation. The values of the other factors such as Catering, Service, Punctuality were taken from Skytrax, the World Airline Site [27]. Figure 15 shows that the recommendation values shows a similar pattern but at different recommendation values. The reason for the similar values is that the data and the graph used for analysis were the same. The combined values from the four above-mentioned factors (Catering, Service, Punctuality, and Reputation) produces the shift of the recommendation values. The amount of shift is determined by the value of the factors and the importance of the factor. By differing the importance of one of the four above-mentioned factors or the mapping values, the amount of shift may differ.

The amount of shift is known as the difference of the combined value of mapping factors derived from the identity of the supplier. Figure 15 shows supplier *Airline A* has the highest recommendation value because it possess the highest values for Service

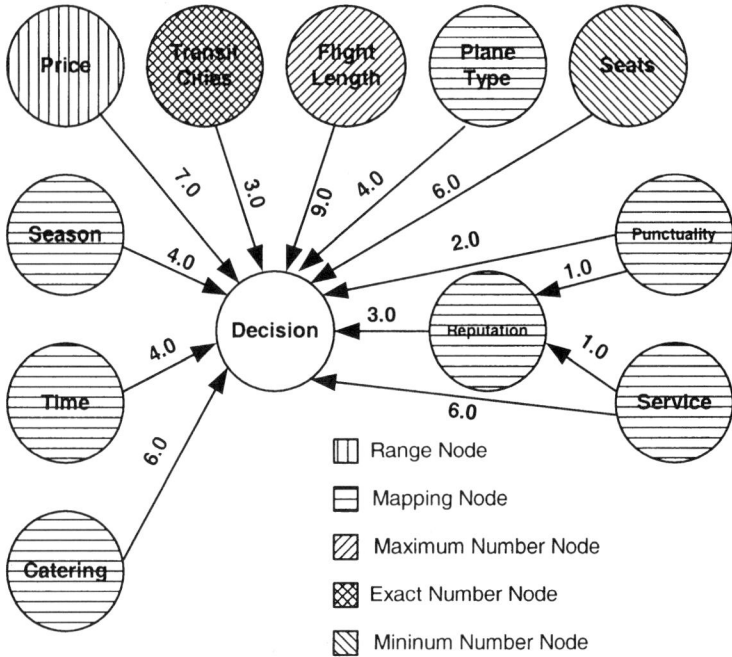

Figure 14. The test graph.

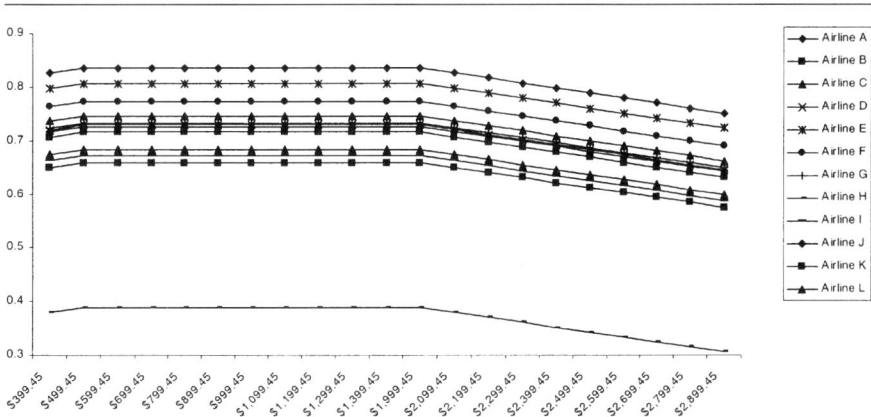

Figure 15. Recommendation between different suppliers.

and Catering factor, which are rated as very important in the graph. Both arcs from Service to the Decision factor, and Catering to Decision are 6.0, out of the maximum weight of 10.

Various testing has been carried out using data collected from different airline websites and the other sites [26, 27]. Variation of the factors and their importance was made to test out the effects on the final recommendation. The recommendation values corresponded with expected results.

8. CONCLUSION

Although the application demonstrated in the project is only an experimental example of the use based on the scenario, the model was able to assist the decision making process. Through the assistance and customisation provided by the agent system, the decision-making process is more efficiently carried out, as consumers are relieved of the tedium of information gathering and analysis. The primary goal of this project, to specify, design, and implement a multi-agent system for B2B eCommerce application, has been met.

The key to this ability is an underlying knowledge base based on AIM graph, which enables the agents to represent both domain and user's knowledge. Compared with rule based and case based knowledge base etc, the graph based knowledge base proposed in this project presents a number of desired customer-centric features such as knowledge visualization, knowledge dynamic, ease to use etc. The entire system is implemented using the proposed multi-agent system architecture for B2B e-Commerce that permits multiple types of e-Commerce agents to share common knowledge thus directly supporting collaboration and knowledge reuse.

REFERENCES

[1] Skinner, S., Business to Business e-Commerce: An Investment Perspective, 2000, http://www.durlacher.com.
[2] Häubl, G. and Murray, K., Recommending or Persuading? The Impact of a Shopping Agent's Algorithm on User Behavior, *Third ACM Conference on Electronic Commerce*, Tampa, Florida, USA, 14–17, October 2001.
[3] Schafer, J. B., Konstan, J. A., and Riedl, J., Recommender Systems in E-Commerce, *ACM Conference on Electronic Commerce (EC-99)*, pp. 158–166, 1999.
[4] Schafer, J. B., Konstan, J. A., and Riedl, J., E-commerce recommendation applications, *Data Mining and Knowledge Discovery*, Vol. 5, pp. 115–152, 2001.
[5] Wooldridge, M., Reasoning about Rational Agents, *The MIT Press*, July 2000.
[6] Wooldridge, M. and Jennings, N. R. Intelligent Agents: Theory and Practice, *The Knowledge Engineering Review*, Vol. 10(2), pp. 115–52, 1995.
[7] Russell, S. and Norvig, P. Artificial Intelligence, A Modern Approach, *Prentice-Hall*, NJ, 1995.
[8] Papazoglou, M. P., Agent Oriented Technology in Support of E-Business, *Communications of the ACM*, Vol. 44, No. 4, 2001.
[9] Maes, P. R. and Moukas, A., The Role of Agents as Mediators in Electronic Commerce *Special Issue of Knowledge Engineering Review on Practical Applications of Agents*, B. Crabtree, Ed., 1998.
[10] Stone, P. and Veloso, M., Multi-agent Systems: A Survey from a Machine Learning Perspective, Autonomous Robots, Vol. 8, No. 3, pp. 345–383, 2000.
[11] Jennings, N. R., Sycana, K., and Wooldridge, M., A Roadmap of Agent Research and Development, *Autonomous Agents and Multi-Agent Systems*, Vol. 1, Issue 1, pp. 7–38, 1998.

[12] Curet, O., Jackson, M., and Tarar, A., Designing and Evaluating a Case-Based Learning and Reasoning Agent in Unstructured Decision Making, *1996 IEEE International Conference on Systems, Man and Cybernetics*, Vol. 4, pp. 2487–2492, 1996.

[13] Clancey, W. J., The Epistemology of a Rule Based Expert System: A Framework for Explanation, *Artificial Intelligence*, Vol. 20, pp. 215–251, 1983.

[14] Hayes-Roth, F., Rule-based systems, *Communications of the ACM*, Vol. 28, No. 9 September 1985.

[15] Cercone, N., An, A., and Chan, C., Rule Induction and Case-based Reasoning: Hybrid Architectures appear Advantageous, *IEEE Transactions on Knowledge and Data Engineering*, Vol. 11, No. 1, pp. 166–174, 1999.

[16] Lenz, M., Burkhard, H. D., Bartsch-Sporl, B., and Wess, S., Case-Based Reasoning Technology: From Foundations to Applications, *Lecture Notes in Artificial Intelligence*, Springer Verlag, 1998.

[17] Goodwin, R., Keskinocak, P., Murthy, S., Wu, F., and Akkiraju, R., Intelligent Decision Support for the e-Supply Chain, *AIEC 99*, Orlando, Florida, 1999.

[18] Grosof, B. N. and Labrou, Y., An Approach to using XML and a Rule-based Content Language with an Agent Communication Language", *Proceedings of the Agent Communication Languages Workshop 99*(ACL-99), 1999.

[19] F. Stuart, The Changing Face of E-Commerce: Extending the Boundaries of the Possible, *IEEE internet computing*, Vol. 4, No. 3, 2000.

[20] A. Lin, A Multi-Agent Business Process Management System, *Proceedings of 15th International Conference on Computers and Their Applications*, March 29–31, 2000, New Orleans, Louisiana, USA.

[21] A. Pivk and Gams M., Intelligent Agents in E-Commerce, Electrotechnical Review, Vol. 67(5), pp. 251–260, 2000.

[22] Serenko, A. and Detlor, B., Agent Toolkits for eBusiness: Towards a Typology, *The 4th World Congress on the Management of Electronic Business 2003*, Ontario, Jan. 15–17, 2003.

[23] Giorgini, P., Kolp, M., and Mylopoulos, J., Multi-Agent and Software Architecture: A Comparative Case Study, *Proceedings of the 1st International Conference on Autonomous Agent and Multi Agent Systems (AAMAS'02)*, Bologna, Italy, July 2002.

[24] Dellarocas, C. and Klein, M., A Knowledge-Based Approach for Handling Exceptions in Business Processes, *Information Technology and Management*, Vol. 1, No. 3, pp. 155–169, January 2000.

[25] Miao, C. Y., Goh, A., Miao, Y., and Yang, Z. H., Agent that Models, Reasons and Makes Decisions, *Knowledge-Based Systems*, Vol. 15, No. 3. Elsevier Science, 2002.

[26] Fortune Website. http://www.fortune.com/lists/globaladmired/indsnap_3.html.

[27] Skytrax, the World Airline Site. http://www.airlinequality.com, 2002.

[28] FIPA (Foundation for Intelligent Physical Agent). http://www.fipa.org.

[29] JADE Specification for Interoperable Multi-Agent System. http://jade.cselt.it/

[30] Scott, A. DeLoach, Mark F. Wood, and Clint H. Sparkman, Multi-agent Systems Engineering, *International Journal of Software Engineering and Knowledge Engineering*, Volume 11 no. 3, June 2001.

[31] R. Scott et. al., An Agent-based Infrastructure for Enterprise Integration, *Proceedings of First International Symposium on Agent Systems and Applications* (ASA'99), California, USA, 1999.

FROM ROLES TO AGENTS: CONSIDERATIONS ON FORMAL AGENT MODELING AND IMPLEMENTATION

IVAN ROMERO HERNANDEZ AND JEAN-LUC KONING

1. INTRODUCTION

1.1. Complex systems

Nowadays agent-oriented systems are attracting increasingly more attention from the industry of software development. Such growing interest stems from many reasons, among them there is the multi-agent systems' capacity to almost naturally represent complex systems made of "intelligent" interacting entities. As growing complexity is more of a concern as time passes, this capacity to represent complex systems is a most welcome help.

Systems grow complex for many reasons: first the demand for extended features, or greater usability/intuitiveness increase the size of the source code and therefore, the work necessary to develop it. Next, there is the increasing demand for network aware systems and utilities.

This demand for network aware applications leads to a proliferation of application level protocols in the development cycle, resulting in still another complexity level added to those traditionally found in software engineering.

As protocols are usually a very complex piece of software, needing a careful analysis and design by themselves, it could be useful to have methodological frameworks proposing more straightforward processes for protocol engineering than those proposed nowadays, both via non formal development methodologies as UML and also by formal techniques (LOTOS [Courtiat and Saidouni, 1995], Promela/SPIN [Holzmann, 1997], etc.).

These development processes could be either notational improvements over preexisting notations, methodological or even reflected in the very syntax and semantics of programming languages.

1.2. Application protocols

As the network capacities of final user applications grow steadily but surely, there is also a growing need to use development tools fit for such tasks, i.e., we need tools capable to model, validate and develop communication protocols.

Communication protocols are not a new concept at all, for they exist from almost the very beginning of computer technology. But unfortunately they also are largely absent from most current development approaches.

In a strict sense, protocols are algorithms that define a communication process between entities, and as most algorithms, they could be specified, analyzed and developed using a set of specific purpose methodologies and notations, most of them grounded strongly on finite state automata theory.

Unfortunately, the methodological approaches for protocol engineering are out of the usual domain of software developers who are more concerned with the problem of system understanding/subdividing and implementation than with network related details. Most protocols are *really* complex and with *very recurrent* functionality (to take data packet X from A to B, by instance).

So, the usual approach is (1) to leave protocol development to protocol's specialists and once these protocols have been adequately specified and implemented, (2) to use them in a traditional approach of high level encapsulation of system services. Thus, most of the time, protocols become operating systems' low level services and are used correspondingly, through a high-level interface which hides the internal functionality and confusing details inherent to most protocol's complex functionality.

However, this approach reveals itself increasingly less satisfactory, as the number of application level protocols increases. The concept of application level protocols comes in a straightforward way from the once practical, now theoretical, OSI multi-layered model for networked systems [Tillman and Yen, 1990].

It is out of the scope of this paper to discuss the OSI multi-layered approach for protocol development. It is enough to say that we call application level protocols those who make always use of other protocols to fulfill their task and that exist in a conventionally named *high level* (e.g., they are user applications, they are not OS services).

These application level protocols become increasingly common as developers face the migration from monolithic-centered systems to distributed network-aware ones.

It is a fact that current development techniques and methodologies are object oriented, and so they are strongly focused on a top-down problem subdivision, they do that through the creation of sets of modules with specific capabilities and competencies; each object is intended to be specialized and solves only a subset of the final problem, delegating the solution as a whole to a concerted cooperation among objects via message calling.

When we take this approach to a networked scenario, software developers continue indeed to see the whole system as made of objects or modules. It is easy to see why. Problem subdivision comes more naturally in a distributed system than in a monolithic one, because *there always are* clear-cut independent modules in a distributed system. This subdivision is inherent to the problem and gives a stronger hint to problem modularization than a somewhat artificial subdivision of competencies within a single monolithic system.

1.3. Distributed objects

Object-oriented systems are intended to be centered applications. This restriction comes from the fact that objects are basically abstract data types. Every class is created in order to establish an abstract link between data and the functions that modify it.

This modularization is helpful in more than one way, because we could relate better to events where personified entities (even abstract ones) interact one with each other than with mere sequences of instructions and control statements.

So, most object-oriented languages and methodologies assume that every object is directly accessible via a simple function calling (method invocation is an instance of local function calling).

Continuous advancement have led to a increased awareness of the similarities between the object method invocation and communication protocols. From the beginning of the object-oriented approach it was clear that the pre-existing remote procedure call (RPC) infrastructures [Birrell and Nelson, 1983] could be perfectly well used to represent a method invocation. There are many examples of distributed object platforms with their own RPC schemes, some of them widely used so far [Sankar, 1996; Microsystems, 2001], where objects executed in different systems can execute methods on remote objects.

However, a remote procedure call infrastructure imposes severe restrictions to the system to be developed with it. Any remote procedure call scheme is a virtualization of a whole communication protocol enabling the invocation, parameter and result exchange between the interacting network hosts.

This yields the problem of platform incompatibility, every RPC scheme defines its own protocol and functionality, and at the same time, isolates almost completely the objects from the actual communication mechanism they use to interact. It is true that the motivation of any RPC mechanism is actually to isolate the object from all those excruciatingly repetitive communication details, but the shielding is so efficient that any interaction among distributed objects via RPC mechanisms could hardly be named *a protocol*.

Obviously, any RPC scheme could be fooled using the appropriate message passing scheme only by emulating the right fine-grained protocol definition, but tat the price of a considerable grow in complexity.

2. AGENT-ORIENTED PROGRAMMING

The object-oriented approach has shown to be satisfactory enough for most modern software development. However, there are some kinds of applications that even when using an object migration approach from centered to distributed infrastructures, have many properties that are either impossible to address using an object-oriented approach, or very complex to do.

Industry shows a steadily but surely increase of interest on agent-oriented systems which are commonly believed to be the next programming framework for computer science, right after the current object-oriented approach. Whether they really are the *heirs* of objects is (still) debatable, it is certain that they have many interesting properties as a conceptual framework for programming, even in the case that they are mere object-oriented and/or extensions of parallel programming. This interest goes further, for it has motivated the proposition of special-purpose languages specifically devised to cover the aspects usually related to a multi-agent system [Shoham, 1990; Shoham, 1991].

It is important to note that when we talk about an "*agent*" we are using the definition given by Odell et al. [Odell et al., 2000a]. This definition says that an agent is a independent communicating entity (equivalent to a system process) with the capacity to answer "*no*" to a petition based on its own internal functionality or rules (non observable behavior), and also able to say "*go*" using internal mechanisms in a way that would look "spontaneous" for an external observer of the entity.

This definition is wide enough to cover most multi-agent systems, but restrictive enough to get rid of many object-oriented and structured systems. What there is, indeed, is a wide intersection with those we call "distributed systems", but that is not an issue because it happens that any networked modules taking initiatives—even if it was not designed with agency in mind—could be thought of as an *avant garde* agent.

2.1. Sub-protocols

In [Koning et al., 2001a] we have a proposal for the concept of subprotocol, sub-protocols are partial, reusable sequences of communication acts defining the temporal ordering of the later within a specific communication process between *roles*. Roles represent the behavior that a given entity holds within the protocol. While roles convey an agent's behavior and are related to this agent's definition, they are not limited to that specific entity. For example, roles are not equivalent to the object-oriented concept of a *class*. An entity A of type B could have a role C, while an entity D of type E could also have the same role C and still be two different agents.

We consider roles to be stereotyped behaviors that could be taken by an entity to accomplish a meaningful task, or the sequence of communication acts an entity sends and receives through a specific interaction. The most important aspect is to know which module sends what to whom, and exactly when it does it.

2.2. Agent-UML

Agent-UML (AUML) [Odell et al., 2000b] is an agent extension for UML designed to represent the specific requirements of an agent-oriented analysis and design process that UML as it is cannot adequately represent. It is not really surprising to find that AUML strongly focuses on interaction protocols.

The AUML proposal divides interaction protocol specifications on three closely related phases or *layers* (in fact, they call their proposition *a layered approach to protocols*) [Bauer et al., 2001]:

Overall protocol representation Everything related to the creation of a general view of the protocol. The package notation is used and extended to represent the existence of interactions among related agents (roles) instead of simple class conglomerates semantically linked, as in UML. The UML template notation is quite useful here, as interactions are very often patterns of behavior repeated more than once in the final system behavior (e.g., session opening and closing), thus enabling an explicit representation of reusable protocol blocks.

Interaction among agents representation UML sequence diagrams are extended to be more expressive, thus allowing a richer notation for object lifeline branching and communication. In order to do this, a counterpart of execution operators found on some process algebra based languages are created, but they are separated into two kinds: those that affect the agent's lifelines and those that affect the communication acts. To a lesser extent, collaboration diagrams, activity diagrams and statecharts are also extended.

Agent's internal processing representation UML activity diagram and statecharts are used to enable a further understanding of the agents' internal behavior. However, such notation is not extended.

2.3. From objects- to agent-oriented programming

In spite of appearances, there is always some trade-off between new technologies and experience, methodological frameworks for software development being in any case not an exception. As no new approach for problem solving is completely new or completely free from the many concepts shown to work in practice, computer languages following a certain approach to problem solving tend to include as much capabilities as possible from previous ones. Obviously, there is too the pragmatic idea that it is easier to learn something one already is familiarized to.

C++ is an example of a successful language that knew how to balance the needs of structured C programmers with a new programming framework, it did so by making the C language a subset of itself (including its structured orientation), and by adding some specific object-oriented structures it enabled the creation of classes and objects "on C". Its philosophy could be expressed as *freedom of choice*, meaning that a programmer should be able to use classes and objects, but not obliged to; joined to that, the huge amount of pre-existing C source code, made C++ the language of choice for those willing to do a painless migration from a structured to an object-oriented programming framework.

Sun took the example, designing its Java language intentionally similar to C++ to profit of its large developers base. New agent-oriented languages should benefit

Agent oriented language

Object oriented language

Structured language

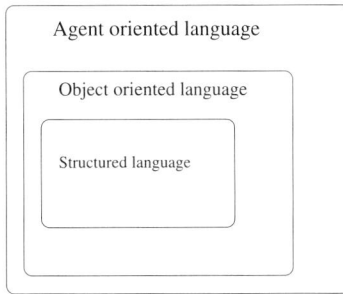

Figure 1.1. General structure of an agent-oriented language.

from examples like that, not in the sense of copying languages, but to encourage the creation of languages that do not get rid of many features already present in previous tools.

In [Huget, 2002], some interesting wishes and petitions for agent-oriented language developers are formulated. These wishes express reasonable concerns about the lack of support for many programming artifacts on agent-oriented platforms and languages. Agent-oriented systems are yet too specific and too agent-conceptualization centered to attract non-agent specialists. Agent languages should become more friendly and more inclusive.

For doing this, we believe as others do [Singh, 1996], that agent-oriented programming languages should focus on their similarities with object-oriented systems rather than upon their differences. It could be interesting to design new agent-oriented languages having a syntax and semantics allowing them to express agent-oriented, object-oriented *and* structured programs (see fig. 1.1).

This recently gained freedom to accept everything that existed before agents as a part of them, makes possible to do and think things like this: an agent that only waits for input from anyone and only reacts after that input, behaves exactly as an object and should likely be one, unless there is a very good reason for that. Agents and objects are not so far apart from each other to justify a total rupture.

If we accept the notion that the progressive focus towards system encapsulation and weak interfaces, found in software engineering, represents a migration from method calling between objects to controlled interaction executions among agents, then roles could be viewed as macro-definitions of temporally ordered interactions. In fact, we believe that roles could be translated to programming artifacts analogous but different at the same time to the concept of class, or better, to the concept of *interface* found in the Java programming language.

Java interfaces are class-like entities that define attributes and methods working upon them, but that are unable to generate any executable instance or object without any explicit attachment to a class. A role is analogous to an interface in this sense: they are always attached to agents, but add the notion of state controlled execution of interactions.

With the aforementioned hypothesis, we can suggest the following steps towards an interaction-oriented language for multi-agent systems:

1. To unify object methods and protocol individual messages in a single concept: the communication act.
2. To add support for state controlled execution of communication acts: this enables the specification of temporary ordered sequences of communication acts or protocols, and gives the possibility to handle errors through careful state control.
3. To add support for template protocols and role specification using an interface-like syntax: this could be done by creating the concept of role as an agent unable to generate instances.
4. To enable the entities to explicitly use defined roles.

2.4. Method and message passing unification

The distributed systems view on communication is often very simplistic: an atomic communication consists mainly on transmitting a symbol from a sender to a willing receiver. This simplification comes naturally because in most theoretical approaches there is no need to include more implementation details than necessary in order to solve problems. Communication protocols are at the most basic level, algorithms or well defined behavioral patterns representing a sequence of message exchanges between willing parties, in order to achieve a goal.

While in practice this is quite the contrary; they are heavily dependent upon the target implementation's details. However, and fortunately for us, the wild complexity of network standard protocols and their corresponding implementations, show some generic properties allowing us to create an abstract understanding of similar problems on similar situations despite the specific differences.

Communication, even in theory, could be viewed in many different ways, depending on what we are interested in, or the meaning of the problem itself. For example, a communication act could be viewed as synchronous or asynchronous, depending on system's behavior during message transmission, or one could be interested in more abstract aspects like how the developer perceives the communication infrastructure provided by the system he/she is to program.

If we were interested in those last abstract levels, we could easily see that programming languages provide two main approaches to communication between distributed entities: remote procedure call (RPC) and message passing.

While RPC schemes allow parametrized function calling by name through a network, message passing schemes are more raw data packet oriented, allowing much more flexibility at the cost of complexity. In the RPC schemes one knows exactly what one wants from the another party (a function is called by its explicit name) and how to do it (a mutually common RPC protocol is used) while in the message passing schemes the agreement between parties is supposed to be of a lower level (one agrees on the exchange of data, and hopefully, a certain protocol to do so).

It is worth to note that in both cases there is always a *de facto* agreement: in order to exchange even packets of data one needs to agree first about how to exchange this information. In fact RPC schemes are by themselves an agreement about how to exchange data and are always constructed using lower level message passing oriented schemes.

However, there are some important implications, at least on the way we perceive their utility: while RPC schemes are a matter of software engineering interest, message passing schemes are usually considered as too complex to be designed with the usual structured or object-oriented methodologies.

Why is that?

There are many reasons. Let us focus on some relevant ones:

- RPC schemes usually assume stateless interactions. Message passing schemes are most of the time strongly oriented towards state controlled execution.
- RPC schemes are more "intuitive" or "conversational" because a function is called by its abstract name and variables or objects in a very well defined fashion, while message passing schemes leave a lot of implementation details on developer's shoulders because the exchanged data format is totally free.

2.5. Internal state control of an agent

Most object-oriented methodologies focus on the objects' internal state. While the notion of an object's "state" is slightly different from its match found on distributed systems, it is an interesting approximation of both worlds.

An object state space consists of all the possible values its internal variables could take in response to every possible method-call the object could receive through its life-cycle. This state could eventually define the way any given object will react facing a certain stimulus. It is easy to see that given the huge quantity of values some variables could take, an object state space could be quite difficult to define clearly.

In distributed systems, the notion of "state" is usually more related to an actual finite state machine's state [Estelle, 1997], the internal one controlling the protocol's execution. However, a protocol execution is usually controlled by more than a mere automaton. It is not unusual to have many internal variables in the object-oriented/structured programming sense of whatever type is fit to the problem's semantics, that affect or even control some portion of the protocol execution. This is the reason for most agent-oriented languages and techniques supporting the notion of internal variables [Adorni and Poggi, 1993b; Adorni and Poggi, 1993a; Sijelmassi and Strausser, 1993; Sijelmassi and Strausser, 1990].

The resulting automata controlled by input, state and internal variables are not finite extended machines in the strict sense of the word, but are quite useful to represent the behavior of any given entity taking a role inside a protocol, and have been widely used in many formal and semi-formal methodologies for protocol engineering.

However, finite state machines and their extended versions are seldom used as nothing more than a comfortable specification artifact to be used inside a more extended development process. It is easy to see that current object-oriented programming languages do not have any kind of explicit support for the notion of state controlled execution, and that these notions must be implemented "by hand" using one of the usual techniques for finite state machine (FSM) representation on actual programming language's source code.

In this sense, we believe it could be interesting to have explicit support for state-oriented execution of objects not only within the context of formal specification techniques but also within the syntax and semantics of a pragmatic programming language.

3. ROLES AND SCENARIOS

3.1. Definitions

As it is implied by our introductory material, we are looking for a programming approach linking object-oriented programming with the agent-oriented approach, specially focusing on interaction.

In order to enable this migration of approaches, we need to define a set of artifacts that could be useful for our particular purposes. First, let us define the concept of role. As far as we are concerned, a role R is a stereotypical behavior expressing the temporal ordering of the message exchange between an agent and others, in an analogous way to the concept of role in a theater piece where every actor has a well defined and ordered dialog. In fact, we consider the role to be an attribute *assigned* to a single agent.

There is another interesting analogy. If each agent has a *role* to perform, we could say that a set of interacting roles make a *Scenario*. This analogy could prove useful as a specifying and even, as a programming device, as we will see later.

Let $r = \{s, Q, C, \Sigma, T, F, \}$ be a role, where $Q = \{q_1, q_2, \ldots, q_n\}$ is the role's finite state set containing the n possible states of r, $s \in Q$ is the initial state, $C = \{c_1, c_2, \ldots, c_k\}$ is the set of communication channels linking r to its $k \geq 1$ communication parties, $\Sigma = \{s_1 s_2, \ldots, s_j\}$ is the set of all symbols received or sent by r, $T : Q \times C \times \Sigma \times C \times \Sigma \rightarrow Q$ is the transition function that accepts *and* puts out a symbol at every firing and $F \subseteq Q$ is the set of final states.

Each role r is for us an automata expressing the observable behavior of the system, this *role* is any semantically linked sequence of observable messages taken by an agent facing a specific stimulus.

Let us exemplify our definitions on the FIPA definition of the Contract Net protocol as it is represented by means of the Agent-UML notation proposed by Odell et al. [Odell et al., 2000b]. Figure 1.2 shows the aforementioned Contract Net protocol. This scenario holds two roles: the *Initiator* and the *Participant*. The interactions set is

$$I = \{cfp, not\_understood, refuse, propose, reject\_proposal,$$
$$accept\_proposal, failure, inform\_done, inform\_ref\}$$

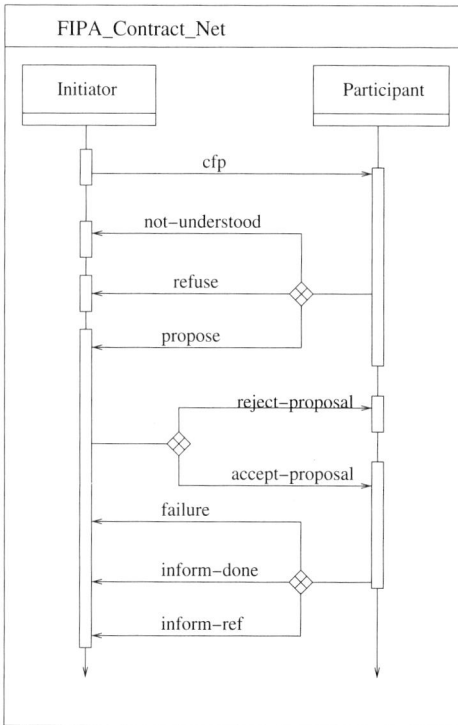

Figure 1.2. AUML representation of the fipa contract net protocol.

The communication channel set C is not showed explicitly, but could be assumed from the moment an interaction takes place between two roles, so we could say that there is a communication channel c_1 linking the *Initiator* and the *Participant*, so $C = \{c_1\}$.

If we continue with the same Contract Net protocol, we could express the behavior of both *Initiator* and *Participants* roles as two distinct EFSM. Figure 1.3 shows a possible modeling for the *Initiator*'s role. As this automata is an extended one, there machine accepts an input and an output symbol at every transition. The notation we use here to represent both kinds of symbols is `<input symbol>/<output symbol>`, if there is no output or input symbol in any given transition, we use a score before (input) or after (output) the dividing slash.

Figure 1.4 is the corresponding automata model for the *Participant* role. As in figure 1.3 the input/output symbols are written separated by a slash and located side by side with their corresponding transitions. The translation from a graphic representation to a formal one, using our definition of *Role* as an extended FSM, is trivial and left out for space reasons.

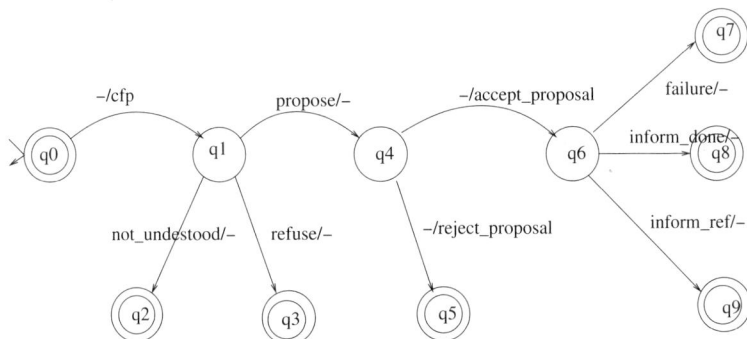

Figure 1.3. The initiator's role automata.

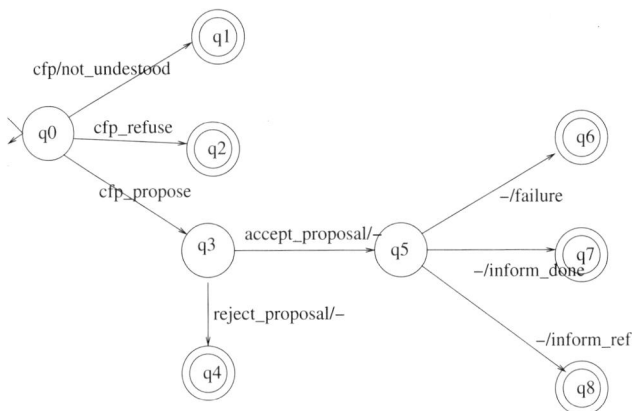

Figure 1.4. The participant's role automata.

3.2. Artifacts for development

The reason for defining roles as extended finite state machines, and scenarios as tuples containing roles, interactions and communication channels, is to propose a way to include them within the context of a generic agent-oriented programming language, centered on the interaction aspect of agency.

In [Koning et al., 2001b] the concept of sub-protocol is proposed, sub-protocols are partial, reusable sequences of communication acts defining the temporal ordering of messages, within a specific communication process between *roles*. Roles, as said before, represent the behavior that any specific agent has through an interaction process.

While all the agents take on certain *roles* inside any given interaction process, the roles are not restricted to any entity, e.g., a function taking from roles to agents is not

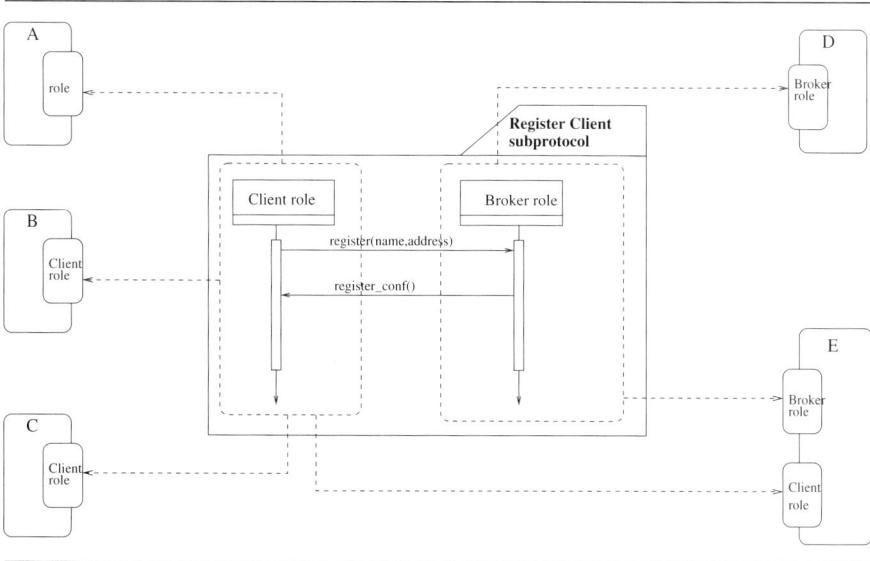

Figure 1.5. Registering a sub-protocol scheme.

bijective. Entity A of type B could take on a role C, while entity D of type E could take on a same role C and still being two different agents.

Figure 1.5 shows a simple AUML package expressing the registering sub-protocol of an agent on a resource broker, this sub-protocol has two roles: **broker** and *client*, both represented with labeled boxes. Communication acts (individual messages) are represented using labeled arrows, where the label expresses the exchanged message and its parameters. The temporal ordering notation is conventional to UML and AUML sequence diagrams. The roles of *client* and *broker* in this sub-protocol are specific, but at the same time, applicable to many different entities (named A, B, C, D and E), represented in the figure as round boxes "containing" inside them the role. The dashed boxes around the roles and the arrow notation linking these roles to the agents the implement them is not AUML at all, but shows the presence of an abstract linking between the sub-protocol generated roles and the agents who take them on.

Odell's AUML notation [Bauer et al., 2001] gives explicit support for template protocols and role specification, but not for specifying role-to-agent links and protocol reuse. It could be useful to have such a notation, in order to extend the expressiveness of AUML. After all, the mapping of roles to agents is done in some way or another, but implicitly.

Figure 1.6 shows the same client registration sub-protocol, but using now our suggested notation based on the UML *generalization* graphical artifact. Other UML artifacts could be used, but we think they do not express adequately the intrinsic behavior modification an agent undergoes when implementing a role. It is likely a good idea

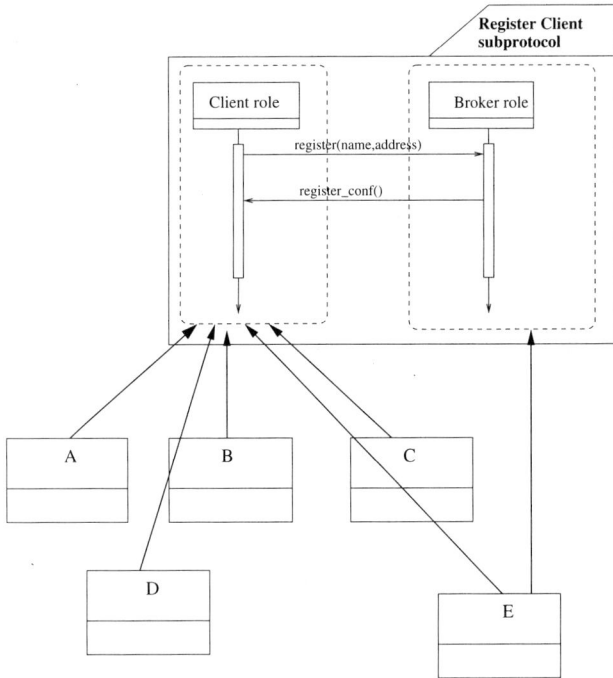

Figure 1.6. Proposal for role generalization.

to slightly change the notation in order to avoid confusion with the actual UML class generalization artifact, but context should get rid of this confusion.

Some authors note that well-designed template protocols and the roles they create could perfectly be used as a reuse mechanism [Huget, 2001]. AUML is expressive enough to represent template protocols and roles, but lacks specific notation to link these roles to the agents that use them.

However, to hide the module's internal behavior as much as possible, and to base the system's functionality representation on weakly-coupled interfaces is not enough to fully model or implement a communicating modular system, either object- or agent-oriented. Even in object-oriented systems, internal variables have a very relevant part upon the system's behavior. Due to the usual presence of complex communication protocols between agents, the need for the agents to have an execution control mechanism increases.

There is always some internal processing involved in order for an agent to know how to react when faced with a specific stimulus and when to take the initiative and begin an interaction without any explicit input.

As roles are indeed partial protocol specifications (they specify only one agent's perspective inside the communication process), we need some internal mechanism to control a role's state whenever we use that role inside an agent. For that purpose we could perfectly use the approach presented on section 1.3 to model *and* implement the final Agent, but how to do this is outside the scope of this paper. Some authors note that well-designed template protocols and the roles they create could perfectly be used as a reutilization mechanism [Koning et al., 2001b; Odell et al., 2000a; Odell et al., 2000b; Singh, 1996]. Agent-UML is expressive enough to represent template protocols and roles, but lacks specific notation to link these roles to the agents that use them.

However, to hide the modules' internal behavior as much as possible, and to base the representation of the system's functionality on weakly-coupled interfaces is not enough to fully model or implement a communicating modular system. Either object or agent-oriented, even in object-oriented systems internal variables, have a very relevant part upon system's behavior. For agents, the need for having an execution control mechanism increases due to the usual presence of complex communication protocols between agents. There is always some internal processing involved in order for an agent to know how to react when faced with a specific stimulus or to know when to take the initiative and begin an interaction without any explicit input.

As roles are indeed partial protocol specifications (they specify only one agent's perspective inside the communication process), on needs some internal mechanism in order to control the role's state whenever an agent makes use of that role. The most widely used artifacts for modeling a protocol execution are finite state machines and variations of them. Although Petri nets or process algebras is also used sometimes [Barbuceanu and Lo, 1999].

3.3. Roles and scenarios as programming artifacts

Having defined the concept of *role* as an extended finite state machine, a *scenario* as a set of roles and the *role inheritance operator* as a product between the ancestor role's automata and the descendant's ones, we can see that these three elements could create a programming artifact equivalent to the *Interface* (instance-less/virtual class) notion present in Sun Microsystem's Java language and now we could see hints about how to implement them.

3.3.1. State control

Most formal specification techniques used for protocol specification, like LOTOS [Courtiat and Saidouni, 1995] and Promela/SPIN [Holzmann, 1997], use algorithms provided by the theory of finite state machines to perform their tasks, even if there is not any explicit programming structure for that purpose.

However, there are previous examples of languages that explicitly enable a state controlled execution of autonomous entities, like for instance, the ISO standard formal description technique ESTELLE [Estelle, 1997].

In ESTELLE, a specification is a text file describing the observable behavior of black-box entities linked by communication channels, ESTELLE's syntax is Pascal-like, allowing a straightforward understanding of the function of every grammatical element.

```
body descrSwitch for Switch;
  state OFF, ON; { Records ON/OFF state }
  initialize to OFF
    begin
    end;
  trans { *** Activate/deactivate switch *** }
    when P.TurnOn
      from OFF to ON
        begin
        output P.TurnedOn
        end;
    when P.TurnOff
      from ON to OFF
        begin
        output P.TurnedOff
        end;
end; { SwitchBody }
```

This is the "body" specification (internal behavior) for a sample switch object in ESTELLE. The first statement declares the set of states of the entity (ON,OFF), the next one specifies which one is the initial state (OFF). The following part specifies the transitions and the input symbols that triggers them. There are only two transitions, from ON to OFF with a symbol P.TurnOn and from ON to OFF with an input symbol P.TurnOff. The begin-end pairs allow to insert code to be executed right after the preceding event expressed has been triggered.

ESTELLE is neither an object-oriented technique (there is no inheritance, polymorphism or method invocation) nor a pragmatic programming language (it lacks many usual programming facilities like I/O features, dynamic memory allocation and so on). However, it does have some interesting similarities to some well known and widely used object-oriented languages, with a strong emphasis on data encapsulation and interface design, while at the same time it proposes a clear syntax for state-controlled execution. It was designed to be a formal specification language capable to verify a set of properties on the modeled system through the use of specialized software tools.

Having programming artifacts that enable the representation of state-controlled execution paths, does not provide with any significant advantage over formal description techniques like ESTELLE. There are already some well known and used techniques to translate a finite state machine onto machine-compilable source code, most of them are used to implement compiler-compilers [Waite and Goos, 1984] or produce executable versions of formally specified systems, like for instance, ESTELLE to C translators [Thees, 1998].

However, if we could represent a communicating automata inside a class, nothing forbids to extend this same concept toward internal automata inheritance.

3.3.2. State space inheritance

Now, state space inheritance among agents is an interesting problem in itself, because if one accepts the notion of multiple parents for a single entity, it arises a number of internal state inconsistencies that are difficult to trace and eliminate. How does one "join" two automata in a purposeful way?

In order to answer this question, we could analyze the semantical meaning of *state inheritance*, and look for some formal equivalent in the finite state machine theory. For instance, one could take three basic automata-related operations and a fancy-defined one to use them: be it union, concatenation, cross product and the composition of finite state machines.

The union of n languages is represented by $L(D_1) \cup L(D_2) \cup \cdots \cup L(D_n)$, and generates an automata that accepts any string s recognized by any of the automata $D_1, D_2, \ldots, D_n$. The union of languages could be used to represent any case where one wishes an entity to behave in different ways depending on the first input it receives. The automata resulting from a union should recognize all the sequences of messages recognized by the original languages, but only one at a time. So, any entity inheriting the behavioral automata of a third one using the union operator, would choose to behave as its ancestor or as its eventual new definition, depending on the first symbol it receives (i.e., the first symbol of any string $s \in L(D_i)$ where $i = 1, 2, \ldots, n$).

The concatenation of n languages is represented by $L(D_1)L(D_2) \cdots L(D_n)$, and generates an automata that accepts any string $s_1 s_2 \cdots s_n$ where $s_i \in L(D_i)$ any $i = 1 \ldots n$. This operator could be useful for creating sequenced scenarios, sub-protocols or something one could call *sequenced roles*. The behavioral automata of a role R_1 could be concatenated to that of a role R_2 to produce the combined behavior $L(R_1)L(R_2)$ that accepts the inputs and generates the outputs of both roles in a sequenced manner.

The cross product has the property of representing the parallel behavior of two or more FSM $D_1, D_2, \ldots, D_n$, thus allowing us to create an automata which recognizes the languages $L(D_1) \cup L(D_2) \cup \ldots \cup L(D_n)$ in a *pseudo-parallel fashion*, interleaving the symbols that form any string $s \in L(D_i)$ where $i = 1, 2, \ldots, n$. But the cross product could be inconvenient in many cases, first because two or more of the ancestors could react to one single stimulus, thus being unable to decide which behavior should the joint automata take. Second, even in the case that there is no non-determinism on the input, the semantics associated to a multi-parented agent could dictate that reacting to a stimulus is incorrect in certain states, likely rendering the behavior of the agent formally correct but semantically senseless. And last but not least, one faces the unavoidable exponential growth of the state space.

The composition, this operation takes two languages $L(D_s), L(D_i)$ and a non-empty string $s \in L(D_i)$, and generates a new language $L(D_r) = (L(D_i) - \{s\}) \cup \{\{s\}L(D_i)\}$ that accepts all the strings of $L(D_i)$ minus s, plus all the strings resulting in the concatenation of s with all the strings of $L(D_s)$. This fancy-defined operator would allow the representation of some kind of *behavior composition*. That is, an automata that behaves as another under certain circumstances (which in this definition is represented by the presence of the former string—now prefix—s).

Our definition of a scenario as a set of roles, and of a role as an extended finite state machine is completely arbitrary. Its principal advantage is that it enables to propose a formal language, to express which kind of programming artifacts could be implemented, once the concept of scenario and role are viewed as programming artifacts, and overall, how they could be actually implemented.

3.3.3. Genericity and composability

AUML on its actual definition [Odell et al., 2000b; Odell et al., 2000a] provides specific notation to model *template interaction protocols*, which are meta-definitions of interaction sequences between parametrized roles, in this context, parameters within a template protocol are undefined values that need to be provided in order for the protocol to function. The motivation for this facility is to create fully reusable protocols that express a stereotypical interaction process using unknown typed entities.

To exemplify this idea of template interaction protocol, we could refer again to the aforementioned ContractNet.

Figure 1.7 shows the same protocol FIPA Contract Net shown before in figure 1.2, only with a slight modification. In the upper right corner of the class box there is a dashed box containing the label *cfp*. The presence of that box implies that the Contract Net protocol is a template that needs one parameter to fully define its behavior, in this case the parameter is the context dependent *cfp* message, that is, the offer specific to every Contract Net interaction process.

The idea of genericity is quite attractive for those looking for reutilization mechanisms. We have decided to adopt it in our proposal. We have also decided to add another level of parametrization: role-level parameters.

The meaning of this is not difficult to understand at all, once one can relate it to the notion of component. Components have many definitions. Most of these definitions agree to consider these components as exchangeable modules that offer a uniform interface to the external world. The minimum set of properties that any entity within a Components context must satisfy, is the component's composability.

If one wants to put forward roles and interaction protocols as artifacts for reuse, one needs to put forward composability restrictions that ensure that every part of the system could interact with each other without presenting synchronization or sequence related problems during the exchange of messages. After all, our definition of role could be reduced to a tree of sequenced messages.

As far as we are concerned, the first and most important problems that establishes the composability of any role, is the *matching* of message exchanges between any given role and its peers and the need for roles that always terminate.

3.4. On state inheritance

Having programming artifacts that enable us to represent state-controlled execution paths does not provide any significant advantage. There are already some well known and used techniques for translating a finite state machine into some machine-compilable source code [Sijelmassi and Strausser, 1993]. Most of them implement

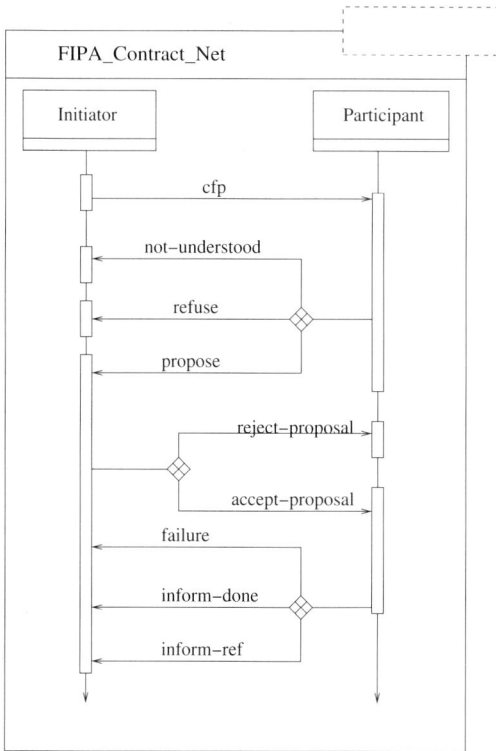

Figure 1.7. Template FIPA contract net in AUML.

compiler-compilers [Waite and Goos, 1984] or produce executable versions of formally specified systems, as for instance ESTELLE to C translators [Thees, 1998].

As said in section 1.2.1, sub-protocols are partial, stereotypical and reusable sequences of communication acts defining the temporal ordering of the later, within a specific communication process between *roles*. It is evident that this separation of protocols and sub-protocols is completely arbitrary: sub-protocols are protocols too but with much *lesser ambitions*.

The most usual image about a sub-protocol is that of a procedure or a function. Functions usually have a semantic unity justifying their very existence, but at the same time they are like building blocks that can be arranged in different ways. Sub-protocols could also be arranged like pieces in a puzzle in order to build a bigger and far reaching protocol with them, or at least, this is the ideal.

However, there are a number of problems associated with this approach: protocols are temporary ordered sequences of messages that may—or may not—have a final state. What we mean here is that not every protocol has a well defined set of internal states such there is no next state. We all know perfectly well that *in practice*, every program has an end, but in *theory* we could imagine perfectly well iterative processes going on forever.

If we want a rigorous validation of any protocol specification, such subtle differences become important. So, we need to improve our definition of sub-protocol, and its related formal meaning.

Refined sub-protocol definition: Let $r = \{s, Q, C, \Sigma, T, F, \}$ be a role as defined in section 1.3, it is possible to say that r is a subprotocol if and only if for any state s and t where $s \in Q$ and $t \in F$, it is true that $s \xrightarrow{*} t$. If there is a sequence of messages taking from any state s to a final state f, we could say that this protocol has certainly *an end*, thus it satifies the notion of *composability*.

4. THE DHELI TOOL

4.1. The interaction-oriented programming framework

Our current research exists within the framework of a multi-layered project, this project has some parts or layers that are of a theoretical nature (e.g., methodology and programming approaches), and others that are more pragmatical (software tools). We could say that this project has three main operational levels:

1. The Interaction-Oriented Programming Framework (IOPF): This part of the project is a proposal of a programming approach for multi-agent systems based on *interaction*. There are many interesting works proposing agent-oriented languages based on specific aspects of agency, many of them are based on knowledge modeling and logical inference, the well known Agent1 by Shoham [Shoham, 1993] is an example of an agent-oriented language focusing knowledge modeling. There is a second kind of agent development platforms, which provide facilities of infrastructre for communication among heterogeneous systems in the form of language libraries. However, there are few platforms taking seriously in count the problem of communication of multi-agent systems from an *internal* programming perspective (i.e., proposing ad hoc languages for this problem). Our proposal involves the creation of a set of criteria defining the properties to be represented inside an *agent-oriented programming language*.

2. A lightweight methodology following the aforementioned programming framework. This methodological proposition will be adjusted to cope the new requirements of an interaction-oriented language, and at the same time it will look for easy integration with the Agent-UML proposal, in order to test AUML in the context of a CASE development testbed.

3. An Agent-UML/UML-like assisted CASE tool suite implementing the methodology.

Every one of those operational layers will be mentioned more than once, so for clarity's sake they will be called the *programming layer*, the *methodological layer* and the *testbed*

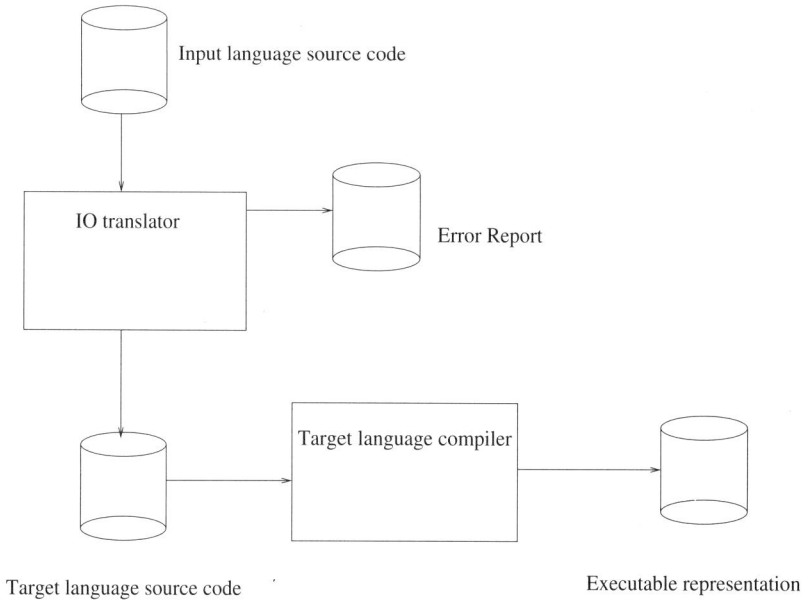

Figure 1.8. Overall system structure.

layer. Note that these "layers" are not directly related to the actual implementation of any of the referenced projects or tools whatsoever, they define only three different work levels involved in our research proposal.

The DHELI system is a part of the aforementioned Interaction-Oriented Programming Framework (IOPF). The DHELI system is a semi-independent project. It has an independent functionality of its own (it could be executed separatedly from the other parts), but its inputs, functionality and outputs are also closely related to the inputs, functionality and outputs of other systems inside the aforementioned case tool.

Figure 1.8 shows the general structure of the DHELI system. It shows the expected inputs and the generated outputs. The DHELI translator system is intended to be an *independent process/program/class* executed on whatever subjacent platform we use.

4.2. System runtime interfaces

The system's functionality does not require special purpose system interfaces. All the interaction with the system is done through the function calls available on the system's development and/or runtime platform.

Figure 1.9 shows the runtime interfaces of the DHELI system. The DHELI system is a standalone Java application and correspondingly, it needs a Java 2 Virtual Machine (Java Runtime Environment or JRE 2) installed on the system in order to be executed.

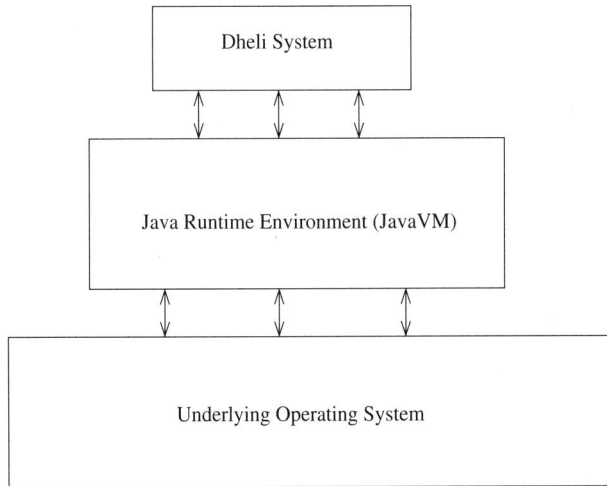

Figure 1.9. Runtime system interfaces.

The Java runtime set of system calls and libraries is rich enough for our purposes, and provides the portability associated to the Java platform, thing that is not of minor importance in a research project designed to be, eventually, reviewed by a third party.

In Figure 1.8, the cylinder labeled *Input Language Source Code* represents a text containing statements expressed in our specific purpose language. The arrow linking the *Input Language Source Code* file to the DHELI translator system box implies that the system waits for a text file expressed on *Input Language* syntax at its input. For space and clarity reasons, the Input Language (DHELI) is defined in another whole section.

Following the aforementioned conventionalism about input/output files and processes, it is easy to see that the translator has two probable outputs: a file expressed on a target language's syntax and semantics (an accurate translation of the input) and a error report file if error there is.

The *Target Language Source Code* file is a translation of the input expressed on a target language. The target language in this state of the project is XML. The target language in this state of the project is a XML representation of a finite state machine and a Promela/SPIN source code representing the same finite state machine.

The function of this XML code is to be interpreted by a specific-purpose DOM parser which reads it and performs an *animation* of the specification itself. This feature was added in order to provide a fast prototyping tool for protocol development. The DOM parser and interpreter was made in Java. The choice of Java 2 for the interpreter implementation comes for pragmatic reasons: Java 2 proposes a mature development environment, corresponding adequately to our development needs but without the strong license restrictions associated with other tools for languages like C or C++. Java compilers are available for free thanks to Sun Microsystems community license.

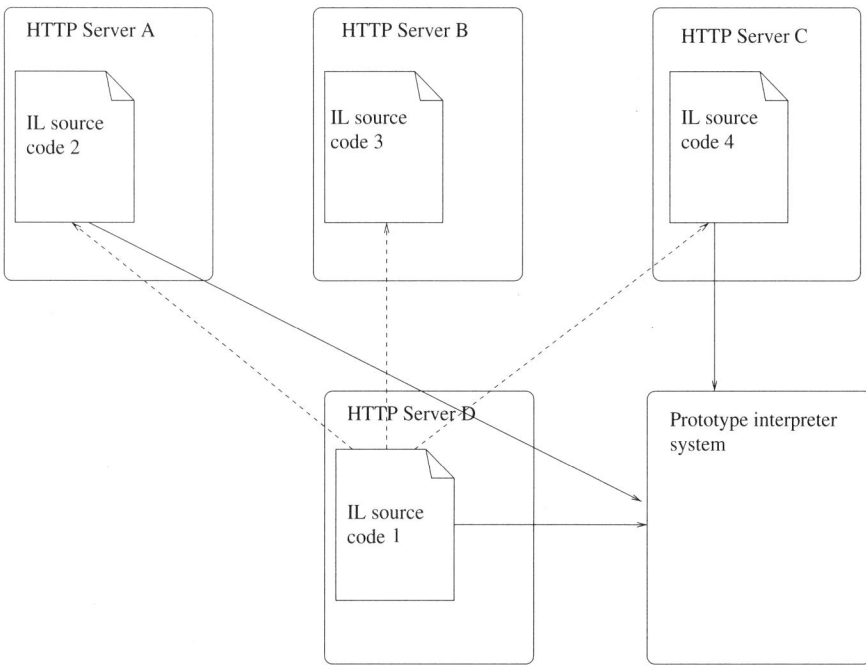

Figure 1.10. Interpreter system communication interfaces.

4.3. Communication interfaces

The prototype interpreter sub-system retrieves remote objects by URL using the W3C HTTP protocol and the IETF standard FTP protocol. So, this chosen development platform for system deployment provides *many* facilities for that purpose. This is one of the main motivations to choose Java as development platform for the system: Java provides a rich set of classes to easily manage the retrieval of URIs using the W3C HTTP and IETF FTP protocols.

Figure 1.10 shows the communication insfrastructure of the generated *prototype interpreter system*. The labeled rounded boxes represent processes or independent programs (HTTP servers and the DHELI interpreter sub-system itself), while the rectangular sheets represent Input Language source code files to access/read/write.

In this figure we could see some dashed lines going from DHELI *Source Code 1* to DHELI *Source Code 2*, DHELI *Source Code 3* and DHELI *Source Code 4*. These lines represent a kind of source level "inclusion" relationship, analogous to the concept of source inclusion present on the C and Java language specifications.

It is necessary to note that in the current DHELI language specification, all the entities are identified by W3C URIs, even those files accessible through the local file system. So, in order to retrieve any file referenced by a URI with a `http://` header, the DHELI system is very likely going to need to use either the HTTP or FTP protocol. In figure 1.10, the inclusion relationships are represented by dashed arrows directed towards the included files, the *effective* file inclusion done by the IOT compiler whenever that file is referenced by a third one, is represented by solid arrows, that are, in fact, resource retrievals by URI via the HTTP protocol.

This does not mean that the interpreter system could not or should not use the file I/O system calls proposed by the runtime environment (the Java VM), by instance in the case of URIs with the header `file://`, there is not need to use HTTP or FTP for file retrieval.

4.4. The DHELI language

In [Koning and Romero-Hernandez, 2002a; Koning and Romero-Hernandez, 2002b] we presented a tool called AtoS (AUML to Promela/SPIN), which takes a textual representation of visual of AUML sequence diagrams, and generates an equivalent Promela source code to validate with the SPIN tool.

Very soon, it was evident to us that an almost full AUML equivalence would be quite restrictive in certain cases, specially when we wanted to represent whole communication scenatios where it was mandatory to use operations not defined by the AUML definition (e.g., interation, life line collapse).

To cope with the functional holes of AUML, we made further advancement in the same sense, through notational enhancements, and this resulted in the creation of the DHELI tool. DHELI stands for Double-approach Hybrid Experimental Language for Interaction representation.

4.4.1. Entities

The DHELI language is made to represent structures that are equivalent in expressivity to AUML sequence diagrams, but adding another level of expressivity through the use of state controlled execution and four types of "automata inheritance".

As most extended automata-based formal description techniques and notations, the tool is based on the notion of *module* or *entity* and correspondingly, there is a set of statements to specify the temporal sequence of messages exchanged between these entities.

In our language, entities are named *Roles*, whose behavior is internally represented as defined in section 1.3. Every *Role* exists within an specific context, called a *Scenario*, which contains always a minimum of two roles. This limitation comes from common sense, as we need at least two entities communicating one with each other to have an interesting multi-agent system. Agents talking only to themselves are of not much interest for us.

The code in algorithm 1 shows the declaration of one scenario called *ContractNet* containing two roles (*Initiator* and *Participant*). A specification may contain as many scenarios as we wish, but every one must have a different name. Inside a scenario, there could be too as many roles as we desire, with the restriction that every role name must be unique within a single scenario—e.g., there could be other roles called *Initiator* and *Participant* within other scenarios.

Algorithm 1 First Level Entities.

```
scenario ContractNet {
  role Initiator {
    state={q0};
    init=q0;
    when(q0) ( interaction, nil, Participant, nil, true, cfp,
      q0 ) {
      ...
    }
  }
  role Participant {
    state={s0};
    init=s0;
    when(s0) ( interaction, Initiator, nil, cfp, true, nil,
      s0 ) {
      ...
    }
  }
}
```

To allow a fine grained control of the state space, the language has a set of statements to declare explicitly a finite state machine, the notation to do so is strongly inspired on ESTELLE. In algorithm 1, the set of states of every internal automata are declared by name within the two statements `state={q0}` and `state={s0}`, if there were more states to declare, they could be enounced separated by commas. The function of the init statement is to set automata's initial state.

Once we define the set of states and the initial state, we could proceed to define the actions that change it. The statement when defines the beginning of a series of actions that could only happen at that state; the series of actions that could happen in current state are limited only by the insertion of another when statement, that on its turn, will begin the enumeration of actions that could happen when the automata is on another state. The notation used to represent a explicit—and implicit—state change are explained below.

4.4.2. Communication acts

The basic element of every DHELI specification (as it was for AtoS and every AUML sequence diagram) is the *Communication Act* [Odell et al., 2000b], e.g., the atomic event of an entity sending or receiving a message to/from another one. For DHELI, a communication act is a tuple $E = (CA_{type}, A, B, C)$, where $CA_{type} = \{int, xor\ out, or\ out, and\ out, sync\}$ is the set of all communication act types supported by DHELI, a and B are sets representing the source and destination roles of current communication act, and $C = (I, E, O)$ is another tuple, where I is an input symbol to receive, E a logical expression(guard) and O an output symbol to send whenever the messages specified on I have arrived and E is true.

In the language, there are two sorts of communication acts:

1. Implicit state-change communication acts. We call so those acts that define an execution path equivalent to a AUML's sequence diagram.
2. Explicit state-change communication acts. We call explicit state-change communication act those that modify the state of the system explicitly. Their structure differs slightly from their implicit equivalents, they have the next structure: $(CA_{type}, A, B, C, next_{state})$, where $next_{state}$ is the label of one state defined in the state list.

Next we show the different kind of Communication Acts proposed by AUML that DHELI can handle, and their equivalence on tuples:

- Message sending: (`interaction, nil, target, <nil,true,msg_out>`), in this case, the source an the input message set to *nil* (not waiting for messages) and the guard expression evaluated as *true*, enable the immediate occurrence of this output event.
- Message receiving: (`interaction, source, nil, <msg_in,true,nil>`).
- Message sending triggered by input (causality): (`interaction, source, target, <msg_in, true,msg_out>`).
- XOR message sending: (`xor-out, nil, [T1,...,Tk], <nil,true, [msg1,..., msgk]>`)
- OR message sending: (`or-out, nil, [T1,...,Tk], <nil,true,[msg1,..., msgk]>`).
- AND message sending: (`and-out, nil, [T1,...,Tk], <nil,true, [msg1,...,msgk]>`).
- Synchronization: (`sync, [S1,...,Sk], nil,<[msg1,...,msgk],true,nil>`), this notation means that current agent waits to receive every single message in the list from its corresponding source list, in a one-to-one correspondence.

AUML proposes four branching operators to represent the subdivision of life-lines, DHELI provides them all and adds a fifth one, created in order to cover some of the original notational deficiencies of AUML. The four operators originally taken from AUML are:

- Sequential composition: if we want to express that the communication act E_1 happens before E_2, we use the statement `seq(E1,E2,no branches)` reserved phrase no branches is mandatory whenever we want to say there is not further life-line subdivision.
- XOR choice: if either E_1 or E_2 communication acts happen, but not both, we use the statement `seq(nil,xor(seq(E1,no branches), seq(E2, no`

branches))); AUML's branching operators (like XOR) happen always at the end of a sequential composition. This restriction is imposed by AUML itself.

- OR choice: the OR branching operator between two communication acts E_1 and E_2, means that either E_1 and E_2 happen inter-leavedly, or only E_1 happens but not E_2, or that E_1 do not happen but E_2 does. This is represented by `seq(nil, or(seq(E1, no branches),seq(E2, no branches)))`
- AND choice (parallelism): if both E_1 and E_2 happen, we use the syntax `seq(nil,and(seq(E1, no branches),seq(E2, no branches)))`.

4.4.3. Variables, role variables and meta-roles

DHELI gives limited support for internal variable manipulations. For the system, every variable is either an integer or a symbol (a string). It also provides a small set of operations capable of doing some minimal logical operations between variables (equality and logical comparisons).

Variables could be exchanged between entities both at the output and input part of every interaction. This allows the exchange of dynamically generated values. The syntax used to declare a variable in DHELI is straightforward. It is very similar to its analogous on most structured and object-oriented languages. The statements `var x=1;var y= "string";` declare two variables x and y and initialize them as two string values ("1" and "string"). Variables must be declared before used.

The tool also provides the notion of *role variable*, which is a reference to a specific instance of any given role. The difference between a *Role* and a *Role Variable* is significant, because a role represents the behavior of a whole set of entities, while the *role variables* are single entities that follow the behavior specified by the Role. We could find an analogy in the notion of class and object from object-oriented programming.

Role variables could be exchanged between roles as normal variables are, and they may be declared within *roles* too. Even more, they could be acquired through an interaction process with an external entity. The interest of role variables is to provide the capacity of interaction with entities whose behavior is well known, while its precise identity is not.

Algorithm 2 A template role with a role variable acquisition.

```
role Client {
   state={q0};
   init=q0,q1;
   Host @host;
   when(q0) (interaction, $User, nil, [connect, @host], true,
     nil, q0) {
     ...
   }
}
```

The last entity type allowed by the language is the meta-role. Meta-roles are variables that could reference roles themselves. Their function is to provide a genericity mechanism for protocol reuse.

Algorithm 2 shows a parametrized role called *Client*. Such template role declares the role variable *@host* that belongs to the explicit role *Host* (Role variables always begin with the character '@'. The language is case-sensitive.), and it receives a message from a meta-role called $User (meta-roles always begin with character '$'). The meaning of this interaction is that any other role in the system could interact with *Client*—or any of its instances—as long as it respects the matching criteria imposed by composability restrictions, and sends it a message with the symbol "connect" and a correct value for *@host*.

If we decide to use the explicit name of a Role to indicate the source or the target of any interaction, we are in fact using some kind of *role literals*.

5. CONCLUSION AND FUTURE WORK

In the context of this paper, we propose a definition of role that enables the creation of development artifacts that could be included within an AUML-like development process. The concept of role we provide has a greater expressiveness than AUML sequence diagrams, and still tries to keep the graphic inspiration of the later.

We also put forward some general criteria to assure the composability of roles if they are considered as programming artifacts. The first property was the matching of messages between peers and the second one, the finite behavior of every role. Both properties could be proved with the assistance of a formal description technique tool, like Promela/Spin.

In order to do so, we have constructed a tool that is capable of taking a specification expressed in a specific purpose language of our invention, and thus obtain in the end an equivalent Promela/Spin translation that enables the verification of those two properties of peer-message matching and finite behavior.

Unfortunately, some features are lacking in the current state of the tool. While we think of providing support for meta-roles, the tests and algorithms to prove the peer message-matching is not complete yet.

REFERENCES

Adorni, G. and Poggi, A. (1993a). MAP—A language for the modelling of multi-agent systems. In Torasso, Pietro, editor, *Advances in Artificial Intelligence: Proceedings of the 3rd Congress of the Italian Association for Artificial Intelligence (AI*IA '93)*, volume 728 of *LNAI*, pages 154–159, Torino, Italy. SV.

Adorni, Giovanni and Poggi, Agostino (1993b). An object-oriented language for distributed artificial intelligence. *International Journal of Man-Machine Studies*, 38(3): 435–453.

Barbuceanu, Mihai and Lo, Wai-Kao (1999). Conversation oriented programming in COOL: Current state and future directions. In *Autonomous Agents'99, Special Workshop on Conversation Policies*.

Bauer, B., Muller, J., and Odell, J. (2001). Agent UML: A formalism for specifying multiagent interaction. In Ciancarini and Wooldridge, editors, *International journal of software engineering and knowledge engineering*, volume 11, pages 91–103. Springer, Berlin.

Birrell, A. D. and Nelson, B. J. (1983). Implementing remote procedure calls. In *Proceedings of the ACM Symposium on Operating System Principles*, page 3, Bretton Woods, NH. Association for Computing Machinery.

Courtiat, Jean-Pierre and Saidouni, Djamel-Edine (1995). A case study on protocol design. In *Lotosphere: Software Development with LOTOS*, pages 201–217. Kluwer Academic Publishers.

Estelle (1997). *Information processing systems—Open systems interconnection—Estelle—A formal description technique based on an extended state transition model.* International Organization for Standardization, Geneva. 9074.

Holzmann, Gerard J. (1997). The model checker SPIN. *IEEE Transactions on Software Engineering,* 23(5):279–295.

Huget, Marc-Philippe (2001). *Une ingénierie des protocoles dans les systèmes multi-agents.* PhD thesis, Université Paris Dauphine.

Huget, Marc-Philippe (2002). Desiderata for agent oriented programming languages. Technical Report ULCS-02-010, University of Liverpool, Liverpool, UK.

Koning, J.-L., Huget, M.-Ph., Wei, J., and Wang, X. (2001a). Engineering electronic commerce interaction protocols. In Mohammadian, M., editor, *International Conference on Intelligent Agents, Web Technology and Internet Commerce (IAWTIC'2001),* Las Vegas, USA.

Koning, J.-L., Huget, M.-Ph., Wei, J., and Wang, X. (2001b). Extended modeling languages for interaction protocol design. In Wooldridge, M., Ciancarini, P., and Weiss, G., editors, *Second International Workshop on Agent-Oriented Software Engineering (AOSE-2001),* Montreal, Canada.

Koning, J.-L. and Romero-Hernandez, I. (2002a). Generating machine processable representations of textual representations of auml. In Odell, J., editor, *Third International Workshop on Agent-Oriented Software Engineering (AOSE-2002),* Bologna, Italy. Springer-Verlag.

Koning, J.-L. and Romero-Hernandez, I. (2002b). Thoughts on an agent oriented language centered on interaction modeling. In *Second IEEE International Symposium on Advanced Distributed Systems (ISADS-2002),* Guadalajara, Mexico. IEEE, Springer-Verlag.

Microsystems, Sun (2001). *Jini Architecture Specification.* 901 San Antonio Road, Palo Alto, CA 94303 USA.

Odell, James, Van Dyke Parunak, Harry, and Bauer, Bernhard (2000a). Extending UML for agents. In Wagner, Gerd, Lesperance, Yves, and Yu, Eric, editors, *Proceedings of the Agent-Oriented Information Systems Workshop at the 17th National conference on Artificial Intelligence,* Austin, Texas. ICue Publishing.

Odell, James, Van Dyke Parunak, Harry, and Bauer, Bernhard (2000b). Representing agent interaction protocols in uml. In Ciancarini, Paolo and Wooldridge, Michael, editors, *Proceedings of First International Workshop on Agent-Oriented Software Engineering,* Limerick, Ireland. Springer-Verlag.

Sankar, S. (1996). Introducing formal methods to software engineers through OMG's CORBA environment and interface definition language. *Lecture Notes in Computer Science,* 1101:52–61.

Shoham, Y. (1990). Agent-oriented programming. Technical Report STAN-CS-1335-90, Computer Science Department, Stanford University, Stanford, CA 94305.

Shoham, Y. (1991). Agent-oriented programming. In *Proceedings of the 11th International Workshop on DAI,* pages 345–353.

Shoham, Yoav (1993). Agent oriented programming. *Journal of Artificial Intelligence,* 60(1):51–92. Elsevier Science Publishers Ltd.

Sijelmassi, Rachid and Strausser, Brett (1990). NIST integrated tool set for Estelle. In Quemada, Juan, Mañas, José A., and Vázquez, Enrique, editors, *FORTE, Formal Description Techniques, III, Proceedings of the IFIP TC6/WG6.1 Third International Conference on Formal Description Techniques for Distributed Systems and Communication Protocols, FORTE '90,* pages 543–546, Madrid, Spain. North-Holland.

Sijelmassi, Rachid and Strausser, Brett (1993). The PET and DINGO tools for deriving distributed implementations from Estelle. *Computer Networks and ISDN Systems,* 25.

Singh, M. P. (1996). Toward interaction oriented programming. In *Second International Conference on Multi-Agent Systems (ICMAS-96),* Tokyo, Japan.

Thees, J. (1998). Protocol implementation with estelle—from prototypes to efficient implementations. In Budkowski, S., Fischer, S., and Gotzhein, R., editors, *Int'l. Workshop on the Formal Description Technique Estelle (Estelle'98),* Evry, France.

Tillman, Matthew A. and Yen, David Chi-Chung (1990). SNA and OSI: Three strategies for interconnection. *Computing Reviews,* 31(10).

Waite, W. M. and Goos, G. (1984). *Compiler Construction.* Springer-Verlag, Berlin, Germany.

AGENT-BASED eLEARNING SYSTEMS: A GOAL-BASED APPROACH

ZHIQI SHEN, ROBERT GAY AND YUAN MIAO

1. INTRODUCTION

With the development of Internet applications, E-commerce/E-business revolution-ized the way companies sold their products and services and the way businesses ad-dressed customer needs and concerns [1]. These applications increased productivity and reduced cost while increasing customer satisfaction and maintaining their com-petitiveness. E-learning, as another type of Internet applications, is now becoming very popular as companies rethink almost every aspect of the way their employees work in the enterprise [2]. In this era of rapid change, large amounts of new products, market, and competitive information are emerging. Employees are expected to learn frequently so as to compete effectively. However, employees usually have different skill sets and have different learning requirements. Traditional instructor-led training and on-line training cannot scale to meet these new learning challenges. E-learning, defined as Internet-enabled or Internet-enhanced learning, provides the tools to create person-alized learning path and to be able to dynamically readapt learning paths according to user feedbacks in order to optimize the acquisition of needed competencies [2][3].

Unlike on-line training where thousands of static pages of content were posted on the web, E-learning sites contain a variety of media and course components, from many different subject matter experts. Employees or learners will be able to choose what, when, where, how, and how much of the course components they are to under-take. A course component is a self-contained, tagged object. These learning objects will be targeted to learners when they need them and only to those who need them.

Pre-assessments will identify the gap between what learners already know and what they need to know to effectively do their jobs. Post-assessments will confirm if they have retained the knowledge. In short, E-learning provides individualized learning roadmaps for employees or learners to track learning progress based on business objectives. E-learning is moving from a content-centric model such as on-line training, to a rich, personalized, learner-centric model that will touch everyone associated with the enterprise, including its partners and customers.

On the other hand, E-learning systems are more complex than other on-line training systems. Recent advances in the field of E-learning systems have proposed the use of Artificial Intelligence through architectures based on agents' societies [2][3][4]. E-learning systems based on Multi-Agent architectures make it possible to support the development of more interactive and adaptable systems.

Agent technology, a combination of artificial intelligence and software engineering, represents an exciting new means of analyzing, designing and building complex software systems [5]. From 1990s, agents have become one of the most important research areas in the soft computing. Agent based systems have been successfully used in many areas such as information collection/filtering, personal assistants, network management, electronic commerce, intelligent manufacturing, health care, entertainment, and etc. [6][7]. Agent technologies are also well suited to carry out the main activities involved in E-learning. In fact, most of the E-learning systems are distributed systems. Those activities involved in E-learning systems require communications between distributed course components, sensing and monitoring of the environment and autonomous operations. E-learning agents have the ability to reason. They are proactive, interactive, adaptive and autonomous. They can easily perform complex operations based on their goals, messages received and environment changes.

An agent works towards its goals. It takes proper actions to reach its goals autonomously. Goal modeling is one of the most important aspects in a successful agent development. A goal model of an agent ensures the agent will do the right thing on the right time. Goal modeling of agents is the key of successful agent applications. In this chapter, the agent composite goal modeling method [8] is used to model the complex goals of E-learning agents. Furthermore, the model is extended in two directions: 1) Integrate an action selection scheme into the goal model; 2) Promote the goal model for agent identification and coordination in a multi-agent system environment. Therefore, this chapter introduces a complete goal based approach for developing E-learning systems.

Following this introduction, section 2 gives the overview of the composite state goal model. Section 3 describes an extension of the composite agent goal model. Section 4 presents the E-learning model via the goal-based approach. Section 5 illustrates the agent development and a prototype system. Finally the conclusion is reached and the future work is discussed in section 6.

2. OVERVIEW OF THE AGENT COMPOSITE GOAL MODEL

A goal is a desired state which the agent is to reach. In order to reach the goal, an agent must reason about its environment, generate plans and execute these plans. Therefore

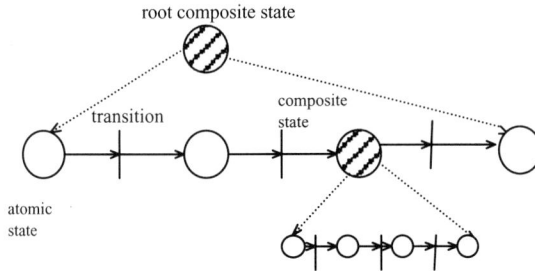

Figure 1. An example of the composite state goal model.

the activities for reaching the goal request many processes or stages, each of which has its own objective. That is, a goal can be divided into many sub goals. Similarly, a sub goal can be further divided into sub goals according to the complexity of the processes for reaching the sub goal. So, the overall goal, sub goals and their relationships form a hierarchical structure. The root of the structure is called final goal. An agent has many sub goals during its pursuing the final goal.

A state is a situation description when an agent is acting to pursue its goal. A goal is a state. Therefore it is the state that indicates the goal of an agent is reached or not.

The *composite state goal model* was proposed based on Petri Net theory [9][10] and object oriented methodology [11]. As it is illustrated in [8], the composite state goal model is composed of five basic objects: *states, transitions, arcs, branches,* and *tokens.*

States, represented by circles, are used to represent different status that agents need to go through to reach their goals. *Transitions,* represented by vertical bars, are used to represent tasks to evolve the agent from one state to another state. A state is connected to transitions via *arcs* or a transition is connected to states via *arcs,* represented by arrows. Each transition has at least an *input state* and an *output state.* Each transition is associated with a task list that defines the tasks an agent may perform in order to fire a transition. When certain conditions are satisfied, the transition fires, and the agent will evolve from the input states to the output states.

There are two kinds of state objects in the model: the *atomic state object,* represented by a blank circle, accommodates a single state which could not be split any more; the *composite state object,* represented by a shadowed circle, may be split into other state objects (either composite or atomic i.e. sub goals) connected via transitions. Figure 1 presents a hierarchical structure of the goal model. The root composite state object in the highest level of the hierarchical structure represents the overall goal of the agent and the composite state objects in lower levels of the hierarchical structure represent sub goals of the agent. A higher level of composite state objects (goal or sub goals) can be split into lower-level state objects connected by transitions.

There are three types of transitions in the model: *direct_to transition, concurrent_with transition, jump_to transition.*

- *Direct_to* transition designates a direct connection in sequence from one state to another state. It defines a successive relationship between two states.
- *Concurrent_with* transition specifies a concurrent occurrence between one state and another states. It defines concurrent relationship between states.
- *Jump_to* transition specifies a jump connection from one state to another state. It defines a jump relationship between states. The inhibitors are used to solve the conflict introduced by this type of transitions.

Both state objects and transition objects have their own properties and behaviors. Besides *state Id* and *description*, a state object has a time counter which records the *duration* of a state, a *local distance value* and a *global distance value* to indicate how close the current state is to the state of the sub goal and final goal respectively. One of the state object's behaviors is that it can compute the *worth value* through the worth value function. The worth value function of a state object gives a quantitative value for specifying the partial goal that the agent has reached. With the above measurements, an agent is able to choose its next sub-goal autonomously based on its available resources.

A transition object has *input states* and *output states*. It is associated with a task list and a *fire condition* function. The fire condition function specifies the fire condition of the progress from the input states of a transition to its output states. The most important behavior of a transition is when the fire condition is satisfied, it can *fire* to remove the tokens from its input states and add tokens to its output states. Therefore, the evaluation of the fire function enables the agent to decide its behaviors autonomously.

Apart from defining the states and the transitions, the model also defines a set of firing rules, which provides a mechanism for capturing and denoting dynamic characteristics of the goal model. In particular, firing rules of the model can be summarized as follows:

1) A transition is enabled when all the input states are active, i.e. hold tokens;
2) A transition fires as soon as the agent has successfully carried out the tasks specified in the task list;
3) When a transition fires, its input states become inactive, and its output states are activated;
4) A jump_to transition is enabled when certain conditions of the transition are met;

The goal pursuing of an agent starts from the top state, which represents the overall goal of the agent; then goes through the hierarchical model; and finally goes back to the top state. The goal of the agent is regarded to have been reached at this time. Then the agent will start from the top state again for the next round pursuing.

With different combinations of direct_to, concurrent_with and jump_to transitions, a wide range of complicated relationships between states can be represented, which could accommodate various complex goals of the intelligent agents.

3. EXTENSION OF THE AGENT COMPOSITE GOAL MODEL

3.1. Action selection

A transition contains many actions to drive the agent from one state to next state. In the ideal situation, an agent can take a fixed sequence of actions to go from one state to the next state. But in the real world, the external environment is always changing. In order to move to next the state, an agent has to consider both internal states and external states to select actions. For example, one may go to work from home to office every weekday by bus. In the case it is raining or he is late, he has to choose other rapid transportation tools such as taxi. He may need to ask somebody's help (lift) if there is no taxi available. So, external states are important factors for the action selection. There are many internal or external factors affecting the action selection. As human beings, we make decisions according to the real situation by considering many factors. If only a few important factors are considered by the agent, it is hard for the agent to select right actions. Agents must also be able to handle the uncertainty, as human beings do. In the above example, the way he finally chose to go to his office is uncertain. It depends on the situation he faces. Whether it is raining, he is leaving home late, a taxi is not available, or he can find help from other sources, are all uncertain factors. With incomplete information, human beings usually make decisions based on probability. For example, in above situation, if the probability that no taxi is available is low, he may choose to wait for a taxi. Otherwise, he may call his friends for help.

Bayesian networks [12] have been used in many areas for processing uncertainty. It is also adopted here to help agents make decisions on action selection.

In the proposed composite goal model, transitions are associated with tasks, each of which involves many actions. There are three types of action selection strategies:

- Fixed sequence of actions: This is the simplest situation. There is no action selection needed. Agents can move from one state to the next states by finishing the execution of the fixed sequence of actions.
- Rule-based reasoning: In this situation, complete information for action selection presents. Agent can make decision according to the rules and the current values of all the factors or states.
- Probabilistic reasoning: In this situation, information for action selection is not complete. But a Bayesian network that represents the causal relationships between factors and actions can be constructed. Agent then reasons its actions through Bayesian network inference.

3.1.1. Bayesian inference

Suppose $E = \{E_1, E_2, \ldots, E_n\}$ is the external factor set, $I = \{I_1, I_2, \ldots, I_m\}$ is the internal factor set, $A = \{A_1, A_2, \ldots, A_k\}$ is the action group set and $R = \{(C, D)|C, D \subseteq (E \cup I \cup A)\}$ is the set of causal relationships between external factors, internal factors and action groups. The target states are internal factors. Every element of A can fulfill the tasks associated with a transition. The function U is an utility function to measure the achievement by performing a group of actions. If the achievement is higher than the predefined threshold, the transition fires. The agent will move to the next state. The action selection through Bayesian inference is to find out an action group in the current situation that will gain a satisfied (or the best) result so that the transition would fire.

Assuming the prior probabilities of the internal and external factors of a transition are known. When the transition is enabled, with the evidence of all the factors, the post probabilities can be computed. Then the action group with the biggest probability would be selected. Such action group with the highest probability does not mean that it will generate big enough achievement to make the transition fire. If this group fails, the action group with the second highest probability will be selected. This process can be continued until the transition fires or all the groups have been tested. If the transition cannot fire at the end of the tests, the agent will interact with human beings (or other agents) to ask for help. There are many ways human beings can interfere the decision making of agents. For example, in this case human beings can adjust the threshold value to a lower value. Then the agent can restart to try the action groups from the one with the highest probability.

Upon finishing the transition, a learning process is needed to adjust the prior probabilities of the factors.

3.1.2. Discussion

The complexity of the action selection based on Bayesian network includes the network learning and the action group evaluation, which affect the execution time and cost, i.e. performance of the agent. One of the solutions to this problem is to train Bayesian networks outside the agents.

3.2. Multi-agent modeling

When a problem is so complex that a single agent cannot resolve it with an acceptable performance, a multi-agent system will be considered. In a multi-agent system, many agents work together to solve the problem (to reach the common goal). Agent identification and agent coordination are two important issues in multi-agent modeling. The composite state goal model is extended in this section to systematically address these two issues.

In a composite state goal model, a composite state together with its decompositions can be regarded as a standalone goal model. This model can be identified as a goal model of a separate agent. If there is another composite state in the new model, this state together with its decompositions can be further identified as a goal model of another agent. So a sub goal pursuing by a single agent becomes the goal pursuing of a group of agents in the generated multi-agent system. A higher level agent becomes a coordinator of lower level of agents at the time it is pursuing its own goals. The transition between one composite state and another composite state or atomic state defines the coordination tasks and schedules.

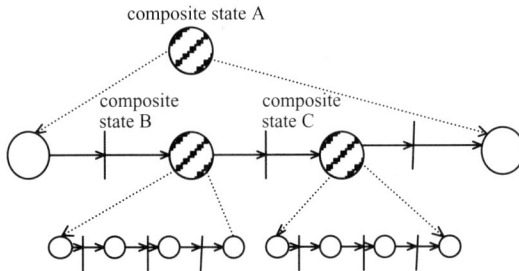

Figure 2. A composite state goal model.

3.2.1. Agent identification

A composite state together with its decompositions in a composite goal model can be selected to form the goal model of a new agent. This composite state becomes the goal of the new agent and it becomes the root node of the goal hierarchy. This new agent goal model can be further extended based on the requirement as long as the root node that represents the goal, is not changed.

While a composite state and its decompositions are selected to form a new agent, the composite state is replaced by a connection state in the original model. The connection state is an atomic state that represents the state of a composite state, which is split from the goal model. There is a connection between the connection state and the newly derived root state. When a connection state starts to hold a token, a copy of the token will be sent to the agent pointed by the connection state. The generated agent will then initialize its goal model with this token, and start to pursue its goal. After the goal is reached, the generated agent will send back the token to the original agent. The original agent extracts information from the token received from the generated agent and discards this token.

3.2.2. Coordination

In a multi-agent system modeled by the composite state goal model, agents are organized in a hierarchical structure. The structure can be derived from the goal model. For example, Figure 2 is a goal model while Figure 3 is the organization structure of the multi-agent system modeled by the goal model presented in Figure 2.

An agent is active when it holds tokens. Otherwise it is idling. Suppose composite state B is decomposed state A. The state B together with its further decompositions forms a model of a new agent B. The state A together with its rest members of its decompositions forms agent A. The agent A is then called the parent agent of agent B according to the hierarchical structure. For example, in Figure 3, the agent A is the parent agent of the agent B and the agent C. The agent A has its own goal. It needs agent B's work to reach the goal. It at the same time becomes a coordinator of its child agents. The child agents start to work when they receive tokens from their parent agent. The goal model of agent A can be regarded as a coordinator for the entire multi-agent system.

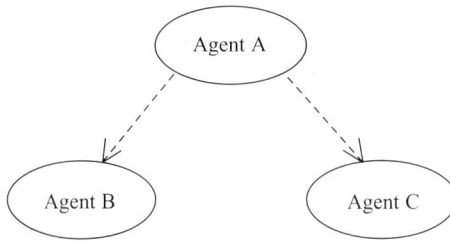

Figure 3. Derived agent organization from goal model in Figure 2.

3.2.3. Communication

Agents in a multi-agent system cooperate through the communications with each other. There are three types of communications in the multi-agent system modeled by the composite state goal model.

- Interaction: An agent interacts with other agents or human beings. For example, the agent may need human beings' assistance about the action selection. This type of communication is done through the message exchange mechanism.
- Coordination: A parent agent coordinates its child agents. This type of communication is done through token transferring.
- Notification: The coordination between agents is done asynchronously. When a parent agent sends a token to a child agent, it does not wait. Instead, it save the state of the current goal and continue to pursue another goal. After the child agent reaches its goal, it will notify its parent agent that it has finished the job and then sends the token back to its parent agent. The parent agent will restore hung goal and handle the token received from the child agent. This type of communication is done through the signal mechanism.

3.2.4. Summary

In summary, there are many advantages to use the composite state goal model for multi-agent system modeling. In details, with the modeling method:

- Agents can be identified easily,
- Coordinations can be derived, and
- Job schedulers can also be derived.

4. E-LEARNING MODEL

4.1. Goal-based modeling

Goal-based modeling is to model a multi-agent system using the extended composite state goal model. To work out a multi-agent system model with the goal-based approach, customer satisfaction has to drive all actions and decisions within the design process. This demands that goals, i.e. the customer wishes, have to be used as design criteria through the whole process of the system modeling. The role of goals has to evolve from a starting point of a top-down satisfaction to central criteria driving all decisions within the design process. Goals have to be used to estimate the current models, to evaluate single alternatives, and thus help to guide the development process according to the visions on the information system to be built.

Goal-based development starts from the problem decomposition and requirement analysis [13]. The development stages include problem analysis, goal modeling, agent identification, and agent development. Following is the list of the development stages and the procedures included in each stage.

- Problem Analysis
  - Decompose the problems into processes
  - Identify goals of each process
  - Define tasks, constraints and context of each process
- Goal Modeling
  - Draw goal model diagram according to process work flows
  - Identify composite states, states and tasks
- Agent Identification
  - Decide strategies in terms of number of agents, task balance and complexity
  - Identify agents by splitting the goal models.
  - Refine individual agent models
- Agent Development
  - Define system architecture
  - Design agent actions
  - Implement the agent system
  - Deploy the system

Next sub section will detail each stage of the goal-based modeling. Agent development will be elaborated in section 5.

4.2. E-learning modeling

In general, e-learning is the delivery of education and training courses over the Internet and/or Intranets. It can be defined as a mixture of content (on-line courses or courseware) and communications (reaching online, emails, discussion forums). But it is not just about placing classes online to address *training* issues. E-learning encompasses training, education, information, communication, collaboration, knowledge management and performance management. It addresses *business* issues such as reducing costs, providing greater access to information and accountability for learning, and increasing employee competence and competitive agility. E-learning is a critical element of enterprise workforce optimization initiative.

The key e-learning stakeholders can be divided into two broad categories—the consumers and the providers.

- The consumers of an e-learning system are:
  - **Learners** are those who are seeking knowledge, including the internal employees of the organization, and the customers, channel partners, supply chain vendors that are external to the organizations.
  - **Knowledge officers** are responsible for guiding and managing the learning and the development of individuals and/or organizations.
- The providers of an e-learning system are:
  - **Content provider**s include instructors, subject matter experts and instructional designers who perform needs analysis to determine the learning objectives required. This group of people also includes course component developers, who look at job roles and tasks, and then specifically define the competencies (skills, behaviours, and knowledge) required to do them.
  - **Administrators** are responsible for managing catalogue items, schedules, and resources. They maintain the content servers and networks. They may also identify generic curricula for an organization and register content in the content servers.

An advantage of e-learning system is its ability to help enriching, sharing and circulating organization knowledge. Because of the dynamism of the market, the business may change, products need to be improved or upgraded, and new products need to be made, organizations often need to enrich enterprise knowledge, refresh skills of employees to gain new competencies in the dynamic market. Therefore an appropriate and properly utilized e-learning system becomes an important component of the Enterprise Knowledge Management.

Given a requirement for a role in a project, the e-learning system should be able to suggest a team member or a list of possible team members based on their profiles stored in the knowledge base of the organization. A suitable employee will then be selected by the manager. The e-learning system should be able to measure the competence gaps and to reduce them by creating personalized learning paths for the selected employee. Moreover, the system should be able to refine the learning path according to feedbacks the employee provides in order to optimize the acquisition of needed competencies. Based on the learning path, the training courses and material should be delivered to the employee site. The system should also be able to assess the learning results of the employee and readapt the learning path to cater for the progress of the employee. The learning cycle will be repeated until the assessment of the learning results meets the requirement of the role in the project.

An e-learning process can be decomposed into two sub processes: a learner preparation process and learning process. The learner preparation process can be further decomposed into a role identification process, an employee selection process and a pre-assessment process. Learning process can also be further decomposed into a learning path generation process, a course delivery process and a post-assessment process. The processes and their goals are listed in Table 1.

The E-learning service process is a main process that provides flexible training services to individual employees. The services are completed through the layered sub processes.

Table 1 E-learning processes and their goals

Process	Goal
E-learning service	Employee is well trained
Learner preparation	Learner is ready to learn
Learning	Learning is proceeded
Role identification	Role in a project is identified
Employee selection	Employee is selected for a specific role
Pre-assessment	Feedbacks from the employee are obtained
Learning path generation	Learning path is generated for the particular employee
Course delivery	Courses are delivered
Post-assessment	Results of self-learning are measured

- Learner preparation process is to find employees who need to be trained and to make assessment for the employees selected.
- Learning process is to the generate personal learning path for individual employees and complete the training processes.
- Role identification process is to identify roles that make up a project team according to the project specification. The responsibility of each role and the technical requirement for each role are defined.
- Employee selection process is to select employees for each role identified in the previous process. The selection is done by matching the technical requirement of each role to the user profile of each employee. Each role may have one or many candidates. The most suitable one should be selected based on all the factors that affect the availability of employees. In the case there is no employee is selected for a particular role within the organization, a request for recruitment should be made.
- Pre-assessment process is to obtain feedbacks from each of the selected employees. The assessment is made based on the user profile, technical requirement for the role in the project and the training course materials. The user profile may not contain complete information about an employee and may not be up-to-date. This process is necessary to gain an optimized learning path.
- Learning path generation process is to generate learning paths for all the employees selected for the project. It is done according to the user profile, the feedback of each employee and the course materials. The generated learning path will then be stored in the user profile of individual employees.
- Course delivery process is to deliver the corresponding course materials to the employee site over the Internet or intranet. It is done according to the learning path generated for the employee. Each employee can make his own arrangement for the training courses.
- Post-assessment process is to measure the achievement of the employee by the training courses. If the results have met the requirements of all the courses, the training for this employee is finished. His user profile will be updated accordingly. If the employee fails to pass any of the courses, a new learning path will be generated. He needs to continue the course work until he passes all the courses in the learning path.

Figure 4.1 shows the Goal based E-learning Model. The E-learning service is a composite state that is decomposed to sub states. The six states at the bottom layer can

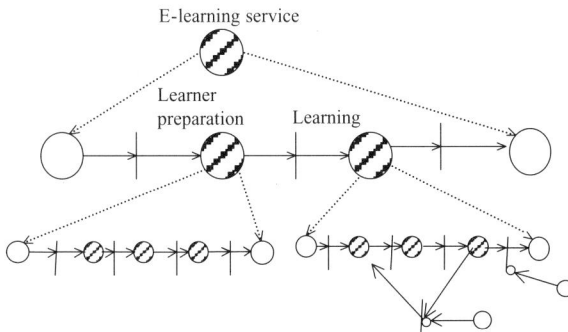

Figure 4. An e-learning goal model.

be further decomposed. For simplicity, this figure only shows the top three layers of the model.

As mentioned in section 3, each composite state together with its decomposition can be identified as an agent. Based on Figure 4.1 we have nine agents: learning service agent, learner preparation agent, learning agent, role identification agent, learner selection agent, pre-assessment agent, learning path generation agent, course delivery agent and post-assessment agent.

5. E-LEARNING SYSTEM DEVELOPMENT

5.1. E-learning system architecture

After an e-learning problem is modeled with the composite state goal model, multiple e-learning agents are identified and thus a multi-agent system environment is needed for those multiple agents to live in. Figure 5 represents the multi-agent based e-learning system architecture.

As showed in this figure, a multi-agent based e-learning system contains an agent administration server, an ontology server, a communication server, a business management server, a course management server, a knowledge bases, a database systems and many agents.

The agent administration server provides various services for agents. The services include agent naming service, directory service, agent registration, information service, and task administration.

When an agent is running, the first thing it will do is to register itself with its personal information, such as goal model identifier, parent id, etc., to the agent administration server. The server will then assign an agent name, a group identifier and an unique identifier to this agent. The agent name, identifier, and the reference of this agent are also registered into the naming service and directory service by the agent administration server automatically. When the agent is stop running its records in agent administration server are deleted from the server. Obviously, the agents are organized in a group based on the underlining hierarchical structure of the goal model.

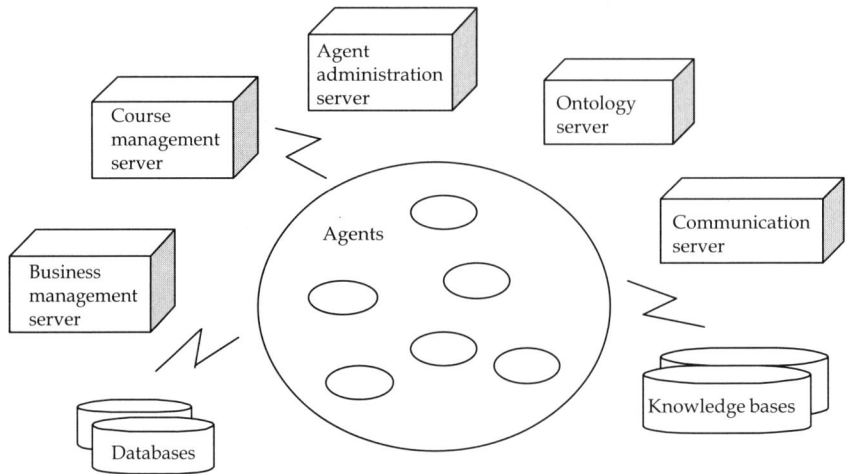

Figure 5. The e-learning system architecture.

Directory service provides agent information for other agents or other applications. Agents or other applications can search a particular agent through the directory service. Once the agent is found, the other agent or applications can request service from or communicate with this agent by obtaining the agent reference from the naming service.

Information service contains all the variables or factors of the real world. The variables and factors reflect the current states of real world. Agents may use them to select suitable actions during their goal pursing.

Task administration manages tasks assigned by the users. They tasks are dispatched to the master agents of different groups. The master agents will then conduct the member agents to fulfill the tasks. That is, when a new project is initialized, a project team needs to be formed. The task for each employee's training will be assigned to the e-learning service agent through the agent task administration service.

The Communication server provides services for agent communications. The services include communication channels, user interaction services, message coordination, and communication administration.

Communication channels provide a communication mechanism for agents to communicate. The channels can be TCP/IP network services, CORBA event channels message queues, or their combinations. They are application dependent and will be decided in real applications.

User interaction service provides a mechanism for user to communicate with agents. Agents communicate through a specific language, such as the Agent Communication Language (ACL) or the Knowledge Query Manipulate Language (KQML). The user interaction service of the communication server translates, converts and formats the messages between users and agents. The user interaction service provides a such a GUI interface. When a message is given by the user, the communication server will translate this message to the agent language through the ontology server, then convert it to the agent communication language format and finally send it to the target agent. The process will be reversed when an agent sends a message to a user.

The message coordination provides services for the communication between agents. It plays a message coordination role. It works with the agent administration server to dispatch messages to the right agent.

The communication administration provides general services for agent communication. For example, communication administration can have a connection pool to facilitate agent communication. It can provide language translation and conversion services to facilitate user interactions. It can also provide services to handle communication failures.

The ontology server provides vocabulary translation services for agent communication. For example, it is used to map the terms in the course work to the terms in the business environment.

The course management server manages all the course work. It provides services to add new course components, delete course components or modify course components. It also provides functions for course retrieval, query and course component meta data management. Course provider manage the course work through the course management server. E-learning agents access the course management server to generate personal learning paths, retrieve course components or assess learners learning progress.

The business management server manages all the business related information including the user profiles of all the employees, project specifications, role definitions, technical requirements, and etc. E-learning agents access this server to search for suitable employees for new projects, obtain information for learning path generations and monitor employees' skills to make training suggestions.

The knowledge bases include a business knowledge base and an agent knowledge base. The business knowledge base stores the enterprise knowledge of the organization. For example, the knowledge base can store user profiles technical skills, experiences of the employees, business strategies, business plans and information of the customers or partners. The agent knowledge base stores agent knowledge such as goal models, Bayesian networks, application computational models and other model parameters, factors. Each agent has its own knowledge.

The databases are used to store all the other data, including the project information, application specific data, etc.

The agents are e-learning agents that are modeled using the composite state goal model. They are grouped by goal models. The master agent of each group is the agent whose goal is the root state of a goal model before it is split into other agents.

5.2. E-learning system development

There are many agent development tools provide agent management service, ontology service and communication service. We selected Java Agent DEvelopment Framework (JADE) [14] as the development tool in our current prototype e-learning system. JADE was developed to comply with the Foundation for Intelligent Physical Agents (FIPA) specifications. It supports agent management, agent communication and ontology server implementation.

A goal based agent model includes four layers [8]: the environment layer, the goal model layer, the function layer and the interface layer.

- The environment layer: Java is a portable programming language. The e-learning agents are developed with Java on JADE platform. JADE also provides the communication mechanism. Oracle database system is used for the knowledge bases and databases.
- The goal-model layer: The goal model is derived based on the problem decomposition, requirement analysis, process workflow and business logic of the e-learning application. The goal model will create the execution plan of an agent when the agent is running. The framework for goal model implementation was also developed with Java.
- The function layer: E-learning functions and agent functions were implemented based on the goal model framework and agent framework [15].
- The interface layer: This layer facilitates the agent to interact with users and other agents. The user interface of agents was developed to support web environment so that learners can access the e-learning agents through either the Internet or the Intranet.

6. CONCLUSION AND FUTURE WORK

6.1. Conclusion

In this chapter, we have presented a practical new approach to model the goals of the e-learning agent. An e-learning problem can be represented by composite state goal models in different level of the hierarchical structure. The composite state goal model is further extended to support multi-agent modeling. Therefore agents can be easily identified from the model and the agent coordination can also be derived from the model.

It has been shown that the goal based approach proposed in this chapter for developing e-learning systems not only provides an easy way for agent development but also enables agents to present both behavior autonomy and goal autonomy.

6.2. Future work

The ongoing research consists of both theoretical and practical aspects: 1) Implementation of a multi-agent system based on the proposed composite goal model for a real e-learning application. 2) Further enhancement and evaluation of the composite goal model with Bayesian inference.

REFERENCES

[1] Wilderman, J., The Es have it: E-business, E-commerce, E-tailing and the web, *Gartner Group Research Report*, 2000.
[2] Osmar, R. and Zaïane, Building a Recommender Agent for e-Learning Systems, in *Proceedings of the International Conference on Computers in Education*, pp. 55–59, Auckland, New Zealand, December 2002.

[3] Garro, A. and Palopoli, L., An XML Multi-Agent System for e-Learning and Skill Management, in *Proceedings of the 3rd International Symposium on Multi-Agent Systems, Large Complex Systems, and E-Businesses (MALCEB'2002)*, pp. 283–294, Erfurt, Germany, October, 2002.

[4] Silveira, R. A., Improving interactivity in e-learning systems with Multi-Agent architecture, De Bra P., Brusilovisky P., and Conejo R. (Eds.): *Lecture Notes in Computer Science, Biarritz*, Vol. 2347, Springer-Verlag Berlin Heidelberg, 2002.

[5] Wooldridge, M. and Jennings, N. R., Intelligent agents: Theory and practice, *The knowledge Engineering Review*, Vol. 10, Issue 2, pp. 115–152, 1995.

[6] Jennings, N. R., Sycana, K. and Wooldridge, M., A roadmap of agent research and development, *Autonomous Agents and Multi-Agent Systems,* Vol. 1, Issue 1, pp. 7–38, 1998.

[7] Guttman, R., Moukas, A. and Maes, P., Agent-mediated electronic commerce: A survey, *Knowledge Engineering Review*, Vol. 13, pp. 147–159, 1998.

[8] Shen, Z. Q., Gay, R. and Tao, X. H., Goal-Based Intelligent Agents, *International Journal of Information Technology*, Vol. 9, No. 1, pp. 19–30, 2003.

[9] Murata, T., Petri Net : Properties, Analysis and Applications, in *Proceedings of IEEE*, 1989.

[10] Jensen, K., An Introduction to the Practical Use of Coloured Petri Nets, Reisig W. and Rozenberg G. (eds.): *Lectures on Petri Nets II: Applications, Lecture Notes in Computer Science*, Vol. 1492, Springer-Verlag, 1998.

[11] Martin, J. and Odell, J. J., Object-Oriented Methods: A Foundation, 2nd ed., Prentice-Hall, Upper Saddle River, 1998.

[12] Mayo, M. and Mitrovic, A., Optimising ITS Behaviour with Bayesian Networks and Decision Theory, *International Journal of Artificial Intelligence in Education*, Vol. 12, pp. 124–153, 2001.

[13] Van Lamsweerde A., Goal-Oriented Requirements Engineering: A Guided Tour, in *Proceedings of the Fifth IEEE International Symposium on Requirements Engineering (RE '01)*, pp. 249–262, Toronto, Canada, August, 2001.

[14] JADE Specification for Interoperable Multi-Agent System, http://jade.cselt.it/.

[15] Shen, Z. Q., Gay, R., Li, X. and Yang, Z. H., An Agent Approach for Intelligent Business Forecasting, Leondes, C. T. (eds.): *Chapter of Intelligent Systems: Technology and Applications, Volume V: Manufacturing, Industrial and Management Systems*, CRC Press/Lewis Publishers, Boca Raton, FL, USA, 2002.

COMBINING TEMPORAL ABSTRACTION AND DATA MINING METHODS IN MEDICAL DATA ANALYSIS

TU BAO HO, TRONG DUNG NGUYEN, SAORI KAWASAKI AND SI QUANG LE

1. INTRODUCTION

Medicine has been a traditional domain for artificial intelligence (AI) research and application. It can be observed that the focus on expert systems (ES) in medicine in early days of AI has been changed to intelligent data analysis (IDA) in medicine, especially by machine learning and data mining techniques [Kononenko 01], [Lavrac et al. 97], [Cios 01]. At least, two reasons for the new trend are the bottleneck of knowledge acquisition and the explosive growth of medical databases. Intelligent data analysis in medicine has its own features because of the characteristics of medical data. These characteristics include the incompleteness (missing values), incorrectness (noise in data), sparseness (few and/or non-representable patient records available), and inexactness (inappropriate selection of parameters for a given task). Moreover, medical databases are characterized by the particular constraints and difficulties of the privacy-sensitive, heterogeneous, but voluminous, data of medicine [Cios and Moore 02].

Methods for intelligent data analysis in medicine can be classified into two main categories of data abstraction and data mining [Lavrac et al. 97]. While data abstraction is concerned with the interpretation of raw, mostly numerical data by extracting useful symbolic abstractions, data mining is concerned with analysis and discovery of patterns/models hidden in data [Hand et al. 01].

Recently, data abstraction methods have been mostly concerned with the interpretation of temporal data (temporal abstraction). Temporal abstraction (TA) aims to transform time-stamped data into an interval-based representation of data by extracting their most relevant features. The TA process concerns with abstracting time-stamped data within episodes and it typically extracts states (e.g., low, normal, high) and/or trends (e.g., increase, stable, decrease), as well as finding temporal relationships between findings. Typical TA works include the knowledge-based TA framework [Shahar and Musen 96], [Shahar 97]; methods for context-sensitive and expectation-guided TA [Larizza et al. 97], [Miksch et al. 96], [Horn et al. 97], [Horn 01]; methods for combining statistical and probability techniques with TA [Bellazzi et al. 98], [Bellazzi et al. 00].

Knowledge discovery and data mining (hereafter called data mining)—the rapidly growing interdisciplinary field of computing that evolves from its roots in database management, statistics, and machine learning—aims at finding useful knowledge from large databases. The data mining primary goals of prediction and description are concerned with different tasks such as characterization, discrimination, association, classification, and clustering. Also, there are different tasks of data cleaning, integration, transformation, and reduction in the preprocessing step; and those of interpretation, evaluation, exportation, and visualization of results in the post-processing step [Fayyad et al. 96], [Han and Kamber 01], [Hand et al. 01].

It can be observed that most work on data abstraction and data mining have been done in separation. Most methods on temporal abstraction function on a single attribute and some rather simple analysis can be applied to interpret the abstracted attribute. On the other hand, data mining methods have usually been developed to directly process temporal data [Antunes and Oliveira 01]. However, in some sense, temporal abstraction can be seen as a powerful approach to data preprocessing that could give interpretable and understandable results of data mining. Motivated by a temporal data analysis work in the hepatitis domain, we propose a framework in which the multi-variable temporal data will first be transformed into symbolic ones by temporal abstraction methods, and the abstracted data can then be analyzed by different data mining methods for symbolic data. Within this framework, we developed a novel method of temporal abstraction in the hepatitis domain in which the temporal data were irregularly collected in long periods. Different data mining methods have been applied to abstracted hepatitis data to find patterns/models whose statistical significance were carefully evaluated according to a recent method [Bruzzese and Davino 01].

The hepatitis database collected during 1982–2001 at the Chiba university hospital was recently given to challenge the data mining research [Motoda 02]. It contains results of 771 patients on 983 laboratory tests. The tests are divided into two groups: tests that can suddenly change in short-terms (several days or weeks) and tests that only smoothly change in long-terms (months and years). The hepatitis database is a large un-cleansed temporal relational database consisting of six tables of which the biggest has 1.6 million records. The typical characteristics of these data are their irregularity and long periods of gathering (e.g., twenty years). The doctors posed a number of problems on hepatitis that are expected to be solved by data mining techniques. All existing methods of temporal abstraction are suitable for regular temporal data but not for the hepatitis data.

This chapter presents the framework that links temporal abstraction and data mining methods and its application in the hepatitis domain with a cooperation of between computer scientists and medical experts.

2. TEMPORAL ABSTRACTION AND DATA MINING METHODS

In [Lavrac et al. 97] the authors classified methods for intelligent data analysis in medicine into two main categories:

— *Data abstraction methods*, intended to support specific knowledge-based problem solving activities (data interpretation, diagnosis, prognosis, monitoring, etc.) by extracting useful abstractions from the raw, mostly numeric data. Temporal data abstraction methods represent an important subgroup where the processed data are temporal. The derivation of abstractions is often done in a context sensitive and/or distributed manner and it applies to discrete and continuous supplies of data. Useful types of temporal abstractions are trends, periodic happenings, and other forms of temporal patterns. Temporal abstractions can also be discovered by visualization. The abstraction can be performed over a single case (e.g., a single patient) or over a collection of cases.
— *Data mining methods*, intended to extract knowledge preferably in a meaningful and understandable symbolic form. Most frequently applied methods in this context are supervised symbolic machine learning methods. For example, effective tools for inductive learning exist that can be used to generate understandable diagnostic and prognostic rules. Symbolic clustering, discovery of concept hierarchies, qualitative model discovery, and learning of probabilistic causal networks fit in this framework as well. Sub-symbolic learning and case-based reasoning methods can also be classified in the data mining category. Other frequently applied sub-symbolic methods are the nearest neighbor method, Bayesian classifier, and (non-symbolic) clustering.

2.1. Temporal abstraction methods

The research on data abstraction is motivated by the gap between the highly specific, raw patient data and the highly abstract medical knowledge. On the one hand, data on a particular patient mostly comprise numeric measurements of various parameters at different points in time. On the other hand, medical explicit knowledge is usually expressed in a form of symbolic statements which is as general as possible. To perform any kind of medical problem solving, patient data have to be "matched" against medical knowledge. The process of data abstraction aims to bring the raw patient data to the level of medical knowledge in order to permit the derivation of diagnostic, prognostic or therapeutic conclusions [Lavrac et al. 97]. The notion of data abstraction has the root in the work on heuristics classification [Clancey 85] in which the author defined three types of data abstraction: definitional that involves the essential features of a class of objects; qualitative that involves abstraction over quantitative measures, and generalization that involves abstraction in a hierarchy. These in fact can be considered simple types of data abstraction that are atemporal and often involve a single datum, which is mapped to a more abstract concept. The dimension of time adds a new aspect of complexity to the derivation of (temporal) abstractions. Most temporal abstraction works focus on the derivation of trend abstractions, whereas few is concerned with periodicity abstractions.

In the Shahar and Musen's approach [Shahar and Musen 96], [Shahar 97] the authors have developed a knowledge-based framework for the creation of abstract, interval concepts from time-stamped clinical data. The principles underlying this framework are generality and reusability where the use of knowledge is emphasized. This proposal has been realized in the system RÉSUMÉ. A significant novelty of this approach is the dynamic derivation of interpretation contexts. Interpretation contexts are induced by events, such as therapeutic actions. Abstractions are generated on the basis of interpretation contexts, thus the interpretation of the patient data is context sensitive.

In the Miksch et al. approach [Miksch et al. 96], [Horn et al. 97], unlike the approach by Shahar and Musen, the aim is not to formulate in generic terms a knowledge-based temporal abstraction task. This proposal has been realized in VIE-VENT, a system for data validation and therapy planning for artificially ventilated newborn infants. The overall aim is the context-based validation and interpretation of temporal data, where data can be of different types (continuously assessed quantitative data, discontinuously assessed quantitative data, and qualitative data). The interpretation contexts are not dynamically derived, but they are defined through schemata with thresholds that can be dynamically tailored to the patient under examination. The context schemata correspond to potential treatment regimes; which context is actually active depends on the current regime of the patient.

In the Bellazzi and his colleagues' approach [Larizza et al. 97], [Bellazzi et al. 98], [Bellazzi et al. 00], the authors focus on using and combining statistical and probability techniques in/with temporal abstraction, and applied them to process the diabetes mellitus domain.

Recently, the distributed temporal abstraction system RASTA to facilitate knowledge-driven monitoring of clinical databases has been developed and available at the Stanford University School of Medicine [Connor et al. 01].

2.2. Data mining methods

Knowledge discovery and data mining (KDD, hereafter also called data mining)— the rapidly growing interdisciplinary field of computing that evolves from its roots in database management, statistics, and machine learning—aims at finding useful knowledge from large databases [Fayyad et al. 96b], [Han and Kamber 01], [Hand et al. 01].

The goal of knowledge discovery and data mining is to find interesting patterns and/or models that exist in databases but are hidden among the volumes of data. Concerning the target of data mining, the *interestingness* is characterized by several criteria. Evidence indicates the significance of a finding measured by a statistical criterion. Redundancy amounts to the similarity of a finding with respect to other findings and measures to what degree a finding follows from another one. Usefulness relates a finding to the goal of the users. Novelty includes the deviation from prior knowledge of the user or system. Simplicity refers to the syntactical complexity of the presentation of a finding, and generality is determined [Fayyad et al. 96a].

Knowledge discovery and data mining is done through a complicated *process* containing several steps [Mannila 97], [Fayyad et al. 96a]. The first step is to understand the application domain, to formulate the problem, and to collect data. The second step is to preprocess the data. The third step is that of data mining with the aim of extracting useful knowledge as patterns or models hidden in data. The fourth step is to post-process discovered knowledge. The fifth step is to put discovered knowledge in practical use. These steps are inherently iterative and interactive, i.e., one cannot expect to extract useful knowledge by just pushing a large amount of data into a black box once without the user's participation.

The two primary goals of KDD are *prediction* and *description*. These goals are concerned with different tasks in the data mining step, typically those for characterization, discrimination, association, classification, and clustering. Also, there are different tasks of data cleaning, integration, transformation, and reduction in the preprocessing step; and those of interpretation, evaluation, exportation, and visualization of results in the post-processing step. Moreover, each of these tasks can be done with different methods and algorithms. To solve a given discovery problem, the user usually has to go through these steps several times, each time corresponding to an exploitation of a series of algorithms. KDD methods basically include the following [Fayyad et al. 96a], [Han and Kamber 01]:

– Classification: learning a function that maps a data item into one of several predefined classes.
– Regression: learning a function that maps a data item to a real-valued prediction variable.
– Clustering: a common descriptive task where one seeks to identify a finite set of categories or clusters to describe the data.
– Summarization involves methods for finding a compact description for a subset of data.
– Dependency modeling: consists of finding a model that describes significant dependencies between variables.
– Change and deviation detection: focuses on discovering the most significant changes in the data from previously measured values.

3. THE HEPATITIS DATABASE AND A FRAMEWORK FOR COMBINING TEMPORAL ABSTRACTION WITH DATA MINING METHODS

3.1. The hepatitis database and problems

The database collected during 1982–2001 at the Chiba university hospital was given recently to challenge the data mining research. This temporal relational database contains results of 771 patients on 983 laboratory tests for hepatitis. It is a large uncleansed temporal relational database consisting of six tables of which the biggest has

1.6 million records. Collected during a long period with progress in test equipments, the database also contains inconsistent measurements, many missing values, and a large number of non unified notations. The doctors posed a number of problems on hepatitis that are expected to be investigated by KDD techniques (http://www.cs.helsinki.fi/events/eclpkdd/challenge.html).

The database is broadly split into two categories. The first includes administrative information such as patient's information (age and date of birth), pathological classification of the disease, date of biopsy, result of biopsy, and duration of interferon therapy. The second includes temporal records of blood examination and urinalysis that can be further split into two subcategories, in-hospital and out-hospital examination data. In-hospital examination data contain the results of 230 examinations that were performed using the hospital's equipment. Out-hospital examination data contain the results of 753 examinations, including comments of staffs, performed using special equipment on the other facilities. Consequently, the temporal data contain the results of 983 types of examinations. The database consists of 6 tables in CSV format. A key attribute called MID (masked ID) is included in each of the tables except for *labn_e.csv.*

Table 1. Basic information of patients: pt.csv (total 771 records).
> *Example*: 2, M, 19590220.
> *Meaning*: the patient with MID 2 is male and his birthday is February 20, 1959.

Table 2. Results of biopsy: bio.csv (total 960 records)
> *Example*: 37, 8900, C, 19980611, CAH2B, 1 naika, F3, A2.
> *Meaning*: the patient with MID 37; the specimen collected at 1 naika on June 11, 1998, and assigned an ID of 8900; the type of hepatitis was C, and chronic active hepatitis 2B (CAH2B). The stage of fibrosis was F3, the activity of virus was A2.

Table 3. Information on interferon therapy: ifn.csv (total 198 records)
> *Example*: 2, 1, 19920615, 19921129
> *Meaning*: the record shows the interferon therapy for a patient MID 2; this was his first administration with duration of 6 months (June 15, 1992–November 29, 1992).

Table 4. Results of out-hospital examinations: olab.csv (total 30,243 records)
> *Example*: 1, 19871202, 1, AFP, 1.75, NG/ML 1, 19871202, 1, HBE-AB, 100, +
> *Meaning*: two records of out-hospital examinations for the patient with MID 1, among others; measurements of alpha-fetoprotein (AFP) and hepatitis B virus e antibody (HBE-AB) on December 2, 1987; the measurement units and additional comments are not shown here.

Table 5. Results of in-hospital examinations: ilae.csv (total 1,565,877 records)
> *Example*: 2, 20000228, 1, ALB, 4.1, 2, 20000228, 1, ALP, 170
> *Meaning:* two records of in-hospital examinations for a patient with MID 2, among others; measurements of albumin (ALB) and alkaline phosphatase (ALP) on February 28, 2000; Units and normal values of the measurements are described in the table labn_e.csv.

Table 6. Information about measurements in in-hospital examinations: labn.csv (total 459 records)

Example: ALB, N, 3.9, 5.1, 5, 0, g/dl

Meaning: information regarding the measurement of albumin. The datatype code is N; the normal value of ALB is from 3.9 to 5.1; parameters scale=5 and origin=0 can be used to display the result on a console screen. The unit of ALB measurement is gram per deciliter.

Note that the history of each patient is described as a set of time stamped records which can be obtained by the join operation among tables with keys of patient id and experiment date. The doctor posed the following problems:

P1. Discover the differences in temporal pattern between hepatitis B and C.
P2. Evaluate if laboratory tests can be used to estimate the stages of liver fibrosis.
P3. Evaluate whether the interferon therapy is effective or not
P4. Discover the relationships between the stage of liver fibrosis and the onset of hepatocarcinoma.
P5. Discover the relationships between hematological status and time to the onset of hepatocarcinoma.
P6. Validate if GOT and GPT can be used to measure the inflammation speed.

Each problem requires a special sub-dataset derived from the original hepatitis database.

3.2. Preprocessing for hepatitis data

As the hepatitis database has been collected during a long period with progress in test equipments, it also contains inconsistent measurements, many missing values, and a large number of non unified notations. Such incompleteness has to be handled before any further analysis in order to avoid the misdirection. Our preprocessing includes data cleaning, integration, reduction, and transformation, as well a special preprocessing for extracting sub-datasets for problems under investigation. Table 1 shows a part of integrated data that comprise of temporal sequences.

3.2.1. Feature selection and data reduction

Each patient is described by 983 temporal sequences corresponding to the 983 hospital tests. As the complexity of learning generally increases with the number of tests under investigation, a small number of selected tests is expected. After selecting 41 tests from 983 tests by statistical frequency check and medical background knowledge, we firstly focus on the 15 most typical tests as suggested by medical experts. These tests can then be divided into two groups depending whether their values can change in a short term or long term.

Table 1 Part of integrated table of temporal data

MID	Data	Sex	IFN	GOT	GPT	ALB	ALP	F-ALB	F-B.GL	...
1	19810219	M	n	55	65	5.4	134	n/a	7.0	...
1	19810316	M	n	54	87	5.2	141	n/a	7.7	...
1	19810423	M	n	47	64	5.2	122	68.9	7.1	...
...	...	...		...	...	...	...	...	...	...
1	19920629	M	y	68	100	5.5	123	68.6	7.3	...
...	...	...	...	...	...	...	...	...	...	...
1	20010726	M	n	77	114	4.4	n/a	66.2	5.8	...
2	19920721	F	n	54	82	4.5	304	65.7	7.3	...
...	...	...		...	...	...	...	...	...	...

1. The short-terms changed tests: The tests in this group, GOT, GPT, TTT, and ZTT, in particular GOT and GPT, can rapidly change (within several days or weeks) their values to high or even very high values when liver cells were destroyed by inflammation.
2. The long-term changed tests: The tests in this group can slowly change (within months or years). Liver has the reserve capacity so that some products of liver (T-CHO, CHE, ALB, and TP) do not have low values until its reserve capacity is exhaustive (the terminal state of chronic hepatitis, i.e., liver cirrhosis). Two kind of tests in this group are:
   – Going down tests: T-CHO, CHE, ALB, TP, PLT, WBC, and HGB.
   – Going up tests: D-BIL, I-BIL, T-BIL, and ICG-15.

3.2.2. Extraction of data subsets

The data extraction aims to create an appropriate dataset for solving each of problems P1-P3. These are supervised datasets where each patient's data correspond to temporal sequences of test values and the patient has a value of the class attribute such as "type B" or "type C" of hepatitis (problem P1); "F0", "F1", "F2", "F3" and "F4" of fibrosis stages (problem P2); "response", "partial response", "aggravation", and "no change" of the interferon therapy (problem P3). These class values for P1 and P3 can be directly extracted from the original database, while those for P2 need to be derived from temporal sequences according to the conditions defined by experts.

The extraction of data subsets deeply depends on the domain context. It is important to recall that the result of temporal abstraction also strongly depends on how episodes on which data are abstracted were taken. In this research we usually investigated the episode of 5 years (with some other trials up to 10 years) according to the suggestion of medical doctors. As the goal of the problem P1 is to find the set of historical sequences of some tests to explain hepatitis B or C, the sequence of each test was forwardly taken from its beginning point to the point where the sequence reaches the episode length. In cases of problems P2 and P3, the sequences were backwardly taken from the biopsy date or the starting day of interferon therapy, respectively, to the point where the sequence reaches the episode length.

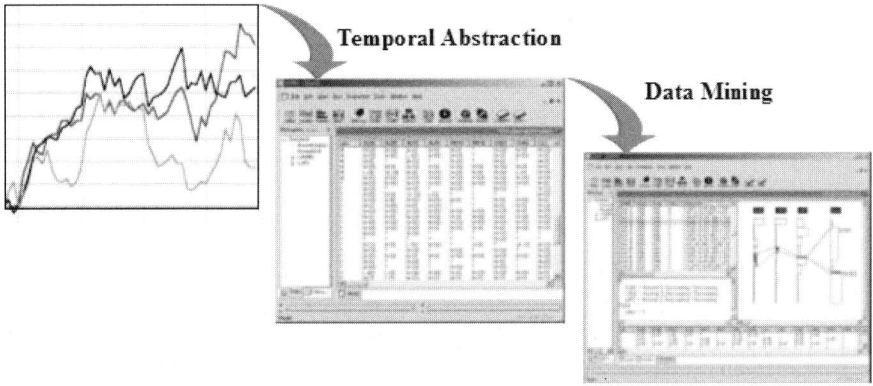

Figure 1. Framework for combining temporal abstraction and data mining methods.

The complete solution to these problems requires different TA methods for processing short-term changed tests and long-term changed tests.

3.3. A framework on combining temporal abstraction and data mining methods

Figure 1 presents our framework for analysis of medical temporal data. The framework comprises of two steps. The first is to abstract temporal data into abstracted symbolic data, and the second is to use suitable symbolic data mining methods to analyze the abstracted data. Though temporal abstraction methods are context-sensitive, the framework is applicable to different situations when the temporal abstractions methods are appropriate. In next sections we described an application to the hepatitis domain.

4. A TEMPORAL ABSTRACTION METHOD IN THE HEPATITIS DOMAIN

After having the preprocessed data subsets with test sequences taken in the given episodes, the task of basic TA is to find abstractions of those sequences. Our basic idea to abstract a sequence is to map it into a set of abstraction patterns viewed as combinations of TA primitives in subsequences. To this end, our method consists of two parts: (1) to determine typical abstraction patterns; and (2) to assign each test sequence into one of abstraction patterns.

4.1. Determination of typical abstraction patterns

This problem can be stated as follows: Is it possible to determine a small number of typical abstraction patterns to be used to characterize most real sequences observed. In our opinion, the solution to such a problem can be well obtained by a combination of TA primitive computation with human inspection using visual tools.

4.1.1. The TA primitives

The TA primitives are commonly used in temporal abstraction and mainly concern with the states and trends of sequences.

A test value can lie in the normal region determined by medical doctors (with upper and lower bounds) or out of the normal region (high or low regions). Consequently, the state of any sequence or subsequence can be judged with the following TA state primitives: N (normal), L (low), VL (very low), XL (extreme low), H (high), VH (very high), and XH (extreme high). Note that the thresholds to determine these primitives are greatly different with respect to different tests.

The thresholds to distinguish the state primitives of tests are given by medical doctors, for example, those to distinguish values N, H, VH, XH of "total protein" are 5.5, 6.5, 8.2, 9.2 where (5.5, 6.5) is the normal region. The long-term changed tests, whose values tend to gradually and smoothly change, usually have values of "N", "L" and "H" of the state primitives because the extremely far values hardly occur. The values of "VH", "XH", "VL" and "XL" basically can be observed in short-term changed tests.

In this work we consider the following TA trend primitives of long-term changed tests: S (stable), I (increasing), FI (fast increasing), D (decreasing), and FD (fast decreasing).

4.1.2. Observation and determination of abstraction patterns

In case of hepatitis data, the sequences taken in long episodes usually have complex changes. Our approach to determination of abstraction patterns is based on careful observations and analysis of various real sequences. To this end, we created a simple tool in MATLAB for visualizing the sequences of tests in a given episode. As preliminary work, we observed almost sequences of patient's test values in the hepatitis database to get an idea about the possible abstraction patterns.

In case of long-term changed tests, we have observed two main groups of sequences. One is a group of sequences that greatly fluctuate between the boundaries of the normal range. The other is a group of sequences that smoothly change between the normal, high or low regions. In case of short-term changed tests, the move is sometimes very rapid and the deviation from the base line of the sequence is very big. The baseline of a sequence often keeps a same level from the boundary in case it is out of the normal region but the distance from the normal boundary varies.

Our basic views in abstraction patterns is the proposed notions "change of state" to characterize long-term changed tests sequences, and the notion of "base state" and "peaks" to characterize the short-term changed tests sequences. For the short-term changed tests, a new state primitive, denoted by "P", indicates whether peaks appear in a given sequence.

4.1.3. Relations between TA primitives

By observations and visual analysis we detected and formulated four kinds of relations between primitives:

"change state to" (>): shows that the state of a sequence changes from one region to another region. This relation can occur in long-term changed tests.
"and" (&): connects a state primitive and the peak primitive, and occurs in short-term changed tests.

<pattern> ::= <state primitive>

<pattern> ::= <state primitive> <relation> | <state primitive> | <trend primitive>

<pattern> ::= <state primitive> <relation> <peak>

<pattern> ::= <state primitive> <relation> <state primitive> <relation> |

<state primitive> | <trend primitive>

Figure 2. Structure of abstraction patterns.

"**and then**" (−): connects a state primitive and a trend primitive in long-term changed tests. It expresses a trend in the sequence that does not change to another state ever after.

"**majority/minority**" (/): connects two adjoining states for describing sequences of long-term changed tests that fluctuate in the boundary of two regions. The state before the primitive "/" is the state where majority of points in the sequence belong to. For example, "X/Y" means that the majority of points are in state X and the minority of points is in state Y.

By analyzing various available sequences, we formulated four possible structures of abstraction patterns that can be used to represent most hepatitis sequences.

Here are examples of abstraction patterns:

"ALB = N" (ALB is in the normal region),

"CHE = H-I" (CHE is in the high region and then increasing),

"GPT = XH&P" (GPT is extremely high and with peaks),

"I-BIL = N>L>N" (I-BIL is in the normal region, then changed to the low region, and finally changed to the normal region).

Figure 3 shows the procedure developed and used to identify typical abstraction patterns.

After applying the procedure and consulting medical doctors, we tentatively determined 8 typical abstraction patterns were determined for short-term changed tests as shown in Figure 4, and 22 typical patterns for long-term changed tests shown in Figure 5.

Our key idea is to use the "change of state" to characterize sequences of the long-term changed tests. The "change of state" contains information of both state and trend, and can compactly characterize the sequence. We firstly distinguish two kinds of sequences: those fluctuate around the boundary of the normal region and those do not. The latter can then be observed if at their beginning, the first data points take which of the three states "N", "H", or "L". It will happen that either the sequence changes from one state to another state, smoothly or variably (at boundaries), or the sequence remains in its initial state without changing.

1. Consider the abstraction patterns structures as formulas and the <state primitive>, <trend primitive> and <relation> as their variables. Create all possible candidate abstraction patterns by replacing the <state primitive>, <trend primitive> and <relation> with their possible values.

2. Randomly take a large number of sequences from the datasets, visualize and manually match them with the candidate abstraction patterns to see each of them matches which candidate abstraction pattern.

3. Eliminate the candidate abstraction patterns that have no or a small number of matched sequences.

Figure 3. Procedure for determining typical abstraction patterns.

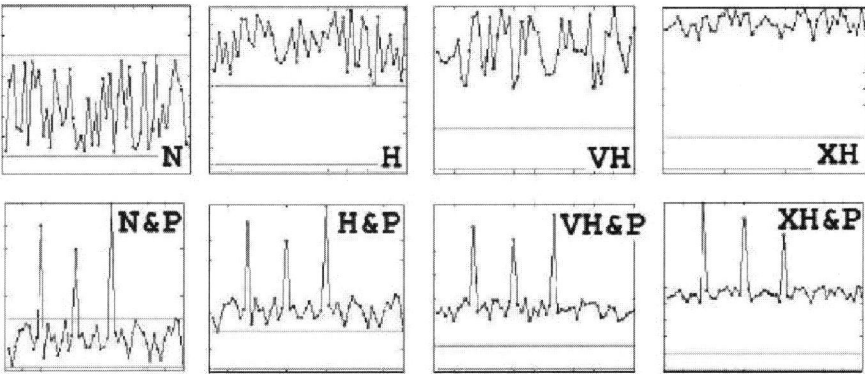

Figure 4. Typical abstraction patterns for short-term changed tests.

We determined four groups of abstraction patterns for long-term changed tests:

– "Varying states": Consisting of patterns that fluctuate around the boundary of the normal region (N/H, H/N, N/L, L/N):
– "Change from high state": Consisting of abstraction patterns H−S, H−I, H−D, H>N, H>N>H;
– "Change from low state": Consisting of abstraction patterns L-S, L−D, L−I, L>N, L>N>L;
– "Change from normal state": Consisting of abstraction patterns N, N>H, N>H−D, N>H>N, N>L, N>L>N, N>L−I.

4.2. Temporal abstraction algorithms for extracting abstraction patterns

The second step in our TA method is to assign each test sequence into one of abstraction patterns. The algorithm described in Figure 6 and Figure 7, which is intrinsically based

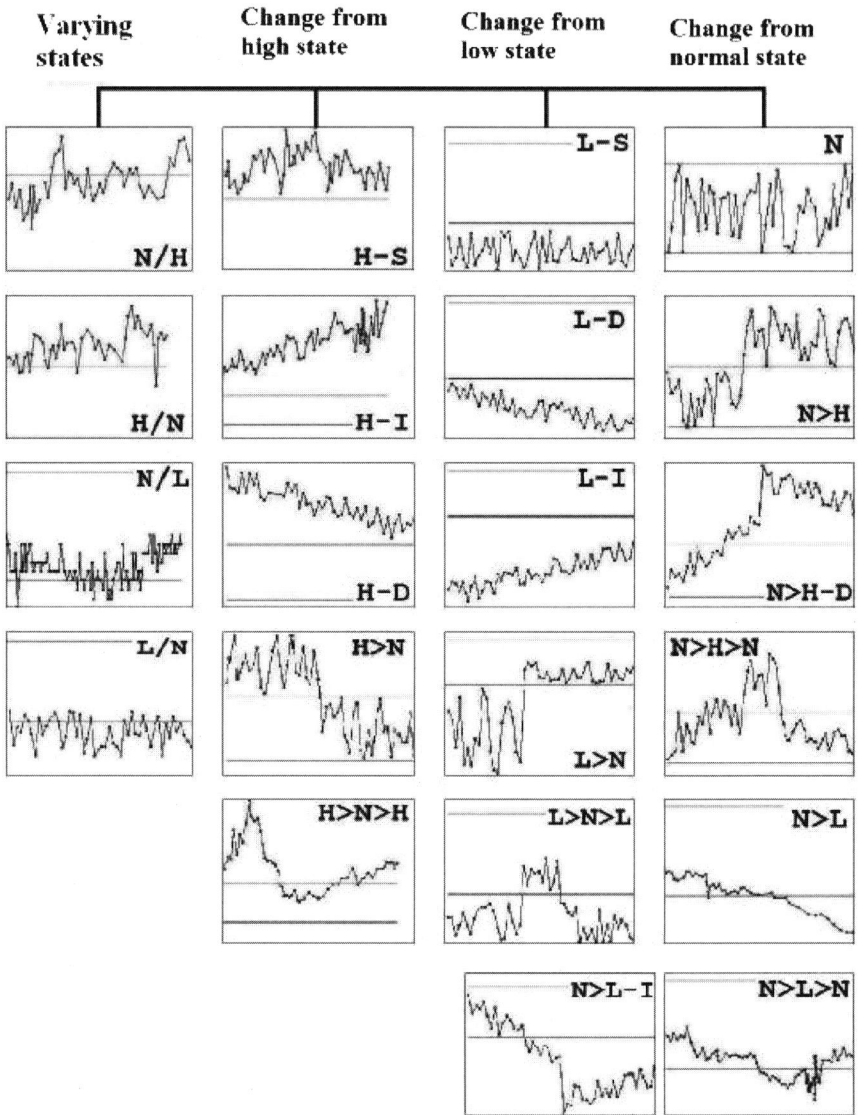

Figure 5. Typical abstraction patterns for long-term changed tests.

on the properties of hepatitis long-term and short-term changed tests, allow to us to do this task.

4.2.1. Notations and parameters used in the algorithms

The basic idea of the algorithm is as follows: If the sequence is not fluctuated around the boundary of the normal region, specify its state at the beginning and at the end

Algorithm 1 (for short-term changed tests)

Input: A sequence of values of a test (of a patient) with length N denoted as $S_{00} = \{s_1, s_2, \ldots, s_n\}$ in a given episode.

Output: A base state, a set of peaks PE_i, and an abstracted pattern derived from the sequence.

Parameters: NU, HU, VHU, XHU: upper thresholds of normal, high, very high, extreme high regions of a test, and α (real).

A. Searching for the base state

1. Based on NU, HU, VHU, and XHU, calculate the corresponding populations Normal(S), High(S), VeryHigh(S), and ExtremeHigh(S).
2. MV = max {Normal(S), High(S), VeryHigh(S), ExtremeHigh(S)}. **If** MV/Total(S) $\geq \alpha$ **then** BS = MS.
3. Else BS := NULL

B. Searching for peaks

4. **For** every element s_i of S, **if** $s_i > s_{i-1}$ and $s_i > s_{i+1}$ **then** s_i is a local maximum of S.
5. **For** every element ms_i of the set of local maximum points, $PE_i = ms_i$ will be a peak if one of the following conditions is true, where V(x), S(x) is the value and state of x, respectively:
    i.   BS = N $\wedge$ S(ms_i) = VH or higher
    ii. BS = H $\wedge$ S(ms_i) = XH or higher
    iii. BS = VH $\wedge$ V(ms_i) $\geq$ 2*XHU
    iv. BS = XH $\wedge$ V(ms_i) $\geq$ 4*XHU

C. Output the basic temporal abstraction pattern

6. **If** BS = N $\wedge$ there is no peak, **then** N
7. **If** BS = N $\wedge$ there is at least a peak, **then** N&P
8. **If** BS = H $\wedge$ there is no peak, **then** H
9. **If** BS = H $\wedge$ there is at least a peak, **then** H&P
10. **If** BS = VH $\wedge$ there is no peak, **then** VH
11. **If** BS = VH $\wedge$ there is at least a peak, **then** VH&P
12. **If** BS = XH $\wedge$ there is no peak, **then** XH
13. **If** BS = XH $\wedge$ there is at least a peak, **then** XH&P
14. **If** BS = NULL **then** Undetermined.

Figure 6. Basic TA algorithm for short-term changed tests.

subsequences as well as the changes in the middle in order to match it with the abstraction patterns. To this end, a number of intermediate functions are defined on the sequence S.

Functions

- High(S): # points of S in the high region
- VeryHigh(S): # points of S in the very high region
- ExtremeHigh(S): # points of S in the extreme high region
- Low(S): # points of S in the low region
- VeryLow(S): # points of S in the very low region
- Normal(S): # points of S in the normal region
- Total(S) = High(S) + VeryHigh(S) + ExtremeHigh(S) + Normal(S) + Low(S) + VeryLow(S)
- In(S) = Normal(S)/Total(S)

Input: A sequence of patient's values of a test $S_{00} = \{s_1, s_2, ..., s_n\}$ in a given episode.

Output: An abstracted pattern of the sequence derived from the sequence.

Parameters: α, δ, ε, σ (integer), β (real)

Notations: $S_{10} = [s_1,$ median$]$, $S_{20} = [$median$, s_n]$, $S_{11} = [s_1,$ 1st quartile$]$, $S_{12} = [$1st quartile, median$]$, $S_{21} = [$median, 3rd quartile$]$, $S_{22} = [$3rd quartile, $s_n]$

A. Identification of patterns with many crosses

2. **If** $Cross(S_{00}) > \alpha \wedge In(S_{00}) > Out(S_{00}) \wedge High(S_{00}) > Low(S_{00})$ **then** N/H
3. **If** $Cross(S_{00}) > \alpha \wedge In(S_{00}) > Out(S_{00}) \wedge High(S_{00}) < Low(S_{00})$ **then** N/L
4. **If** $Cross(S_{00}) > \alpha \wedge In(S_{00}) < Out(S_{00}) \wedge High(S_{00}) > Low(S_{00})$ **then** H/N
5. **If** $Cross(S_{00}) > \alpha \wedge In(S_{00}) < Out(S_{00}) \wedge High(S_{00}) < Low(S_{00})$ **then** L/N

B. Identification of patterns without many crosses

6. **If** $In(S_{00}) > \beta$ **then N**
7. **If** $Out(S_{00}) > \beta \wedge State(S_{00}) = H \wedge Trend(S_{00}) = S$ **then** H–S
8. **If** $Out(S_{00}) > \beta \wedge State(S_{00}) = H \wedge Trend(S_{00}) = I$ **then** H–I
9. **If** $Out(S_{00}) > \beta \wedge State(S_{00}) = H \wedge Trend(S_{00}) = D \wedge Last(S_{22}) = H$ **then** H–D
10. **If** $Out(S_{00}) > \beta \wedge State(S_{00}) = L \wedge Trend(S_{00}) = S$ **then** L–S
11. **If** $Out(S_{00}) > \beta \wedge State(S_{00}) = L \wedge Trend(S_{00}) = D$ **then** L–D
12. **If** $Out(S_{00}) > \beta \wedge State(S_{00}) = L \wedge Trend(S_{00}) = I \wedge Last(S_{22}) = L$ **then** L–I

C. Identification of patterns with changes from the normal region

12. **If** $First_\sigma(S_{00}) = N \wedge Cross(S_{00}) < \alpha \wedge Last_\sigma(S_{22}) = H \wedge Trend(S_{22}) = I \wedge Low(S_{00}) < \varepsilon$ **then** N>H
13. **If** $First_\sigma(S_{00}) = N$ & $Cross(S_{00}) < \alpha$ & $Last_\sigma(S_{22}) = H$ & $Trend(S_{22}) = D \wedge Low(S_{00}) < \varepsilon$ **then** N>H–D
14. **If** $First_\sigma(S_{00}) = N \wedge Cross(S_{00}) < \alpha \wedge High(S_{00}) > \delta \wedge Last_\sigma(S_{22}) = N \wedge Trend(S_{22}) = D \wedge Low(S_{00}) < \varepsilon$ **then** N>H>N
15. **If** $First_\sigma(S_{00}) = N \wedge Cross(S_{00}) < \alpha \wedge Last_\sigma(S_{22}) = L \wedge Trend(S_{22}) = D \wedge High(S_{00}) < \varepsilon$ **then** N>L
16. **If** $First_\sigma(S_{00}) = N \wedge Cross(S_{00}) < \alpha \wedge Last_\sigma(S_{22}) = L \wedge Trend(S_{22}) = I \wedge High(S_{00}) < \varepsilon$ **then** N>L–I
17. **If** $First_\sigma(S_{00}) = N \wedge Cross(S_{00}) < \alpha \wedge Low(S_{00}) > \delta \wedge Last_\sigma(S_{22}) = N \wedge Trend(S_{22}) = I \wedge High(S_{00}) < \varepsilon$ **then** N>L>N

D. Identification of patterns with changes from the high region

18. **If** $First_\sigma(S_{00}) = H \wedge Cross(S_{00}) < \alpha \wedge Last_\sigma(S_{22}) = N \wedge Low(S_{00}) < \varepsilon$ **then** H>N
19. **If** $First_\sigma(S_{00}) = H \wedge Cross(S_{00}) < \alpha \wedge Normal(S_{00}) > \delta \wedge Last_\sigma(S_{22}) = H \wedge Trend(S_{22}) = I \wedge Low(S_{00}) < \varepsilon$ **then** H>N>H

E. Identification of patterns with changes from the low region

20. **If** $First_\sigma(S_{00}) = L \wedge Cross(S_{00}) < \alpha \wedge Last_\sigma(S_{22}) = N \wedge Low(S_{00}) < \varepsilon$ **then** L>N
21. **If** $First_\sigma(S_{00}) = L \wedge Cross(S_{00}) < \alpha \wedge Normal(S_{00}) > \delta \wedge Last_\sigma(S_{22}) = L \wedge Trend(S_{22}) = D \wedge High(S_{00}) < \varepsilon$ **then** L>N>L
22. **If** NULL **Then** Undetermined.

Figure 7. Basic TA algorithm for long-term changed tests.

– Cross(S): # times S crosses the upper and lower boundaries of the normal region
– $First_\sigma$(S): State of the subsequence with length σ from the first point of S
– $Last_\sigma$(S): State of the subsequence with length σ from the last point of S
– State(S): State of S (one of the state primitives)
– Trend(S): Trend of S (one of trend primitives)

Parameters

The following parameters (thresholds) α, δ, ε, σ (integer), and β (real) are used in the algorithm whose values are dynamically and experimentally specified in relation with the length n of the sequence.

α : Threshold regarding the number of times the sequence crosses the boundaries of the normal region.

$$\alpha = \begin{cases} 0.3 \times n & \text{if } n \in \{10, \ldots, 30\} \\ 0.2 \times n & \text{if } n \in \{31, \ldots, 60\} \\ 0.11 \times n & \text{if } n \in \{61, \ldots, 100\} \\ 0.1 \times n & \text{if } n > 100 \end{cases}$$

β : Threshold regarding the ratio of points in the sequence being in or out of the normal region.

δ : Threshold regarding the number of sequence points that are in the high region. We employed $\delta = \alpha$

ε : Threshold regarding the number of sequence points that are in the low region. We employed $\varepsilon = \alpha/2$

σ : Threshold regarding the length of the first or last subsequences. By default we take σ as 6 months.

The algorithms are context-sensitive and depend on the parameters. With the parameters taken as mentioned above, most testing sequences were correctly identified, and only a few sequences were undetermined.

4.2.2. Abstraction of short-term changed tests

Our observation and analysis showed that the short term changed tests, especially GPT and GOT, can go up in some very short period of time and then go back to some "stable" state. We found that the two most representative characteristics of these tests are that of a "stable" state, called *base state* (BS), and the position and value of *peaks*, where the tests suddenly go up. Based on this remark, we develop the following algorithm to find the base state and peaks of a short term changed test (Figure 6).

For the sake of simplicity, we have used 9 above values for abstraction. They would be extended in future work for representing more complex situations.

4.3. Abstraction of long-term changed tests

The key idea is to use the "change of state" as the main feature to characterize sequences of the long-term changed tests. The "change of state" contains information of both state and trend, and can compactly characterize the sequence.

At the beginning of a sequence, the first data points can be at one of the three states "N", "H", or "L". It will happen that:

– Either the sequence changes from one state to another state, smoothly or variably (at boundaries),
– Or the sequence remains in its state without changing.

As changes can generally happen in long-term, it is possible to consider the trend of a sequence after changing of the state.

The complex temporal abstractions in our framework are achieved by applying data mining algorithms to the datasets obtained by basic TA algorithms. The data mining systems to be applied here are the rule induction program LUPC of system D2MS [Ho et al. 01] and association rule in the system Clementine [SPSS 02].

5. MINING ABSTRACTED DATA BY DATA MINING METHODS

5.1. The statistical significance of discovered knowledge

The complex temporal abstractions in our framework are achieved by applying data mining algorithms to the datasets obtained by basic TA algorithms. The data mining systems to be applied here are the rule induction program LUPC of system D2MS [Ho et al. 01] and the association mining program in system Clementine. As usual, large numbers of association rules or prediction rules were found. A critical question is which of them are statistically significant and were not found due to chance?

Several works have been done on this topic of evaluating the statistical significance of discovered prediction rules or pruning discovered associations. In [Megiddo and Srikant 98] the authors tested the hypothesis on the proportion of database that contains a given item in association rules. In [Liu et al. 99] the authors tested the independence of associations summarized them as DS rules. Also, in [Liu et al. 01] they proposed to test the stability of rules over time by evaluating rules obtained on data subsets partitioned in by sub-periods of time. In [Gediga and Duntsch 02] the authors considered the null hypothesis that objects are randomly assigned to classes and a randomization technique was developed to evaluate the significance of rules. In this work we employed the method of evaluation of statistical significance in [Bruzzese and Davino 01] that performs three kinds of hypothesis testing:

1. the significance of the consequence of the rule;
2. the significance of antecedent of the rule; and
3. the significance of the accuracy/confidence of the rule.

The method can be summarized as follows. An association rule R is an implication of the form $A \rightarrow C$ where the antecedent part A and the consequence part C are conjunctions of attribute-value pairs (items), and $A \cap C = \emptyset$. Two main measures of support and confidence of R are computed by $S_R = \frac{n_R}{n}$ and $C_R = \frac{n_R}{n_A}$, respectively, where n_R is the number of instances that contain $A \cup C$ and n_A is the number of instances that contain A.

Table 2 Statistically significant associations by using four tests

Problems	# discovered rules	# rules after pruning	# rules pruned by M1	# rules pruned by M2	# rules pruned by M3	# rules pruned by M4
Type B and C	33,447	27 (0.08%)	6,231	7,073	15,979	4,135
Fibrosis stage	15,563	43 (0.28%)	5,419	4,250	5,780	71
Interferon	22,870	28 (0.12%)	19,171	2601	982	88

The first test for the significance of the rule consequence is to compare the rule confidence (C_R) with the rule consequence part (S_C) by the hypotheses $H_0 : C_R = S_C$, $H_1 : C_R > S_C$, and the test statistic $V_{cons} = \frac{C_R - S_C}{\sqrt{\frac{S_C(1-S_C)}{n_A}}}$.

The second test for significance of rule antecedence when different rules share the same antecedent part by comparing the observed frequencies n_R with the theoretical uniform frequencies. The χ^2 statistic is used $\chi^2 = \sum_{i=1}^{R_A} \frac{(n^*_{R(i)} - \hat{n}_{R(i)})^2}{\hat{n}_{R(i)}}$ with $R_A - 1$ degrees of freedom. The third test significance of the accuracy/confidence of the rule is to compare the rule support S_R with the rule antecedent part support S_A by the hypotheses $H_0 : S_R = S_A$, $H_1 : S_R > S_A$ and the test statistic $V_{conf} = \frac{S_R - S_A}{\sqrt{\frac{S_A(1-S_A)}{n}}}$.

We applied four different tests M1 [Liu et al. 99], M2 and M3 (the first and the third tests in [Bruzzese and Davino 01], and M4 (our proposed test to associations that have the antecedent parts included in each others) to the set of all discovered associations in order to select the statistically significant ones.

Table 2 shows the summary of statistically significant associations obtained by applying these four tests. There is a small number of associations remained after the tests. For example, there are only 0.08%, 0.05% and 0.11% of huge numbers of discovered associations are considered statistically significant with level 95%, 2.47% and 2.65% for the problems P1, P2, and P3, respectively.

5.2. Mining abstracted hepatitis data with system D2MS and Clementine

D2MS is a visual data mining system with visualization support for model selection [Ho et al. 01]. D2MS facilitates the trials of various alternatives of algorithm combinations and their settings. The data mining methods in D2MS consists of programs CABRO for tree learning and LUPC for rule learning. CABRO produces decision trees using R-measure and graphically represents them in particular with T2.5D tool (trees 2.5 dimension). LUPC is a separate-and-conquer algorithm that controls the induction process by several parameters that allow obtaining different results. This ability supports the user plays a central role in the mining process.

For the problem P1, different datasets were found by using LUPC with different parameters. Figure 8 illustrates one of rules describing the type C of hepatitis found by LUPC in D2MS. Table 3 shows typical discovered associations considered as statistically significant by the four tests with levels 95%, 90%, and 85%. Each rule in the table is

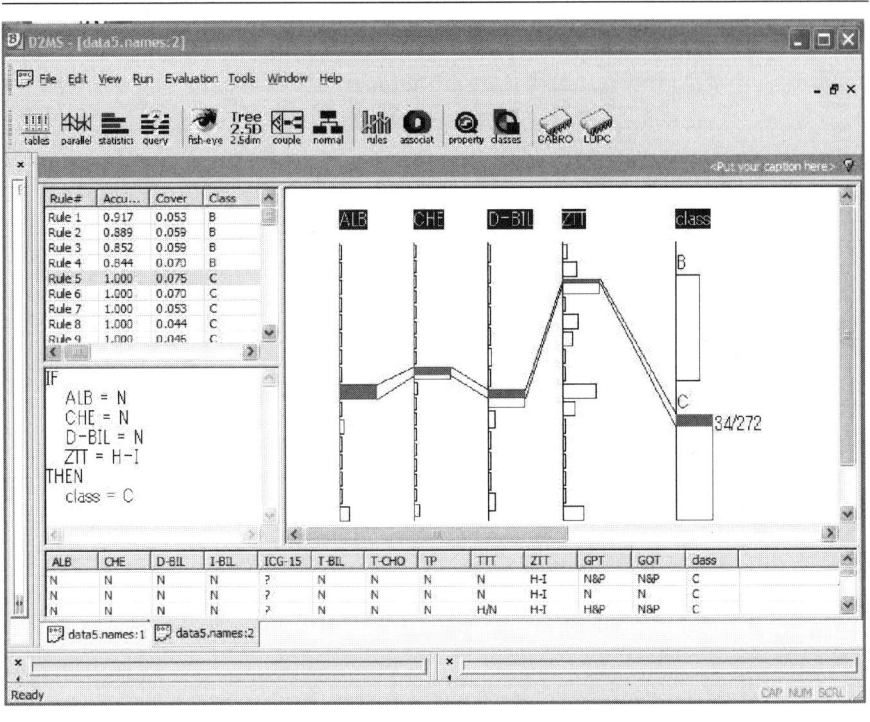

Figure 8. A rule describing type C of hepatitis.

shown with the class B or C and the statistically significance level, a conjunction of attribute-values pairs, the accuracy, the numbers of corrected and covered cases.

Some remarks can be drawn among others:

- A few rules found are statistically significant in terms of the employed evaluation methods. The 27 rules, selected from 33,447 discovered rules, passed all the four tests and they are considerable findings on hepatitis.
- Several simple rules such as No. 2, CHE = N→HCV (α = 95%), No. 10 and 11, CHE = H/N or N/H→HBV (α = 90%) give a rough distinction of groups of HBV and HCV.
- The tests GOT, GPT, CHE, D-BIL, TTT, and ZTT often occur in rules that distinguish types B and C of hepatitis.
- Rules for type B often cover a smaller number of cases than those for type C.

For the problem P2 and P3 we also found a number of statistically significant rules by D2MS. Figure 9 presents a decision tree learnt by CABRO for the problem P2, and represented in tree visualizer T2.5D. In the T2.5D representation, some sub-trees

Table 3 Some statistically significant discovered rules for types B and C

No.	class	T-CHO	CHE	GOT	GPT	CHE	TTT	ZTT	D-BIL	T-BIL	I-BIL	TP	acc	ratio
1	C (95%)	N											0.66	171/260
2	C (95%)		N										0.72	183/256
3	C (95%)			H					N				0.73	180/248
4	C (95%)				H								0.76	89/117
5	C (95%)					N							0.76	78/103
6	C (95%)								N				0.82	142/173
7	C (95%)						N	H/N					0.92	11/12
8	C (95%)				H					N/H			0.93	14/15
9	B (95%)				H&P			H/N					0.92	11/12
10	B (90%)							N					0.68	63/93
11	B (90%)		H/N										0.7	14/20
12	B (90%)		N/H										0.74	23/31
13	B (90%)			N&P	H&P								0.7	16/23
14	B (90%)							N/H	N				0.88	7/8
15	C (90%)		N				N						0.8	67/84
16	C (90%)		N					H-I	N				0.95	63/66
17	C (90%)			H	XH								0.92	11/12
18	C (90%)		N	N						N			0.93	26/28
19	C (90%)						H-I					N/H	0.81	35/43
20	C (90%)						N				N		0.93	25/27
21	C (85%)			N	N&P								0.69	33/40
22	C (85%)		N	H									0.84	41/49
23	C (85%)		N										0.87	58/67
24	C (85%)				XH		H/N				N		0.79	23/29
25	C (85%)												0.72	18/25
26	C (85%)	N/L											0.8	28/35
27	C (85%)							H-D					0.83	33/40

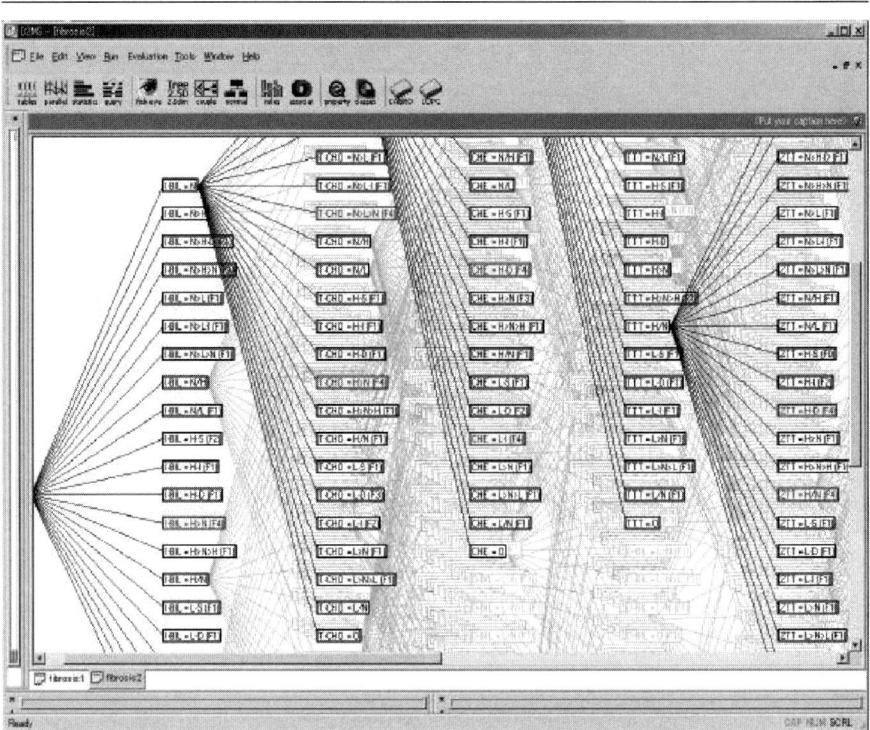

Figure 9. A decision tree learned by CABRO for describing fibrosis stages.

of interest are displayed in a 2D space while the whole tree is displayed in a virtual 3D space. The figure shows a focus on paths leading to fibrosis stage F4 (read leaf nodes). In next section we analyze the results of P2 obtained by association rule learning.

The complex temporal abstraction can be done by different data mining and machine learning methods depending on the purpose. Together with using D2MS we also used Clementine and See5 [SPSS 02] to investigate the abstracted hepatitis data, in particular the association rule mining for problems P2 and P3 because the number of patients taking biopsy (P2) or interferon therapy (P3) is much smaller than the number of hepatitis types B or C, and consequently there are less cases to investigate P2 and P3.

Using the Apriori program we have discovered several interesting properties of hepatitis. Table 4 shows a number of statistically significant associations on fibrosis stages (P2). Among these only one association was considered as statistically significant for the fibrosis state F4 while more associations were statistically significant for the fibrosis stage F1. Table 5 shows selected associations obtained when investigating the problem P3 on the effectiveness of interferon therapy. Only associations for the class "response" were validated with statistical significance among them many are with high support and confidence.

Table 4 Statistically significant associations on fibrosis stages (significance level 90%)

Class	ALB	CHE	GOT	GPT	D-BIL	I-BIL	T-BIL	T-CHO	TP	TTT	ZTT	acc	cover
F3			H&P	H&P	Z		Z	Z				0.8	0.019
F3	N		H&P	H&P	Z		Z	Z				0.8	0.019
F3		N	H&P	H&P	Z	Z	Z	Z				0.8	0.019
F3	N		H&P	H&P	Z	Z	Z	Z				0.8	0.019
F3	N	N	H&P	H&P	Z	Z	Z	Z	Z			0.8	0.019
F3		N	H&P	H&P	Z	Z	Z	Z	Z			0.8	0.019
F4					Z			N/L	Z			0.8	0.019
F4	N				Z			N/L	Z			0.8	0.019
F4	N			VH&P	Z			N/L	Z			0.8	0.019
F1	N	N	N&P	VH&P					Z			0.67	0.036
F1	N	N	N&P					N	Z			0.67	0.036
F1		N	H	H		Z	Z		Z	Z		0.67	0.036
F1	N		H	H			Z		Z	H-I		0.67	0.036
F1			H	H		Z	Z		Z	Z		0.67	0.036
F1	N		H	H			Z		Z	Z		0.67	0.036
F1	N	N	H	H		Z	Z		Z	Z		0.67	0.036
F1			H	H			Z		Z	Z		0.67	0.036
F1	N	N	H			Z	Z		Z	Z		0.67	0.036
F1	N		N&P				Z			Z		0.67	0.036
F1			N&P							Z		0.9	0.04
F1	N					Z	Z			Z		0.9	0.04
F1		N				Z				Z	H-I	0.67	0.045
F1	N	N				Z	Z			Z	H-I	0.67	0.045
F1	N					Z	Z			Z	H-I	0.67	0.045
F1		N				Z	Z			Z	H-I	0.67	0.045
F1	N	N								Z	H-I	0.67	0.045
F1	N	N								Z	H-I	0.67	0.045
F1	N	N								Z	H-I	0.67	0.045
F1		N								Z	H-I	0.67	0.045
F1	N				Z				Z	Z	H-I	0.67	0.045
F1	N				Z				Z	Z	H-I	0.67	0.045
F1	N	N	N&P									0.65	0.058
F1	N		N&P									0.65	0.058

Table 5 Statistically significant associations on effectiveness of interferon therapy (significance level 90%)

Class	ALB	CHE	GOT	GPT	D-BIL	I-BIL	T-BIL	T-CHO	TP	TTT	ZTT	acc	cover
response				H					N		H-I	0.95	0.15
response	N			H					N		H-I	0.95	0.15
response				H		N					H-I	0.95	0.15
response	N	Z	H				Z	Z			H-I	0.95	0.15
response		Z	H			N	Z	Z			H-I	0.95	0.15
response	N	Z	H			N	Z	Z			H-I	0.95	0.15
response			H		N		Z	Z			H-I	0.96	0.18
response			H		N	N	Z	Z			H-I	0.96	0.18
response	N		H				Z	Z			H-I	0.96	0.19
response	N		H				Z	Z			H-I	0.96	0.19
response		Z					Z	Z			H-I	0.93	0.2
response	N	Z	H	H			Z	Z	N			0.93	0.2
response	N	Z	H	H			Z	Z	N			0.93	0.2
response			H			N	Z	Z	N			0.93	0.2
response	N	Z	H	H		N	Z	Z			H-I	0.93	0.2
response	N					N	Z	Z				0.93	0.2
response			H	H		N	Z	Z	N		H-I	0.93	0.2
partial response		Z	H						H/N			0.67	0.02
partial response		Z	H	H					H/N	Z		0.67	0.02
partial response					N				N/H	Z		0.67	0.02
partial response			H						N/H		H-I	0.67	0.02
partial response			H						N/H	Z		0.67	0.02
partial response				H					H/N		H-I	0.67	0.02
no response			H		N	N					N	0.67	0.02
no response			H		N						N	0.67	0.02
no response					N/H			Z			H-I	0.67	0.02

6. CONCLUSIONS

Both data abstraction and data mining are key technologies receiving considerable attentions in medical data analysis. The framework introduced in this chapter to combine methods of temporal abstraction and data mining in analyzing medical data has shown its practical value. In particular, we developed a novel temporal abstraction method for data irregularly collected in long periods in the hepatitis domain, and we applied mining methods to data abstracted. The findings by this combination were positively evaluated by medical doctors in terms of novelty, acceptability and utility. The results were considered new and interesting, and the sets of rules partially answered the problems in hepatitis research.

The temporal abstraction approach presented in this paper is carried out in the scope of an on going project in collaboration with medical doctors. The issues to be investigated in the next step include refinement of abstracted patterns (for example, positions of peaks or parameters for abstraction), the post-processing and interpretation of obtained temporal abstractions. The framework can be extended to similar circumstances in medical data analysis.

7. ACKNOWLEDGMENTS

This research is supported by the project "Realization of Active Mining in the Era of Information Flood", Grant-in-aid for scientific research on priority areas (B). The authors would like to express their sincere thanks to doctors Katsuhiko Takabayashi and Hideto Yokoi of Chiba University Hospital for their guidance and collaboration.

REFERENCES

[Antunes and Oliveira 01] Antunes, C. M. and Oliveira, A. L., "Temporal data mining: an overview", *Workshop Temporal Data Mining, ACM International Conference on Knowledge Discovery and Data Mining, August 2001.*

[Bellazzi et al. 98] Bellazzi, R., Magni, P., Larizza, C., De Nicolao, G., Riva, A., Stefanelli, M., "Mining biomedical time series by combining structural analysis and temporal abstractions", *Journal of American Medical Informatics Association* Vol. 5, 160–164, 1998.

[Bellazzi et al. 00] Bellazzi, R., Larizza, C., Magni, P., Monntani, S., and Stefanelli,M., "Intelligent Analysis of Clinic Time Series: An Application in the Diabetes Mellitus Domain", *Artificial Intelligence in Medicine*, 20, 37–57, 2000.

[Bruzzese and Davino 01] Bruzzese, D. and Davino, C., "Statistical Pruning of Discovered Association Rules", Computational Statistics 16 (3), pp. 387–398, 2001.

[Cios 01] Cios, K. J. *Medical data mining and knowledge discover* (Ed.) Physica-Verlag, 2001.

[Cios and Moore 02] Cios, K. J. and Moore, G. W., "Uniqueness of medical data mining", *Artificial Intelligence in Medicine*, 26, 1–24, 2002.

[Clancey 85] Clancey, W. J., "Heuristic classification," *Artificial Intelligence*, 27: 289–350, 1985.

[Connor et al. 01] O'Connor M. J., Grosso W. E., Tu S. W., Musen M. A., "RASTA: A distributed temporal abstraction system to facilitate knowledge-driven monitoring of clinical databases", In MedInfo; 2001; London, 2001.

[Fayyad et al. 96] Fayyad, U,. Piatetsky-Shapiro, G., Smyth, P., and Uthurusamy, R. (Eds.), *Advances in Knowledge Discovery and Data Mining*, AAAI/MIT Press, 1996.

[Gediga and Duntsch 02] Gediga, G. and Duntsch, I., "A fast randomisation test for rule significance", Technical Report, Brock University, 2002.

[Han and Kamber 01] Han, J. and Kamber, M., *Data Mining: Concepts and Techniques*, Morgan Kaufmann, Palo Alto, CA, 2001.

[Hand et al. 01] Hand, D. J., Mannila, H. and Smyth, P., *Principles of Data Mining,* MIT Press, 2001.

[Ho et al. 01] Ho, T. B., Nguyen, T. D., Nguyen, D. D., and Kawasaki, S., "Visualization Support for User-Centered Model Selection in Knowledge Discovery and Data Mining", *International Journal of Artificial Intelligence Tools*, World Scientific, Vol. 10, No. 4, 691–713, 2001.

[Ho et al. 03] Ho, T. B., Nguyen, T. D., Kawasaki, S., Le, S. Q., Nguyen, D. D., Yokoi, H., Takabayashi, K., "Mining Hepatitis Data with Temporal Abstraction", *ACM International Conference on Knowledge Discovery and Data Mining KDD-03*, Washington DC, 24–27, August 2003.

[Horn et al 97] Horn, W., Miksch, S., Egghart, G., Popow, C., and Paky, F., "Effective Data Validation of High-Frequency Data: Time-Point-, Time-Interval-, and Trend-Based Methods", *Computer in Biology and Medicine, Special Issue: Time-Oriented Systems in Medicine*, 27(5), 389–409, 1997.

[Horn 01] Horn, W., "AI in medicine on its way from knowledge-intensive to data-intensive systems", *Artificial Intelligence in Medicine*, 23, 5–12, 2001.

[Jensen 02] Jensen, D., "Knowledge evaluation", in *Handbook of Dat Mining and Knowledge Discovery*, Klosge, W. and Zytlow, J. M. (Eds.), Oxford, 475–489, 2002.

[Kononenko et al. 98] Kononenko, I., Bratko, I., and Kular, M., "Application of machine learning to medical diagnosis", *Machine Learning and Data Mining. Methods and Applications*, Michalski R. S. et al. (Eds.), Wiley, 389–408, 1998.

[Kononenko 01] Kononenko, I., "Machine learning for medical diagnosis: history, state of the art and perspective", *Artificial Intelligence in Medicine*, 23, 89–109, 2001.

[Larizza et al. 97] Larizza, C., Bellazzi, R., and Riva, A., "Temporal abstractions for diabetic patients management", *Artificial Intelligence in Medicine*, Keravnou, E. et al. (eds.), Proc.AIME-97, 319–330, 1997.

[Lavrac et al. 97] Lavrac, N., Keravnou, E., and Zupan, B., *Intelligent Data Analysis in Medicine and Pharmacology* (Eds.), Kluwer. 310 pages.

[Lavrac 99] Lavrac, N., "Selected Techniques for Data Mining in Medicine", *Artificial Intelligence in Medicine*, 16, 3–23, 1999.

[Liu et al. 99] Liu, B., Hsu, W., Ma, Y., "Pruning and Summarizing the Discovered Associations", *ACM International Conference on Knowledge Discovery and Data Mining KDD 99*, 125–134, 1999.

[Liu et al. 01] Liu, B., Ma, Y., Lee, R., "Analyzing the interestingness of association rules from the temporal dimension", *IEEE International Conference on Data Mining ICDM 2001*, 377–382, 2001.

[Mannila 97] Mannila, H., "Methods and problems in data mining", *International Conference on Database Theory*, Springer-Verlag, Heidelberg, 41–55, 1997.

[Megiddo and Srikant 1998] Megiddo, N. and Srikant, R., "Discovering Predictive Association Rules", *ACM International Conference on Knowledge Discovery and Data Mining KDD 98*, 274–278, 1998.

[Miksch et al. 96] Miksch S., Horn W., Popow C., and Paky F., "Utilizing temporal data abstraction for data validation and therapy planning for artificially ventilated newborn infants", *Artificial Intelligence in Medicine*, 8, 543–576, 1996.

[Motoda 02] Motoda, H., *Active Mining: New directions of data mining* (Ed.), IOS Press, 2002.

[Pyle 99] Pyle, D., *Data Preparation for Data Mining*, Morgan Kaufmann, 1999.

[Shahar and Musen 96] Shahar, Y. and Musen, M. A., "Knowledge-Based Temporal Abstraction in Clinical Domains", Artificial Intelligence in Medicine, 8, 267–298, 1996.

[Shahar 97] Shahar, Y., "A Framework for Knowledge-based Temporal Abstraction", Artificial Intelligence, 90, 79–133, 1997

[SPSS 02] *Clementine 7.0 User's Guide*, SPSS, 2002.

DISTRIBUTED MONITORING: METHODS, MEANS AND TECHNOLOGIES

ANTONIO LIOTTA

1. INTRODUCTION

Monitoring has been described by Joyce *et al.* as "the process of dynamic collection, interpretation and presentation of information concerning objects or software processes under scrutiny" [64]. In his book on network and system management, Sloman has later defined distributed monitoring as "the essential means for obtaining the information required about the components of a distributed system in order to make management decisions and subsequently control their behavior" [72].

Monitoring is an essential function of virtually any engineering system. It is needed to perform a large variety of tasks such as program debugging, testing, visualization and animation. In the context of networking, monitoring is fundamental to network operation, maintenance and control. Network monitoring, for instance, entails the collection of traffic information used for a range of performance management activities such as capacity planning, traffic flow predictions, congestion detection, quality of service monitoring and so forth. In general, monitoring is of paramount importance for fault, configuration, accounting, performance and security management.

The importance of effective monitoring dramatically increases alongside the *size*, *level of distribution*, and *dynamics* of the monitored system. Each of these factors affects the ability to extract information in a timely, reliable and efficient manner, and without loading the monitored system itself.

Modern networked systems in fact rely on a combination of fixed, mobile and cellular inter-networks that have inevitably assumed a global scale and a high level of dynamics. As an example we may consider the scenario envisaged by pervasive networks in which a range of devices (e.g. cellular phones, televisions, thermostats, PDAs etc.) are all accessible across the net. Distributed services and applications also rely on large-scale inter-networked systems. Some examples are: distributed gaming, collaborative work, and tele-conferencing, and particularly the forthcoming 3G mobile services.

Most of these networked devices and applications will need constant monitoring for the purpose of operation, management and control. Researchers have therefore been facing the challenge of designing monitoring systems that could cope with very stringent constraints including *scalability, flexibility*, and *adaptability*. This chapter provides an insight into monitoring methods, means and technologies. We start from conventional approaches and protocols, and review some of most recent approaches which make use of software code mobility for increased distribution, flexibility and scalability. We make particular reference to architectures, protocols and standards developed in the context of the Internet and of telecommunication networks.

2. FEATURES AND FUNCTIONS OF MONITORING SYSTEMS

In general, four monitoring activities are performed in a loosely-coupled, object-based distributed system [72]:

1. *Generation:* Important events are detected and event and status reports are generated. These monitoring reports are used to construct monitoring traces, which represent historical views of system activity.
2. *Processing:* A generalized monitoring service provides common processing functions such as merging of traces, validation, database updating, combination, correlation, and filtering of monitoring information. They convert the raw and low-level monitoring data to the required format and level of detail.
3. *Dissemination:* Monitoring reports are disseminated to the users, managers or processing agents who require them.
4. *Presentation:* Gathered and processed information is displayed to the users in an appropriate form.

Monitoring data is generated in the form of *status* and *event reports*, and according to different modalities. For example status reporting can be either *periodic* or *on request*, and events can be detected by either software or hardware *probes* and reported in a variety of different *formats*. A sequence of such reports is used to generate a *monitoring trace*. Finally, monitoring data can be generated according to two different models: the *polling* model and the *event-driven* model.

As far as processing of monitoring data is concerned, the basic operations include *merging* of monitoring traces, *combining* of monitoring information (i.e. to increase the level of abstraction of data), *filtering* of monitoring information (i.e. to reduce the amount of data), and *analysis* of monitoring information (e.g. to determine average or mean variance values of particular status variables, trend analysis, diagnosis etc.).

The simplest dissemination scheme consists of broadcasting all reports to all users. This scheme only works for a relatively small monitoring system. In general more sophisticated dissemination schemes based on *subscriptions* are necessary ([72] page 321). In that case, specific reports are sent only to those management entities that have previously expressed an interest in (i.e. they have subscribed to) those reports.

An important characteristic of monitoring systems is their *intrusiveness,* which can be defined as "the effect that monitoring may have on the behavior of the monitored system" [72]. Intrusiveness results from the monitoring system sharing resources with the observed system (e.g. processing power, communication channels, storage space). Intrusive monitors may alter the timing of events in the system in an arbitrary manner and can lead to problems such as: degradation of system performance; a change of the global ordering of these events; incorrect results; an increase in the execution time of the application; and masking or creating deadlock situations. Delays in transferring information from the place it is generated to the place it is used means that it may be out of date. For this reason it is very difficult to obtain a global, consistent view of all components in a distributed system.

A fundamental property of monitoring systems is therefore their *scalability*. This is defined in [17] as "the ability to increase the size of the problem domain with a small or negligible increase in the solution's time and space complexity". Hence, in our context scalability can be defined as the ability to increase the size of the monitored system and the accuracy of the monitoring system, with a small or negligible decrease in performance.

It should be mentioned that accuracy is related to scale because a higher level of accuracy usually results in larger resource consumption. For instance, if polling is used to collect monitoring information, higher polling rates are necessary to increase the system accuracy.

Scalability is strongly dependent on the architectural design of the monitoring system that is, in turn, part of a more general management system. Hence, the next sections review the key management architectures and management paradigms. We should note that this chapter addresses more directly the first two of our four abovementioned monitoring activities—i.e. generation and processing—looking at different ways to realize them in the context of network and telecommunications management.

3. MONITORING ARCHITECTURES

Similarly to management systems, monitoring systems can use various architectural approaches to implement their functions. A typical classification includes three different architectures—centralized, hierarchical, and distributed [5]—that are described below. Typical technologies, protocols and standards for each of the three categories are described in Section 6.

3.1. Centralized monitoring

A centralized architecture employs a management platform operating on a single computer system and responsible for all management duties. The monitoring system collects all alerts and events and stores them on a single database for further processing (Figure 1).

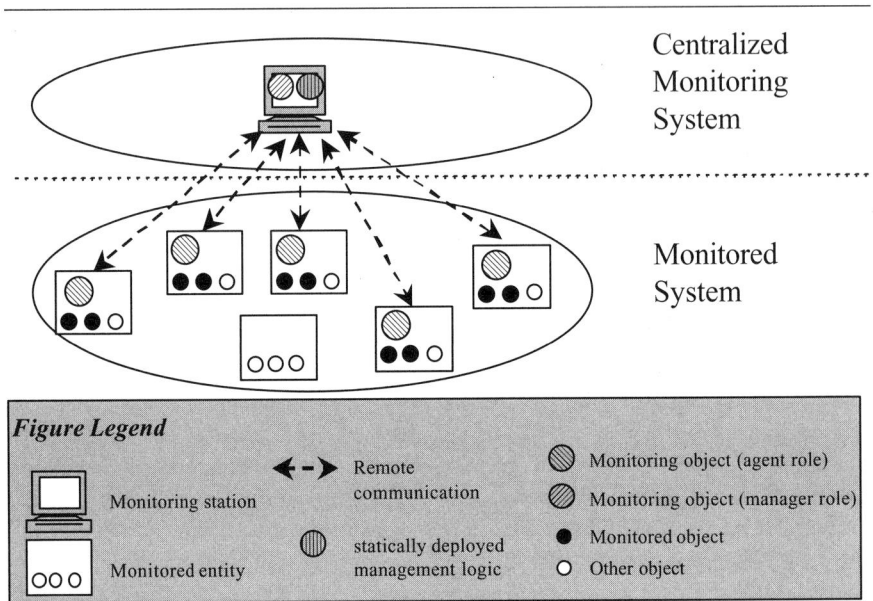

Figure 1. Centralized monitoring.

The system generally requires pre-installed, static software components both in the monitoring system and in each of the monitored entities. Similarly to most large-scale networked systems, telecommunication networks adopt a manager-agent paradigm as well as the object oriented abstraction concepts. Physical resources are made accessible as software objects (i.e. *monitored objects*) with associated parameters whose values can be obtained through specific methods.

However, in order to decouple the monitoring system from the monitored system and to pursue technology independency, the monitored objects are often not exposed directly to the monitoring system. Specific, standardized *monitoring objects*, acting in the role of *agents*, are locally instantiated for this purpose.

Other monitoring objects play the role of *manager objects*, although their functionality is equivalent to that of their agent counterparts, and are instantiated in the management station. The *management logic*, required to process the monitoring data, is statically installed at the management station.

Having all the management applications and information at one point is advantageous because it is useful for troubleshooting and problem correlation and provides convenience, accessibility and security for the manager. However, this architecture is weak for various reasons, as pointed out in [32] [39] [63]. First, it *does not scale*. As the number of elements of the monitored system grows, monitoring traffic, in turn, increases and tends to overload the network resources located in the proximity of the management station. In addition, the processing load at the management station increases. Thus, this model suffers from both communication and processing bottlenecks caused by the need to transmit and process large amounts of data at the management station. There can also be an 'implosion effect', with all the responses traversing the small area of the network adjacent to the management station.

Another problem is that the centralized architecture *is not robust* because the management station is a single point of failure. If the connection from the management station to the network gets severed, all management capabilities are lost. In addition, this approach can be *expensive* because it requires powerful management stations in terms of memory and processing capability.

Furthermore, centralized management tends to be *static* and *inflexible* for different reasons. One is that it may not be able to respond rapidly to dynamic changes in the state of the underlying network infrastructure. It is in practice unfeasible for a central station to have an accurate snapshot of the network status especially if the system is characterized by high-frequency variations.

The other reason is that, in practice, systems following this approach concentrate all the management intelligence in the management station and rely on pre-defined management functions which require a complicated software update procedure when they are changed. In network management this approach is exemplified by protocol-based SNMP management ([83] [97]), as described in Section 6.1.

3.2. Hierarchical monitoring

One way to pursue increased performance and scalability is to adopt a *hierarchical* management architecture, which uses multiple systems with one system acting as a central server (the main management station) and the others working as clients (Figure 2). Some of the functions of the management system reside within the server; others run on the clients, which act in the role of 'area managers'. For instance, in network management separate client systems can be configured to collect and pre-process raw data from different portions of the network.

Hierarchical monitoring can be realized in the Telecommunications Management Network (TMN) [18], which uses OSI Systems Management (OSI-SM) as the base management technology [101] and CMIP/S as management protocol [83] (Section 6.2). In a similar fashion, in the context of Internet management, simple monitoring and statistical probes can be introduced using RMON [82] [97] (Section 6.1), which is equivalent to an area manager that collects monitoring information about a number of elements within a sub-network.

The common denominator between centralized and hierarchical architectures is the adoption of simple, pre-defined functions that can result only in a limited level of decentralization of management intelligence. Monitoring functions that can actually be decentralized are restricted to operations such as low-level filtering of monitoring data, generation of alarms on the basis of simple conditions, and collection of rudimentary statistical information. In addition, these decentralized area managers operate in pre-defined network locations, which means that they cannot easily adapt to network changes. Therefore, conventional hierarchical schemes, despite coping with the scalability problem to a certain extent, inherit the other problems of centralized management and cannot easily cope with frequently changing dynamic environments.

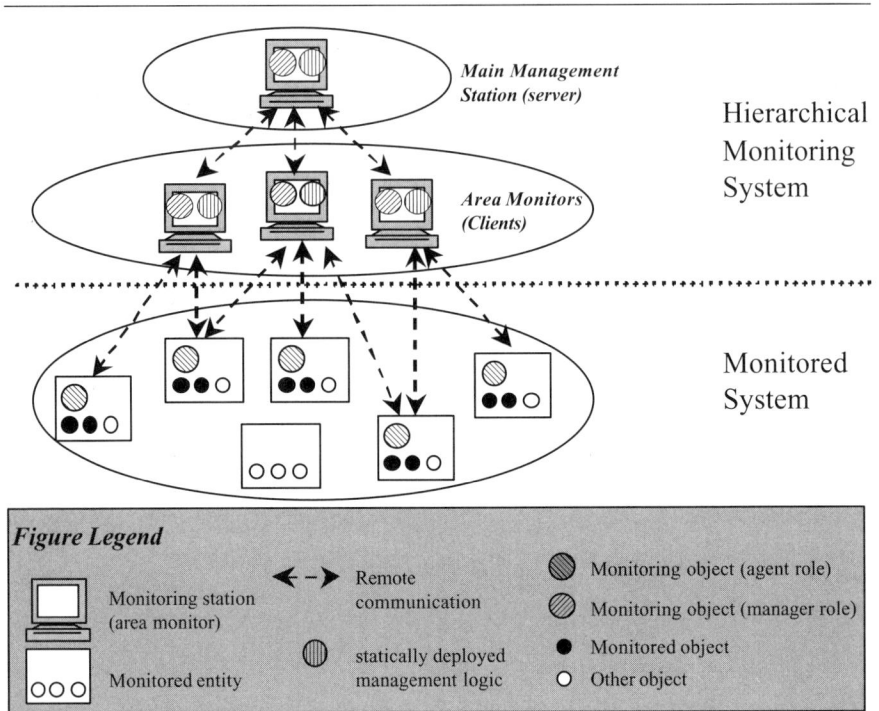

Figure 2. Hierarchical monitoring.

They are still inflexible and static solutions. For instance, once a task has been defined in an agent (e.g. via RMON, or CMIP/S with M_ACTION), there is no way to modify it dynamically; it remains static. Moreover, those systems have a limited range of pre-defined actions which can be invoked but cannot be programmed in an arbitrary way.

3.3. Distributed monitoring

The *distributed* architecture combines the centralized and hierarchical approaches. Instead of having one centralized system or a hierarchy of area managers controlled by a main station, the distributed approach uses multiple peer management systems; that is a network of managers in which there is no clear-cut allocation of resources to management systems (Figure 3). The type of allocation depends on many factors. For instance, the same resources can be allocated to several managers with, say, one manager responsible for security management and the other one for performance management.

A key aim of the distributed approach is to pursue flexibility and adaptability, along with increased scalability. This is why distributed approaches are usually associated with techniques that allow dynamic deployment of management logic instead of relying on

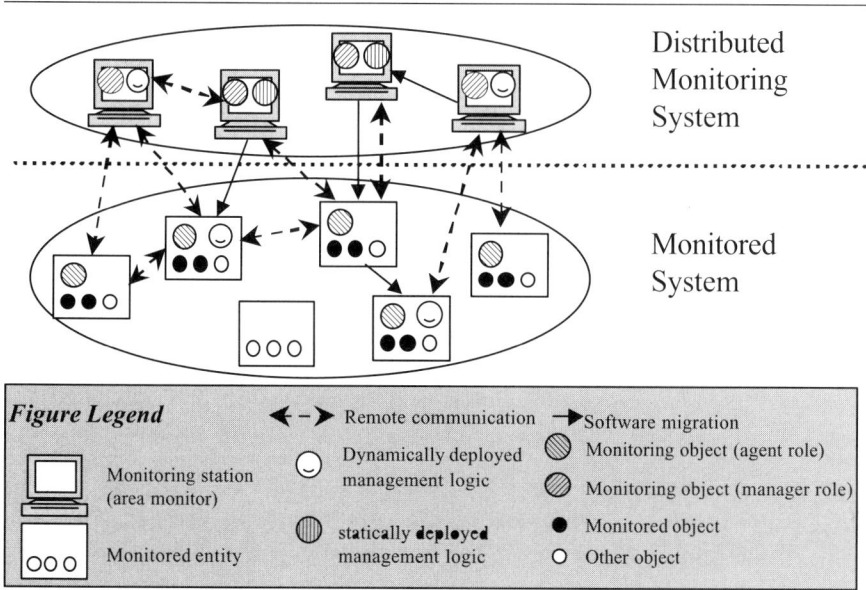

Figure 3. Dynamic, distributed monitoring.

pre-installed mechanisms. Object and software mobility as well as mobile, intelligent or co-operating software agents are practical means for the realization of distributed monitoring system (Section 4 and 5).

Because of their potential, distributed architectures have been the subject of intensive research in recent years. Martin-Flatin *et al.* have further categorized distributed approaches as follows [61] [62] [63]:

• Weakly distributed hierarchical paradigms;
• Strongly distributed hierarchical paradigms;
• Strongly distributed co-operative paradigms.

Weakly distributed hierarchical paradigms are substantially equivalent to the hierarchical approach described in Section 3.2. These are characterized by a management logic concentrated in few managers, with numerous agents limited to the role of dumb data collectors. Along with centralized management, weakly distributed hierarchical approaches can be regarded as traditional management paradigms.

Strongly distributed paradigms, instead, encompass the more recent approaches to network and system management. They decentralize management processing down to every agent. Management tasks are no longer confined to managers: both agents and managers take part in the management application processing.

Research on strongly distributed hierarchical paradigms has been sparked by Yemini *et al.* in 1991 when they first introduced the concept of Management by Delegation

(MbD). They devised a manager-to-agent delegation model which allowed dynamic reprogramming of network devices, promoting them from dumb data collectors to the rank of managing entities (Section 7.1).

MbD triggered extensive research work that led to the development of many technologies for strongly distributed management paradigms. *Mobile code* and *distributed object* technologies have been used so far to realize strongly distributed hierarchical management systems (Sections 5 and 6).

On the other hand, strongly distributed co-operative paradigms have mainly been investigated in the area of software intelligent agents. In this case, the area manager functionality and logic (Figure 3) are realized through techniques borrowed from the areas of Distributed Artificial Intelligence (DAI) and Multi-Agent Systems [73] [74]. In order for such techniques to be applicable to network management it is necessary to achieve a uniform, standard approach to agent management and communication. The Foundation for Intelligent Physical Agents (FIPA) consortium is working on such standards ([69] [27]).

Several researchers have been working on the applicability of DAI to network and system management as can be seen from the review presented in [76]. However, in the remainder of this chapter we shall focus on paradigms and technologies for weakly and strongly distributed hierarchical paradigms but we shall not look into further detail at strongly distributed co-operative paradigms.

4. SOFTWARE PARADIGMS FOR MONITORING

Another important dimension of monitoring systems is represented by the software design paradigm used to realize them. Many authors have looked at software paradigms for distributed systems and applications, and particularly those tailored to network management—e.g. [31] [71] [3] [4] [14] [70]. The most important paradigms relevant to distributed monitoring are summarized below.

4.1. Client-Server

In the *Client-Server* (CS) paradigm, a server component exports a set of services that are statically deployed and installed, i.e. before the service request. The code implementing those services (or *service logic*) is owned by the server component—i.e. the server holds the *know-how* (Figure 4). It is the server who executes the services; thus, it has the *processor* capability. The server also has the *resources* (or *data*) which are accessed by the client through the server.

The CS paradigm is one of the most widely used paradigms. It is the bases of the Internet (protocols and applications) and is also adopted in network-centric applications. In management, it underlies the manager-agent paradigm adopted by both Internet and OSI management (Section 6). One of the limitations that have been associated with the CS mode of operation is that it does not support code mobility (i.e. mobile computations) and it is, therefore, limited in terms of flexibility and dynamic programmability. The software paradigms described below address this shortcoming.

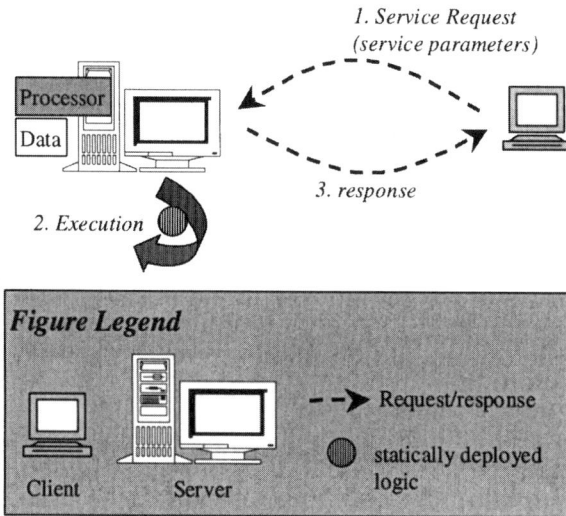

Figure 4. The client-server (C-S) software paradigm.

4.2. Remote Evaluation (or code pushing)

Remote Evaluation (REV) has been introduce by Stamos and Gifford in their pioneering work described in [60] [59]. In REV, an application in the client role can dynamically enhance the server capability by sending code to the server (Figure 5). Subsequently, clients can remotely initiate the execution of this code that is allowed to access the resources collocated within the server (the service request can include a combination of statically and dynamically deployed code). Therefore, this approach can be seen as an extension of the CS paradigm whereby a client, in addition to the name of the service requested and the input parameters, can also send code implementing new services. Hence the client owns the code needed to perform a service, while the server offers both the computational resources required to execute the service and the access to its local resources. The REV principles have led to the more recent approach usually referred to as *code pushing*. This design paradigm usually relies on the object migration mechanism or on the weak mobility mechanism described in Section 5.3 below.

4.3. Code on Demand (or code pulling)

In *code on demand (COD)* a client downloads (or pulls) the required code from a code repository (or code server) and links it dynamically in order to perform a task (Figure 6). Hence, the client owns the resources needed to perform a service but lacks part of the code (or logic) required to perform it. The COD principles have led to the more recent approach usually referred to as *code pulling*. Similarly to REV, COD usually relies on the object migration mechanism or on the weak mobility mechanism described in Section 5.3 below.

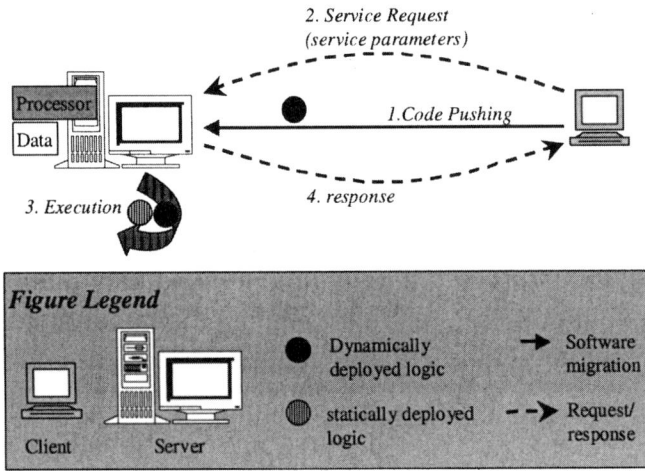

Figure 5. The Remote Evaluation (REV) software paradigm (code-pushing).

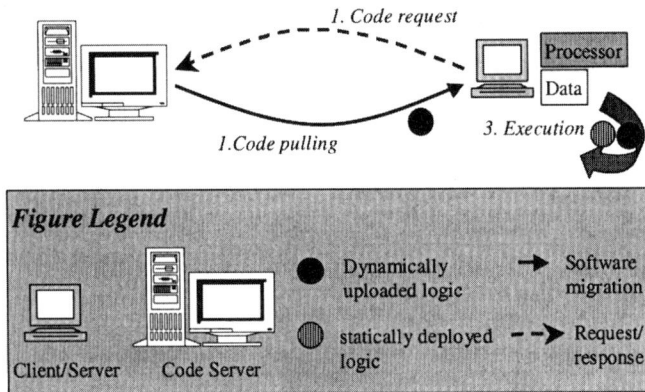

Figure 6. The Code on Demand (CoD) software paradigm (code pulling).

4.4. Mobile Agents

A *mobile agent* (MA) is essentially an autonomous execution unit containing the logic to perform a given task and migrate under its own control from machine to machine in a heterogeneous network (Figure 7). While in execution at a given node, the MA is able to suspend its execution at an arbitrary point, transport itself to another machine, seamlessly resume execution from the point of suspension, and possibly gain local access to the resources of the new node. Hence, the agent owns the code to perform a service but lacks the resources needed to accomplish it. The server owns those resources and provides an environment to execute the code sent by the client.

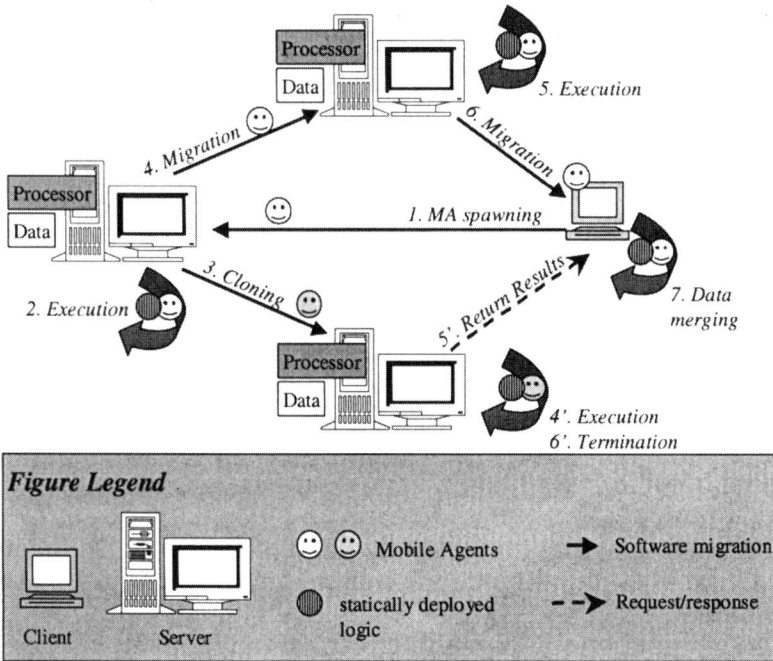

Figure 7. The Mobile Agent (MA) software paradigm.

In addition to being able to roam the network, MAs can also spawn, or *clone*, other MAs characterized by equivalent functionality but operating in separate threads of execution. Cloning is used to increase the level of parallelism in a distributed system and can be particularly useful in distributed monitoring [8] [9]. The mobility mechanisms adopted to realize this design paradigm are weak, strong, or higher-order mobility, as explained in Section 5.3.

5. SOFTWARE MOBILITY FOR DISTRIBUTED MONITORING

Following the rapid availability of relatively low-cost fixed and mobile network-ing infrastructures, networked systems can potentially assume very large scales. This poses stringent demands on the monitoring system that will have to cope with *size* (i.e. number of monitored objects), *distribution* (i.e. geographically dispersed moni-tored objects) and *dynamics* (i.e. mobile objects abstract resources that are volatile or mobile).

Various techniques have been adopted to build monitoring systems that would be sufficiently flexible and efficient to meet these demands. The natural approach has been to look at software mobility at various levels, as illustrated below.

5.1. Location transparency and location awareness

The code mobility concept originates in work aimed at supporting the migration of active processes and objects (together with their state and associated code) at the operating system level. For instance, migratory systems such as Locus [42] and Cool [79] support transparent process and object migration, respectively, regardless of the underlying hardware substrate. Transparent migration at operating system level addresses the issues that arise when *code* and *state* are moved among the hosts of a loosely coupled, small-scale distributed system. This approach does not tend to be suitable for large-scale networks and systems, particularly those of the scale of the Internet. Papaioannou in his recent PhD thesis builds an argument against *location transparency* in large-scale systems [92]. He argues that location transparency, by creating the illusion that all components exist within the same machine, breaks the fundamental concepts of layering and abstraction adopted in computer networks.

A more recent approach for large-scale distributed systems is the one of *location-aware programming* based on Mobile Code. This approach contrasts with the philosophy of location transparency, and exhibits several innovations [4]:

- *Code mobility is exploited on a large rather than small scale.* In large-scale systems networks are composed of heterogeneous hosts, managed by heterogeneous authorities, connected by heterogeneous links.
- *Programming is location aware and mobility is under the programmer's control.* Location of computational entities may have a significant impact on heterogeneous, large-scale systems. Location-aware applications may take actions based on the knowledge of the locations of the other application components.
- *Mobility is not performed just for load balancing.* Contrarily to operating system level migration, mobile code systems are oriented towards service customization, dynamic extension of application functionality, and support for nomadic computing.

5.2. Mobile code systems

The main difference between traditional systems—e.g. those supporting location-transparent migration at operating system level—and Mobile Code Systems (MCSs) is that the former provide network transparency by means of a *True Distributed System* layer; whereas the latter manifest to the programmer the structure of the underlying computer network. An example of the first case is CORBA in which the programmer is never aware of the network topology and always interacts with a single well-known object broker [58]. Conversely, in MCSs a *Computational Environment* (CE) is layered upon the network operating system of each network host. The CE maintains the identity of the host where it is located and provides the application with the capability to dynamically relocate computation onto different hosts.

Fugetta distinguishes the components hosted by the CE as the *Executing Unit* (EU) and the *resources* [4]. EUs represent sequential flows of execution, such as single-threaded processes or individual threads of multi-threaded process. Resources are entities which can be shared among multiple EUs, such as a file or an object shared by different threads. In turn, an EU may be modeled as a composition of a *code segment*, which provides the static description of a computation behavior, and a *state* composed of a *data space* and an *execution state*. The data space is the set of references to resources that can be accessed by the EU. The execution state contains private data that cannot be shared, as well as control information related to the EU state, such as call stack and instruction pointer.

5.3. Mobility mechanisms

Considering the concepts and definitions provided above, we can identify five different types of mobility mechanisms:

- *Process Migration*. Concerns the transfer of an operating system process from the machine where it is running to a different one. Process migration facilities manage the binding between the process and its execution environment and operate at operating system level. This has been used in loosely coupled, small-scale distributed systems to achieve load balancing across network nodes.
- *Object Migration*. Object migration makes it possible to move objects among address spaces, implementing a finer grain mobility than that of systems that provide migration at the process level. In some cases object migration is achieved transparently, that is without user intervention or knowledge. Technologies supporting object migration have now become mature and widely available, which makes this mechanism a good candidate to realize distributed monitoring systems.
- *Weak Mobility*. Weak mobility is the ability of an MCS to allow code movement, along with its initialization data, across different CEs. This is a powerful mobility mechanism that suits the requirements of large-scale, dynamic monitoring systems. Its applicability to distributed monitoring has been demonstrated by Liotta *et al.* [7] [8] [9], as described in Section 7.
- *Strong Mobility*. Strong mobility is the ability of an MCS to allow migration of both the code and execution state of an EU between different CEs. This mechanism involves significant migration overheads related to the need to save and transport the execution state along with the code. These overheads may be contained with *discrete migration*, i.e., if migration is triggered only at particular moments when the execution state is relatively small. However, despite its potential, strong mobility has not yet been employed for the development of distributed monitoring systems.
- *Higher-order Mobility*. Higher-order mobility is the ability of an MCS to allow migration of code, execution state, and data space of an EU between different CEs. The overheads associated to this mechanism are even heavier than those of strong mobility. Hence, higher-order mobility is not exploited in distributed monitoring. An in-depth study of higher-order mobility is presented in [19].

6. TECHNOLOGIES AND STANDARDS FOR MONITORING

Having described concepts, paradigms and techniques that can be used for building management and monitoring systems, we now take a closer look at the most widespread technologies and standards available today. The technologies presented in this section can be regarded as the conventional ones—they are well established and widely used. Some of them are, however, the technologies that are showing significant shortcomings and are, hence, evolving towards the new approaches presented in Section 7.

6.1. Internet/IETF monitoring

In the Internet there are typically two ways to gather performance monitoring information:

- *Passive measurements*: information is gained as a result of the analysis of the traffic passing through network elements (e.g. for measurements of utilized bandwidth, packet loss ratios, etc.)
- *Active measurements*: information is gained by injecting small test streams (e.g. for measurements of delay, jitter, etc.)

Typical performance parameters of interest are described in [96]. For example, in a router utilization can be measured through the packet forwarding rate, processor load, percentage of dropped frames, or packet queue length. Important indicators of the level of service are the following parameters:

- *Total response time*: the time elapsed between a packet entering the network for processing and a response being issued by the network. A description of how to achieve round-trip times and one-way delays has been provided by the IETF (Internet Engineering Task Force) IPPM working group [44] and is documented in [29] and [30].
- *Rejection rate*: the percentage of time the network cannot transfer information because of poor performance or lack of resources. Most devices provide information on the number of frames rejected by specific interfaces.
- *Availability*: the percentage of time the network is accessible for use. This is usually measured as a function of the Mean Time Between Failure (MTBF). Most devices and links hold information on how long they have been operational.

A *de facto* IETF standard is represented by the Simple Network Management Protocol (SNMP) that is used to collect management information from the network elements [97]. The IETF has also standardized the Management Information Base (MIB), that is the objects representing network element manageable resources [66] [65]. What has not been standardized, however, is the Internet Management Architecture.

SNMP follows a manager/agent model of operation which involves a management station interacting with agents executing in the network elements. Each station stores and manipulates information in the MIB, i.e. the local information base.

Monitoring is mainly achieved by polling raw information obtained from the agents and processing it at the management station. This fine-grained client-server interaction between management station and remote agents is often referred to as micro-management because it involves exchange of raw, unprocessed data which tends to incur substantial traffic in the vicinity of the station and to overload the management station.

In addition to polling, which is the main monitoring mechanism, SNMP also supports an elementary event-based approach by means of *traps*. These allow SNMP agents to report the occurrence of specific events to the manager.

Therefore, SNMP can be characterized as follows:

- *Simplicity*: one of the strengths of SNMP is its extreme simplicity which means that it is easy to use and puts a relatively limited load on the network element. Simplicity, however, comes with limited semantics. Shortcomings include the absence of high-level MIBs, a limited set of protocol primitives, and a purely data-oriented information model.
- *Scalability*: SNMP was meant for private networks (LANs and MANs) and for the Internet backbones. That is reflected by its polling-based, simple 'remote-debugging', centralized approach. Because of these features, SNMP does not suit the requirements of large inter-networks. Simple and static hierarchical monitoring can be performed with SNMPv2 [97], which introduces intermediate level managers. In addition, with the Remote Monitoring (RMON) MIB [97] part of data pre-processing can be performed at the network elements, resulting in a certain level of decentralization. However, SNMP remains a poorly performing protocol in large-scale networks.
- *Reliability*: SNMP relies on the User Datagram Protocol (UDP), a connectionless, unreliable transport protocol. While this has the advantage of allowing management even under faulty conditions, it also has the disadvantage of not supporting reliable management/monitoring. Trivial causes such as router buffer overflows may, for instance, result in loss of critical management information.
- *Security*: SNMPv1 and SNMPv2 adopt a weak security scheme. SNMPv3 promises to address this limitation but is, however, being deployed very slowly.
- *Flexibility*: SNMP capabilities at network nodes are fixed, being embedded by the manufacturer. SNMP inflexibility is being addressed by the IETF Script MIB proposal which allows a certain level of programmability through the use of mobile code servers [25] [24] [56], as explained in Section 7.2.

6.2. OSI monitoring

The Open Systems Interconnection (OSI) Network Management Forum (NMF) was established in 1988 to promote the development, acceptance and implementation of OSI management standards. OSI management has been gradually standardized by ITU-T (International Telecommunication Union—Telecommunication Standardization Sector) under the X.7xx document series. The fundamentals are described in the OSI Management Framework (X.700) [46] and in the OSI System Management Overview (X.701) [47] and are illustrated in [41].

OSI management is split into five functional areas, commonly referred to as FCAPS: Fault, Configuration, Accounting, Performance, and Security management.

Monitoring has been recognized as fundamental to each of the FCAPS functions and has been specified in the following ITU-T documents:

- X.739 *Metric objects and attributes*. Describes mechanisms for the processing of scanned processed information and a model for emitting notifications [52].
- X.738 *Summarization function*. Describes mechanisms for gathering and examining collections of performance information [51].
- X.733 *Alarm reporting function*. Describes alarm mechanisms with indications of the severity of a situation, each time network conditions change [50].

The OSI has also defined the Common Management Information Protocol (CMIP) in X.711 [49], which follows a manager/agent model similar to that of SNMP. It assumes a client network management station that remotely polls the agents in the network elements. CMIP is used to implement a number of network management capabilities, referred to as the Common Management Information Services (CMIS) and defined in X.710 [48].

In comparison to SNMP, CMIP agents are much more sophisticated and capable. However, they are also more difficult to program and require a larger amount of computational resources. In summary, the advantages of CMIP over SNMP are:

- CMIP variables not only relay information but can also be used to perform tasks
- CMIP is safer because it has built in security supporting authorization, access control and security logs
- CMIP provides more powerful primitives that allow management applications to accomplish relatively sophisticated tasks with a single request
- CMIP provides better monitoring and event notification mechanisms

Despite these benefits, CMIP/S failed to gain popularity mainly due to a combination of long standardization cycles, the significant overheads at the network elements, and its programming complexity. The high level of standardization achieved by CMIP/S is also its major drawback since all functionality is statically pre-determined and cannot be easily changed.

Finally, OSI management allows hierarchical, static monitoring and adopts the client-server paradigm.

6.3. CORBA

While protocol-based approaches to management are specific to particular management frameworks, a more generic approach to the client-server model can be provided through a distributed object framework. The Common Object Request Broker Architecture (CORBA) [78] proposed by the Object Management Group (OMG) has been regarded as a potential framework to realize distributed management. Its object-oriented nature and the fact that management systems are composed of distributed, interacting objects suggests that CORBA could effectively be used for management.

In fact, OMG CORBA has been chosen by the Telecommunication Information Network Architecture (TINA) initiative as the basis for their Distributed Processing Environment [98].

Pavlou has dedicated significant effort to assessing the viability of CORBA-based management, presenting his arguments in [41] and [38]. He has come to the conclusions that CORBA's fully object-oriented model is largely compatible with that of OSI management. Likewise, it adopts a reliable connection-oriented communication approach and supports client-server, decentralized management.

Interworking and coexistence among CORBA, CMIP and SNMP has also been looked at by Pavlou, as well as being the task of the Joint Interdomain Management (JIDM) group. Interworking between CORBA and SNMP would be necessary in order to manage SNMP-capable network elements in a TINA environment. However, after so many years since its conception and despite its enormous potential, TINA does not seem to have become a commercial reality. Interworking with CORBA would be needed in both TMN and TINA environments. However, both architectural frameworks seem to be losing momentum.

Finally, similarly to CMIP, a CORBA approach is complex and management functionality is statically pre-determined at design time. It is with approaches based on code mobility that it is possible to pursue distribution and dynamic programmability. These are described in Section 7.

6.4. Java

After the Java Remote Method Invocation (RMI) [90] was released in 1997 a new way of managing networks and systems gradually emerged. Java RMI makes it possible to program a management application like a distributed object-oriented application. However, unlike CORBA with its support for multiple languages, Java-RMI is tightly coupled with Java. While this feature may be seen as a drawback, it in fact enables enhanced interactions between distributed objects. Further, when Java-RMI is combined with Object Serialization [89]—which allows objects to be transferred from host to host—management application designers have a powerful technology that allows exploitation of combinations of mobile code and distributed object technologies.

Java-based APIs and toolkits specialized for management have already appeared within the following frameworks:

- *The Java Management Extensions (JMX) initiative* [88] (formerly JMAPI): The JMX technology represents a universal, open technology for managing and monitoring devices, applications and service-driven networks. It supports MIB II by mapping all managed objects onto Java objects [66].
- *The Java Dynamic Management Kit (J-DMK)* [87]: is a component-oriented management toolkit based on JavaBeans [84] which comes with a library of core management services and can communicate via RMI, HTTP, and SNMP. This is the first implementation of the JMX specification. This toolkit allows to both 'push' and 'pull' code and offers a very powerful way of building strongly distributed management applications.

6.5. SOAP

The Simple Object Access Protocol (SOAP) is a technology-independent, lightweight protocol for exchange of information in a decentralized, distributed environment [99]. It is based upon the Extensible Markup Language (XML) [26] consisting of three parts: an envelope that defines a framework for describing what is in a message and how to process it; a set of encoding rules for expressing instances of application-defined datatypes; and a convention for representing remote procedure calls and responses.

Besides being technology neutral, SOAP presents other advantages with respect to CORBA and Java-RMI. These use binary remote procedure calls (RPCs) which pose compatibility problems with the widely used HTTP protocol that was not designed for this kind of traffic. Furthermore, binary RPCs present security constraints as firewalls and proxy servers will normally block binary traffic. On the contrary, SOAP uses text-based communication through XML messages transferred by HTTP.

Because of its features, SOAP can potentially be used in combination with a variety of other protocols and has, therefore, a good potential for being employed for building efficient, distributed network monitoring systems.

6.6. OSA, Parlay and Jain

The 3rd Generation (3G) communication systems will be formed by a collection of heterogeneous networks, both fixed and mobile. Monitoring and managing such networks will therefore pose the ambitious hurdle of gaining unified access to a myriad of network devices independently of protocols and technologies. Technology-neutral network services will be offered to service providers and developers by creating a standardized layer, which abstracts network capabilities. In this context, we often hear that network abstraction is realized by 'opening up' networks, a term that used to be unpopular among network operators.

The most eminent consortia that are driving the specification of open network interfaces allowing cross-domain and cross-technology operation and management are:

- *The 3rd Generation Partnership Project (3GPP)* [93]: is specifying the Open Service Access (OSA) architecture [1] for 3G fixed, mobile, and cellular networks. This allows a complete decoupling between the application and the network layers, with technology-independent network functions being exposed to the application in the form of Service Capability Features (SCF).
- *The Parlay Group* [95]: has initially started working merely on fixed networks but has more recently started working with 3GPP towards a unified OSA architecture.
- *The JAIN community* [86]: is developing a number of Java APIs that abstracts the details of network and protocol implementations, facilitating the development of portable applications. In this sense, JAIN is working in the same direction as OSA/Parlay but is adopting a pragmatic, Java-oriented approach. Open APIs offering monitoring and management functionality have initially been specified as part of the JAIN Connectivity Management framework [85]. This specification work seems, however, to have been interrupted in late 2000. It is most probable that the specification of

open connectivity management interfaces will be carried forward in the context of OSA/Parlay.

The 3GPP efforts on OSA/Parlay represent an important attempt to open up networks. The work on the specification of network management capabilities, although still at its infancy, promises interesting developments as it is being closely followed by the major network operators.

7. EMERGING APPROACHES TO DYNAMIC MONITORING

The technologies and standards presented in Section 6 are either well established (e.g. SNMP, CMIP, CORBA) or in the process of gaining significant momentum (JAVA, SOAP, OSA/Parlay). Other more revolutionary approaches are at the same time being looked at in the management research community. This section describes some of the most influential studies on management and monitoring approaches based on code mobility. The innovation is represented by the following aspects:

- adoption of the code pushing, code pulling, and mobile agent software paradigms as opposed to the conventional client–server approach (these have been described in Section 4);
- adoption of location-aware programming as opposed to location-transparency (these have been described in Section 5.1);
- use of mobile code systems as execution environments instead of more conventional distributed object oriented frameworks (these have been described in Section 5.2);
- exploitation of object migration and weak mobility mechanisms to pursue enhanced flexibility, adaptability and programmability of the monitoring system (these have been described in Section 5.3).

7.1. Management by Delegation (MbD)

A seminal work on *strongly distributed hierarchical management* is the one introduced in [100] by Yemini *et al.* with their Management by Delegation (MbD) framework. MbD also represents one of the first concrete attempts to make use of Mobile Code in Network Management. Its inventors claim that MbD is not only a technique that allows for dynamic decentralization and automation of management functions, but it also introduces a paradigm shift in the management arena [35].

The basic underlying principle of MbD is that management processing functions can be delegated dynamically to the network elements and executed locally rather than centrally. Thus, instead of moving raw data from the elements to a central management application, the application itself is moved and executed at the elements where data actually resides. Thus, the MbD concept follows the *code pushing* software paradigm described in Section 4.2 and exemplified in Figure 5.

An MbD platform is implemented as a set of *elastic servers* residing in the network elements. An elastic server is a multithreaded process whose *program code* and *process state* can be modified, extended and/or contracted during its execution [33]. *Server elasticity* contrasts with the traditional *client-server* paradigm, which does not provide support for such a dynamic transfer of functionality between client and server. Thus elastic servers introduce a new paradigm of interaction between components in distributed applications and provide a powerful mechanism to dynamically compose distributed applications by connecting and integrating independently delegated programs.

A manager can dynamically dispatch *delegated agents* to remote elastic servers using a *delegation protocol* and can then control their execution. This protocol includes service primitives to delegate, instantiate, suspend, resume, abort and remove delegated programs. Thus, by using this protocol, a manager application can, during execution time, augment the functionality of a subordinate element, allowing it to perform an open-ended set of management programs. Delegated agents can monitor, analyze, and control devices independently from the manager, except where explicit co-ordination is required.

MbD supports *dynamic delegation*[1] [75] and provides mechanisms for both *spatial* and *temporal distribution*[2] [34]. Several applications have been prototyped on this MbD platform [32], showing the advantages, and some of the fields of applicability for the delegation framework. Examples include an application for real-time monitoring of the *health* of large-scale networks [36] and another one for the management of *stressed* networks [67]. Further, some considerations describing how MbD can reduce the *management control loop* and thus make networks more *reliable*, are reported in [67] [32]. More generally, a class of applications which might benefit from MbD is described in [67] [32]. Therefore, in this MbD framework, delegated scripts can operate independently from the manager, and on behalf of it, whilst managers are concerned with the management of delegated scripts. Thus, this platform is a feasible base-framework for autonomous, hierarchical, and delegated management.

Because of its potential, MbD has been studied and applied to concrete management and monitoring applications by a number of researchers. Examples have been reported in [9] (Section 3.1.1) and [13]. The standardization process, fundamental to the widespread adoption of MbD, has however been slow. Sections 7.2 and 7.3 below look at the recent developments of MbD in the context of Internet and OSI management, respectively.

7.2. MbD in the context of internet management

The Distributed Management (DISMAN) working group of the IETF was chartered to define an architecture where a main manager can delegate control to several distributed

---

[1] With *static delegation*, the management functionality is pre-allocated to distributed entities at management design time and cannot be dynamically expanded or changed without reprogramming and recompilation of the code on the remote entity. This approach is usually acceptable for standard, routine management tasks, such as low level monitoring operations with RMON [97]. On the other hand, with *dynamic delegation* functions can be delegated during the operational phase of management, which improves the flexibility of the management system.

[2] Mechanisms for dynamic delegation can support both spatial and temporal distribution. *Spatial distribution* involves delegation of functionality over different nodes for the purpose of reducing the latency in the access of remote data. It provides, for instance, the means to distribute the monitoring functions, perform local data compression, and relay only sensitive information to the main monitoring station. *Temporal distribution* is the ability to dynamically delegate new management code to a device as soon as it is needed. It can assist the manager in modifying management or monitoring policies as administrative requirements change or as the monitored environment evolves.

management stations. The DISMAN framework provides mechanisms for distributing scripts which perform arbitrary management tasks to remote devices. To the DISMAN group, distributed management does not mean management functions distributed in a statically set way, but something that is 'movable'. The objective is to allow the 'distributed management' application to keep pace with the changing needs of large, distributed systems.

Proposals for several related Management Information Bases (MIBs) already exist. Among these are DISMAN-SERVICES-MIB, TARGET-MIB (to express targets for traps and script transfer), EVENT-MIB (based on the RMON alarm and event groups), Notification LOG-MIB, Expression MIB, Schedule MIB (definition of managed objects for scheduling management operations), Remote Operations MIB, and Script-MIB.

In particular, Script-MIB defines an SNMP-compliant Management Information Base and a standard interface for the delegation of management functions based on the Internet management framework [24] [55] [56] [57]. This comprises capabilities to transfer management scripts; for initiating, suspending, resuming, and terminating scripts; to transfer arguments and results; and to monitor and control running scripts.

Script-MIB assumes that management functions are defined in the form of executable code (scripts) that can be installed in network nodes. The MIB supports arbitrary programming languages and makes no assumptions about code formats. It may also allow the delegation of compiled native code.

The technology supports two different ways to transfer management scripts to a distributed manager. The first approach follows the "push model" and requires that the manager pushes the script to the distributed manager. The second approach follows the "pull model", requiring that the manager informs the distributed manager of the location of a particular script. This is followed by the retrieval of the script by the distributed manager. The delegation protocol proposed by the IETF is the Script-MIB Extensibility protocol (SMX) [56].

An evaluation of the Script-MIB performance and functionality has been carried out based on the Jasmin platform [94], the first implementation of Script-MIB. Schonwalder *et al.* report their findings in [55]. More recently, Bohoris has carried out a comparative study among Java-RMI, CORBA, Grasshopper, and Script-MIB, prototyping a performance monitoring system based on each of these technologies [13]. His analysis highlights that overheads associated with software migration are considerably smaller if a management-orientated platform such as Script-MIB is used instead of a general-purpose mobile agent framework such as Grasshopper. He also demonstrates that, once deployed, Script-MIB scripts perform comparably to (although slightly worse than) CORBA- and Java-based performance monitoring applications.

7.3. MbD in the context of OSI management

MbD has also attracted interest in the OSI management community, though significantly less than in the Internet community. Perhaps the reasons for that originate in the different philosophy of OSI management, which is more complex and relies on a high degree of standardization.

An early study towards the realization of MbD in the context of OSI management has been carried out by Vassila *et al.* [10]. Upon discussing the need for programmable management facilities within the TMN (Telecommunications Management Network) environment, the authors propose the concept of Active Managed Objects (AMOs) as opposed to the standardized, static Managed Objects (MOs). AMOs offer the means to specify and express arbitrary management functions along with a mechanism to dispatch and control management scripts to the Network Element (NE) using existing TMN mechanisms. AMOs may be delegated to a TMN application in the agent role and function close to other MOs they access.

The authors describe also a pilot implementation of AMOs [11] within the OSIMIS TMN platform [40]. They present two APIs which need to be available to program scripts; one provides access to the local environment in which the script is embedded; the other provides access to MOs in local and remote systems. The control of the script execution is effected by representing the script and its execution as an MO.

Since AMOs use the normal TMN mechanisms for information modeling and access they might have been standardized. However, this never happened, although a similar approach was pursued by the ISO/ITU that designed the CMIP command sequencer [53] [45]. Again, management functions are delegated as scripts which are transferred to the location where they are to be executed. These scripts can be started remotely; arguments can be passed to them; and results can be returned to the initiator. The scripts can communicate in the agent role with the delegating manager.

In contrast to Script-MIB that supports arbitrary programming languages, the CMIP Command Sequencer approach chose to define a special script language, the Systems Management Script Language (SMSL), in order to facilitate interoperability at the script level. Further, in CMIP command sequencer script results are 'pushed' to the manager. This contrasts with Script MIB, in which it is the manager who 'pulls' the results.

7.4. Mobile agents for distributed monitoring

While MbD is already entering the realm of practical network management, MA-based management has inspired a plethora of research work without, however, crossing the boundary of academia. The excitement surrounding MA-based management was sparked by the idea that if MbD (i.e. single-hop code mobility) was adding the extra gear of dynamic programmability, multiple-hop agent mobility may have had the potential of providing the means for designing even more powerful strongly distributed management systems.

The interested reader may refer to [9] (and references quoted therein) for a comprehensive review of the MA-based management applications proposed during the last decade. These encompass each of the five functional areas of management, the FCAPS, particularly fault management, configuration management, QoS management, distributed routing, information gathering, and network monitoring.

It is the last of these that has proved to benefit the most from the combination of agent features (autonomy, pro-activity, reactivity, cloning, etc.) and multiple-hop mobility. In fact, with the exception of distributed network monitoring, most work on MA-based management degenerates to either MbD, single-hop mobility or static multi-agents. Not many have shown how to fully exploit the real essence of MA—i.e. run-time, multiple-hop mobility—beyond the realm of monitoring or monitoring-related functionality.

MA-based distributed monitoring is analyzed in depth in [9] [13] [23]. Important hurdles that have been faced in this area can be summarized as follows:

- *Mobility patterns.* A variety of agent mobility patterns have been looked at together with their suitability for different monitoring operations and different network conditions. Agents may for instance jump from node to node on the basis of specific parameter values (found in the node or assumed by the agent). Alternatively, they may have pre-determined itineraries. They may fork parallel operations by cloning new agents or merge the results of different agents.
- *Agent dissemination/deployment.* Difficult tasks include populating the monitoring system with the 'right' number of MAs; appropriately partitioning the monitored system; and placing each agent in a 'good' location. Too many agents may overload the system unnecessarily. On the other hand, an insufficient number of MAs may result in lack of task distribution. Agents should also be placed in 'strategic' locations so as to incur minimal overheads e.g. when they periodically poll the objects within their catching area.
- *Adaptation through agent migration/cloning.* Migration and cloning are two important means for building adaptable systems. In the face of dynamic relocation of monitored objects (e.g. objects representing mobile resources), monitoring agents may react by self-relocating in order to keep monitoring traffic at low levels and preserve small values of latency. As the monitored system grows, the agent system may instead react by creating, i.e. cloning, new agents in charge of these new objects.
- *Control of MA systems and stability.* Agent cloning and agent migration do tend to cause serious instability problems. For instance, agent cloning may overpopulate and, hence, overload the monitored system. Inconsiderate agent migration may instead cause instability, with the agent-based monitoring system spending most of its time and resources trying to adapt through migration rather than performing its due tasks.

The author of this book chapter has studied the above problems and has demonstrated the feasibility of MA-based distributed and dynamic monitoring, identifying and quantifying also the benefits of this approach [8] [9]. We have demonstrated the applicability of *weak mobility* (Section 5.3) for dynamic distributed monitoring, assessing the advantages in terms of performance, scalability and adaptability.

What has not been demonstrated so far is the applicability to network management and monitoring and the practical use of *strong mobility* and *higher-order mobility* (Section 5.3). After so much effort dedicated to studying MA-based management we can therefore conclude that these two forms of mobility are most probably not suited to network management.

In the following two sections we illustrate some of the key advantages of MA-based management and the most apparent open issues, respectively.

7.5. Potential benefits of MA-based management

Because MA-based management is still at a research level, it is important to identify and keep in mind its potential advantages. These have been largely discussed in the literature, for instance in [16] [22] [81] [68] [2] [54] [21] [20] [92] [91]. The unanimous conclusion is that the real advantages arising from MAs are related to 'aggregate' rather than 'individual' advantages. It is, therefore, a combination of the following individual advantages that makes MA-based management so interesting:

- *They reduce network load.* MAs allow users to package a conversation and dispatch it to a destination host where interactions take place locally. MAs are also useful when reducing the flow of raw data in the network by moving the computation to the data rather than the data to the computation.
- *They overcome network latency.* For critical, real-time systems network latency may be not acceptable. MAs offer a solution, because they can be dispatched from a central controller to act locally and execute the controller's directions directly.
- *They can offload low-powered devices.* MAs allow a low-powered client such as a small mobile device to offload work to a high-powered proxy or an overloaded server to offload work to clients.
- *They encapsulate protocols.* As protocols evolve to accommodate new requirements for functionality, efficiency or security, it is cumbersome if not impossible to upgrade protocol code efficiently. As a result, protocols often become a legacy problem. MAs can move to remote hosts to establish 'channels' based on proprietary protocols.
- *They can dynamically enhance server capability.* Because MAs can relocate computational logic, servers become much simpler. Effectively, a server becomes merely an executing environment for hosting MAs. The server capability can be dynamically extended by sending new MAs. More generally, MAs can be used to distribute or upgrade software on demand.
- *They provide a natural approach to disconnected computing.* Mobile devices often rely on expensive or fragile network connections. Tasks requiring a continuously open connection between a mobile device and a fixed network can be embedded into MAs which can operate asynchronously and autonomously. In fact, MAs do not necessarily require a permanent connection during their operation.
- *They adapt dynamically.* MAs can sense their execution environment and react autonomously to changes. MAs can distribute themselves among the hosts to maintain the optimal configuration for solving a particular problem.
- *They are naturally heterogeneous.* MAs are generally computer- and transport-layer-independent, hence can provide optimal conditions for seamless system integration.
- *They are robust and fault-tolerant.* MAs' ability to react dynamically to unfavorable situations and events makes it easier to build robust and fault-tolerant distributed systems. For instance, MAs can be dispatched to a different host upon being warned that their host is about to shut down.
- *They provide natural support for distributed computation.* MAs are inherently distributed and, as such, can be a fundamental enabler for distributed computation.

- *They potentially result in more scalable distributed applications.* Because they can be dynamically located and can maintain location optimality through migration, MAs can result in increased scalability.

7.6. Open issues of MA-based management

In addition to not having reached commercial level, MA-based management is still facing a number of open issues that will probably further delay the maturation of this technology and paradigm. Some of them are summarized below with the intention of stimulating further research; they are also discussed in [16] [22] [68] [80] [92] [9]:

- *Security.* This is one of the most emotive issues raised when discussing MA systems in general and MA-based management in particular. Lack of security guarantees is one of the major arguments against MAs and a driver for a wealth of research in this subject [43]. It should be mentioned that much of the effort in security has been towards host protection, whereas less work has addressed the problem of protecting the MA integrity against malicious hosts and execution environments. Another problem is that security measures often result in performance and functional limitations. Finally, the real success of MAs is conditional upon overcoming security concerns in order to achieve trust on the part of third-party server providers along with their willingness to allow users to customize server behavior.
- *Safety.* A safe environment will make sure that MAs can be executed only 'where' and 'if' a sufficient amount of resources such as processing power and local storage capacity is available and that concurrent and consistent access to the resources manipulated by the MAs is guaranteed. This also relates to the willingness of the third-party service providers to sustain the MA's computational load.
- *Secrecy.* MAs can be entrusted with private information such as user profile information, user authentication data, or user negotiation preferences. Protecting an MA is not simple since agents are invariably interpreted within an execution environment. Mechanisms that ensure that agents maintain the privacy of their originator need further attention.
- *Transactional support.* A considerable part of today's commercial applications require a high degree of robustness. Moreover, transactional support is a pre-requisite for an increasing number of tasks. This will require a tight integration of agent technology and transaction management. There are two challenges to achieve this integration [68]. Firstly, the identification of transaction models which suit the asynchronous nature of agents. Secondly, the development of agent recovery mechanisms.
- *Standardization and interoperability.* Despite the efforts toward standardizing agent systems in order to allow for full interoperability (see [77] [28] [69] [27]), further work is required before agents can fully interoperate and run across different agent execution environments.
- *Limited Availability of agent execution environments.* Agent execution environments are not widespread and it is difficult to propagate them onto the management site, connectivity provider site, service provider site, and optionally also at the terminal site. This is envisioned to happen in the near future but as of today it represents a problem.

- *Complexity*. MA-based management systems are likely to be quite complex to design and debug because it will be difficult to determine their behavior in a real, dynamic network environment. This compares with their strength (in comparison to the CS design paradigm) which resides in easier implementation, deployment, and maintenance. Debugging a distributed system is difficult. An MA system is particularly difficult to assess because it involves mobile autonomous software entities whose behavior is often determined by the environment in which they sit and by their perception of the environment itself. Although some work has been done on agent design [102], on architectural styles for agent distribution [15], and on decomposition patterns for mobile-code based management [6], the application of these design techniques to the field of management has not been investigated so far. Finally, it is not clear how agent-based, delegated management should be used to pursue a real automation of management itself.
- *Limited availability of quantitative performance evaluation*. The ability of the MA paradigm to result in increased performance, scalability and flexibility in comparison to the CS one has been claimed by many authors. Though acceptable in principle, this claim has not corresponded to a widespread application of the MA paradigm across the management arena. One of the reasons is that insufficient work has been carried out to assess its strength in a quantitative fashion. Opponents of the MA paradigm suggest that, in fact, an alternative direction could be to enable RPC-based client-server interactions to match the advantages of MAs.
- *Migration overheads*. Agent migration involves overheads that need careful consideration. With today's platforms, the migration time between two hosts is in the order of seconds (see [12] and [37]); migration traffic depends on agent size and state and on the serialization mechanism; finally, processing overheads are associated with the serialization and de-serialization process. Further study is required to reduce migration overheads which limit significantly the MA application domain.
- *Control structures*. Today's MA systems allow the creation and cloning of agents, while efficient mechanisms for controlling agent migration and termination have not been sufficiently investigated. Algorithms for agent location, termination and for orphan detection are discussed in [54]. Agent autonomous migration is a potential source of instability if the triggered mechanisms are not well thought out and fine-tuned. The stability of MA systems is another interesting subject which requires further investigation. More generally, mechanisms to manage agent mobility in the context of integrated fixed and mobile networks are needed. A mobile networking environment is particularly dynamic as it involves a large number of simple, mobile terminals. Agent control mechanisms are particularly important to prevent instability and require further work.

8. CONCLUSIONS

Monitoring and information gathering functions are fundamental to each and every management-related activity. It is therefore crucial to design and realize monitoring systems that are efficient as well as being able to cope with the stringent requirements imposed by current and future networked systems. Important requirements include *scalability, adaptability, programmability,* and *reliability.* Future networked systems are bound to assume a global scale and to be based upon the Internet as a fundamental networking infrastructure. It is therefore important to consider monitoring techniques and technologies that are compatible with the Internet as well as meeting the requirements of telecommunications operators.

This chapter has provided an overview of a variety of monitoring methods, means and technologies. We have started by reviewing conventional approaches and protocols, looking at their main limitations. We have then directed our attention towards more innovative architectural approaches and software paradigms in order to identify suitable means for realizing distributed and dynamic monitoring systems.

Because of the large *scale* and high *dynamics* associated with fixed and mobile networked systems, centralized, protocol-based approaches such as SNMP, RMON, and CMIP cannot address the requirements of future monitoring systems. A paradigm shift towards decentralized, programmable, and adaptable distributed monitoring is necessary. In parallel, suitable technologies need to be developed.

Since one of the main characteristics of future systems is physical mobility (e.g. terminal, user, and service mobility), many researchers have been looking at various forms of software mobility to build suitable monitoring systems. In this chapter, we have reviewed the most influential and successful form of code mobility for management and monitoring, i.e. Management by Delegation. MbD has so far succeeded in crossing the boundary of academia, reaching the level of standardization in the context of both Internet and OSI management.

The mobile agent approach is even more powerful than MbD, providing a combination of powerful means for dynamic management—i.e. the agent concept and the multiple-hop mobility function. Despite its potential, MA-based management has not, however, yet matured into a feasible technology because of the numerous issues that are still open (the main ones have been reviewed in Section 7.6). Nevertheless, MA-based management seems still an active research area as demonstrated by the numerous international projects and conferences that capture the on-going research efforts. The open issues of Section 7.6 can be considered as a starting point for future research, while many other interesting research questions can be formulated starting from the seeds disseminated in this chapter.

ACKNOWLEDGEMENTS

The material presented in this chapter has been developed in the context of the POLYMICS project, funded by the UK Engineering and Physical Sciences Research Council (EPSRC)—Grant GR/S09371/01.

REFERENCES

[1] 3GPP, Technical Specification group services and system aspects: Virtual Home Environment / Open Service Access, 3GPP TS 23.127, v5.2.0, (June 2002).
[2] A. Bieszczad, B. Pagurek, T. White, *Mobile Agents for Network Management*, IEEE Communications Surveys, Fourth Quarter 1998, vol. 1, no. 1, pp. 2–9, (1998).

[3] A. Carzaniga, G. P. Picco, G. Vigna, *Designing Distributed Applications with Mobile Code Paradigms*. Proceedings of the 19th International Conference on Software Engineering (ICSE'97). pp. 22–32, (May 1997).

[4] A. Fuggetta, G. P. Picco, G. Vigna, *Understanding Code Mobility*, IEEE Transactions on Software Engineering, vol. 24, no. 5, pp. 342–361, (1998).

[5] A. Leinwand, K. F. Conroy, *Network Management, a Practical Perspective*. Addison-Wesley, (1996).

[6] A. Liotta, G. Knight, *Decomposition Patterns for Mobile Code-based Management*. In proc. of HP-OVUA, The Hewlett-Packard Openview University Association Plenary Workshop 1998, ENST de Bretagne, Rennes, France, (April 19–21, 1998).

[7] A. Liotta, G. Pavlou, G. Knight, *A Self-adaptable Agent System for Efficient Information Gathering*, Proceedings of the 3rd International Workshop on Mobile Agents for Telecommunication Applications (MATA'01), Montreal, Canada, Springer-Verlag (August 2001).

[8] A. Liotta, G. Pavlou, G. Knight, Exploiting Agent Mobility for Large Scale Network Monitoring, IEEE Network, special issue on Applicability of Mobile Agents to Telecommunications, Vol. 16, No. 3, IEEE, (May/June 2002).

[9] A. Liotta, *Towards Flexible and Scalable Distributed Monitoring with Mobile Agents*. PhD Thesis, University College London, London UK, (2001).

[10] A. Vassila, G. Knight, *Introducing Active Managed Objects for Effective and Autonomous Distributed Management*. In Proceedings of the 3rd International Conference on Intelligence in Broadband Services and Networks IS&N 95, Heraklion, Crete, Greece, (October 16–20, 1995).

[11] A. Vassila, G. Pavlou, G. Knight, *Active Objects in TMN*. In Proceedings of ISINM '97, (1997).

[12] C. Bohoris, A. Liotta, G. Pavlou, *Evaluation of Constrained Mobility for Programmability in Network Management*, To appear in the proceedings of the 11th IFIP/IEEE International Workshop on Distributed Systems: Operations & Management (DSOM 2000), Austin, Texas, USA, (December 2000).

[13] C. Bohoris, *Network Performance Management using Mobile Agents*. PhD Thesis, University of Surrey, UK, (2003).

[14] C. Ghezzi and G. Vigna, *Mobile Code Paradigms and Technologies: A Case Study*. In Proceeding of the First International Workshop on Mobile Agents '97, Berlin, Germany, (April 1997).

[15] C. Weir, *Architectural Styles for Distribution, Using macro-patterns for system design*. Second European Conference on Pattern Languages of Programming, EuroPLoP'97, (June 1997).

[16] C. G. Harrison., D. M. Chess, A. Kershenbaum, *Mobile Agents: Are they a good idea?* Technical Report, IBM Research Division. Watson Research Center, (March 1995).

[17] Casavant, T. L., Singhal, M., *Readings in Distributed Computing Systems*. IEEE Computer Society Press, (1994).

[18] CCITT Rec. M3010 1991, Principles for a Telecommunications Management Network (TMN), (1991).

[19] D. A. Halls, *Applying Mobile Code to Distributed Systems*. PhD thesis, University of Cambridge, (1997).

[20] D. B. Lange, M. Oshima, *Seven Good Reasons for Mobile Agents*. Communications of the ACM, Vol.42(3), pp. 88–89, (March 1999).

[21] D. B. Lange, *Mobile Objects and Mobile Agents: The Future of Distributed Computing?*, Proceedings of the European Conference on Object-Oriented Programming (ECOOP'98), (1998).

[22] D. Chess, C. Harrison, A. Kershenbaum, *Mobile Agents: Are they a Good Idea?* Proc. of Mobile Object Systems, Towards the Programmable Internet. J. Vitek, C. Tschudin, editors, Springer, pp. 25–47, (1997).

[23] D. Gavalas, *Mobile Software Agents for Network Monitoring and Performance Management*. PhD Thesis, University of Essex, UK, (2001).

[24] D. Levi, J. Schonwalder, RFC2592—*Definitions of Managed Objects for the Delegation of Management Scripts*. The Internet Society, (May 1999).

[25] D. B. Levi, J. Schonwalder, *Script MIB. Definition of Managed Objects for the Delegation of Management Scripts*. IETF Internet Draft, 1st version, (November 1996).

[26] Extensible Markup Language (XML), http://www.w3.org/XML/

[27] FIPA 98 Specification, Version 2.0, Part 2, Agent Communication Language, (October 1998).

[28] Foundation for Intelligent Physical Agents, web page: http://www.fipa.org/

[29] G. Almes, S. Kalidindi, M. Zekauskas, "*RFC2679—A One-way Delay Metric for IPPM*", The Internet Society, September 1999.

[30] G. Almes, S. Kalidindi, M. Zekauskas, "*RFC2681—A Round-trip Delay Metric for IPPM*", The Internet Society, September 1999.

[31] G. Cugola, C. Ghezzi, G. P. Picco, and G. Vigna, *A Characterization of Mobility and State Distribution in Mobile Code Languages*. In Proceedings of the Second Workshop on Mobile Object Systems, Linz, Austria, (July 1996).

[32] G. Goldszmidt, *Distributed Management by Delegation*. PhD Thesis, Columbia University, New York, (1996).

[33] G. Goldszmidt, *Distributed System Management via Elastic Servers*. In Proceedings of the IEEE First International Workshop on System Management, Los Angeles, California, (April 1993).

[34] G. Goldszmidt, Y. Yemini, *Delegated Agents for Distributed System Management*. IFIP/IEEE DSOM 1996 Workshop. L'Aquila, Italy, (October 28–30th 1996).

[35] G. Goldszmidt, Y. Yemini, *Delegated Agents for Network Management*. IEEE Communications Magazine, Vol.36 No.3, (March 1998).

[36] G. Goldszmidt, Y. Yemini, *Evaluating Management Decisions via Delegation*. Integrated Network Management IV. New York: Chapman & Hall, (1995).

[37] G. Knight, R. Hazemi, *Mobile Agent based management in the INSERT project*, Journal of Network and System Management (Mobile Agent-based Network and Service Management), Vol. 7 (3), (September 1999).

[38] G. Pavlou, *"Telecommunications Management Network: a Novel Approach Towards its Architecture and Realization Through Object-Oriented Software Platforms"*, PhD Thesis, University College London, March 1998.

[39] G. Pavlou, G. Mykoniatis, J. Sanchez, *Distributed Intelligent Monitoring and Reporting Facilities*, IEE Distributed Systems Engineering Journal (DSEJ), Special Issue on Management, Vol. 3, No. 2, pp. 124–135, IOP Publishing, (1996).

[40] G. Pavlou, K. McCarthy, S. Bhatti, G. Knight, *The OSIMIS Platform: Making OSI Management Simple*. Integrated Network Management IV—New York: Chapman & Hall (1995).

[41] G. Pavlou, *OSI Systems Management, Internet SNMP and ODP/OMG CORBA as Technologies for Telecommunications Network Management*, in Telecommunications Network Management: Technologies and Implementations, S. Aidarous, T. Plevyak, eds. pp. 63–109, IEEE Press, 1998.

[42] G. Thiel, *Locus Operating System, a Transparent System*. Computer Communications, Vol.14(6), pp. 336–346, (1991).

[43] G. Vigna, (editor), *Mobile Agents and Security*. Lecture Notes in Computer Science, LNCS 1419, Springer-Verlag, (1998).

[44] IETF IP Performance Metrics Workgroup, http://www.ietf.org/html.charters/ippm-charter.html

[45] ISO, Information Technology—Open Systems Interconnection—Systems Management—Command Sequencer. International Standard ISO 10164-21, ISO (1998).

[46] ITU-T Rec. X.700, Information Technology—Open Systems Interconnection—*Management Framework*, (1989).

[47] ITU-T Rec. X.701, Information Technology—Open Systems Interconnection—*Systems Management Overview*, (1992).

[48] ITU-T Rec. X.710, Information Technology—Open Systems Interconnection—*Common Management Information Service Specification (CMIS)*, Version 2 (1991).

[49] ITU-T Rec. X.711, Information Technology—Open Systems Interconnection—*Common Management Information Protocol Specification (CMIP)*, Version 2 (1991).

[50] ITU-T Rec. X.733, Information Technology—Open Systems Interconnection—*Systems Management: Alarm Reporting Function*.

[51] ITU-T Rec. X.738, Information Technology—Open Systems Interconnection—*Systems Management: Summarization Function,* (November 1993).

[52] ITU-T Rec. X.739, Information Technology—Open Systems Interconnection—*Systems Management: Metric Objects and Attributes,* (November 1993).

[53] ITU-T Rec. X.753, Information Technology—Open Systems Interconnection—*Systems Management: Command Sequencer for System Management*. ITU, Geneva, Switzerland, (October 1997).

[54] J. Baumann, *Control Algorithms for Mobile Agents*. PhD Thesis, University of Stuttgart, (1999).

[55] J. Schonwalder, J. Quittek, C. Kappler, *Building Distributed Management Applications with the IETF Script-MIB*, IEEE Journal on Selected Areas in Communications, Vol. 18, No. 5, pp. 702–714, (May 2000).

[56] J. Schonwalder, J. Quittek, *RFC2593—Script MIB Extensibility Protocol Version 1.0,* The Internet Society, (May 1999).

[57] J. Schonwalder, *Network Management by Delegation—From Research Prototypes Towards Standards*. Proc. of the 8th Joint European Networking Conference (JENC8), Edinburgh (May 1997).

[58] J. Siegel, *CORBA Fundamentals and Programming*. John Wiley & Sons, (1996).

[59] J. W. Stamos, D. K. Gifford, *Remote Evaluation*, ACM Transactions on Programming Languages and Systems, 12(4):537–565, (October 1990).

[60] J. W. Stamos, D. K. Gifford, Implementing Remote Evaluation. IEEE Transactions on Software Engineering, Vol. 16, No.7, (July 1990).

[61] Jean-Philippe Martin-Flatin, *A Survey of Distributed Enterprise Network and Systems Management Paradigms*. Submitted to JNSM, Special Issue on Enterprise Network and Systems Management, (November 30, 1997).

[62] Jean-Philippe Martin-Flatin, S. Znaty, *Annotated Typology of Distributed Network Management Paradigms*. Proceedings of DSOM'97, Sydney, Australia, (21–23 October 1997).

[63] Jean-Philippe Martin-Flatin, S. Znaty, *Two Taxonomies of Distributed Network and System Management Paradigms*. In Emerging Trends and Challenges in Network Management, S. Erfani and P. Ray (Eds.), Plenum Publishers, (2000).

[64] Joyce, J., Lomow, G., Slind, K., Unger, B., *Monitoring Distributed Systems*. ACM Trans. Comput. Syst., 5(2), 121–50, (1987).

[65] K. McCloghrie, F. Kastenholz, *"RFC1573—Evolution of the Interfaces Group of MIB-II"*, The Internet Society, January 1994.

[66] K. McCloghrie, M. Rose, *"RFC1213—Management Information Base for Network Management of TCP/IP-based internets: MIB-II"*, The Internet Society, March 1991.

[67] K. Meyer, M. Erlinger, J. Betser, C. Sunshine, G. Goldszmidt, Y. Yemini, *Decentralising Control and Intelligence in Network Management*. Proceedings of the 4th International Symposium on Integrated Network Management, Santa Barbara, CA, (May 1995).

[68] K. Rothermel, F. Hohl, N. Radouniklis, *Mobile Agents: What is Missing?* Proc. of Distributed Applications and Interoperable Systems, DAIS'97, Chapman & Hall, pp. 74–85, (1997).

[69] L. Chiariglione, *Foundations for Intelligent Physical Agents*. FIPA 98 Draft Specification, part 11, http://drogo.cselt.it/fipa/spec/fipa98/fipa98.html, (August 17, 1998).

[70] M. Baldi, G. P. Picco, *Evaluating the Tradeoffs of Mobile Code Paradigms in Network Management Applications*, ACM Transactions on Software Engineering and Methodology, 20th International Conference on Software Engineering (ICSE '98), Kyoto, Japan, (April 1998).

[71] M. Baldi, S. Gai, G. P. Picco, *Exploiting Code Mobility in Decentralized and Flexible Network Management*, Proceedings of the First International Workshop on Mobile Agents, Berlin, Germany, (April 1997).

[72] M. Sloman, *Network and Distributed Systems Management*. Addison-Wesley Publishing Company, (1994).

[73] M. Wooldridge, N. Jennings. *Agent Theories, Architectures, and Languages: A Survey*. In Proc. of ECAI94 Workshop on Agent Theories, Architectures & Languages (eds M.J. Wooldridge & N.R. Jennings) Amsterdam The Netherlands, pp. 1–32, (1994).

[74] M. Wooldridge. *INTELLIGENT AGENTS II: Agent Theories, Architectures, and Languages*. Springer-Verlag Lecture Notes in AI—Volume 1037, (1996).

[75] M. A. Mountzia, G. Dreo-Rodosek, *Delegation of Functionality: Aspects and Requirements on Management Architectures*. Proceedings of the IFIP/IEEE International Workshop on Distributed Systems: Operations & Management (DSOM'06), (October 1996).

[76] M. M. Cheikhrouhou, P. Conti, J. Labetoulle, *Intelligent Agents in Network Management: A State of the Art*. Networking and Information Systems Journal, (June 1998).

[77] Object Management Group, Mobile Agent System Interoperability Facilities Specification, orbos/97-10-05, 1997, ftp://ftp.omg.org/pub/docs/orbos/97-10-05.pdf (1997).

[78] OMG, *The Common Object Request Broker Architecture and Specification* (CORBA), Version 2.0, (1995).

[79] R. Lea, C. Jacquemont, E. Pillevesse, *Cool: System Support for Distributed Object-oriented Programming*. Communications of the ACM, Vol.36(9), pp. 37–46, (November 93).

[80] R. Oppliger, *Security Issues Related to Mobile Code and Agent-based Systems*. Computer Communications, Vol.22, pp. 1165–1170, Elsevier, (1999).

[81] R. S. Gray, *Agent Tcl: A Flexible and Secure Mobile-agent System*. PhD Thesis, Dartmouth College, Hanover, New Hampshire, (June 1997).

[82] S. Waldbusser, Remote Network Monitoring Management Information Base. RFC 1757, (February 1995).

[83] Stallings, W., SNMP, SNMPv2 and CMIP The Practical Guide to Network Management Standards. Addison-Wesley Publishing Company, (1993).

[84] Sun Microsystem, *Enterprise Java Beans* http://java.sun.com/products/ejb/index.html

[85] Sun Microsystem, JAIN Connectivity Management Specification. http://www.jcp.org/en/jsr/detail?id=25

[86] Sun Microsystem, JAIN. http://java.sun.com/products/jain/

[87] Sun Microsystem, *Java Dynamic Management Kit*. http://www.sun.com/products-n-solutions/telecom/software/java-dynamic/

[88] Sun Microsystem, *Java Management Extensions* (JMX). http://java.sun.com/products/JavaManagement/index.html

[89] Sun Microsystems, *Java Object Serialization*, http://java.sun.com/j2se/1.3/docs/guide/serialization/

[90] Sun Microsystems, *Java Remote Method Invocation*, http://java.sun.com/products/jdk/rmi/

[91] T. Papaioannou, *Mobile Information Agents for Cyberspace—State of the Art and Visions*. Proc. of Co-operating Information Agents, (2000).

[92] T. Papaioannou, *On the Structuring of Distributed Systems*. PhD Thesis, Loughborough University, (February 2000).

[93] The 3rd Generation Partnership Project (3GPP), http://www.3gpp.org/

[94] *The Jasmin Platform*, http://www.ibr.cs.tu-bs.de/projects/jasmin/

[95] The Parlay Group, *www.parlay.org*

[96] V. Paxson, G. Almes, J. Mahdavi, M. Mathis, *"RFC2330—Framework for IP Performance Metrics"*, The Internet Society, May 1998.

[97] W. Stallings, SNMP, SNMPv2, and RMON Practical Network Management, Addison-Wesley, (1996).

[98] W. J. Barr, T. Boyd, Y. Inoue, *The TINA Initiative*. IEEE Communications Magazine, Vol 31(3), pp. 70–76, (1993).

[99] W3C, The Simple Object Access Protocol, http://www.w3c.org/TR/SOAP/

[100] Y. Yemini, G. G. Goldszmidt, S. Yemini, *Network Management by Delegation*. Integrated Network Management II, Amsterdam (1991).

[101] Y. Yemini, *The OSI Network Management Model*. IEEE Communication Magazine, Pagg. 20–29, (May 1993).

[102] Yariv Aridor and Danny B. Lange, *Agent Design Patterns: Elements of Agent Applications Design*. Second International Conference on Autonomous Agents (Agents '98), (May 1998).

FINDING PATTERNS IN IMAGE DATABASES

WYNNE HSU, MONG LI LEE AND JING DAI

1. INTRODUCTION

Image is one of the most widely used media in the world. Many real-life applications have been designed to process and analyze large number of images. For example, in the terrain matching applications, we have thousands of images that are returned by the satellite which need to be processed and mapped; in the archaeology domain, all ancient artifacts are photographed and stored for subsequent efficient retrieval; in the medical domain, images such as mammograms, ultrasound images, X-ray images, MRI-images are already a standard part of health care industry. Finding meaningful patterns from large sets of images is necessary for automatic indexing, categorizing, retrieving, and analyzing these images.

While there have been much efforts in applying data mining techniques to image databases, there is a lack of pattern discovery algorithms specifically designed to generate patterns unique to images. One such class of image patterns is what we called the viewpoint patterns. Viewpoint patterns refer to the invariant relationships, in the form of the relative spatial relationships among the objects in images. These invariant relationships convey critical perceptual information in images.

Figure 1 shows an example of viewpoint pattern based on three kitchen plan images. Each kitchen plan consists of a subset of {cooktop (C), sink (S), refrigerator (R), microwave (M), dishwasher (D)}. A quick inspection reveals that while the absolute positions of the objects in each kitchen plans are unique, there exist a fixed relationship among three objects in these plans, namely,

Kitchen plans (Plan_1, Plan_2, Plan_3)

Viewpoint pattern found in the 3 Kitchen plans

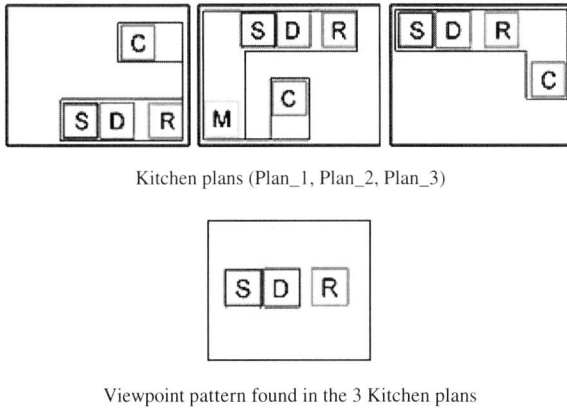

Figure 1. Sample image set and viewpoint pattern found.

$$\text{Sink} \xrightarrow{\textit{Dist 38, Orient Left}} \text{Dishwasher} \xrightarrow{\textit{Dist 51, Orient Left}} \text{Refrigerator.}$$

We call this relationship a viewpoint pattern. Experiments on large image collections, ranging from general category images, to medical images, to architectural design images, demonstrate that viewpoint patterns are meaningful and interesting to human users.

The book chapter is organized as follows. Section 2 reviews related work in image mining. Their main ideas and limitations will be discussed. Section 3 gives the definition of viewpoint pattern and presents our proposed ViewpointMiner. Section 4 gives the results of experiments to evaluate ViewpointMiner. Section 5 draws the conclusion and discusses future work.

2. RELATED WORK

Image mining approaches can be divided into two categories according to their input data: pixel information or objects. Mining based on pixel-level information aims to discover patterns directly from pixel-level features such as color, texture and wavelet coefficients, whereas mining based on object-level information requires objects recognition. The main difference in the two approaches lies in the way they preprocess the input data. The subsequent pattern discovery phase is similar for the two approaches.

2.1. Preprocessing

Preprocessing of images mainly consists of two aspects: image adjustment and feature extraction. The aim of the preprocessing step is to transform the images to a form suitable for the application of traditional data mining techniques.

In general, the approaches based on pixel-level information perform the preprocessing step of image adjustment by applying some mathematical methods to enhance certain pixel data so that their characteristics can be emphasized to generate clear and distinct patterns. For example, principal component analysis is used to reduce the dimensionality of the feature space [5]. This is usually followed by performing a variance maximization of the pixel classes [15]. [2] employs histogram equalization to increase the contrast range of grey levels in medical images. [9] attempts to fix the error of image acquisition by performing geometric correction and radiometric correction on the remotely sensed image. [22] extracts the wavelet coefficients of spectral data as the input to the classifier. To get more information, some approaches extract global or regional features such as color histogram, mean value and deviation [29] in preprocessing. In general, image mining approaches that are based on pixel-level information suffer from the lack of meaningful mapping from the low level pixel patterns to the human perceived meaning in the images.

On the other hand, mining based on object-level information requires objects recognition. To recognize objects from image content, image segmentation techniques have been employed to segment an image into disjoint and usually connected regions. Ideally, each region is expected to represent an object. Errors in image segmentation will be accumulated to subsequent pattern discovery. Examples of image segmentation systems include: Blobworld [12], feature localization in C-BIRD [21], IRM in SIMPLIcity [20] and Delphi2 eCognition [3].

2.2. Pattern discovery

Having preprocessed the images to extract or highlight the relevant features, existing or adapted data mining algorithms are then used to perform the pattern discovery process. In many applications, these input features are prepared in such a way that traditional data mining methods can be used directly with little or no modification. However, to discover patterns involving interesting spatial and semantic information in image sets, special data mining algorithms are needed.

2.2.1. Association mining in image data

Association rule mining in image data as an unsupervised mining method has been used to extract the associations among visual features, text descriptions and objects from image sets.

Based on the extracted objects, Ordonez et al. [23] tries to find associations of the occurrence of the objects after running a preprocessing to identify objects in images and prepare the data in the form of transactions. The preprocessing algorithm places similar objects under one object id. The similarity between two objects is determined by their region descriptions. The cost of this preprocessing is $O(n^2)$ if the number of objects in one image is limited, otherwise it will be $O(n^2m^2)$ where m is the number of possible different objects in one image. This does not seem to be scalable for a large image database. After the preprocessing step, the image data has been transformed into a transactional data set. Traditional association rule mining algorithm can be directly applied to discover interesting patterns. An example of the discovered rules is:

{Object7, Object 10, Object11} => {Object2}; Support = 0.3, Confidence = 1

While this represents a good attempt at discovering associations between objects in image database, it suffers from a number of limitations. First, the algorithm does not consider the case where there are several similar objects in one image. For example, if there are two objects O inside one image, the algorithm may count O only once. Second, the rules discovered are not able to represent the relative object spatial information that is essential for understanding image contents.

Another example of image association rule mining is the MM-Associator module of MultiMediaMiner [31]. This module discovers association rules based on pixel features and text description, not the objects. One possible example rule found by this module can be described as:

is(Image, big) and is(Keyword, sky) => is(Frequent_color, blue);

$$\text{Support} = 0.1, \text{Confidence} = 0.55.$$

[14] discovers associations between active brain areas and brain functions. This is achieved by first deriving a linear formula to describe the relation using regression analysis and then extracting rules from the formula. [8] presents an algorithm that discovers relationships between low-level images features such as autocorrelogram of colors and Fourier description of textures. The relationships are ranked based on conditional probability and implication intensity. The discovered relationships are then used to automatically categorize new images and improve accuracy while retrieving images.

2.2.2. Clustering in image data

Clustering in image data refers to grouping similar image feature vectors together for further analysis. There are many applications that perform clustering of image pixels and/or clustering of image regions.

The SOM Neural Network is a clustering tool that has been used in [9], [15], [32] to cluster image content. Generally, the SOM arranges feature vectors according to their similarity, creating continuous topological of the input layer. In this topological map, the vectors that are similar in the input layer are clustered in the output layer, while those vectors that are different are kept far apart. In [9], after image adjustment, the pixel intensities of satellite remotely sensed images are used as the input data of SOM. After clustering, seven distinct clusters are identified and later labeled as different land types. The clustered image is actually segmented in this way. [15] uses the gray level of the pixel as input to SOM to analyze the properties of typhoon cloud patterns. In [32], SOM is used to cluster images using texture and color features. The images are hierarchically clustered to build an index tree for image retrieval.

A different approach is adopted by Chang et al. [7] where they present a Replicated IMage dEtector system (RIME) that uses a clustering algorithm, Cluster Forming (CF), to detect unlawful copy images on the web. This clustering algorithm is reported to have obtained more natural clusters than K-means and SOM. However, all these techniques do not take into consideration the relative values and spatial information of image objects.

2.2.3. Classification in image data

Image classification is to assign image feature vectors to two or more pre-defined classes. Classification methods such as Bayesian classifier, decision tree, neural network, and classification based on associations have been widely used to classify image data.

Bayesian classification method [4], [22], [24], [29], is a statistics based method to determine the most probable class that a new sample should belong to. This probability of belonging to a class for a feature vector is obtained from the training data. [4] applies the maximum likelihood classifier to analyze remote sensing images. In this work, the spectral responses of the images are used as features to classify land into five classes. They use a training set to estimate the parameters of the classifier. [22] utilizes the wavelet coefficient as the input of Bayesian linear discriminant analysis to classify mineralogical spectral data. [29] uses a Bayesian classifier to classify vacation images into semantic classes. [24] employs a Bayesian learning network to recognize irregular features such as unconstrained handwritten characters. In the learning network, the corresponding pixels are grouped to form an irregular feature vector so that the recognition can be done.

The Sky Image Cataloging and Analysis Tool (SKICAT) [11] applies decision tree learning to classify sky objects. Attributes such as intensity and area are defined by the astronomers and used to classify the objects. The system has successfully classified a large set of photographic plates because this problem is well understood.

In the project CEHDS [17], a classifier SHRINK [18] is used to classify oil spills from radar images. A significant characteristic of this system is that it considers both the positive samples and negative samples to be suitable for the oil spills distribution. Furthermore, the users are allowed to control the rate between true positive and false positive in the classification.

The "template-matching" methods are used to recognize specific objects in image collections [6], [30]. These methods generate a set of templates for destination objects according to the training image data. [6] presents a distributed architecture Diamond Eye which can be used to find certain objects in images via network. This system applies the spatially-deformable configuration of parts models which provides a hybrid of principle component analysis and continuously-scalable template models. The models represent the object hierarchically using whole-parts relationship. After building the models, the system is able to return the set of best matches in the image set. [30] describes a Wavelet Image Pornography Elimination, a system that is capable of detecting objectionable images using wavelet-based shape matching. Among a series of detectors applied in the system, the shape matching with objectionable images in the training database is the final step to determinate whether the image is benign.

Using the Focus of Attention to generate candidates and the Principle Component Analysis to extract features, [5] applies classification methods like Bayesian methods, Neural Network, Nearest Neighbor and decision tree to identify volcanoes in Venus images. [2] classifies mammograms using both Neural Network and association rule mining. The original mammograms are split into small squares, and the grey level statistics of each square is used as features together with the descriptions. The results of two classifiers are compared and analyzed. [10] applies voting strategies to integrate the results from multiple base classifiers to identify tumor cells more accurately in tissue-section images.

2.3. Image-specific considerations

After reviewing the various efforts in applying data mining techniques to image databases, we observe that semantic information and spatial information need to be taken into account in order to generate patterns that are unique to images.

2.3.1. Semantic information

All the image mining prototypes involving semantic information requires the incorporation of domain knowledge either in the form of human expert to build the prototypes of the patterns [28], [29]; or in the form of feedback loops to tune the mining results [16], [19], [27].

An example involving semantic information is the image classification prototype presented by Vailaya et al. [29]. In this work, they manually define semantic hierarchical classes for vacation images. These conceptual image classes are meaningful and mostly exclusive. Having labeled the classes, Bayesian method is used to classify the images into different classes using pixel-level features. Note that according to different node in the hierarchy, different features are also chosen by human experts. [28] presents a hypothesis-driven method to discover associations with color, shape, texture and text of images. The hypotheses are formulated by human in form of association rules and verified by scanning the image database.

In the MARS-2 system [27], after querying by example, users are required to indicate how relevant the retrieved images are to the query. The weights of links from the query image to the result images are then updated according to that feedback. [16] applies the same strategy to train the Bayesian classifier by manually labeling a selected pixel in satellite imageries. Similarly, [19] presents an incremental clustering method involving user's feedback. The image feature weights are updated based on both the clustered database and the relevance feedback.

2.3.2. Spatial relationship

After reviewing the various technologies in the image mining field, we see an obvious gap in discovering image patterns involving spatial information. To date, we are only aware of one work that deals with spatial information of image objects.

Mining based on Attributed Relational Graph (ARG) is recently proposed to extract adjacent relations of image regions. Attributed Relational Graph (ARG) is a powerful model to represent relations between objects in images [25], [26]. It has recently been used to represent frequent patterns in image mining [13]. They use a compact pattern ARG (PARG) model to summarize a large set of sample ARGs which represent the segmented images. The nodes in the ARG are regions in an image and each arc between two nodes shows that the two corresponding regions are connected. Their work is to estimate PARG models with underlying probabilistic distribution function by learning the sample images. However, their work focuses on discovering the adjacent relationships between different regions in images and hence, it is not suitable for finding invariant relationships among disconnected image objects. Moreover, the patterns represented by ARG are not easy to visualize. In this chapter, we propose a new class of mining algorithm that is able to generate invariant spatial relationships that will provide a good understanding of the image contents across large set of images.

3. VIEWPOINT PATTERN DISCOVERY

Viewpoint patterns refer to patterns that demonstrate the invariant relationships of one object from the point of view of another object. This class of patterns is especially relevant to describing the perceptually meaningful relationships among objects in images. Each object is described as a set of attribute value pairs (attribute, value). The 'viewpoint' relationships are represented by relative distance and orientation: $\xrightarrow{Dist\ d,\ Orient\ o}$, from one object to its right neighbor. Formally, a viewpoint pattern involving N objects, each having K attributes can be described as follows:

$$\text{Object}_1((a_{11},v_{11}); (a_{12},v_{12}); \ldots (a_{1K},v_{1K})) \xrightarrow{Dist\ d_1, Orient\ o_1} \text{Object}_2((a_{21},v_{21}); (a_{22},v_{22}); \ldots$$

$$(a_{2K},v_{2K})) \xrightarrow{Dist\ d_2, Orient\ o_2} \ldots \xrightarrow{Dist\ d_{N-1}, Orient\ o_{N-1}} \text{Object}_N((a_{N1},v_{N1}); (a_{N2},v_{N2}); \ldots$$

$$(a_{NK},v_{NK})) \qquad (\text{Support})$$

where

1. (a_{ij}, v_{ij}) denote the jth attribute value pair used to describe *Object$_i$*. Note the object here is an abstract object as defined by the constraints on its attribute values;
2. connects Object$_{i+1}$ with respect to Object$_i$. Note that v_{ij}, d_i and o_i can be null, a single-value, or an interval. We order these objects by imposing the constraint that Object$_i$ must appear to the left of Object$_{i+1}$. With this constraint, each k-object record can form at most one unique k-object viewpoint pattern;
3. *Support* indicates how significant is the pattern. The support of a pattern refers to the number of times the pattern appears in the image collection. If the same pattern appears more than once in an image, then the support will be incremented by 2 for this pattern.

A *frequent viewpoint pattern* is a pattern whose support is larger than a threshold. Frequent viewpoint patterns are what people are interested in and what we want to discover.

While the viewpoint patterns look deceivingly similar to association rules, they are different from association rules. Viewpoint patterns do not have "and" and "→" as in association rule because the entire pattern is one predicate. Further, a viewpoint pattern contains more information than the association rule, because the traditional "and" and "→" have been replaced by distance and orientation relationship. Our goal

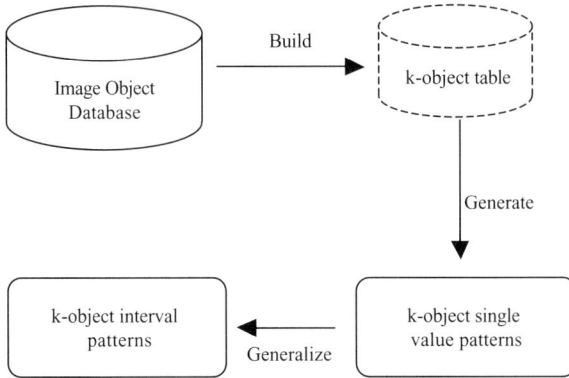

Figure 2. Major steps for mining viewpoint patterns.

is to generate such viewpoint patterns from image databases. The details of the mining algorithm ViewpointMiner are described in the following subsection.

3.1. Overview

Figure 2 shows an overview of the major steps involved in the mining of viewpoint patterns. Given an image object database, we first generate all possible 2-object patterns. This is achieved by building an in-memory 2-object table to store all the object pairs that appear in the same image. Scanning the 2-object table, we generate all frequent 2-object patterns and record their supports. All the frequent 'adjacent' 2-object patterns are merged to form 2-object interval patterns. Next, we proceed to generate k-object patterns from (k-1)-object patterns. The process continues until no new patterns are generated.

3.2. Algorithm ViewpointMiner

Before we describe the algorithm, we first define some terminologies that are used here. Table 1 defines the pattern and relation types that are utilized in the mining process.

Figure 3 presents the ViewpointMiner algorithm. Let D be the image object database which stores the attribute values and locations for all the objects. The preprocessing step in the algorithm discretizes all the continuous value attributes and locations, and prunes away the insignificant objects that are either too small or with low contrast to the background. The pattern generation process begins with k = 2. Line 3 builds the k-object table in memory based on D and the (k-1)-object table. From lines 4 to 14, the program generates the candidates and counts the frequent ones as single-value viewpoint patterns. Line 15 generalizes single-value patterns to interval patterns. Lines 16 and 17 prune the redundant interval patterns and useless k-object records. This process is repeated until no new patterns are generated. Next, we describe in details the six functions that are invoked from within the loop.

Table 1 Patterns and relation types

Terms	Definition
Single-value $S_{k,m}$ Pattern	$S_{k,m}$ are the frequent k-object patterns with the constraint that: when k > 2, there are exactly m values in the set $\{d_{(k-1)}, o_{(k-1)}, v_{kj}, \text{for all } j\}$ that are single-value, while others are all null; when k = 2, there are exactly m values in the set $\{d_1, o_1, v_{kj}, \text{for all } j, k\}$ are single-value, while others are all null.
Interval I_k Pattern	I_k are the frequent k-object patterns where: when k > 2, there are some values in the set $\{d_{(k-1)}, o_{(k-1)}, v_{kj}, \text{for all } j\}$ are interval; when k = 2, there are some values in the set $\{d_1, o_1, v_{kj}, \text{for all } j, k\}$ are interval.
SI_k Pattern	This refers to the union of single-value and interval patterns, that is, $SI_k = I_k \cup S_{k,m}$, for all m.
Cover Relation	Pattern A *cover* pattern B if and only if all the attribute, distance and/or orientation values of A are superset of that of B.

Algorithm ViewpointMiner:
Input: Image object database D;
Output: SI_k patterns for all k;

1) D' = preprocess (D);
2) For (k = 2; $S_{(k-1), 1}$!= NULL; k++)
3)   k-object table = *build (D', (k-1)-object table)*;
4)   If (k > 2)
5) $CS_{k, 1}$ = *candidate-gen1 ($SI_{(k-1)}$, $S_{(k-1), 1}$)*;
6)   Else
7) $CS_{2, 1}$ = set of all attribute value pairs in D';
8)   Endif
9) $S_{k, 1}$ = {c ∈ $CS_{k, 1}$ | is_frequent (c)};
10)   F = # of object attributes + 2;
11)   For (f = 2; f <= F and $S_{k, f-1}$!= NULL; f++)
12) $CS_{k, f}$ = *candidate-gen2 ($S_{k, (f-1)}$)*;
13) $S_{k, f}$ = {c ∈ $CS_{k, f}$ | is_frequent (c)};
14)   Endfor
15) I_k = *generalize ($\cup_f S_{k, f}$)*;
16) SI_k = *prune-pattern (($\cup_f S_{k, f}$) $\cup I_k$)*;
17)   k-object table = *prune-obj (k-object table, SI_k)*;
18) Endfor

Figure 3. Algorithm ViewpointMiner.

build (D', (k-1)-object table): This is the most time consuming part of the algorithm. This function scans the database and records all combinations of k objects that appear in each image into k-object table. The k-object table is indexed by a hash function. The total size of this k-object table is controlled by the preprocessing function. In this function, the distance and orientation among the k objects are calculated and stored after sorting them according to their locations.

candidate-gen1 ($SI_{(k-1)}$, $S_{(k-1),1}$: This function generates the candidates of $S_{k,1}$ patterns. It is similar to the candidate generation function of the Apriori algorithm [1].

The difference is that each candidate is a sequence of objects where the order of the objects is important. In this function, each candidate for $S_{k,1}$ pattern is generated by adding $\text{Object}_{(k-1)}$, $o_{(k-2)}$ and $d_{(k-2)}$ of a $S_{(k-1),1}$ pattern to the end of a $SI_{(k-1)}$ pattern, at the same time the sub-pattern formed by the last k-1 objects and k-2 distances and orientations of the candidate must cover the $S_{(k-1),1}$ pattern. Note that we select a special subset of $SI_{(k-1)}$ and $S_{(k-1),1}$ as the input parameters to the function. This enables us to limit the number of patterns generated. Suppose we have

$$\text{Object}_1((\text{color},3)) \xrightarrow{\textit{Dist 38, Orient 1.57}} \text{Object}_2((\text{color},4)); \text{ and}$$

$$\text{Object}_1((\text{color},4)) \xrightarrow{\textit{Dist 97, Orient null}} \text{Object}_2((\text{color},6));$$

Then the candidate pattern generated is:

$$\text{Object}_1((\text{color},3)) \xrightarrow{\textit{Dist 38, Orient 1.57}} \text{Object}_2((\text{color},4)) \xrightarrow{\textit{Dist 97, Orient null}} \text{Object}_3((\text{color},6)).$$

candidate-gen2 ($S_{k,(f-1)}$): The function generates the $S_{k,f}$ candidate patterns from $S_{k,(f-1)}$ patterns. It is also similar to the candidate generation in the Apriori algorithm. The difference is that it is the attribute, and not the object or item concerned. For each pair of $S_{k,(f-1)}$ patterns with the same first k-1 objects and k-2 dist and orient, the function generates a temporary candidate by combining them together, if they have only one different attribute value in the last object and last dist and orient. If the temporary candidate can be covered by some $S_{k,(f-1)}$ pattern after set any attribute value of the last object or the last dist or orient as null, then it is stored as a candidate pattern.

generalize ($S_{k,j}$): This function generates I_k by merging the adjacent segments in $S_{k,j}$ patterns. It makes use of a sub-generalize function to create the interval range for the selected attribute. Sub-generalize function generalizes a single attribute or dist or orient for all the patterns. Suppose we have two $S_{2,3}$ patterns:

$$\text{Object}_1((\text{color},3)) \xrightarrow{\textit{Dist 2, Orient NULL}} \text{Object}_2((\text{color},4)) \ (\text{Sup}=10); \text{Object}_1((\text{color}, 3))$$

$$\xrightarrow{\textit{Dist 3, Orient NULL}} \text{Object}_2((\text{color},4)) \ (\text{Sup}=5);$$

These patterns can be generalized using sub-generalize function on the attribute dist to

$$\text{Object}_1((\text{color},3)) \xrightarrow{\textit{Dist [2, 3], Orient NULL}} \text{Object}_2((\text{color},4)) \ (\text{Sup}=15);$$

When we want to generalize attributes A and B, we can generate interval-value patterns using sub-generalize function on A first, before using the result patterns to generalize on B using sub-generalize function again. Thus all the result patterns are high level patterns about A and B.

prune-pattern (SI_k): Since function generalize ($S_{k,f}$) produces many interval patterns, there will be some patterns covered by the others. This function prunes away these redundant patterns. Noticing that the patterns with all the attributes are single-value are usually interesting and important to generate candidate patterns in candidate-gen1 function, we keep these patterns in the result pattern set. Suppose pattern P2 covers pattern P1. If they have the same support, then P2 is regarded as redundant, otherwise, P1 is redundant. This pruning step can decrease the number of candidates for the outer loop as well as the final result.

prune-obj (k-object table, SI_k): This function prunes away the records that are not covered by SI_k patterns from D'. If a k-object record is not covered by SI_k patterns, then it implies that the record will not be covered by any $SI_{(k+1)}$ patterns. Thus, after the prune-obj function, only the useful k-object record will be kept in the k-object table to generate the (k + 1)-object table. This is a simple but important part because it decreases the size of the in-memory table which is frequently accessed during mining.

The ViewpointMiner algorithm incurs low I/O cost, since the number of times to scan the image object database is equal to the number of objects in the longest pattern minus one. The most time-consuming part build function can run in almost linear time to the total number of images due to the hash table built. The sizes of both data space and image space are reduced to simplify the computational process. Without the fixed concept hierarchy structure, the flexibility of the patterns is considered and generalization is done.

4. EXPERIMENTS

In this section, we demonstrate how the ViewpointMiner algorithm performs on different types of image databases. Three series of experiments have been done using general category images, retinal images and kitchen plan images respectively. A visualization tool has been implemented for easy understanding of the viewpoint patterns in these experiments. We implemented the algorithm in Java and carried out experiments on a Pentium 4 1.6GHz with 256 MB memory and 20GB hard disk, running Windows XP.

4.1. General category images

The most expensive part of our algorithm is the function *build( )* that requires scanning the image database to construct the k-object records. Theoretically, with an appropriate hash function, the time complexity of the function *build( )* is O(m) where m is the number of images in the database (assuming the number of objects in an image is O(1)). As all the other functions are run in the main memory, they are much faster comparing to the function *build( )*.

In the first set of experiments, we used 5000 images from a general category image collection. Using Blobworld [12], we extracted over 25,000 objects after restricting the number of objects in each image to be 7. Figure 4 shows a sample of the images and their corresponding extracted objects. The minimum support is set to be 0.15% of

Figure 4. Samples from general categorized image set.

the size of the 2-object table. Experiment results show that, in total, we have 57,058 2-object records and 71,602 3-object records, and 51,575 4-object records without object pruning.

Figure 5 gives the time needed to build the k-object table as we vary the number of images from 1000 to 5000. We observe that the time needed to build the k-object tables is linear to the number of images. Building the 2-object table requires almost the same time as building the 4-object table because the number of 2-object records and the number of 4-object records are similar in this image collection.

In order to investigate the effect of varying the minimum support values on the runtime efficiency of the algorithm, we conduct a second set of experiments on 5000 images where the minimum support is varied from 0.15% to 0.35% (Figure 6). The results indicate that the smaller the minimum support value, the greater is the time required to generate viewpoint patterns. This is to be expected because a smaller minimum support value implies the number of frequent patterns will increase. Consequently, more candidates will be generated and the cost will go up.

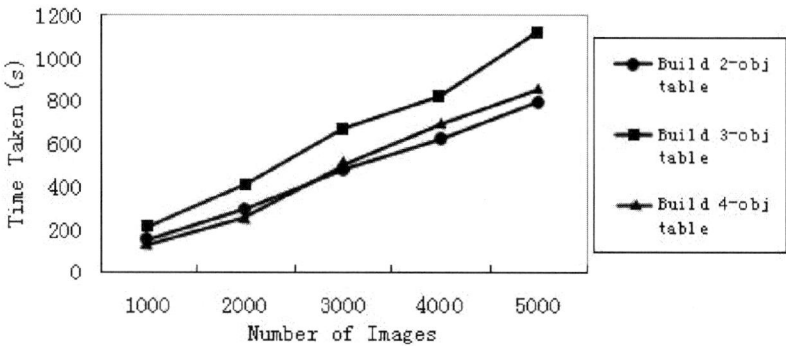

Figure 5. Time taken to build k-object table.

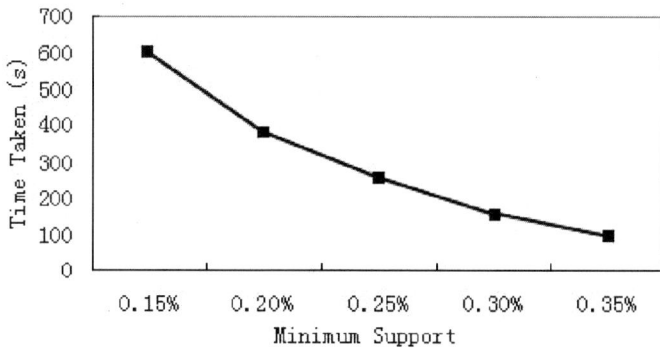

Figure 6. Time taken to generate 2-object patterns.

Our study on the time complexity of the generalization to interval patterns shows that this function is relatively inexpensive. In fact, the generalization process takes less than 0.5 second even in experiments on 5000 images.

Next, we investigate the effect of pruning on the performance of the algorithm (Figure 7). The results showed that after pruning objects using the $S_{2,3}$ patterns, only 14.3% of the 2-object records are left, and 2,978 3-object records are generated as compared to the 71,602 records generated without pruning. This indicates that our viewpoint pattern mining algorithm is scalable and efficient.

Given the variety of images as shown in Figure 4, we did not discover any meaningful viewpoint patterns in this image set. In the next two sets of experiments, we use two real-world domain-specific image databases to discover useful and interesting viewpoint patterns.

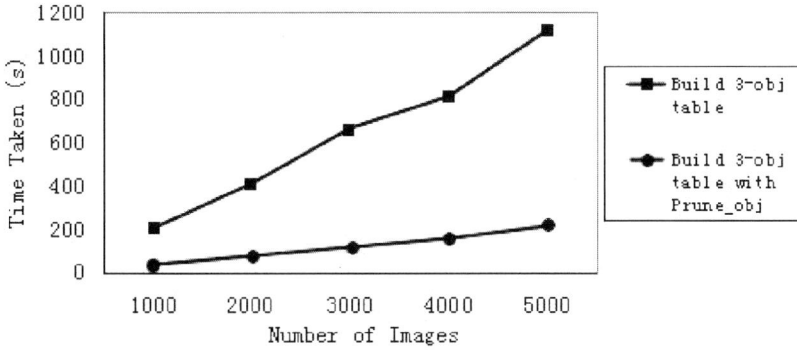

Figure 7. Time taken w/o Prune-obj step.

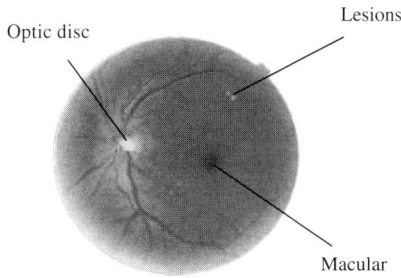

Figure 8. A retinal image.

4.2. Retinal images

In this set of experiments, we run the viewpoint pattern mining algorithm on 153 retinal images. Figure 8 shows an example of a retinal image. The retinal image is represented in LUV color space with each component normalized to [0, 255]. One of the symptoms of the medical condition diabetic retinopathy is the development of yellowish spots called lesions in the retina (see Figure 8). Understanding the distribution of lesions and their patterns may lead to more accurate diagnosis of the disease and better treatment protocol.

We perform two experiments on the retinal images. In the first experiment, we investigate the distribution of lesions from the point of view of the optic disc and macular. In the second experiment, we investigate the relationships among the lesions. We extracted a total of 1256 lesion objects. Each lesion object is denoted by its bounding rectangle (x1, x2, y1, y2) as well as its LUV color information as shown:

(lesion#, image#, bottom, top, left, right, color_L, color_U, color_V)

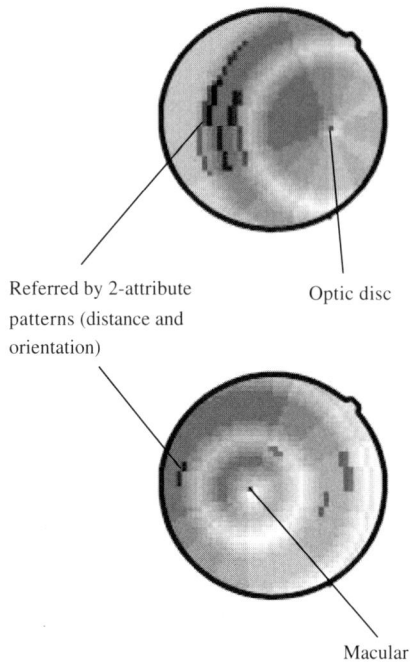

Figure 9. Visualizing the distribution of lesions.

Figure 9 shows the results of performing viewpoint patterns mining from the point of view of the optic disc/macular. Here, we use the optic disc and macular as the reference point, and each viewpoint pattern only contains one reference point and one lesion object. Since we are only interested in the distribution of the lesion objects, the size and color attributes are kept null in these patterns.

Setting the minimum support count to 5, we obtain 261 frequent patterns with respect to the optic disc and 78 frequent patterns with respect to the macular without pruning. The results are then pruned and visualized as shown in Figure 9. We use the level of grey intensities to denote the densities of the frequent patterns—the darker an area is, the more patterns are found to cover the area. Those areas which are much darker than the rest of the area often implies that they are covered by both relative distance and relative orientation viewpoint patterns

The second experiment we performed on the retinal images aims to study the relationships among the lesion objects. In this experiment, we are concerned with the sizes and colors of the lesions. In order to get appropriate number of patterns to analyze, the minimum support is set as 0.4% of 2-object records for 2-object patterns and 0.1% of 3-object records for 3-object patterns.

In this experiment, we reduce the data size first by making use of the size and deviation from the background to prune away 10% of the extracted lesions. This is

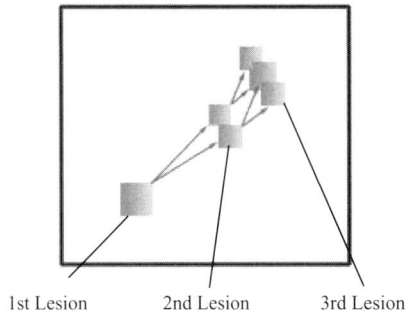

Figure 10. Visualized viewpoint patterns of lesions.

because in the retinal images, about 10% of the extracted lesions are in fact noise. Next, we use $S_{2,3}$ patterns to prune the 2-object records and generate candidates for $S_{3,1}$ patterns. We manage to prune 1102 2-object records.

After the frequent patterns are generated, we visualized the patterns in the way as shown in Figure 10. The objects in the viewpoint patterns are arranged from left to right according to the definition. Note that since intervals are used as values of the attributes, the possible relative positions of a lesion object lie in an area. To denote this area, we use two or more vertexes to mark its bounding box.

In total, 39 2-object viewpoint patterns and 120 3-object viewpoint patterns are found. The lesion objects are divided into two sets: the first set corresponds to the exudates while the second set corresponds to other lesions. Comparing these patterns in the two sets, we found that the relative distance in the patterns from the lesions set is smaller than 8 units, while they are mostly greater than 9 units in the exudates set. This suggests that non-exudates lesion points are usually closer to each other.

4.3. Kitchen plan images

In our final set of experiment, we collected eleven original kitchen plan images from the internet. All the plans include a cooktop (C), a sink (S) and a refrigerator (R), and some of them have microwaves (M) and/or dishwashers (D). Based on these eleven plans, we infer the underlying design principles and generated 40 kitchen plans that adhere to the design principles. In addition, we generated 80 kitchen plan images by randomly placing the five items in each kitchen plan. In total, we have 120 kitchen plan images in which 40 are regarded as meaningful (so-call seeding images).

Setting the minimum support count to 3, we perform the viewpoint pattern mining. The algorithm found 39 2-object patterns, 4 3-object patterns and 1 4-object pattern. Figure 11 illustrates the process of generating a 3-object pattern. The 2-object patterns covered 150 object pairs, in which 104 pairs are from the seeding images, while the 3-object patterns and 4-object patterns can all be traced back to the seeding images. This allows us to conclude that the viewpoint patterns generated do capture the underlying design principles in spite of the 67% random noise introduce to the image collection.

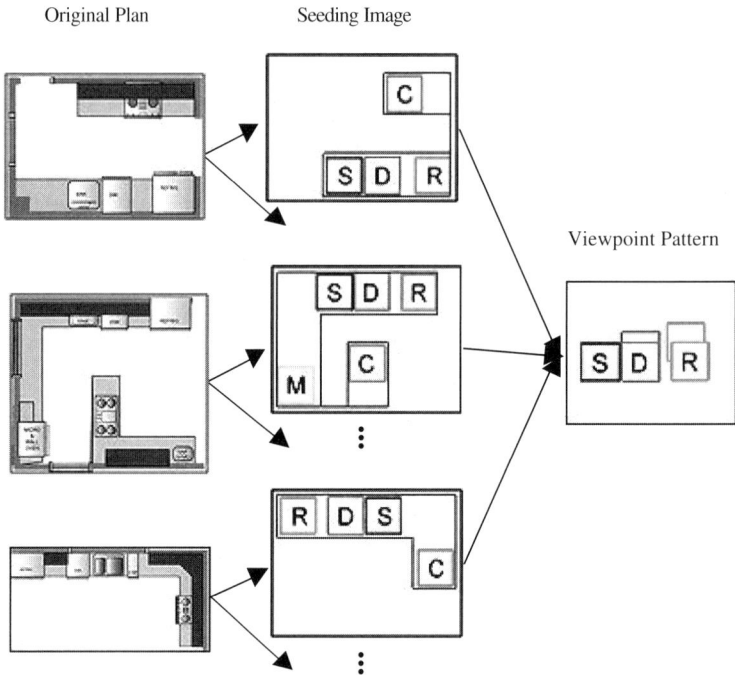

Figure 11. Discovering patterns from kitchen plans.

Based on the discovered viewpoint patterns, we can infer some good kitchen design principles such as: arrange the sink next to the dishwasher and, place the refrigerator next to the microwave.

5. CONCLUSION

This chapter reviews research work related to image mining and presents the concept of a viewpoint pattern. Viewpoint patterns refer to patterns that demonstrate the invariant relationships of one object from the point of view of another object. Viewpoint patterns are particularly useful in images because of the unique nature of image representations. An efficient algorithm ViewpointMiner is designed to discover viewpoint patterns of several objects from large image collections. The algorithm has been tested on general category images, retinal images and kitchen plan images. Experiment results on 5000 general category images show that the time cost is linear to the size of image set. The experiments on retinal images and kitchen plan images have discovered meaningful and interesting patterns from the real-world image collections. Future work includes:

- Discovering viewpoint patterns with shape attribute.
- Improving the performance of ViewpointMiner by parallelizing the algorithm.
- Providing effective visualization and summarization of viewpoint patterns especially when the number of objects in the patterns is large.

REFERENCES

[1] R. Agrawal, and R. Srikant. Fast Algorithms for Mining Association Rules. VLDB-94, 1994.

[2] M. Antonie, O. R. Zaiane, and A. Coman. Application of Data Mining Techniques for Medical Image Classification. Second International Workshop on Multimedia Data Mining (MDM/KDD), 2001.

[3] M. Baatz, and A. Schafe. Delphi2 creative technologies, GmbH, eCognition, Software tutorial. Munchen. 1999.

[4] L. Bruzzone, and D. F. Prieto. Unsupervised Retraining of a Maximum Likelihood Classifier for the Analysis of Multitemporal Remote Sensing Images. In IEEE Transactions on Geosciences and Remote Sensing, VOL. 39, No. 2, 2001.

[5] M. C. Burl, L. Asker, P. Smyth, U. Fayyad, P. Perona, L. Crumpler, and J. Aubele. Learning to Recognize Volcanoes on Venus. In Machine Learning, 30, 165–195, 1998.

[6] M. C. Burl, C. Fowlkes, J. Roden, A. Stechert, and S. Mukhtar. Diamond Eye: A Distributed Architecture for Image Data Mining. In SPIE 13th Intl. Symp. On Aerospace/Defence Sensing, Simulation, and Controls, 1999.

[7] E. Chang, C. Li, J. Wang, P. Mork, and G. Wiederhold. Serching Near-Replicas of Images via Clustering. In SPIE Symp. of Voice, Video and Data Communications, 1999.

[8] C. Djeraba. Relationship Extraction from Large Image Databases. In MDM/KDD, 2001.

[9] I. E. Evangelou, D. G. Hadjimitsis, A. A. Lazakidou, and C. Clayton. Data Mining and Knowledge Discovery in Complex Image Data using Artificial Neural Networks. In 17th International Conference on Logic Programming ICLP 2001, Workshop Proceedings on Complex Reasoning on Geographical Data, 2001.

[10] B. Fang, W. Hsu, and M. L. Lee. Tumor Cell Identification Using Feature Rules. In ACM SIGKDD, 2002.

[11] U. Fayyad, G. Piatesky-Shapiro, and P. Symyth. Mining Science Data. Communication of the ACM, 39(11): 51–57, 1996.

[12] D. A. Forsyth, J. Malik, M. M. Fleck, H. Greenspan, T. Leung, S. Belongie, C. Carson, and C. Bregler. Finding Pictures of Objects in Large Collections of Images. Technical report, U.C. Berkeley, CS Division, 1997.

[13] P. Hong, and T. S. Huang. Mining Inexact Spatial Patterns. In Workshop on Discrete Mathematics and Data Mining, 2002.

[14] M. Kakimoto, C. Morita, and H. Tsukimoto. Data Mining from Functional Brain Images. In MDM/KDD, 2000.

[15] A. Kitamoto. Data Mining for Typhoon Image Collection. In MDM/KDD, 2001.

[16] K. Koperski and G. B. Marchisio. Multi-level indexing and GIS Enhanced Learning for Satellite Imageries. In MDM/KDD, 2000.

[17] M. Kubat, R. Holte, and S. Matwin. Machine Learning for the Detection of Oil Spills in Satellite Radar Images. In Machine Learning, 1998.

[18] M. Kubat, R. Holte, and S. Matwin. Learning When Negative Examples Abound. In Proc. 9th European Conference on Machine Learning, 1997.

[19] K. Lee, and W. Nick Street. Automatic Feature Mining for Personlized Digital Image Retrieval. In MDM/KDD, 2001.

[20] J. Li, J. Z. Wang, and G. Wiederhold. IRM: Integrated Region Matching for Image Retrieval. 2000 ACM Multimedia Conf. LA, October, 2000.

[21] Z. Li, O. R.Zaiane, and Z. Tauber. Illumination Invariance and Object Model in Content-Based Image and Video Retrieval. In Journal of Visual Communication and Image Representation 10(3), pp. 219–244, 1999.

[22] Y. Mallet, D. Coomans, J. Kautsky, and O. De Vel. Classification Using Adaptive Wavelets for Feature Extraction. In IEEE Trans. Pattern Analysis & Machine Intelligence, Vol. 19, No. 10, Oct. 1997.

[23] C. Ordonez, and E. Omiecinski. Discovering Association Rules based on Image Content. In IEEE Advances in Digital Libraries Conference, 1999.

[24] H. Peng, and F. Long. A Bayesian Learning Algorithm of Discrete Variables of Automatically Mining Irregular Features of Pattern Images. In MDM/KDD, 2001.

[25] E. G. M. Petrakis. Fast Retrieval by Spatial Structure in Image Databases. Journal of Visual Languages and Computing, Vol. 13, No. 5, pp. 545–569. 2002.

[26] E. G. M. Petrakis, and C. Faloutsos. Similarity Searching in Medical Image Databases, In IEEE Transactions on Knowledge and Data Engineering, Vol. 9, No. 3, pp. 435–447, 1997.

[27] Y. Rui, T. S. Huang, M. Ortega, and S. Mehrotra. Relevance Feedback: A Power Tool for Interactive Content-based Image Retrieval. In IEEE Transactions on Circuits, Systems and Video Technology, Vol. 9, pp. 644–655, 1998.

[28] Y. Uehara, S. Endo, S. Shiitani, D. Masumoto, and S. Nagata. A Computer-Aided Visual Exploration System for Knowledge Discovery from Images. In MDM/KDD, 2001.

[29] A. Vailaya, M. A. T. Figueiredo, A. K.Jain, and H. Zhang. Image Classification for Content-Based Indexing. In IEEE Transaction on Image Processing, Vol. 10, No. 1, 2001.

[30] J. Z. Wang, J. Li, G. Wiederhold, and O. Firschein. System for Screen Objectionable Images. Computer Communications Journal, 21(15):1355–1360, Elsevier Science, 1998.

[31] O. R. Zaiane, J. Han, Z. Li, S. H. Chee, and J. Y. Chiang. MultiMediaMiner: A System Prototype for MultiMedia Data Mining. In ACM SIGMOD, 1998.

[32] H. J. Zhang, and D. Zhong. A Scheme for Visual Feature Based Image Indexing. In Proc. SPIE Conf. Storage Retrieval Image Video Databases, pp. 36–46, San Jose, CA, Feb. 1995.

COGNITION TECHNIQUES AND THEIR APPLICATIONS

SRIKANTA PATNAIK AND K. KARIBASAPPA

1. EVOLUTION OF THE MODEL OF COGNITION

The word "Cognition" means mental activity, which involves in acquisition, storage, retrieval and use of knowledge. In other word, it is the process of psychological development of human brain. It includes sensing, reasoning, attention, recognition, learning, planning, and task coordination as well as control of activities of a person. Cognitive science is a contemporary field of study that tries to answer questions about the nature of knowledge, it's components, developments and it's use [1]. Cognitive scientists have the opinion that human thinking involves in the manipulation of internal representation of the external world, known as cognitive models. Several models of human cognition have been proposed by different researchers during the last twenty years. Only in recent part, the scientist tried to develop intelligent machines by using cognitive methods/approaches.

The first model of mobile robot [2], rests on the principle of functional decomposition that employs the traditional top–down approach for building the robotic system. In this model the entire task of a mobile robot is divided into few subtasks namely *Sensing, Planning,* Task execution and *Action,* which are realized on separate modules, that together form a chain of information-flow from the environment to the actuators, through sensing, planning and task execution. The model is shown vide Figure 1.

At a later stage, other functional modules such as perception, world modeling and motor control was included in the model. Such a sequential flow of information, through different functional modules, in many circumstances do not reflect the psychological behavior of human mind. Secondly, 'planning' and 'world modeling'

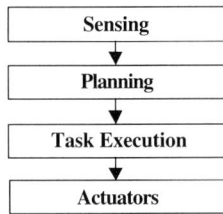

Figure 1. Traditional open loop model of task execution.

turned out to be very hard problem in this model and lastly open loop plan execution was inadequate in the presence of environmental uncertainty and unpredictability.

To overcome these limitations, Rodney A. Brooks came up with a new model of mobile robot [3] that deals with the bottom-up approach for building better robotic systems. This is also referred to as "Behavioral decomposition" model, where the model is first represented by three layered architecture, namely *Sensing, Behaviors*, and *Actuation* shown in Figure 2(a). A behavior consists of number of states. The state transitions within a behavior are autonomous and in a hierarchical order. Further, there exist a possibility of transition of states from a behavior to its higher level of behavior, shown in Figure 2(b). The transition of states that occur from one behavior to another thus represents a possible scope of parallelism among the activities of the agents. For instance, the transition of states from "feel force" in the behavior "avoid object" to the state "avoid" in the behavior "roam around" corresponds to a parallelism of transitions of two or more states, contained in different behaviors.

Rodney Brook's model created a landmark in the modern era of robotics, however it was not free from all limitations [4], [5]. For instance, the model is unable to handle uncertainty of sensory measurements. Secondly, because of the fixed connectivity among the behaviors, it lacks the capability of handling complex real world problem. Further, the model was framed for a static environment and thus is not suitable to model dynamic environments. The model was tested with robot named "HERBERT" for moving around in the environment. It was the beginning of robot cognition.

Let us discuss about another model of *Cognition* that overcomes the earlier limitations. It includes seven mental states: sensing and acquisition, reasoning, attention, recognition, learning, planning, action and coordination and their transitions. There are three cycles embedded in the model. They are Acquisition cycle, Perception Cycle and Learning and Coordination Cycle. The cycles in the model describe concurrent transition of the states. Most of the psychological behavior of living being may be represented by this model. A schematic view of the Robotic Cognition is presented in Figure 3.

1.1. The cycles of model of cognition

There are distinctly three cycles in the model of cognition. They are Acquisition cycle, Perception Cycle and Learning and Coordination Cycle. There are three cycles

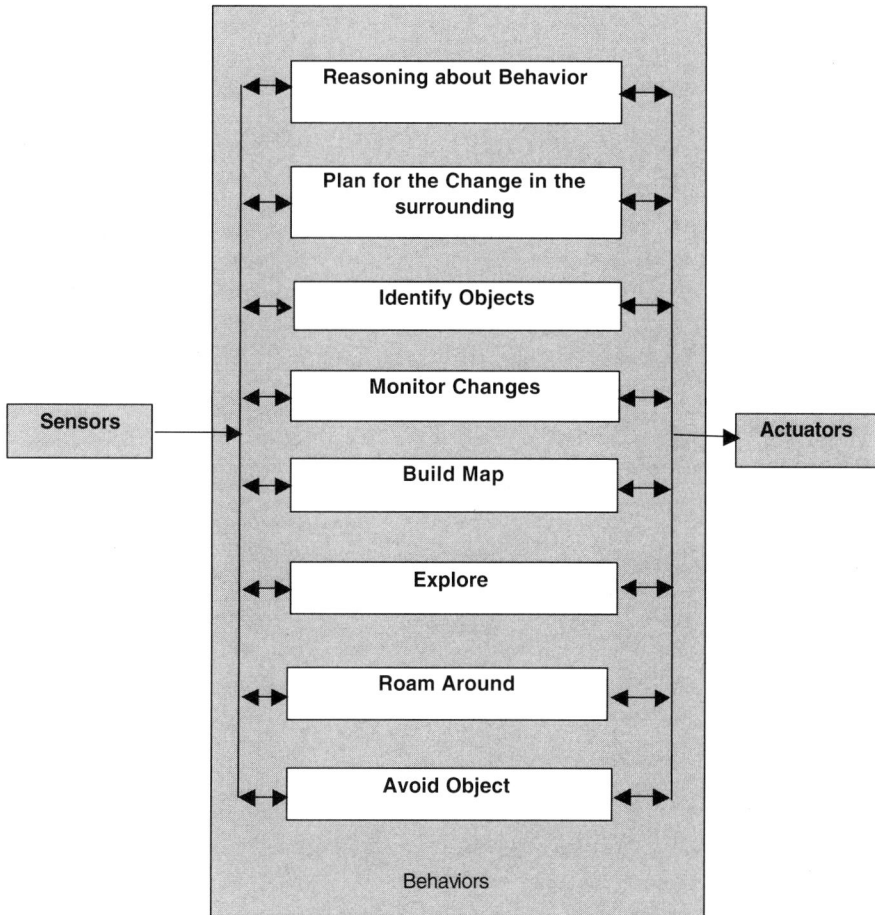

Figure 2(a). Rodney Brook's Three Layered Architecture. Each block with shade signifies one layer in the architecture and the block without shade signifies individual behavior. Each behavior consists of few states which have been shown in the Figure 2(b). Here 'Avoid Object' is the lowest level behavior, and the blocks above it signifies the next level of behavior.

embedded in the model of cognition, shown in Figure 3. First one is the Acquisition cycle, which consist of Sensing, *Short Term Memory*, Attention and *Long Term Memory*. Second one is the Perception Cycle, which consist of three states namely Reasoning, Attention and Recognition along with *Long Term Memory*. The third one is the Learning and Coordination Cycle, which is supervised in nature and consists of Learning, Planning and Action states. They are described as follows:

Acquisition Cycle: The acquisition cycle compares the response of the Short Term Memory (STM) with already acquired and permanently stored information of the Long Term Memory (LTM). The content of LTM, however changes occasionally

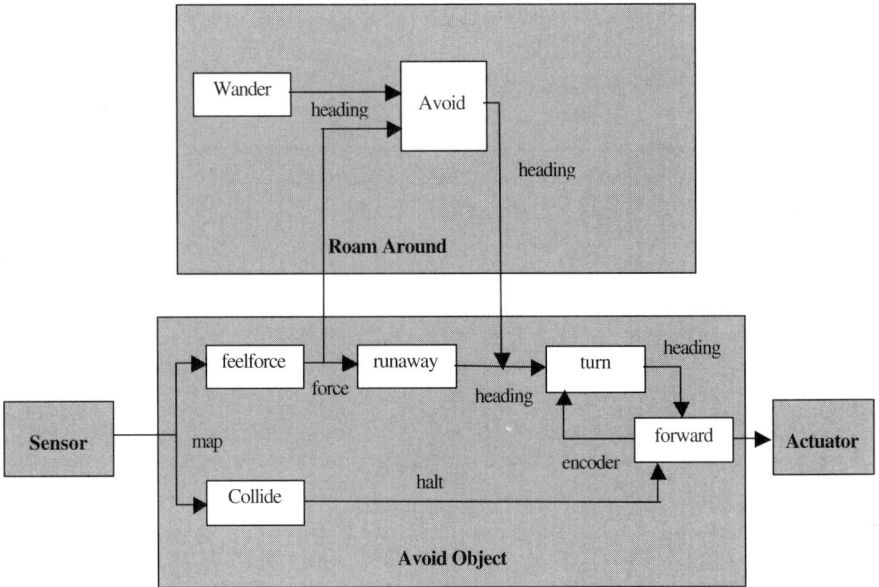

Figure 2(b). Lowest level behavior "Avoid Object" is augmented with the "Roam Around" behavior. Here the shaded block signifies the behavior and the white block inside the behavior signifies the different states within a behavior.

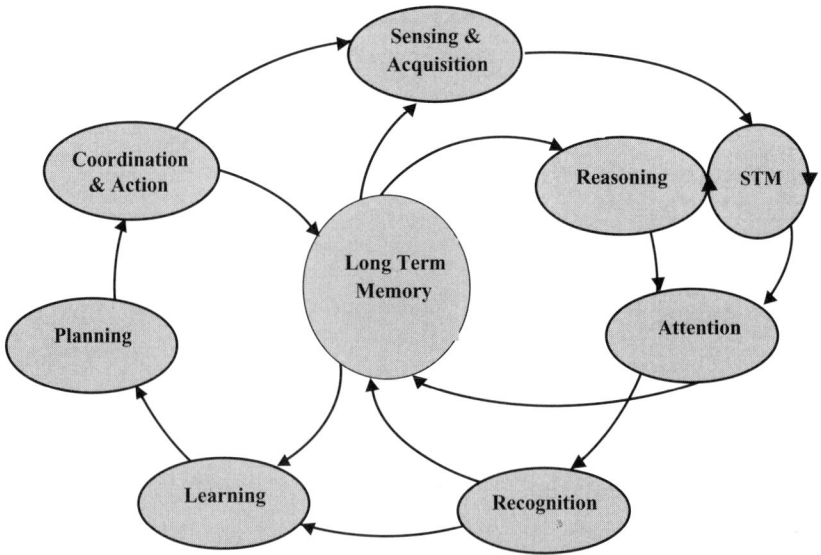

Figure 3. Three Cycles and their states in the model of Cognition.

through the transition of attention and recognition. This process is called refinement of knowledge and generally carried out by a process of unsupervised learning. The learning is unsupervised since such refinement of knowledge is an autonomous process and requires no trainer for its adaptation and therefore not included as a state in the model.

Perception Cycle: It is a cycle or a process that uses the previous knowledge stored in *Long Term Memory* to gather and interpret the stimuli (outside world information) registered by the sensory organs and stored in *Short Term Memory* through reasoning [6]. Three most relevant states of Perception, are which reasoning, attention and recognition. There are various techniques developed for machine perception. They are *Template matching*, *Prototype matching*, *Distinctive feature comparison* and *Computational techniques*. First three techniques are used for recognizing patterns and human faces. *Computation approach* aims at rapid and accurate recognition of three-dimensional objects. The use of computers to simulate these perceptual processes is known as machine vision. We will discuss about the *Computation approach* in detail in this chapter.

Learning and Coordination Cycle: Once a robot perceives the environment around it and stores it in its Long term Memory in a suitable format or data structure, it utilizes for Learning, Planning and Task Coordination. These three states taken together, are known as the Learning and Coordination Cycle. By using this, the robot plans its trajectories of movement in the environment.

These three cycles consists of various states, which are being discussed as follows.

Sensing and Acquisition: Sensing in engineering sciences refers to reception and transformation of signals into measurable form, but has a wider perspective in cognitive science. It is inclusive of pre-processing and extraction of features from the received information along with reception and transformation. For example, visual information on reception is filtered from undesirable noise [7] and the elementary features like size, shape, color etc. are extracted and acquired for storing into *Short Term Memory (STM)*.

Reasoning: This state constructs high level knowledge from acquired information of relatively lower level and organizes it, generally, in structural form for the efficient access of knowledge in subsequent time. The construction of knowledge and its organization are carried out through the process of reasoning that analyses the semantic (meaningful) behavior of the low-level knowledge and their association. It can be modeled by a semantic net [8], [9].

Attention: It is responsible for our more extensive processing of some information, while other information is neglected or suppressed. For instance, finding a face from the scene is an example of attention, which is required for the optimal use of the *Long Term Memory*.

Recognition: It involves identifying a complex arrangement of sensory stimuli, such as a letter of the alphabet, a human face or a complex scene. For example, when one person recognizes a pattern from a large scene, his sensory-organs process transform and organize the raw information provided by the sensory receptors, and he compares the sensory stimuli acquired and stored in *Short Term Memory* with the information stored earlier, in *Long Term Memory* through appropriate reasoning.

Learning: By definition, Learning is a process by which it involves with stimuli from the outside world in the form of examples and classifies these things without given any explicit rules [10]. For instance, a child cannot distinguish between cat and a dog. But as he grows, he can do so, based on numerous examples of each animals, given to him. Learning involves a teacher, who helps classify things by correcting each time, the learner commits a mistake. In machine learning, a program takes the place of a teacher, which discovers the mistake. It is better to mention here that since the invention of computers, it is not clearly known, how to make them learn. Over the period of time, algorithms have been developed that are effective for certain types of learning. There are numerous methods and techniques of learning available in literature [11], [12], [13].

Planning: The state of planning engages itself to determine the steps of action involved in deriving the required goal state from known initial states of the problem. The main task of this state is to identify the appropriate piece of knowledge for application at a given instance, for solving a problem. It executes the above task through matching the problem states with its perceptual model, saved in the semantic memory.

Action and Coordination: This state determines the control commands for actuation of the motor limbs in order to execute the schedule of the action-plan for a given problem. It is carried out through the process of supervised learning, with the required action as input stimulus and the strength of the control signals as the response.

In this chapter we will be discussing the techniques in the development of cognition methods for the mobile robots. A mobile robot senses the world around it by different transducers, such as mono/ stereo camera, drives encoders, ultra sonic sensors, laser range finders and tactile sensors and of course odor and temperature sensors in some robot. The sensory information obtained by a robot is generally mixed with various forms of noise. For instances, the ultrasonic sensors and laser range finders sometimes generate false signals, and as a consequence, determining the direction of obstacle becomes difficult. The acquisition cycle filters the contaminated noise and transfers the noise free information to the permanent storage called Long Term Memory. The perception cycle constructs new knowledge of the robots' world around it from the noise free sensory information is usually referred to as "Map Building". The Learning and Coordination cycle determines the possible trajectories of the robot in both static and dynamic environments and coordinates among the task (a collection of behaviors that purposefully satisfies the requirement of the objective). The subsequent section covers the scope of realization of each cycle of the model of cognition.

2. SCOPE OF REALIZATION OF THE ACQUISITION CYCLE

A mobile robot, as stated earlier, possesses different sensors to perceive its neighborhood world and stores the received information in the STM. The information stored in the STM is usually contaminated with different types of ambiguities. Here we present two different types of ambiguities that result in due to the mis-alignment of the incident and reflected ray from the same Sensor-Detector pair assembly (hereafter called SD unit). In the Figure 4(a), the incident ray from the SD unit is normal to the surface of

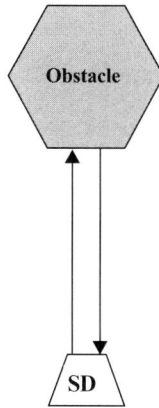

Figure 4(a). Reflected ray is aligned with the incident ray when the surface is normal to the incident ray.

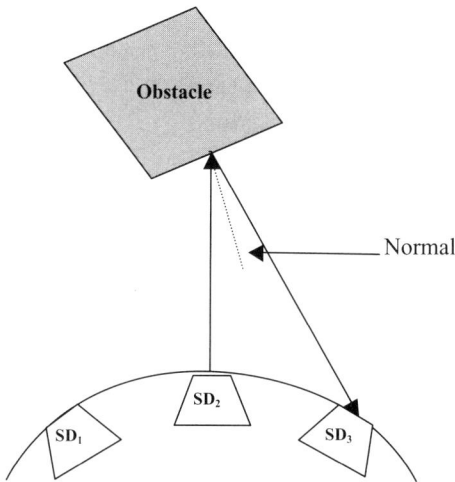

Figure 4(b). Incident rays and reflected rays are non-aligned because of the reflection of the incident rays by an off-normal surface.

the obstacle but there may be cases when the ray is off normal to the surface. Let us see these two cases discussed below.

Type 1: When a ray is off-normal to a surface of an obstacle, the reflected ray is not aligned with the incident ray. Thus the SD unit cannot trace the reflected ray. The reflected ray, if received by another SD unit (shown in Figure 4(b)), causes a false signal to the second S unit.

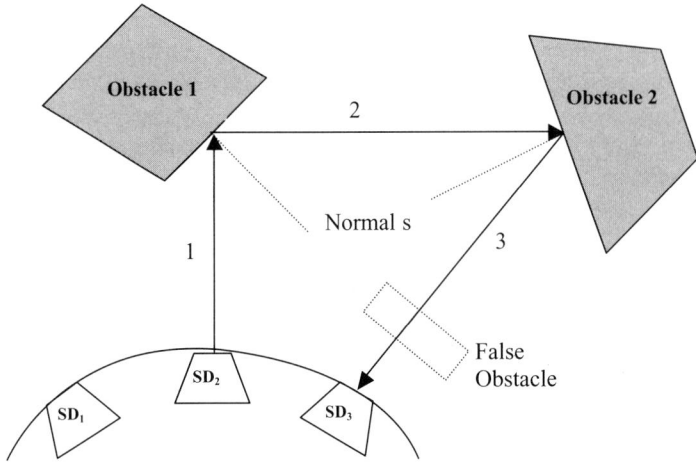

Figure 4(c). Multiple reflection of the transmitted signal from SD_2 by obstacle 1 and 2 in sequence causes the existence of a false obstacle near SD_3.

Type 2: Let 'T' be the time cycle required for the generation of a (light/sound) pulse and reception of the reflected pulse from an obstacle. Now, if the reflected pulse hops through different obstacles it may so happen that it is received at another SD unit after the generation of the second pulse. Thus, the effect of reflection of the first pulse may sometimes occur in the second cycle, thereby misguiding the robot about the existence of a false obstacle in a near vicinity in a wrong direction. This is presented in Figure 4(c).

Various schemes have been devised to overcome these ambiguities from the sensory information. Most researchers are in favor of employing multiple sensors to reduce the scope of ambiguities in the process of detecting obstacles. D. Pagac [14] recently employed the well-known Dempster-Shafer theory to integrate the multi-sensory information received by a mobile robot and called it a "sensor map". They considered the robot's workspace to be partitioned into equal sized grid cells. The robot has to assign a probability mass to all cells within the workspace depending on its position, whether lies on the arc line i.e. arc of uncertainty, within the arc sector, or outside the arc sector. The sensor arc is shown in Figure 5(a).

The basis of assignment, to each cell in the grid characterized by three states: Empty (E) and Full (F) and Ambiguous ($\{E,F\}$). The set of all subset of the field of discernment $= \{E, F, \{E,F\}\}$ and the sum of all probabilities is 1, which may be denoted by the following expression.

$$\sum_{A \subset \Lambda} m_{i,j}(A) = m_{i,j}(E) + m_{i,j}(F) + m_{i,j}(\{E, F\}) = 1$$

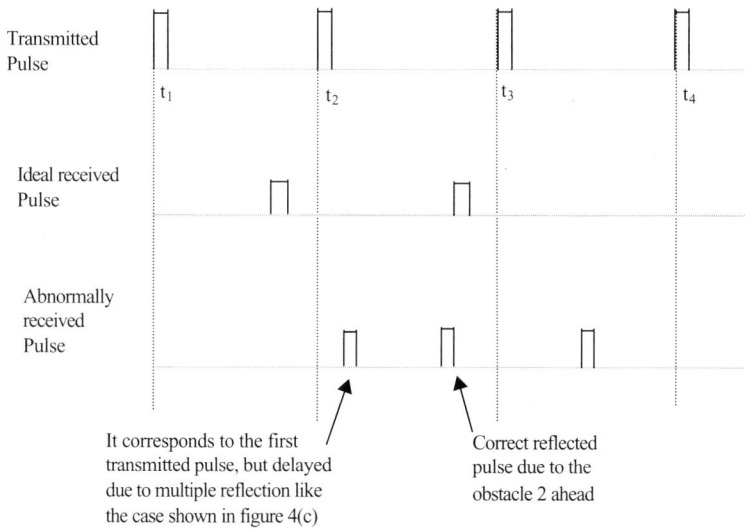

| Transmitted Pulse | | | | |

It corresponds to the first transmitted pulse, but delayed due to multiple reflection like the case shown in figure 4(c)

Correct reflected pulse due to the obstacle 2 ahead

Figure 4(d). Transmission and reception of pulses at SD_3 unit shown in fig. 4(c).

They have characterized the Basic Probability Assignment (BPA) for the cells within the workspace as follows.

(i) For cells on the sensor arc

$$\left.\begin{array}{l} m_{i,j}(E) = 1/n; \\ m_{i,j}(F) = 0 \end{array}\right\} \forall \text{ cells } (i,j) \in \text{ arc}$$

(ii) For the cells within the sector

$$\left.\begin{array}{l} m_{i,j}(E) = \rho \\ m_{i,j}(F) = 0 \end{array}\right\} \forall \text{ cells } (i,j) \in \text{ sector}$$

and (iii) For the cells outside the beam

$$\left.\begin{array}{l} m_{i,j}(E) = 0; \\ m_{i,j}(F) = 0 \end{array}\right\} \forall \text{ cells } (i,j) \notin \text{ arc, sector}$$

where, n is the number of cells on the sensor arc, and ρ is a constant between 0 and 1.

They initialize each cell in the grid with total ignorance i.e. $m_{i,j}(\{E,F\}) = 1$ and $m_{i,j}(E) = m_{i,j}(F) = 0$ and call it the initial map. The composite belief of occupancy of a cell is estimated recursively by taking the orthogonal sum of probability masses assigned to the cell by independent sensors and the probability mass stored in the map.

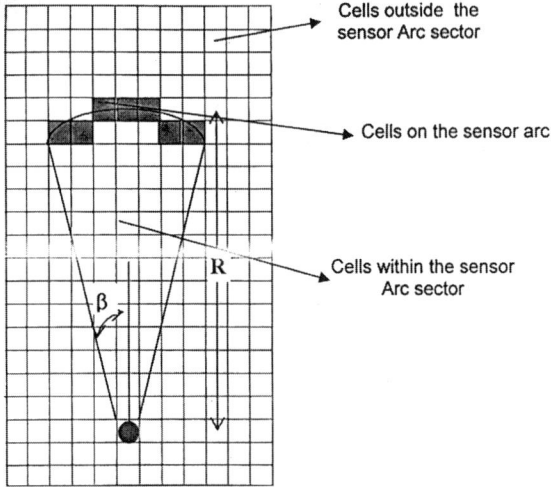

R = the range reading; β = the beam angle as shown in figure and the shaded blocks are the
"cells on the sensor arc", cells within the sensor arc are termed as "cells within the arc sector"
and beyond the arc are termed as "cells outside the sector"

Figure 5(a). Illustrating Dempster-Shafer Technique for ambiguity avoidance by Acquisition Cycle.

Recursive formulation of the Emptiness of the map is presented below, and shown in Figure 5(b).

$$m_{ij}(E_{map}) \longleftarrow m_{ij}(E_{map}) \oplus m_{ij}(E_k)$$

$$= \frac{m_{ij}(E_{map}) \bullet m_{ij}(E_k) + m_{ij}(E_{map}) \bullet m_{ij}(\{E, F\}_k) + m_{ij}(\{E, F\}_{map}) \bullet m_{ij}(E_k)}{1 - m_{ij}(E_{map}) \bullet m_{ij}(F_k) - m_{ij}(F_{map}) \bullet m_{ij}(E_k)}$$

where, k signifies the number of sensors around the robot.

Similarly the state of Filledness and Ambiguousness may be estimated recursively and consequently leads to the composite belief of the map.

Recently, G. Oriolo et al. [15] employed fuzzy membership distribution to avoid ambiguity in the process of detection of obstacle. They designed four different membership functions, in order to counter three sources of uncertainty in the process of finding the position of an object by ultrasonic range finder. The three sources of error are: i) error in the measured distance 'r'; ii) uncertainty in the process of finding angular position within the radiation cone which is 25°; and iii) presence of false obstacle due to the multiple reflection shown in Figure 4(c). They introduced two functions for modeling certainty factor about the state of Occupancy (O) and Emptiness (E) of the cell within the radiation cone from the sensory reading. The membership function of

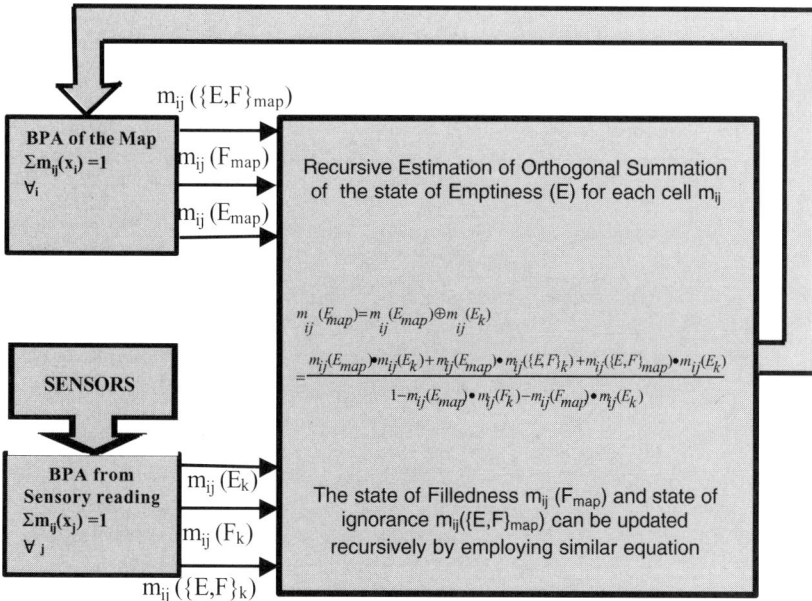

Figure 5(b). Recursive estimation of Dempster-Shafer orthogonal summation of composite basic probability assignment of each cell in the map.

the Emptiness is formulated as:

$$f_E(\rho, r) = \begin{cases} K_E & 0 \leq \rho \leq r - \Delta r \\ K_E(r - \rho/\Delta r)^2 & r - \Delta r \leq \rho \leq r \\ 0 & \rho \geq r \end{cases}$$

and the membership function for the Occupancy (O) is

$$f_O(\rho, r) = \begin{cases} 0 & 0 \leq \rho \leq r - \Delta r \\ K_O(r - \rho/\Delta r)^2 & r - \Delta r \leq \rho \leq r + \Delta r \\ 0 & \rho \geq r + \Delta r \end{cases}$$

where, K_E, K_O are two constants corresponding to the maximum values attained by the functions. 'r' is the range reading and 'ρ' is the distance of the point of assertion from the sensor.

They formulated the third function w.r.t. the radiation directivity from the experimental data as

$$m_1(v) = \begin{cases} D(v) & |v| \leq 12.5 \\ 0 & |v| > 12.5 \end{cases}$$

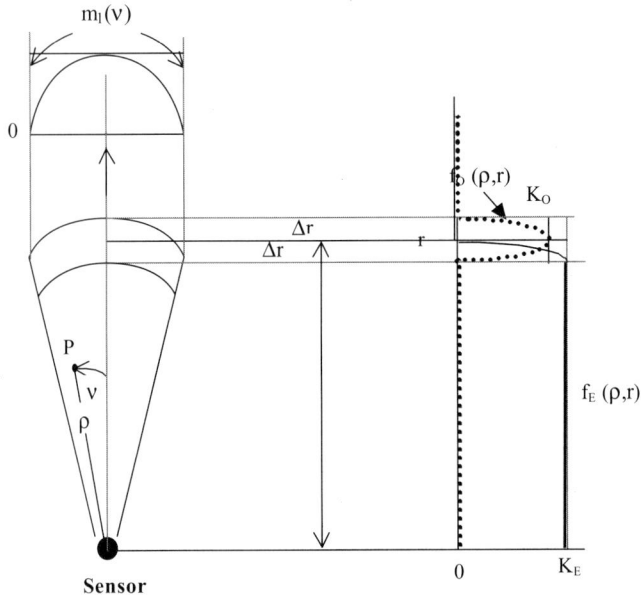

Figure 6. Fuzzy Behaviorist Approach for managing uncertainty in the sonar sensor measurements. Solid line signifies the membership function of the emptiness and dotted line signifies the membership function of the occupancy of the cell.

and the last function is designed to counter the false reflection by using a parameter ρ_v, which they call "visibility radius" i.e. a distance within which there is no uncertainty in the estimation process, which is given by,

$$m_2(\rho) = 1 - ((1 + \tan h(2(\rho - \rho_v))/2).$$

Membership functions are shown in Figure 6. For each range measurement r_i, it is now possible to generate two fuzzy sets E_i and O_i by combining the above four functions.

$$E_i(\rho, v) = f_E(\rho, r) \bullet m_1(v) \bullet m_2(\rho)$$
$$O_i(\rho, v) = f_O(\rho, r) \bullet m_1(v) \bullet m_2(\rho)$$

This two fuzzy sets represents the state of emptiness and occupancy in the radiation cone on the basis of sensory reading r_i. The final reading can be combined by using a fuzzy union operator defined by Dombi [16]

$$E = \cup_i E_i \quad \text{and} \quad O = \cup_i O_i$$

This type of membership function helps to avoid uncertainty in the measurement and acquisition process of sensory data.

Further, a Hopfield neural net may be employed to determine the correct location of the obstacle from their approximate measure. The Hopfield net inputs the measured patterns of the environment as its current state and generates a stable state, representing the ambiguity free location of the obstacles. *A Hopfild net could be of two types: the binary Hopfield net and a continuous Hopfild net. The weights w_{ij} between neuron n_i and n_j in a binary Hopfild net is estimated by*

$$W_{ij} = \sum_s \left(2n_i^s - 1\right)\left(2n_j^s - 1\right)$$

where n_i^s represents set of states for s being an integer 1, 2, ... n

It can be shown by using a Liapunov energy function, that such values of weights lead the network towards the convergence of states.

3. BUILDING PERCEPTION CYCLE

Perception cycle, as discussed earlier, constructs higher level knowledge from relatively lower level data or knowledge. Generally noise free information are stored in LTM by *Acquisition cycle*. The Perception cycle employs reasoning tools on the information recorded in LTM and thus derives new rules for subsequent planning and coordination problems.

A mobile robot constructs its world map from the sensory information stored in LTM and pre-processing that information at different states of perception cycle. For constructing a 2D-world map, the robot has to move around each obstacle. Starting from a given location the robot moves around each obstacle in turn until all obstacles are visited. A two-dimensional world map for the robot is then built with the visited obstacles. There exist a number of literatures on the two-dimensional Map building [17], [18]. Some of these prefer metric based approach, while the rest employs strategies to identify landmark first and then use local search strategy to explore the unvisited obstacles. In this chapter, we will discuss depth first strategy to construct the 2D world map [19]. For navigation purpose, 2D and 3D information of the robot's environment is required. Planning in 3D is a very complex problem. Most of the navigational planning problems therefore deal with 2D map of the robot's world.

In a 2D planning problem, the boundary of the obstacles are generally sensed by ultrasonic sensors or laser range finders, and it is assumed that the top of the obstacles are at a level higher than the mounting point of the sensors. A 3D planning problem, on the other hand requires keeping track of the obstacle surfaces and their height as well. To extend the 3D information, generally additional cameras are employed. These cameras are mounted on a pan-tilt platform, which is fixed with the mobile robot. When more than one camera are used for determining the third dimension of the obstacles, we call it stereo vision.

3.1. Need for map building

As we have discussed in the last section, for perceiving the environment *map building* is an indispensable function of a mobile robot. Over the last twenty years, the *map building* for mobile robots have been attempted by different research laboratories. To mention a few, we are giving a very concise list of successful works carried out at leading research laboratories. Borenstein and Koren [20] of CMU devised a method for probabilistic representation of obstacles in a grid type world model. He defined a scheme for assignment of integer values between 0 to 15 to the grids, based on the sonar measurement about obstacle locations. The value assigned to a cell is called a certainty value (CV) that indicates the measure of confidence of the existence of the obstacle within grid. A heuristic probabilistic function that takes into account the characteristics of a given sensor, is employed to update the CVs. An alternative scheme for determination of the occupancy of grid from multiple sonar maps has been proposed, later by Albeto Elfes [21] of CMU. The uncertainty in measurement, about the obstacle location in the grid structure thus could be solved by this technique.

In another attempt, Dempster Shafer theory has been employed for map building by [22], through multi-sensory sonar images. The mobile robot here computes the possibility of occupancy of a grid point, when seen from a given location in the grid structure. Multiple sonar images taken by the robot from different locations could then, be fused determining the occupancy of the grid point of the obstacle. One of the pioneering works for map building by camera images was proposed by Maja J. Mataric [23]. In her scheme, she evaluated the topological relationship among the landmarks, by employing a compass and one camera. The camera grabs the images of the landmarks and the compass helps in determining the spatial relationships.

Recently, mobile robots have been used commercially, for transporting chemical product, which usually is done by the well-known "road-following algorithm" [24]. The ARPA project scientists devised a scheme of unmanned vehicles [25], which could be used for defense and military actions in the cross-country terrain. The Colorado school of mines brought a new revolution in under mines transportation problem [26] by constructing a mobile robot capable of following the roads inside the mine and handling material for transportation. In manufacturing industries too, robots are currently being employed for pick and placement jobs in connection with material handling and dumping [27]. In the short run, mobile robots will find application in agricultural sector to reduce the strain and monotony of repetitive jobs, presently done by human beings. Mobile robots are also being used for exploration of planetary surfaces [28]. For instance, Rockey-IV, has been used for communicating about the surface characteristics of the MARS. The situations we have discussed so far, deals with more or less static map building. However in a complex environment like a robot repairing the leakage pipeline in a nuclear reactor, or the Mars path finder, a mobile robot is bound to construct a dynamic map of its surrounding to act upon it. The dynamism in the map is present, due to the temporal variations in the spatial relationships of the robot environment. Therefore, a careful and systematic study of the map building is required for mobile robots. We will discuss map building by Depth First Search in the next sub-section.

3.2. Map building by depth first search

By now, it is evident that map building is essential prior to any navigational planning. The objective of map building is to visit all obstacles and their boundaries, if any, and also the inner boundary of the robot's workspace. One classical algorithm that serves the above requirement is presented below. The algorithm uses the following parameters:

S = Set of point mass obstacle;
B = Room boundary;
M = Map;
V = Set of Visited Obstacles;
Procedure Build-map (S,B,V,M)
Begin
V: = ϕ ;
U: = S-V ;
> **While** U $\neq \phi$ do
> **Begin**
> Select an element from U $\cup$ B;
> Visit that obstacle;
> And put it in V;
> U: = S-V
> **End_while;**
End.

The above algorithm selects any point mass obstacles randomly from the set of unvisited obstacle and room boundary. A modification of this classical algorithm can be done, for minimizing the path traversal by employing best first search, which is presented below.

Procedure Build-map by best first search (S,B,V,M)
Begin
V: = ϕ ;
U: = S-V ;
> **While** U $\neq \phi$ do
> **Begin**
> Select the nearest element from U $\cup$ B;
> Visit that obstacle;
> And put it in V;
> U: = S-V
> **End_while;**
End.

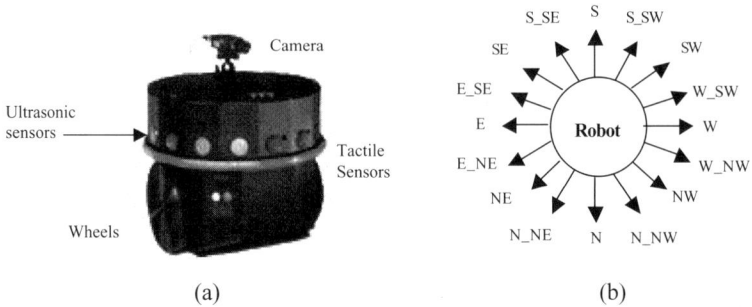

Figure 7(a). The Nomad Super Scoutt II robot; (b) The representation the sixteen ultrasonic sensors around it in sixteen geographical directions.

This algorithm ensures optimality in path traversal, but does not consider minimization of energy during navigation. This can be realized if we prefer a linear traversal from one obstacle to another as far as practicable. For point mass obstacle one simplest algorithm, that supports the above two requirements of optimality in path traversal and energy consumption, is the **Depth First Search** algorithm. Depth first search follows same principle except that, the robot chooses a specific direction for movement until all the obstacles in that direction is visited. Then it started moving in a direction next to the previous direction and so on until all the obstacles as well as the closed room boundary are completely visited.

The experiment has been performed on NOMAD Super Scoutt-II mobile robot shown in Figure 7(a). The Nomad Super Scout-II is equipped with odometric sensors, a tactile bumper ring, 16 ultrasonic sonar sensors and a vision system. The tactile system uses a ribbon switch enclosed in a energy absorbing neoprene channel. The ultrasonic sensors, mounted around its entire periphery, covering a total of 360 degrees, shown in the Figure 7(b). The effective range of ultrasonic sensors is from 15 cm to 650 cm. The Color PCI vision system comes with a color PCI frame-grabber and color camera with 4 mm lens.

Figure 7(b) describes the beam directions of the ultrasonic sensors, where the notations are as follows: N = North; N_NE = North of North-East; NE = North-East; E_NE = East of North-East; E = East; E_SE = East of South-East; SE = South-East; S_SE = South of South-East; S = South; S_SW = South of South-West; SW = South-West; W_SW = West of South-West; W = West; W_NW = West of North-West; NW = North-West; N_NW = North of North-West. For building an algorithm for depth first traversal in the robots world, we use the following structure definition. The structure in Figure 8(a) has four fields; the first two designating the coordinate of the point (x_i, y_i), visited by the robot. The third field corresponds to the pointer to the structure containing the obstacle to be visited next and the last field corresponds the next point to be visited on same obstacle boundary.

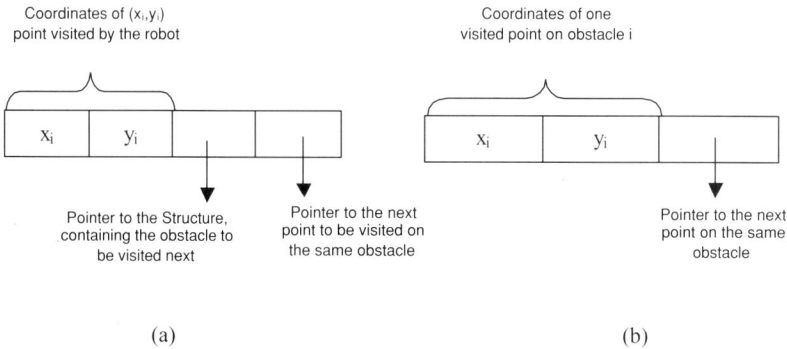

(a)   (b)

Figure 8(a). Definition of one structure with two pointers, used for acquiring the list of visited obstacles. **(b)** Definition of another structure with one pointer for acquiring the boundary points visited round an obstacle.

Another structure having three fields is necessary for storing the information about the boundary of the obstacle, while moving around the polygon shaped obstacle, shown in Figure 2(b). The first two field in the structure corresponds to the coordinate (x_i, y_i) of one point on a visited obstacle-i., and the third field denotes the pointer of the structure of the next location to be visited next of the obstacle-i. The linked list created, records the visited obstacles and their boundaries of the workspace of the robot.

3.2.1. Algorithms for map-building by depth first search

The depth first traversal algorithm employed for the map building problem is now presented below. Traversing around an obstacle and storing the boundary coordinates of the obstacle is one of the important steps in map building. Let us first discuss this algorithm and then we will see how it will be used as a procedure in the map-building algorithm.

Procedure Traverse Boundary (current-coordinates)
Begin
Initial-coordinate = current-coordinate;
Boundary-coordinates: = Null;
   Repeat
   Move-to (current-coordinate) and mark the path of traversal;
      Boundary-coordinates: = Boundary-coordinates ∪ {current-coordinate};
     For (all possible unmarked set of point P)
         Select the next point p ε P, such that
         The perpendicular distance from the next point p to
         Obstacle boundary is minimum;
   Endfor

current-coordinate : = next-coordinate;
   Until current-coordinate = initial-coordinate
   Return Boundary-coordinates;
End.

The above algorithm is self-explanatory and thus needs no elaboration. We now present an algorithm for map building, where we will use the above procedure.

Procedure Map Building (current-coordinate)
Begin
   Move-to(current-coordinate);
   Check-North-direction( );
   If (new obstacle found) **Then do**
   Begin
      Current-obstacle = Traverse-boundary (new-obstacle-coordinate);
      Add-obstacle-list (current-obstacle); //adds current obstacle to list//
      Current-position = find-best-point (current-obstacle) // finding the best take off point from the current obstacle//
      call Map-building (current-position);
   End
   Else do
         Begin
      Check-North of North-East-direction ( );
   If (new obstacle found) **Then do**
   Begin
      Current-obstacle = Traverse-boundary (new-obstacle-coordinate);
      Add-obstacle-list (current-obstacle);
      Current-position = find-best-point (current-obstacle);
      call Map-building (current-position);
   End;
   Else do
         Begin
      Check North-East direction( );
      //Likewise in all remaining directions//
   End
   Else backtrack to the last takeoff point on the obstacle
         (or the starting point);
End.

Procedure Map-building is a recursive algorithm that moves from an obstacle to the next following the depth first traversal criteria. The order of preference of visiting the next obstacle comes from the prioritization of the directional movements in a given order. The algorithm terminates by back-tracking from the last obstacle to the previous one and finally to the starting point. The above algorithm presumes that the obstacles have

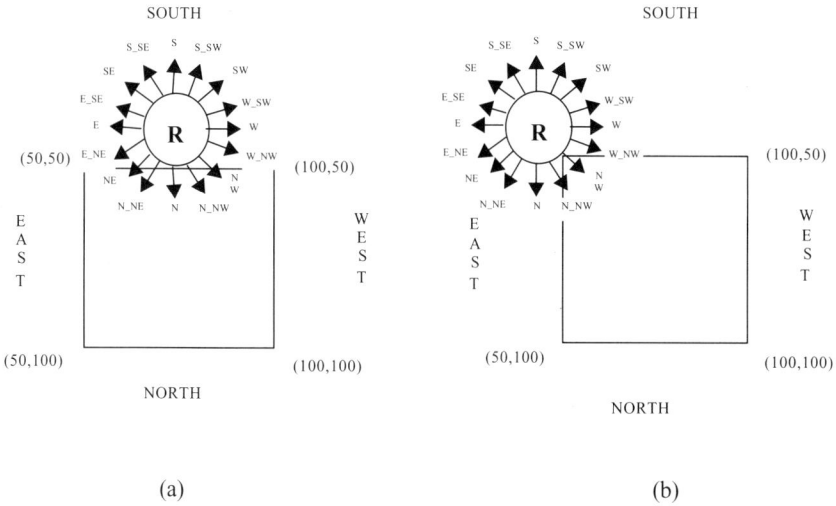

Figure 9(a). The robot near a rectangular obstacle with its sixteen sensors in the specified sixteen directions; **(b)** The robot is at another location near the same obstacle.

polygonal boundaries. A trace of the algorithm for a given robot's world problem is presented below.

3.2.2. An illustration of procedure traverse boundary

Here, the robot's movement around an obstacle is illustrated utilizing the *Procedure Traverse Boundary*. Consider the rectangular obstacle and robot (encircled R), south of the obstacle (shown in Figure 9(a)).

Let the robot's position is at (x = 75, y = 48) on the graphics simulator. The sensor information from the robot's present position in all the sixteen directions are as shown in Table 1(A). The shaded cells in the table are the directions having obstacle regions. Therefore, the robot chooses the point (70.0,48.0), in east of the present position as next location to move, since it is free of obstacle and it is next to obstacle region.

Let us now examine the movement of robot at a corner position i.e. (48.0,48.0) shown in Figure 9(b). The sensory information of the robot, at this new location is given in the Table 1(B). From the Table 1(B), it is clear that the location (48.0,53.0) is in north direction, which is obstacle free point. Therefore, the robot will move to the point (48.0, 53.0) in north direction. Like wise this process will be repeated until the robot, reaches the initial point (75.0,48.0). The coordinates of the boundary of the obstacle are stored in a linked list, which is maintained in a general structure. The process of map building is discussed in the next section, with the help of boundary traversing algorithm.

Table 1(A): Sensory Information at position (75.0, 48.0)

Sensor Direction	Sensory Information
N	(75.0, 50.0)
N_NE	(74.0,50.0)
NE	(73.0, 50.0)
E_NE	(71.0, 50.0)
E	(70.0, 48.0)
E_SE	(71.0, 46.0)
SE	(71.0, 44.0)
S_SE	(73.0, 43.0)
S	(75.0, 43.0)
S_SW	(77.0, 43.0)
SW	(78.0, 44.0)
W_SW	(79.0, 46.0)
W	(80.0, 48.0)
W_NW	(79.0, 50.0)
NW	(77.0, 50.0)
N_NW	(76.0, 50.0)

Table 1(B): Sensory Information at position (48.0, 48.0)

Sensor Direction	Sensory Information
N	(48.0, 53.0)
N_NE	(46.0, 52.0)
NE	(44.0, 52.0)
E_NE	(48.0, 50.0)
E	(43.0, 48.0)
E_SE	(44.0, 46.0)
SE	(44.0, 44.0)
S_SE	(46.0, 43.0)
S	(48.0, 43.0)
S_SW	(50.0, 43.0)
SW	(52.0, 44.0)
W_SW	(52.0, 46.0)
W	(53.0, 48.0)
W_NW	(52.0, 50.0)
NW	(50.0, 50.0)
N_NW	(50.0, 52.0)

3.2.3. An illustration of procedure map building

An example illustrating the creation of linked list to record the visited obstacle and their boundary is present in Figure 11 for an environment as shown in Figure 4.

The search process is started with the north direction of robot. If any obstacle is found, robot will move to that obstacle and records the boundary coordinate information of that obstacle. Again it will start searching into north direction from the recently visited obstacle. In this way it will go as much depth as possible in the north direction only. If no new obstacle is available in north direction, the robot will look for other directions in order to visit a new obstacle. If any new one is found, the robot will visit it and move as much depth as possible in the newly found direction. If in any case it cannot find any new obstacle, it will backtrack to its parent obstacle and starts looking into other directions. The process of generation of the linked list is shown in Figure 11.

3.2.4. Simulation on Superscoutt-II Linux based graphics interface

The algorithm for map building has been simulated and tested by a C++ program, on Linux-based Nomadic Software Development Environment of Superscoutt-II, which includes a graphic interface. An artificial workspace has been created with 9 convex obstacles along with a closed room. The workspace dimension is fixed by four corner points having coordinates (80,80), (400,80), (400,400) and (80,400) in a (640,480) resolution graphic window, shown in Figure 12. The dimensions of the obstacles, described by its peripheral vertices are as follows:

Obstacle 1: (140,120), (170,100), (185,120), (175,140)
Obstacle 2: (240,120), (270,140), (225,164), (210, 135)
Obstacle 3: (178,160), (280,180), (185,200), (170,180)

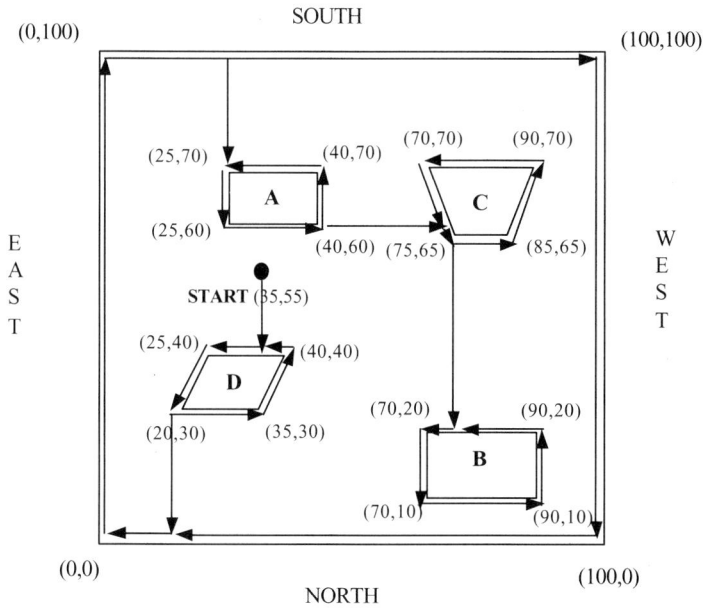

Figure 10. The path traveled by the robot while building the 2D world map using the depth first traversal. The obstacles are represented with literal and the coordinates of the obstacles and the workspace have been shown inside the braces.

Obstacle 4: (245,175), (285,200), (258,204), (230,190)
Obstacle 5: (310,215), (360,240), (330,270), (298,250)
Obstacle 6: (110,245), (130,225), (180,240), (130,280)
Obstacle 7: (230,258), (270,250), (250,280), (220,280)
Obstacle 8: (220,320), (230,300), (250,330), (230,340)
Obstacle 9: (190,330), (210,350), (180,370), (170,350)

The dimension of the soft mobile object is 10 pixel in diameter. The soft object starts at a position (100, 380) and moves as per the map building algorithm, whose sample traces has been displayed through Figures 13–18.

3.3. Construction of 3D world map by depth first search

A mobile robot may sometimes require to know the 3D world around it, for subsequent task planning. One simple way to construct the 3D world is to represent the height of the obstacles at a regular interval of its X and Y space boundaries. The following three data structures shown in Figures 19–21, for instance, may be used to represent the 3D world, of the robot around it.

Coordinates of
starting point

| 35 | 55 | | |

Coordinate of the entry point
of the first visited obstacle

| 35 | 40 | | → | 25 | 40 | → | 20 | 30 | → | 35 | 30 | → | 40 | 40 |

Pointer to the structure of
the next visited obstacle

| 20 | 0 | | → | 0 | 0 | → | 0 | 100 | → | 100 | 100 | → | 100 | 0 |

| 25 | 70 | | → | 25 | 60 | → | 40 | 60 | → | 40 | 70 | → | 25 | 70 |

| 75 | 60 | | → | 75 | 65 | → | 85 | 65 | → | 90 | 70 | → | 70 | 70 |

| 75 | 20 | | → | 70 | 20 | → | 70 | 10 | → | 90 | 10 | → | 90 | 20 |

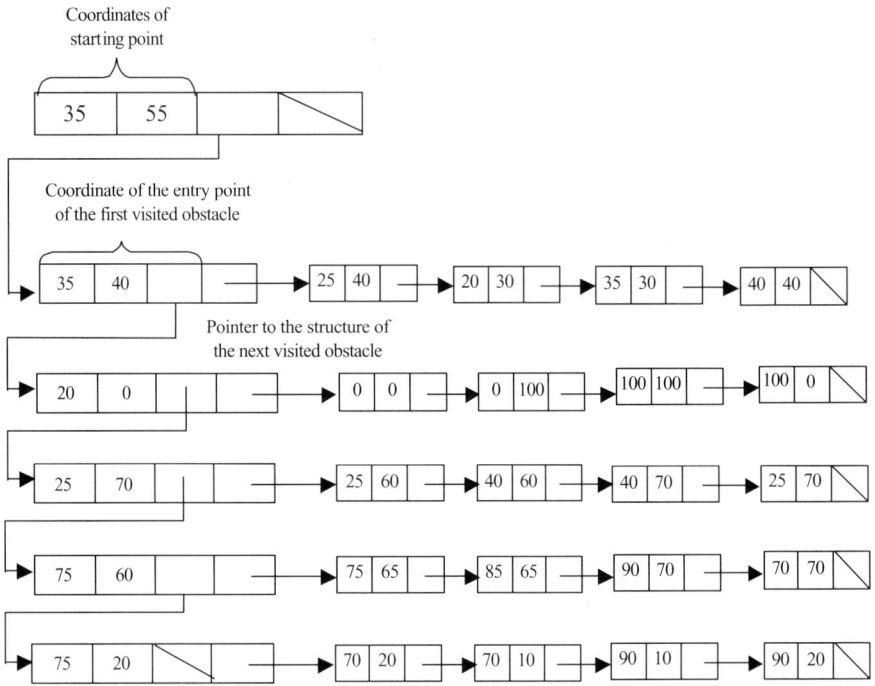

Figure 11. The linked list created to record the visited obstacles and their boundary. Here all the points on the boundary visited by the robot has not been shown in the linked list in order to maintain clarity.

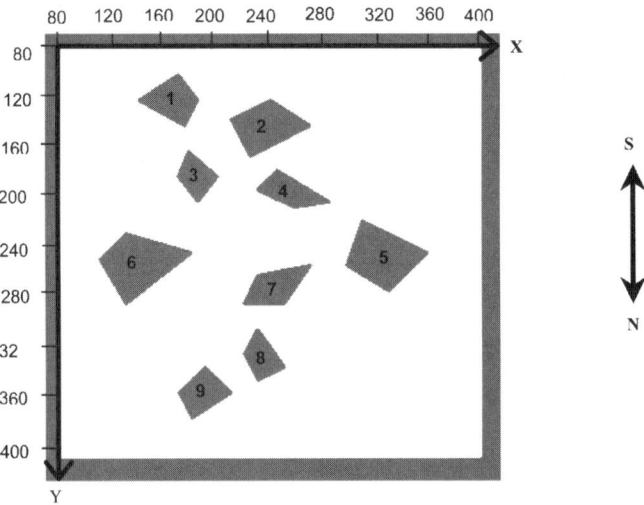

Figure 12. A closed room workspace with 9 (nine) convex obstacles.

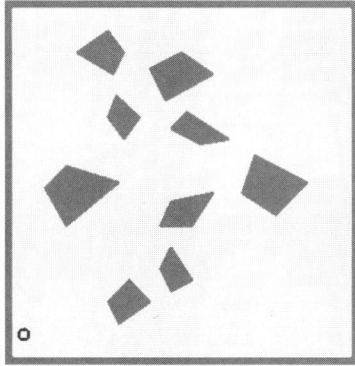

Figure 13. Robot at starting position.

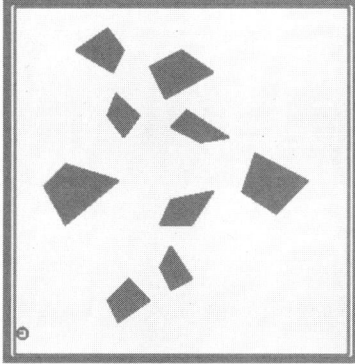

Figure 14. After visiting room boundary.

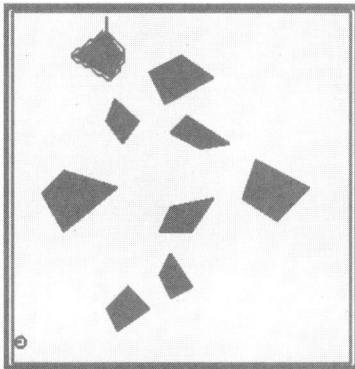

Figure 15. After Visiting the 1st Obstacle.

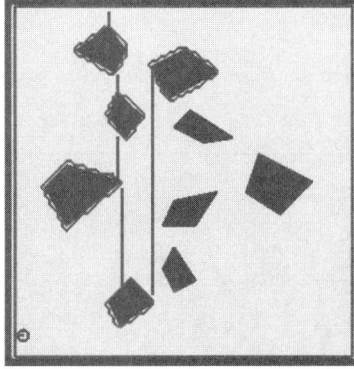

Figure 16. After Visiting 5th Obstacle.

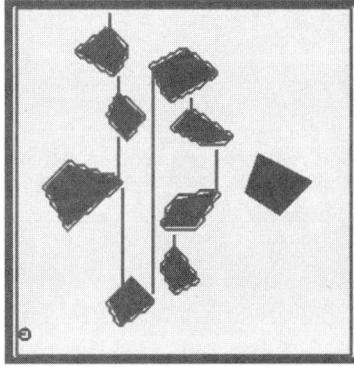

Figure 17. After Visiting 8th Obstacle.

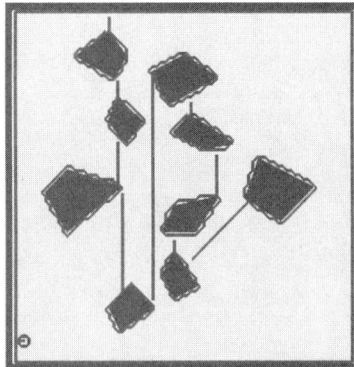

Figure 18. After Visiting 9th Obstacle.

Coordinate of visited point
by the robot

Pointer to the height
information

| x_i | y_i | | | |

Pointer to the Structure,
containing the obstacle to be
visited next

Pointer to the next point to be
visited on the same obstacle

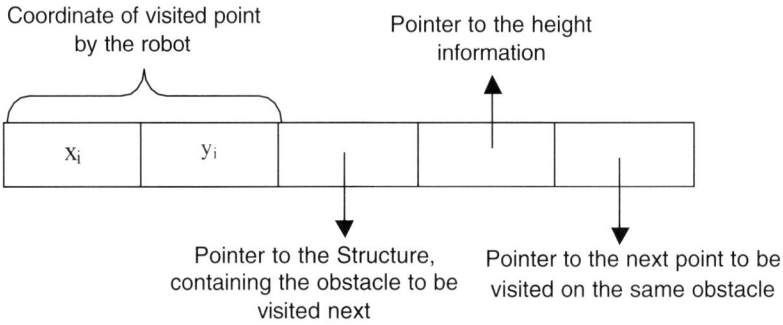

Figure 19. Definition of the data structure with three pointers, used for acquiring the list of visited obstacles and the height information of each obstacle and the boundary information of one obstacle.

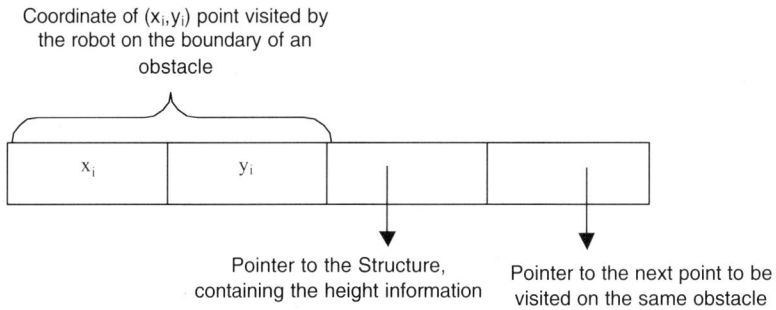

Coordinate of (x_i, y_i) point visited by
the robot on the boundary of an
obstacle

| x_i | y_i | | |

Pointer to the Structure,
containing the height information

Pointer to the next point to be
visited on the same obstacle

Figure 20. Definition of one structure with two pointers, used for acquiring the list of height information and the boundary information of the obstacles.

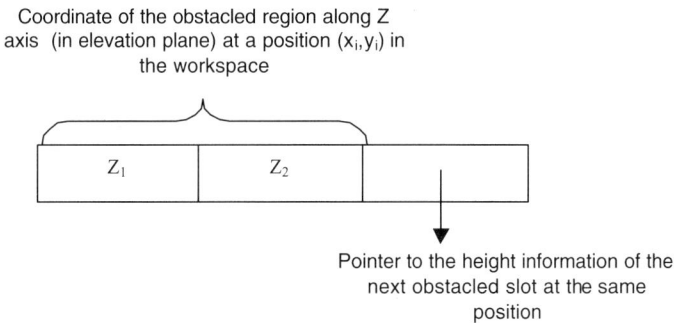

Coordinate of the obstacled region along Z
axis (in elevation plane) at a position (x_i, y_i) in
the workspace

| Z_1 | Z_2 | |

Pointer to the height information of the
next obstacled slot at the same
position

Figure 21. Definition of third structure with one pointer for acquiring the height information at a position (x_i, y_i).

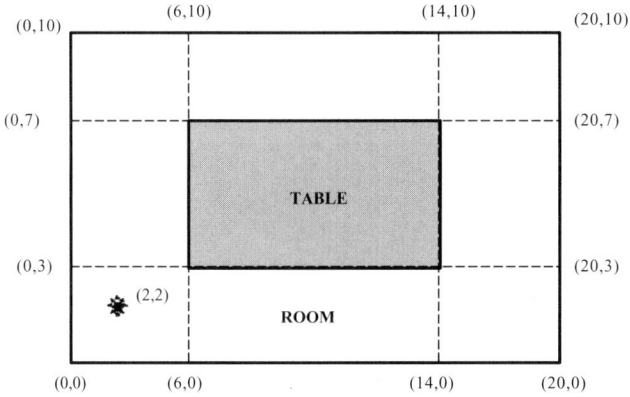

(a)

Table size: Length =8, Width = 4, Height = 6;

Room size: Length =20, Width = 10, Height = 12;

Initially robot is assumed to be at position (2,2) shown in the figure (Drawing is not up to scale)

Figure 22(a). Plan view of a room with a table whose dimensions are given.

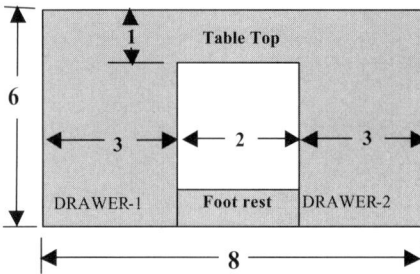

(b)

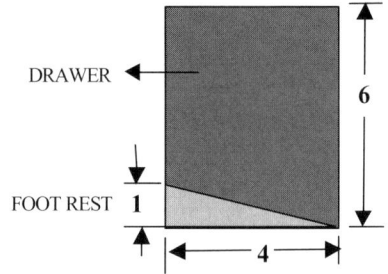

(c)

Figure 22(b). Front view and **(c)** side view of the table.

Let us consider a 3D workspace presented in Figure 22(a) and side views are shown vide Figure 22(b) and (c). This has been encoded by the linked list structure discussed above, and shown in the Figure 23.

4. LEARNING AND COORDINATION CYCLE

In the last two sections, we have seen how a robot perceives its environment around it autonomously and store it in the Long Term Memory in a suitable format/data

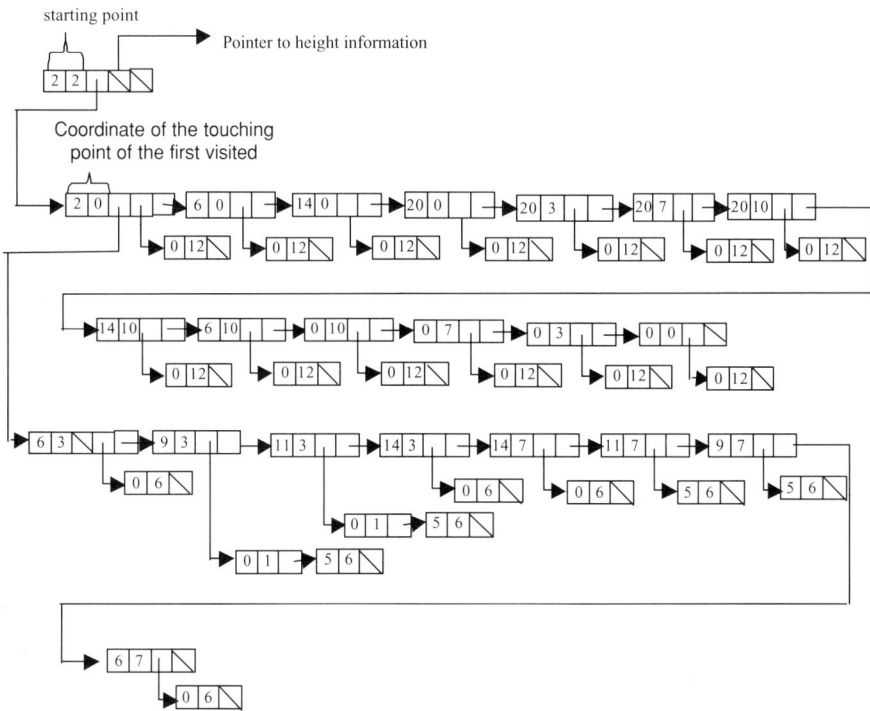

Figure 23. The linked listed structure for the 3D environment shown in Figure 22.

structure. These information can be utilized subsequently for learning, planning and task coordination. Different states of the Learning and coordination cycle have already been defined in the first section. In this section we will discuss how the robot will plan its trajectory of motion from the previously stored information as well as sensory data.

For navigating in the environment, first the robot has to learn how to avoid obstacle. This has been achieved here through supervised learning. We will discuss the supervised learning for obstacle avoidance in the next sub-section. Secondly, for reaching a goal in optimal path and time, the robot needs to do path planning. In this section we will discuss about the navigational planning by Bi-directional Associative Memory and by evolutionary algorithm approach.

4.1. Learning for obstacle avoidance

For navigating in the environment the robot has to learn how to avoid obstacle. It is of course the first behavior in the Rodney Brook's model shown in Fig. 2. It is also required for planning state in the Learning and Coordination cycle of the model

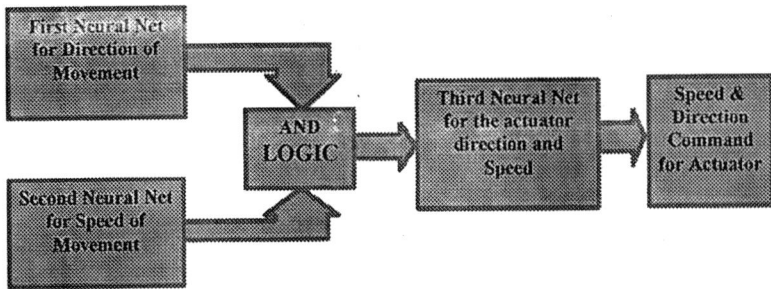

Outputs of the first and second Neural Nets are ANDed together and fed along with the previous direction of movement as input for energy minimization to the AANN and output is supplied to the actuator of the robot for controlling the speed and direction of movement

Figure 24. Outputs of the two Neural nets (Direction and Speed) are ANDed together and fed to the Third Neural Netwrok.

of Cognition. Many techniques for obstacle avoidance are available in literature using various AI and soft computing tools. But most of them suffer from one or more of the following deficiencies [29], [30].

i)   The minimality of distance w.r.t. traversal of path cannot be achieved.
ii) The time constraint for reaching the goal position from a given initial position usually not considered as a significant factor, though for real time systems this is an important issue.
iii) The criteria for minimizing energy-cost is not taken into account in obstacle avoidance problems.

Let us consider the obstacle avoidance model of Meng and Picton [31]. They have partitioned the entire workspace of a mobile robot into non-overlapping blocks and employed an *Artificial Neural Network (ANN)* based algorithm for designing the direction of movement of the robots based on the location of obstacles in its workspace. Here, the minimum time and minimum distance criteria have not been considered. Michalewicz et al. [32] have designed an improved algorithm for path planning in a dynamic environment, that avoids collision, but does not take into account the minimum energy criteria. Let us first discuss a technique that overcomes all the above limitations by employing an *ANN*. For clarity, let us briefly discuss first the constraint in navigation process.

4.1.1. The constraints in the navigation process

The Figure 24 depicts a schematic diagram of obstacle avoidance learning network consisting of the two stage ANN configuration. The first and second network acquires the sensory information stored in LTM and applies the constraints on these data and

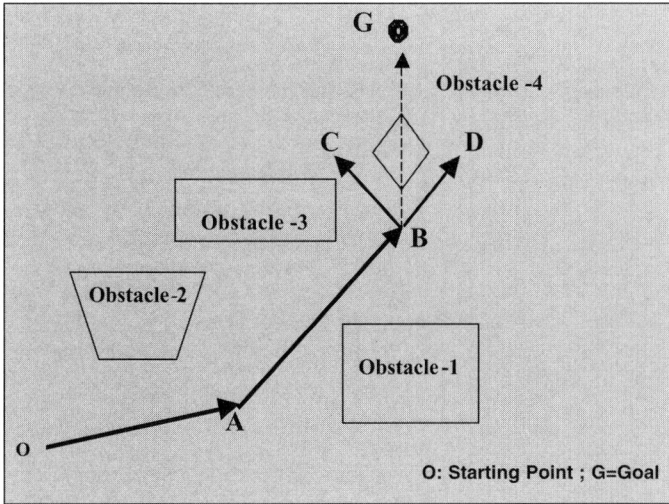

BG is the shortest path between the current position B of the robot and the goal position G. The ultrasonic sensor, however identifies obstacle on this line and attempts to move along the line close to BC by a small angle θ

Figure 25. Minimality in path traversal criteria.

the third network generates control commands for the movement of the motors and the actuators.

The first neural network is designed to support the following criteria:

i) **Minimality in path traversal:** This can be realized by moving always in the direction of goal or along the line, angularly close enough to it from the current position. Formally, the above criteria can be described (vide Figure 25), as the minimization of the angle θ, the direction of movement (say) BD, makes with the shortest route BG.

ii) **Time minimization:** It can be realized by maximizing the speed of movement, along each segment. Thus, the criteria for minimality in time constraint is satisfied if

$$\sum_{\forall i}^{n} v_i \mid v_i = \text{velocity along the line segment i}$$

is minimized.

i) **Energy minimization:** Fewer change in the direction/course of movement, will result in lesser consumption of energy by the robot. The energy minimization

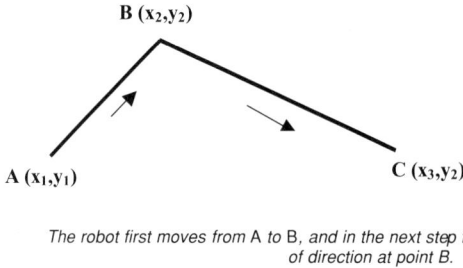

The robot first moves from A to B, and in the next step from B to C, causing a change of direction at point B.

Figure 26. The change of movement direction by the robot.

criteria, formulated based on this strategy, requires movement of the robot on straight line paths as far as practicable. This can be formally realized by minimizing,

$$\sum\nolimits_{v_{i,j}} \{(x_j - x_i)^2 + (y_j - y_i)^2\}$$

where (x_j, y_j) is the next point following (x_i, y_i) when the robot starts changing directions. This is illustrated in Figure 26, where i is 1 and j is 2. This has been realized by taking the previous direction of movement, while finding out the final direction of movement.

4.1.2. Learning for local guidance through Neural Net

The first constraint can be satisfied when the direction of movement is kept aligned to the shortest route (towards Goal) or angularly close to it as far as practicable. It has been realized by the *First Neural Net*, where it takes the *desired direction of movement* (DD) along with the sensory information around the robot in different directions, as input and gives the possible direction of movements as output. These inputs and outputs are shown in the Table-I, which are the information (S_i) about the neighboring environment (shown in Figure 27), while the output variables (d_i) denotes the direction of movement in these specified directions by the robot. In fact, with eight (8) binary input variables $(S_1, S_2, \ldots S_8)$ and one real variable i.e. DD (Desired Direction) which can take 8 values, creates a possible space of $2^8 \times 8$. However, out of this space, less than 100 are significant from the point of view of minimum path deviation of the robot, and has been considered as the samples in Table-I.

The standard back propagation learning algorithm with a gradient descent momentum term and adaptive learning is used for training the *First Neural net*. It has been used 50, 40, 30 and 8 neurons in the hidden layers and output layer with nonlinear functions 'tansig', 'logsig', 'logsig' and 'purelin' respectively. MATLAB 5.0 Neural Network Toolbox is used for training the neural net. At each training phase, the momentum term is set to 0.95 and the learning rate is set to 0.0001 respectively. After 26197 epochs, the network converged to the desired pattern with Sum-Square-Error (SSE) less than 0.001.

Table-I. Sample Training patterns for the First Constraint Neural Net: the sensory information about obstacles along with the desired direction of movement as input and the direction of movement as output

	Input to the Constraint Neural net for direction								Output of the net shows direction of movement							
DD	S_1	S_2	S_3	S_4	S_5	S_6	S_7	S_8	**d1**	**d2**	**d3**	**d4**	**d5**	**d6**	**d7**	**d8**
0	0	0	0	0	0	0	0	0	1	0	0	0	0	0	0	0
0	1	0	0	0	0	0	0	0	0	1	0	0	0	0	0	1
0	0	1	0	0	0	0	0	0	1	0	0	0	0	0	0	0
0	0	0	0	0	0	0	0	1	1	0	0	0	0	0	0	0
0	1	1	0	0	0	0	0	1	0	0	1	0	0	0	1	0
0	0	0	0	0	0	0	1	1	1	0	0	0	0	0	0	0
0	1	0	0	0	0	1	1	0	1	0	0	0	0	0	0	0
0	1	1	1	0	0	0	0	0	0	0	0	0	0	0	0	1
0	1	1	0	0	0	0	1	1	0	0	1	0	0	0	0	0
0	1	1	1	0	0	0	1	1	0	0	0	1	0	1	0	0
0	1	1	0	0	0	0	1	1	0	0	1	0	0	0	0	0
0	1	1	1	0	0	0	0	1	0	0	0	0	0	0	1	0
0	1	1	1	1	0	1	1	1	0	0	0	0	1	0	0	0
0	1	1	1	1	0	0	1	1	0	0	0	0	0	1	0	0
0	1	1	1	0	0	1	1	1	0	0	0	1	0	0	0	0
0	1	0	1	0	1	0	1	0	0	1	0	0	0	0	0	1
0.78	0	0	0	0	0	0	0	0	0	1	0	0	0	0	0	0
0.78	1	0	0	0	0	0	0	0	0	1	0	0	0	0	0	1
0.78	1	1	0	0	0	0	0	0	0	0	0	0	0	0	0	1
0.78	1	0	0	0	0	0	0	1	0	1	0	0	0	0	0	0
0.78	1	1	0	0	0	0	0	1	0	0	1	0	0	0	1	0
0.78	1	0	0	0	0	0	1	1	0	1	0	0	0	0	0	0
0.78	1	1	1	0	0	0	0	0	0	0	0	0	0	0	0	1
0.78	1	1	1	0	0	0	1	1	0	0	0	1	0	1	0	0
0.78	1	1	1	0	0	0	0	1	0	0	0	0	0	0	1	0
0.78	1	1	0	0	0	0	1	1	0	0	1	0	0	0	0	0
0.78	1	1	1	1	0	1	1	1	0	0	0	0	1	0	0	0
0.78	1	1	1	1	0	0	1	1	0	0	0	0	0	1	0	0
0.78	1	1	1	0	0	1	1	1	0	0	0	1	0	0	0	0
0.78	1	0	1	0	1	0	1	0	0	1	0	0	0	0	0	1
−0.78	0	0	0	0	0	0	0	0	0	0	0	0	0	0	0	1
−0.78	0	0	0	0	0	0	0	1	1	0	0	0	0	0	1	0
−0.78	0	0	0	0	0	0	1	1	1	0	0	0	0	0	0	0
−0.78	1	0	0	0	0	0	0	1	0	0	0	0	0	0	1	0
−0.78	1	0	0	0	0	0	1	1	0	1	0	0	0	1	0	0
−0.78	1	1	0	0	0	0	0	1	0	0	0	0	0	0	1	0
−0.78	0	0	0	0	0	1	1	1	1	0	0	0	0	0	0	0
−0.78	1	1	0	0	0	1	1	1	0	0	1	0	1	0	0	0
−0.78	1	0	0	0	0	1	1	1	0	1	0	0	0	0	0	0
−0.78	1	1	0	0	0	0	1	1	0	0	0	0	0	1	0	0
−0.78	1	1	0	0	1	1	1	1	0	0	1	0	0	0	0	0
−0.78	1	1	0	0	1	1	1	1	0	0	1	0	0	0	0	0
−0.78	0	1	0	1	0	1	0	1	1	0	0	0	0	0	1	0
1.57	0	0	0	0	0	0	0	0	0	0	1	0	0	0	0	0
1.57	0	0	1	0	0	0	0	0	0	1	0	1	0	0	0	0

(continue)

Table-I. (continued)

DD	Input to the Constraint Neural net for direction								Output of the net shows direction of movement							
1.57	0	1	1	0	0	0	0	0	0	0	0	1	0	0	0	0
1.57	0	0	1	1	0	0	0	0	0	1	0	0	0	0	0	0
1.57	0	1	1	1	0	0	0	0	1	0	0	0	1	0	0	0
1.57	1	1	1	0	0	0	0	0	0	0	0	1	0	0	0	0
1.57	0	0	1	1	1	0	0	0	0	1	0	0	0	0	0	0
1.57	1	1	1	1	1	0	0	0	0	0	0	0	0	1	0	1
1.57	1	1	1	1	0	0	0	0	0	0	0	0	1	0	0	0
1.57	0	1	1	1	1	0	0	0	1	0	0	0	0	0	0	0
1.57	1	0	1	0	1	0	1	0	0	1	0	1	0	0	0	0
−1.57	0	0	0	0	0	0	0	0	0	0	0	0	0	0	1	0
−1.57	0	0	0	0	0	0	1	0	0	0	0	0	0	1	0	1
−1.57	0	0	0	0	0	1	1	0	0	0	0	0	0	0	0	1
−1.57	0	0	0	0	0	0	1	1	0	0	0	0	0	1	0	0
−1.57	0	0	0	0	0	1	1	1	1	0	0	0	1	0	0	0
−1.57	0	0	0	0	1	1	1	0	0	0	0	0	0	0	0	1
−1.57	0	0	0	0	0	0	1	1	0	0	0	0	0	1	0	0
−1.57	0	0	0	0	1	1	1	1	1	0	0	0	0	0	0	0
−1.57	1	0	1	0	1	0	1	0	0	0	0	0	0	1	0	1
2.36	0	0	0	0	0	0	0	0	0	0	0	1	0	0	0	0
2.36	0	0	0	1	0	0	0	0	0	0	1	0	1	0	0	0
2.36	0	0	1	1	0	0	0	0	0	0	0	0	1	0	0	0
2.36	0	0	0	1	1	0	0	0	0	0	1	0	0	0	0	0
2.36	0	1	1	1	0	0	0	0	0	0	0	0	1	0	0	0
2.36	0	0	0	1	1	1	0	0	0	0	1	0	0	0	0	0
2.36	0	1	1	1	1	1	0	0	1	0	0	0	0	0	1	0
2.36	1	1	1	1	1	1	1	0	0	0	0	0	0	0	0	1
2.36	0	1	0	1	0	1	0	1	0	0	1	0	1	0	0	0
−2.36	0	0	0	0	0	0	0	0	0	0	0	0	0	1	0	0
−2.36	0	0	0	0	0	1	0	0	0	0	0	0	1	0	1	0
−2.36	0	0	0	0	0	1	1	0	0	0	0	0	1	0	0	0
−2.36	0	0	0	0	1	1	0	0	0	0	0	0	0	0	1	0
−2.36	0	0	0	1	1	1	1	0	0	0	0	1	0	0	0	1
−2.36	0	0	0	1	1	1	1	0	0	0	0	0	0	0	0	1
−2.36	0	0	0	0	1	1	1	1	0	0	0	1	0	0	0	0
−2.36	0	0	0	1	1	1	1	1	1	0	1	0	0	0	0	0
−2.36	0	1	0	1	0	1	0	1	0	0	0	0	1	0	1	0
3.14	0	0	0	0	0	0	0	0	0	0	0	1	0	0	0	0
3.14	0	0	0	0	1	0	0	0	0	0	0	1	0	1	0	0
3.14	0	0	0	1	1	0	0	0	0	0	0	0	0	1	0	0
3.14	0	0	0	0	1	1	0	0	0	0	0	1	0	0	0	0
3.14	0	0	0	1	1	1	0	0	0	0	1	0	0	0	1	0
3.14	0	0	1	1	1	1	0	0	0	0	0	0	0	0	1	0
3.14	0	0	0	1	1	1	1	0	0	0	1	0	0	0	0	0
3.14	0	0	1	1	1	1	1	0	0	1	0	0	0	0	0	1
3.14	1	0	1	0	1	0	1	0	0	0	0	1	0	1	0	0

DD = Desired Direction in angle (radian);

$\forall_i S_i$ = Sensor readings, which will be 1, if the reading is 0.5 or more and 0 if the reading is less than 0.5 (where '0' means obstacle free & '1' means occupied by obstacles)

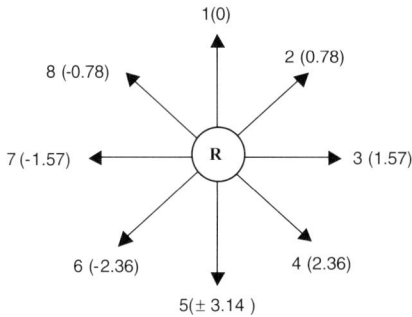

The number 1 through 8 denotes directions, where the angle between two successive directions is 45°.
Direction 1(0) is the forward movement of robot. The information within parenthesis denotes the angles
of the corresponding positions in radians w.r.t. the reference direction 1.

Figure 27. Direction of the Robot estimated in angle (radian).

The second constraint i.e. time minimization can be satisfied, if the speed in the different path segment can be maximized. This has been realized by *Second Neural Net* by taking the distance of the obstacles in the different as the input and the predicted speed in these directions as output. The input variable (S_i) of this net is the measured distance of the obstacle from the robot R, while the output variable (V_i) denotes the velocity in the respective direction of movement of the robot. Here, input variables (S_i) from eight (8) sensors, have been quantified into 11 possible values (0, $0.1V_{max}$, $0.2V_{max}$, $0.3 V_{max}, \ldots, V_{max}$), which could have a possibility space of 11^8. However, out of this space, only few tens of the input patterns may be trained to give a generalized output, which has been shown in Table-II.

The second CNN for finding the speed, is trained by a similar learning algorithm with a gradient descent momentum term and adaptive learning. It has been used 40, 20 and 8 neurons in the hidden layers and output layer with non-linear transfer function 'tansig', 'logsig' and 'purelin' respectively. The momentum term is set at 0.95 and the learning rate is fixed at 0.0001 respectively. The network converged with a SSE less than 0.001 after 7063 epochs.

4.1.3. Building the Third Neural Net

The third constraint i.e. energy minimization has been formulated here by considering the direction of movement of the previous step. The first and the second *Neural Nets* work concurrently for producing direction and speed. Their outputs are ANDed and fed as the input to the Third Neural Net. The input of the Third neural network includes 8 possible velocity movement in prescribed directions and the last direction of movement as well. The output of the network identifies the final direction and speed of movement. The input–output patterns of the Third Neural Net is given in Table-III.

Table-II. Sample Training patterns for Second Constraint Neural Net: The distance of obstacle form the robot as input and possible speeds in different directions as output

Input from sensor								Output from the Speed Constraint Net							
S_1	S_2	S_3	S_4	S_5	S_6	S_7	S_8	v1	v2	v3	v4	v5	v6	v7	v8
0	0	0	0	0	0	0	0	1	1	1	1	1	1	1	1
1	0	0	0	0	0	0	0	0	1	1	1	1	1	1	1
1	1	0	0	0	0	0	1	0	0	1	1	1	1	1	0
1	1	1	0	0	0	1	1	0	0	0	1	1	0	0	0
1	1	1	1	0	1	1	1	0	0	0	0	1	0	0	0
1	0.7	0.5	0.3	0	0.3	0.5	0.7	0	0.3	0.5	0.7	1	0.7	0.5	0.3
1	1	0.8	0.4	0	0.4	0.8	1	0	0	0.2	0.6	1	0.6	0.2	0
1	1	1	0.5	0	0.5	1	1	0	0	0	0.5	1	0.5	0	0
0	1	0	0	0	0	0	0	1	0	1	1	1	1	1	1
0.8	1	0.8	0.5	0.2	0	0.2	0.5	0.2	0	0.2	0.5	0.8	1	0.8	0.5
0	0	1	0	0	0	0	0	1	1	0	1	1	1	1	1
0.5	0.7	1	0.7	0.5	0.2	0	0.2	0.5	0.3	0	0.3	0.5	0.8	1	0.8
0.3	1	1	1	0.3	0	0	0	0.7	0	0	0	0.7	1	1	1
1	1	1	1	1	0.7	0.4	0.7	0	0	0	0	0	0.3	0.6	0.3
0	0	0	1	0	0	0	0	1	1	1	0	1	1	1	1
0	0.3	0.7	1	0.7	0.3	0	0	1	0.7	0.3	0	0.3	0.7	1	1
0.2	0.5	1	1	1	0.7	0.3	0	0.8	0.5	0	0	0	0.3	0.7	1
0.3	1	1	1	1	1	0.2	0	0.7	0	0	0	0	0	0.8	1
0	0	0	0	1	0	0	0	1	1	1	1	0	1	1	1
0	0.3	0.5	0.8	1	0.7	0.6	0.2	1	0.7	0.5	0.2	0	0.3	0.4	0.8
0	0.4	0.7	1	1	1	0.6	0.3	1	0.6	0.3	0	0	0	0.4	0.7
0	0.3	1	1	1	1	1	0.4	1	0.7	0	0	0	0	0	0.6
0.3	0.8	1	1	1	1	1	0.4	0.7	0.2	0	0	0	0	0	0.6
0	0	0	0	0	1	0	0	1	1	1	1	1	0	1	1
0.5	0	0.5	0.8	1	1	1	0.8	0.5	1	0.5	0.2	0	0	0	0.2
0.4	0	0.5	1	1	1	1	1	0.6	1	0.5	0	0	0	0	0
0.6	0.3	0.6	0.8	1	1	1	1	0.4	0.7	0.4	0.2	0	0	0	0
0	0	0	0	0	0	1	0	1	1	1	1	1	1	0	1
0.5	0.3	0	0.3	0.5	0.8	1	0.8	0.5	0.7	1	0.7	0.5	0.2	0	0.2
0.8	0.6	0.1	0.6	0.8	1	1	1	0.2	0.4	0.9	0.4	0.2	0	0	0
1	0.4	0	0.5	1	1	1	1	0	0.6	1	0.5	0	0	0	0
1	1	0.1	1	1	1	1	1	0	0	0.9	0	0	0	0	0
0	0	0	0	0	0	0	1	1	1	1	1	1	1	1	0
0.7	0	0	0	0	0	0.7	1	0.3	1	1	1	1	1	0.3	0
1	0.4	0	0	0	0.4	1	1	0	0.6	1	1	1	0.6	0	0
1	1	0.5	0	0.4	1	1	1	0	0	0.5	1	0.6	0	0	0
1	1	1	0.1	1	1	1	1	0	0	0	0.9	0	0	0	0
0	0.7	0.6	0.9	0.6	0.3	0.2	0.4	1	0.3	0.4	0.1	0.4	0.7	0.8	0.6
0.6	0.4	0.3	0.2	0.2	0.5	0.7	0	0.4	0.6	0.7	0.8	0.8	0.5	0.3	1

$\forall_i S_i = (2 - d_i)/(2 - 0.2)$, where d_i is the distance of the obstacle from the robot.
v_i = Speed in respective direction as shown in Figure 27.

Table-III. Training Pattern of AANN: 8 possible velocity movement as well as the last direction of movement as input and actuator speed and direction as output.

INPUT to the Ambiguity Avoidance Neural Net									OUTPUT	
LD	Vd1	Vd2	Vd3	Vd4	Vd5	Vd6	Vd7	Vd8	V	D
0	1	0	0	0	0	0	0	0	1	0
0	0.8	0.6	0	0	0	0	0	0.5	0.8	0
0	0.7	1	0.8	0	0	0	0	0	1	0.78
0	0.3	0.8	0	0	0	0	0	0	0.8	0.78
0	0	0	0	0	0	0.7	0	1	1	−0.78
0	0	0	0.2	0	0	0	0	0.8	0.8	−0.78
0	0	0.8	0	0	0	0	1	0	1	−1.57
0	0	0.5	0	0	0	0	0.7	0	0.7	−1.57
0	0	0	1	0	0	0	0	0	1	1.57
0	0	0	0.8	0	0	0.2	0	0	0.8	1.57
0.78	0	1	0	0	0	0	0	0	1	0.78
0.78	1	0	0	0	0	0	0	0	1	0
0.78	0.8	0	0	0	0	0.3	0	0	0.8	0
0.78	0.7	0	0.9	0	0	0	0	0	0.9	1.57
0.78	0.8	0.8	0	0	0	0	0	0	0.8	0.78
0.78	0	0.8	0.8	0	0	0	0	0	0.8	1.57
−0.78	1	0	0	0	0	0	0	0	1	0
−0.78	0	0	0	0	0	0	0	1	1	−0.78
−0.78	0.9	0	0	0	0	0	0	0.9	0.9	−1.57
−0.78	0	0.8	0	0	0	0	0	0.8	0.8	−0.78
−0.78	0	0.9	0	0	0	0.8	0	0	0.8	−2.36
−0.78	0.8	0	0	0	0	0	0.9	0	0.9	−1.57
1.57	1	0	0	0	0	0	0	0	1	0
1.57	0	0.8	0	0	0	0	0	0.9	0.8	0.78
1.57	0	0.8	0	0.9	0	0	0	0	0.9	2.36
1.57	0.8	0	0	0	0.7	0	0	0	0.7	3.14
−1.57	1	0	0	0	0	0	0	0	1	0
−1.57	0	0	0	0	0	0	1	0	1	−1.57
−1.57	0	0.8	0	0	0	0	0	0.8	0.8	−0.78
−1.57	0.9	0	0	0	0	0	0.8	0	0.8	−1.57
−1.57	0.9	0	0	0	0.7	0	0	0	0.7	3.14
−1.57	0	0	0	0	0	0.9	0	0.8	0.9	−2.36
2.36	1	0	0	0	0	0	0	0	1	0
2.36	0	0.8	0	0	0	0	0	0.9	0.8	0.78
2.36	0	0	0.8	0	0	0	0.8	0	0.8	1.57
2.36	0	0.8	0	0.9	0	0	0	0	0.9	2.36
2.36	0	0	0.8	0	0.8	0	0	0	0.8	3.14
2.36	0	0.8	0	0	0	0.7	0	0	0.7	−2.36
2.36	0	0	0.6	0	0	0	0.8	0	0.6	1.57
−2.36	1	0	0	0	0	0	0	0	1	0
−2.36	0	0.8	0	0	0	0	0	0.9	0.9	−0.78
−2.36	0	0	0.8	0	0	0	0.6	0	0.6	−1.57
−2.36	0.9	0	0	0	0	0	0.7	0	0.7	−1.57
−2.36	0	0.9	0	0	0	0.6	0	0	0.6	−2.36
−2.36	0	0	0	0	0	0.8	0	0.9	0.8	−2.36
3.14	1	0	0	0	0	0	0	0	1	0
3.14	0	0	0	0.9	0	0.8	0	0	0.9	2.36
3.14	0	0	0.9	0	0	0	0.7	0	0.9	1.57

(continue)

Table-III. (continued)

INPUT to the Ambiguity Avoidance Neural Net										OUTPUT
3.14	0	0	0.9	0	0.8	0	0	0	0.9	1.57
3.14	0	0.8	0	0	0	0	0	0.6	0.6	−0.78
0	0	0	0	0	0	0	0	0	0	0
0.78	0	0	0	0	0	0	0	0	0	0.78
1.57	0	0	0	0	0	0	0	0	0	1.57
2.36	0	0	0	0	0	0	0	0	0	2.36
3.14	0	0	0	0	0	0	0	0	0	3.14
−2.36	0	0	0	0	0	0	0	0	0	−2.36
−1.57	0	0	0	0	0	0	0	0	0	−1.57
−0.78	0	0	0	0	0	0	0	0	0	−0.78

LD = Previous direction of movement of the robot;
$\forall_i vd_i$ = ANDed result of the outputs of TABLE-I and TABLE-II
V = Speed of movement and D = Direction of movement sent to the actuator

A similar BP neural net is used for training this *Neural net*. It has been used 100, 90, 80 and 7 neurons in the hidden layers and output layer with nonlinear functions 'tansig', 'logsig', 'logsig' and 'purelin' respectively. For the purpose training the AANN, the analog values presented in the column V and D are multiplied by a scale of 10 and then converted into 4 and 3 bit binary numbers respectively. At each training phase, the momentum term is set to 0.95 and the learning rate is set to 0.0001 respectively. After 35611 epochs, the network converged to the desired pattern with SSE less than 0.001.

Training time of the various neural nets mentioned above are reasonable, because this learning is done off-line and once the neural net is trained, the outputs can be computed in msecs, after the presentation of the inputs. Once the learning is over, this state can send control signals to the actuator directly from the sensory data received from the sensors.

4.2. Planning by bi-directional associative memory

In this section, we will present a new approach for navigational planning by using a specialized neural topology called the *Bi-directional Associated Memory* (BAM). A BAM is a two layer neural net, where each neuron at one layer is connected bi-directionally to all the neurons in the other layer. BAM was proposed by Prof. Kosko of the University of South California in late 80's [33] [34]. In his elementary model he considered a two layered neural net, where neuron at each layer are connected to the neurons at the other layer through bi-directional links. The signal associated with the neurons can assume $\{-1, +1\}$ values and the weights, describing connectivity between neurons possess signed integer values. The basic problem in BAM was to design a single set of weight matrix W, such that the difference between the transformed vector and the output vector is minimum.

$$\sum_{\forall i}(A_i W - B_i) + \sum_{\forall i}(B_i W^T - A_i) \tag{1}$$

Prof. Kosko considered a Liapunov function, describing a nonlinear surface to show that there exist a single W matrix, for which the minima of expression (1) can be attained. This also proves that if B_i can be computed by taking product of A_i and W, then A_i too can be evaluated by multiplying B_i by W^T.

In one of his later work [34], Prof. Kosko extended the concept of BAM for memorizing a sequence of causal events, which is popularly known as *Temporal Associative Memory* (TAM). For instance, given a set of weight matrix W, if one knows the causal relationships:

$A_1 \rightarrow A_2$

$A_2 \rightarrow A_3$

....

....

$A_{n-1} \rightarrow A_n$

Then A_n can be inferred from A_1 through the chain sequence $A_1 \rightarrow A_2 \rightarrow A_3........... \rightarrow A_n$. Now remembering the weight matrix W and the input vector A_1, one can reconstruct the entire chain leading to A_n. Now, let us consider a case where there exists a bifurcation in the chain at the event A_j. The sequence describing the bifurcation is presented below.

$$A_1 \rightarrow A_2 \rightarrow \ ...... \rightarrow A_j \rightarrow A_{j+1} \rightarrow \ .... \rightarrow A_{n+1}$$
$$\searrow B_1 \rightarrow B_2 \rightarrow B_3...........B_k$$

Let us assume that the whole sequence from A_i through A_n and from A_j through B_n are stored. Now it has been detected that the path from A_{j+1} somehow is blocked. The system under this configuration will backtrack from A_{j+1} to A_j by the operation $A_j = A_{j+1} W^T$ and then proceed for an alternative path through B_1 by the transformation $B_1 = A_j \cdot W$. This property of TAM motivated us to employ it in navigation of a mobile robot.

4.2.1. Temporal associative memory in mobile robot navigation

It has been pointed out in the last section, TAM can be successfully used for navigation in a known world [35]. Here the robot has to determine all possible paths between each pair of given locations, and encode it for subsequent usage. For instance, to traverse the path from A_1 to A_n, the robot has to memorize only the weight matrix W, based on which it can easily evaluate the entire trajectory passing through A_1 and A_n. In fact, we can derive $A_2, A_3, \ldots A_n$ by post multiplying A_1 by $W, W^2,........W^{n-1}$. For determining backtrack path from known A_n, we could go on multiplying it by W^T. Because of the inherent feature of bi–directionality, the above problem can be modeled with TAM.

Encoding and Decoding Process: The possible paths between any two given nodes in the world map are known a priori from the Long Term memory (LTM). The encoding scheme in this context is to evaluate the weight matrix W that satisfies the criteria of minimality of the function denoted by equation (2).

$$\sum_{\forall i}(A_i W - A_{i+1}) + \sum_{\forall i}(A_{i+1} W^T - A_i) \qquad (2)$$

The decoding process evaluates A_i, when A_{i+1} is known or vice-versa. Let us represent the motion of an autonomous vehicle on a path by a set of ordered vectors, such as $A_1 \rightarrow A_2 \rightarrow \ldots\ldots A_k \rightarrow A_{k+1} \rightarrow \ldots \rightarrow A_n$, assuming the temporal patterns are finite and discrete. The feature of the bi-directionality in BAM can be utilized here to memorize the associative matrix between $A_i \rightarrow A_{i+1}$. The following steps can be used to encode the weight matrix of the TAM given by equation (3).

i)   Binary vectors are converted to bipolar vectors
ii) The contiguous relationship $A_i \rightarrow A_{i+1}$ is memorized by forming the correlation matrix $X_i^T \cdot X_{i+1}$
iii) All the above correlation matrices are added point wise to give

$$W = \sum_i^n X_i^T \cdot X_{i+1} \qquad (3)$$

Decoding of the output vector A_{i+1} is estimated by vector multiplication of A with W and applying the following threshold function

$$A_{i+1}^k = \begin{cases} 1, \ldots\ldots & if \quad A_i W_i \geq 0 \\ 0, \ldots\ldots & if \quad A_i W_i < 0 \end{cases}$$

$$A_1^k = \begin{cases} 1, \ldots\ldots & if \quad A_{i+1} W_i^T > 0 \\ 0, \ldots\ldots & if \quad A_{i+1} W_i^T \leq 0 \end{cases}$$

An Illustration in a semi-dynamic environment: The trajectories traversed by the soft mobile object along two alternative paths, shown in Figure 28 are represented by the following set of sequences in decimal number and later converted to binary values, where the number of bits depends on length and resolution.

$A_1 = (X_1, Y_1) = (1, 1) = (0\ 0\ 1\ 0\ 0\ 1);$ $A_2 = (X_2, Y_2) = (1, 2) = (0\ 0\ 1\ 0\ 1\ 0);$
$A_3 = (X_3, X_3) = (1, 3) = (0\ 0\ 1\ 0\ 1\ 1);$ $A_4 = (X_4, Y_4) = (2, 4) = (0\ 1\ 0\ 1\ 0\ 0);$
$A_5 = (X_5, Y_5) = (3, 4) = (0\ 1\ 1\ 1\ 0\ 0);$ $A_6 = (X_6, Y_6) = (4, 4) = (1\ 0\ 0\ 1\ 0\ 0);$
$A_7 = (X_7, Y_7) = (5, 5) = (1\ 0\ 1\ 1\ 0\ 1);$ $A_8 = (X_8, Y_8) = (5, 6) = (1\ 0\ 1\ 1\ 1\ 0);$
$A_9 = (X_9, Y_9) = (6, 7) = (1\ 1\ 0\ 1\ 1\ 1);$ $A_{10} = (X_{10}, Y_{10}) = (7, 7) = (1\ 1\ 1\ 1\ 1\ 1);$

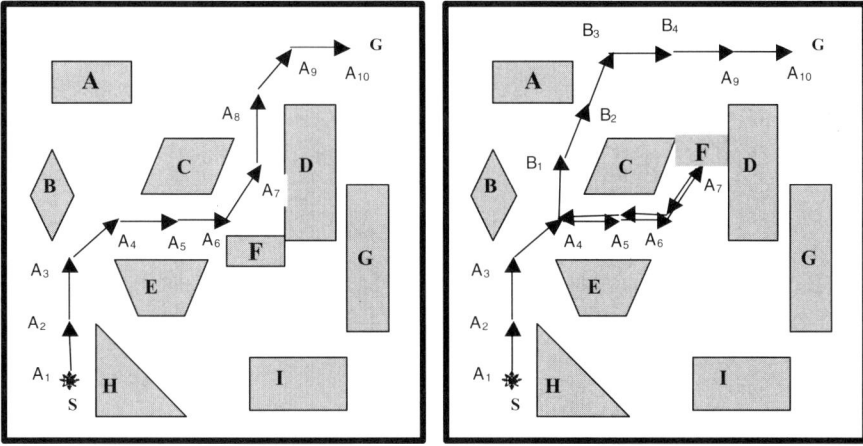

Figure 28(a). Sample path between starting position (S) and goal position (G) though a charted path A_1, $A_2, \ldots A_{10}$; **(b)** Mobile object traverses in an alternate path after back tracking from node A_7 to A_4 as the semi-dynamic obstacle F has shifted its position and then navigate through the charted path from B_1 to B_4 and then taken normal path to reach the goal within the workspace.

Encoding the above sequences into bipolar values is necessary according to the TAM procedure, which is derived below:

$$A_1 = (X_1, Y_1) = (-1 \ -1 \ 1 \ -1 \ -1 \ 1); \quad A_2 = (X_2, Y_2) = (-1 \ -1 \ 1 \ -1 \ 1 \ -1);$$
$$A_3 = (X_3, X_3) = (-1 \ -1 \ 1 \ -1 \ 1 \ 1); \quad A_4 = (X_4, Y_4) = (-1 \ 1 \ -1 \ 1 \ -1 \ -1);$$
$$A_5 = (X_5, Y_5) = (-1 \ 1 \ 1 \ 1 \ -1 \ -1); \quad A_6 = (X_6, Y_6) = (1 \ -1 \ -1 \ 1 \ -1 \ -1);$$
$$A_7 = (X_7, Y_7) = (1 \ -1 \ 1 \ 1 \ -1 \ 1); \quad A_8 = (X_8, Y_8) = (1 \ -1 \ 1 \ 1 \ 1 \ -1);$$
$$A_9 = (X_9, Y_9) = (1 \ 1 \ -1 \ 1 \ 1 \ 1); \quad A_{10} = (X_{10}, Y_{10}) = (1 \ 1 \ 1 \ 1 \ 1 \ 1);$$

The calculation of a sample correlation matrix W_1 is shown below.

$$W_1 = A_1^T \cdot A_2 = (-1 \quad -1 \quad 1 \quad -1 \quad -1 \quad 1)^T \cdot (-1 \quad -1 \quad 1 \quad -1 \quad 1 \quad -1)$$

$$= \begin{bmatrix} 1 & 1 & -1 & 1 & -1 & 1 \\ 1 & 1 & -1 & 1 & -1 & 1 \\ -1 & -1 & 1 & -1 & 1 & -1 \\ 1 & 1 & -1 & 1 & -1 & 1 \\ 1 & 1 & -1 & 1 & -1 & 1 \\ -1 & -1 & 1 & -1 & 1 & -1 \end{bmatrix}$$

The weight matrix W is estimated by adding the contiguous matrices $W_1, W_2, \ldots W_8$.

$$W = W_1 + W_2 + W_3 + W_4 + W_5 + W_6 + W_7 + W_8 + W_9$$
$$= A_1^T \cdot A_2 + A_2^T \cdot A_3 + A_3^T \cdot A_4 + A_4^T \cdot A_5 + A_5^T \cdot A_6 + A_6^T \cdot A_7 + A_7^T \cdot A_8$$
$$+ A_8^T \cdot A_9 + A_9^T \cdot A_{10}$$

$$= \begin{bmatrix} 7 & 1 & 1 & 3 & 3 & 5 \\ 1 & 3 & -1 & 1 & -3 & -01 \\ -1 & -3 & -3 & -1 & 3 & -3 \\ 7 & 1 & 1 & 7 & -1 & 1 \\ 1 & 5 & -3 & -1 & 3 & 5 \\ -1 & 1 & 1- & 1 & 3 & -3 \end{bmatrix}$$

Each successive step of movement can be estimated by the expression $A_i \cdot W$, which can be easily verified. The second objective of the net is to backtrack, in the presence of obstacle on a particular route. For instance, when the robot finds an obstacle after seventh step of movement on the right side path of obstacle C, then it retrace back to A_4 node, which is a junction and takes an alternative path by means of an alternative TAM weight matrix W', which has been estimated by considering the four nodes which surrounds the obstacle C, on the top and left side. Here from the node A_4, two alternate weight matrices are available. If the robot finds obstacle in one of the paths, it will back track and proceed again from the node A_4 on the other path. The weight W' can be estimated, as follows by considering the node points:

$A_4 = (2, 4) = (0\ 1\ 1\ 1\ 0\ 0\ )$; $B_1 = (2, 5) = (\ 0\ 1\ 0\ 1\ 0\ 1)$;
$B_2 = (3, 6) = (0\ 1\ 1\ 1\ 1\ 0)$; $B_3 = (4, 7) = (1\ 0\ 0\ 1\ 1\ 1)$;
$B_4 = (5, 7) = (1\ 0\ 1\ 1\ 1\ 1)$; $A_9 = (6, 7) = (1\ 1\ 0\ 1\ 1\ 1)$;
$A_{10} = (7, 7) = (1\ 1\ 1\ 1\ 1\ 1)$;

Encoding the above sequences into bipolar values gives the following:

$A_4 = (-1\ 1\ 1\ 1\ -1\ -1\ )$; $B_1 = (-1\ 1\ -1\ 1\ -1\ 1)$; $B_2 = (-1\ 1\ 1\ 1\ 1\ -1)$;
$B_3 = (1\ -1\ -1\ 1\ 1\ 1)$; $B_4 = (1\ -1\ 1\ 1\ 1\ 1)$; $A_9 = (1\ 1\ -1\ 1\ 1\ 1)$;
$A_{10} = (1\ 1\ 1\ 1\ 1\ 1)$;

$$W' = A_4^T \cdot B_1 + B_1^T \cdot B_2 + B_2^T \cdot B_3 + B_3^T \cdot B_4 + B_4^T \cdot A_9 + A_9^T \cdot A_{10}$$

$$= \begin{bmatrix} 4 & 0 & 2 & 0 & 2 & 2 \\ -2 & 2 & 0 & 2 & 0 & 0 \\ 0 & 0 & -6 & 0 & -2 & 2 \\ 2 & 2 & 0 & 6 & 4 & 4 \\ 6 & -2 & 0 & 2 & 4 & 4 \\ 2 & 2 & 4 & 2 & 4 & 0 \end{bmatrix}$$

Previous simulation shown in Figures 27 and 28, was repeated after memorizing path segments with the help of TAM. Figure 29 shows that the robot is momentarily blocked by the obstacle F, and then find path by utilizing TAM matrix for different path segments. The final route is shown in Figure 30. While training the W matrix

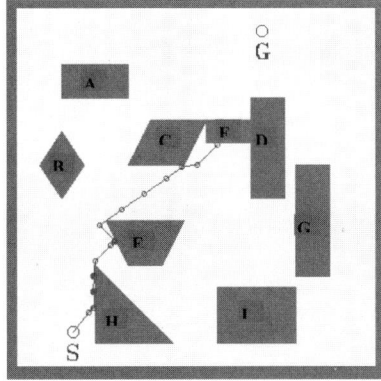

Figure 29. Robot is blocked momentarily by obstacle F.

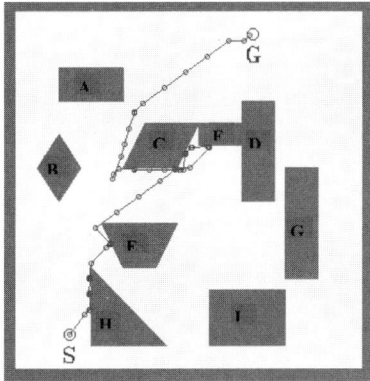

Figure 30. Robot finds alternate path by TAM matrix to reach the goal.

for different path segment, only 8 successive node points are considered for better approximation.

The most significant application of TAM based re-planning is in Automatic guided vehicle for the handicapped people. Given a set of nodes $n_1, n_2, \ldots n_n$, one can employ TAM for determining a path emanating from one node to another fixed node. This technique also have potential application in i) handling cargo in an air terminal; ii) medicine distribution to patient in indoor hospital.

4.3. Planning using evolutionary algorithm

In this section, we will discuss Evolutionary algorithm as a useful tool for navigational planning. The evolution program is a probabilistic algorithm, which maintains a population of individuals, $P(i) = \{x_1^i, \ldots, x_n^i\}$ at iteration i. Each individual represents a potential solution to the problem at hand, and each solution x_i^t is evaluated to give some measure of its "fitness". Then, a new population at iteration (i + 1) is formed by selecting the better suited individuals. Some members of these population undergo transformations by means of unary transformations m_i (mutation), which create new individuals by a small change in a single individual (m_i: S→S), and higher order transformations c_j (crossover), which create new individuals by combining parts from several (two or more) individuals, (c_j: S × S → S). After some number of generations, the program converges. Hopefully, the best individual represents a near optimum solution. The structure of an evolution program is shown below.

Algorithm evolution program
   Begin
       i ← 0;
       Initialize population P_i;
       Evaluate population P_i;
       While (not termination–condition) do
           For i = 1 to n
               i ← i + 1;
               Select population P_i from previous population P_{i-1};
               Apply genetic operators i.e. cross over and mutation on population P_i;
               Evaluation of population P_i by the predefined criteria;
           End For;
       End While
   End;

Evolutionary algorithm have been successfully employed in three classical problems in AI: i) Intelligent search; ii) Optimization and iii) Machine learning. Further many Constraint Satisfaction Problem (CSP) formulated as an intelligent search problem, have been solved by using evolutionary algorithms. The navigational planning problem of a mobile robot, which is formulated as a CSP, can thus be solved using the evolutionary algorithms.

Machalewicz [36] first successfully applied Genetic Algorithm (GA) [37] in navigational planning of mobile robots. In their evolutionary planner algorithm, Michalewicz considered a set of operators including crossover and mutations. An operator is selected based on its probability of occurrence and the operation is executed. The fitness evaluation function is then measured and proportional selection is employed to get population in the next generation. We will discuss a new technique of navigation by evolutionary algorithm.

In the Machalewicz algorithm [38], much of the computation time is wasted for planning a complete path, which later is likely to be disposed off. An alternative method for path planning in dynamic environment can be to select the next point and the path up to that point only in one genetic evolution. This is extremely fast and thus can take

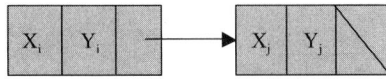

Figure 31. Representation of the chromosome for our simulation.

care of movable obstacles of speeds comparable to the robot. The first step in this path planning is to set up the initial population. For this purpose, instead of taking random coordinates, the sensory information around the robot stored in LTM is taken into account and the coordinates obtained from those data are used to set up the initial population. With this modification it is assured that, all the initial population are feasible, in the sense they are obstacle-free points and the straight line paths between the starting point and the computed subsequent points are obstacle free. Since only one genetic iteration is used for the path planning up to the computed next point, the data structure to represent the chromosome becomes extremely simple, as shown in Figure 31.

Here (X_i, Y_i) is the starting point and (X_j, Y_j) is the one of 2D points, obtained from the sensor information. All these chromosomes form the initial population. The next step is to allow crossover among the initial population. If we choose the cross-site randomly, it is observed that the most of the off-springs generated in the process of crossover are not feasible, as those paths may fall, either in the obstacle region or outside the 2D workspace. So instead of binary crossover, we have chosen for integer crossover. The crossover process is shown in Figure 30. Consider the two chromosomes as shown in Figure 32 and the crossover point is set between the third and the fourth integer for every chromosome. After making crossover between all pairs of initial population, the new population is generated, which are feasible points i.e., they are reachable from the starting point by the straight line path or not. The next step is mutation, which makes fine tuning of the path, such as avoiding the sharp turns. In this process a binary bit is selected randomly on the bit stream of the sensor coordinates and alter that binary bit value, such that the feasibility should not be lost for that chromosome.

Next step is to estimate the fitness of each and every chromosome out of the total present population (both for the initial and new populations). Estimation of the fitness involves finding the sum of the Euclidean distance from the starting point to the coordinate obtained from the sensor information and the distance from that sensor coordinate to the goal point.

Fitness of a chromosome $(X_i, Y_i, X_{jk}, Y_{jk})$

$$= \frac{1}{((\text{distance between } (X_i, Y_i) \text{ and } (X_{jk}, Y_{jk})) + (\text{distance between } (X_{jk}, Y_{jk}) \text{ and } (X_{goal}, Y_{goal}))}$$ for $\forall k$, generated after the crossover.

After finding the fitness value of the chromosomes, the best fit chromosome is evaluated, i.e., for which the fitness is the best. In this case, the best fit chromosome represents the predicted shortest path from the starting point to the goal. The number

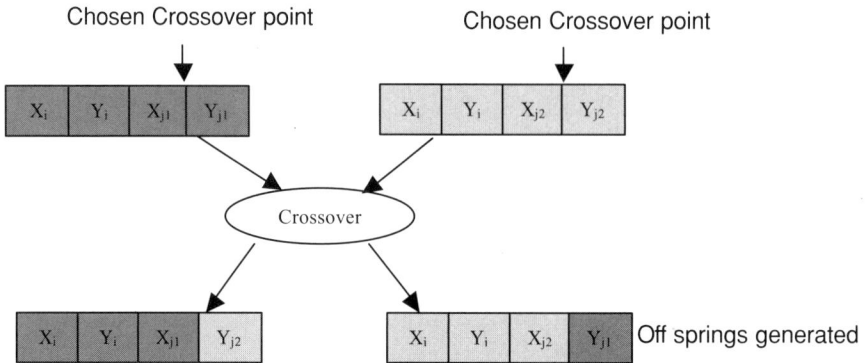

Figure 32. The crossover operation used in the proposed algorithm.

of generations is restricted to one, since in the first generation itself, a near optimal intermediate point is achieved. The third and fourth integer fields of the best fit chromosome will become the next intermediate point to move. Then the starting point is updated with the best fit point and the whole process of the GA, from setting up the initial population is repeated, until the best fit chromosome will have its third and the fourth field equal to the x- and y-coordinates of the goal location. The algorithm is formally presented below.

Procedure Evolutionary Algorithm for Navigational Planning:
// (x_i, y_i) = starting point;
  (x_g, y_g) = goal point; //
add-pathlist (x_i, y_i) ;
Repeat
  i) Initialization:
     Get sensor information in all possible directions
     $(x_{j1}, y_{j1}), (x_{j2}, y_{j2}), \ldots, (x_{jn}, y_{jn})$.
     Form chromosomes like (x_i, y_i, x_j, y_j);
  ii) Crossover:
     Select crossover point randomly on the third and the fourth
     fields of the chromosome.
     Allow crossover between all chromosomes and get new
     population.
     $(x_i, y_i, x_{j1}, y_{j1}), (x_i, y_i, x_{j2}, y_{j2}), (x_i, y_i, x_{j1}^i, y_{j1}^i), (x_i, y_i, x_{j2}^{ii}, y_{j2}^{ii})$;
  iii) Mutation:
     Select a mutation point in bitstream randomly and
     complement that bit position for every chromosome.
  iv) Selection:
     Discard all chromosomes (x_i, y_i, x_j, y_j) from population

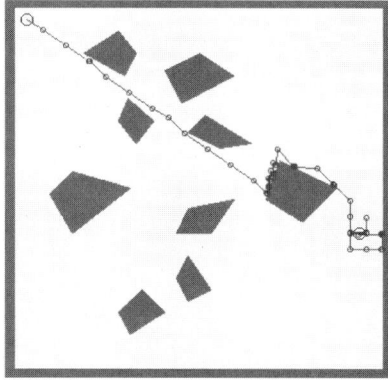

Figure 33. Apriory Known obstacle; S = Starting position (90,90); G = Goal Position (380,280); Time to search the path = 0.604 msec. Distance covered = 507 units.

     whose line segment is on obstacle region
     For all chromosomes in population find fittness using
        Fittness $(x_i, y_i, x_j, y_j) = 1/((x_j - x_i)^2 + (y_j - y_i)^2 + (x_g - x_j)^2 + (y_g - y_j)^2)$;
        Identify the best fit chromosome $(x_i, y_i, x_{bf}, y_{bf})$;
        Add-pathlist (x_{bf}, y_{bf});
        $x_i = x_{bf}$; $y_i = y_{bf}$;
    End for,
  Until $(x_i = x_g) \&\& (y_i = y_g)$;
End.

4.3.1. Simulation for EC planning

This algorithm has been simulated and tested by using C++ program on the Nomadic Superscoutt-II graphical interface. The results of the simulation are shown in the Figures 33–34.

   Here only 2 degree of freedom (DOF) has been considered for the motion of the obstacle. Figure 33 shows a case of navigation in a static environment, where the environment is already stored in the Long Term Memory (LTM). Figure 34 shows a case of an unknown obstacle, which was not stored in LTM prior to navigation. Therefore robot takes quite a large amount of time also moves around extra distances before reaching the goal.

5. CONCLUSIONS

In this chapter, we have discussed a new model of cognition for mobile robots, which consist of three cycles namely *Acquisition cycle*, *Perception cycle* and *Learning and coordination cycle*. Acquisition cycle senses data and puts them into Short Term Memory after filtering and processing. Only the selective portions of the whole image/ scene is stored into the Long Term Memory (LTM) after the attention and recognition state.

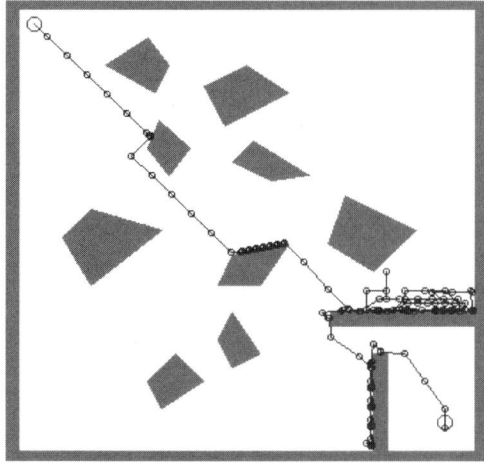

Figure 34. With two unknown Obstacle; S = Starting position (90,90); G = Goal Position (380,380); Time to search the path = 1.703 msec. Distance covered = 1232.58 units.

Perception cycle of the robot perceives its environment from the data stored in Long Term Memory and data comes from the various sensory unit by the help of reasoning and recognition states and is stored in a suitable format/data structure in the LTM. Map building is special type of *Perception* of mobile robot, which has been covered in more detail in this chapter. In *Learning and coordination cycle*, robot learns how to avoid obstacle, navigate amid static/moving obstacles and coordinate various tasks.

For navigation in the workspace, the locations of the obstacles has to be known apriory. Here a robot with 16 ultrasonic sensors is used for the map building. These sensors determine the obstacles directed along the sensor beams. Determination of the exact location of obstacle is affected due to reception of false signal within the sensing range of the robot. In fact when a transmitted ultrasonic signal is reflected in tandem by more than one obstacle, it may be received by a second detector as a false obstacle within the sensing range of the robot. Fuzzy decision theory has been discussed to remove the ambiguity in the detection of obstacles. Membership curve can be designed to assign a lower membership value to a detected obstacle beyond a threshold distance marked as the visibility radius of the robot. If the measured distance of the obstacle is R, the membership of that obstacle to occupy a position in the range $(R - \Delta R)$ to $(R + \Delta R)$ has a bell shaped distribution with a peak at $x = R$. The third source of uncertainty in the process of sensing by ultrasonic sensors arises due to the variation of the strength of the transmitted signal from the principal axis of the transmitted beam. The higher is the deviation from the principal axis, the lower will be the membership value of the obstacle to lie in that zone. Finding the appropriate location of the obstacle within the angular beam width of the radiator, thus is a problem of uncertainty management [39]. A measure of the degree of the occupancy of a location in a robot's environment, can be obtained by constructing a composite function of the three memberships discussed above. Some aspects of these issues have been briefly outlined in the chapter.

The chapter also covers the issue of navigational planning of mobile robots, by neural and evolutionary computing algorithms. It has been observed experimentally that the neural (BP) algorithms converge at a faster rate than the evolutionary computing approaches. Further both the neural and evolutionary computing algorithm are applicable to dynamic environments. Thus after each movement of the obstacle, the algorithm can generate navigational plan in a dynamic environment. The bi-directional associative memory when employed to navigational planning problem helps the robot back track to its previous location, if blocked by an obstacle towards the current sub-goal.

It may be noted that if at any time the robot would be trapped by a dead zone, evolutionary computation is helpful to come out of the trap, which is clear from the Figure 32. The algorithms have been tested with examples as well as computer simulations. It is apparent from the discussion that the evolutionary computing algorithm has a better scope in optimizing the time and path traversal jointly. A realistic algorithm that combines the above two issues into a single selection criteria of the evolutionary algorithm, however, remains an open problem till date.

REFERENCES

[1] Matlin, Margaret W., *Cognition*, Harcourt Brace Publishers & Prism Books Ltd., 1995.

[2] Nilson, Nils J., *Principles of Artificial Intelligence*, Morgan Kaufman Inc., 1980

[3] Brooks, Rodney A., "A Robust Layered Control System For A Mobile Robot", *IEEE Journal of Robotics and Automation*, Vol. 2, No. 1, March, 1986. pp. 14–23.

[4] Lee, Sukhan, and Ro, Sookwang, *Robotics with Perception and Action Net*, appeared in the book Control in *Robotics and Automation: Sensor-Based Integration*, edited by B. K. Ghosh, Ning Xi and T. J. Tarn., Academic Press, 1999.

[5] Patnaik, S., Konar, A., and Mandal, A. K., "Visual perception for navigational planning and coordination of mobile robots", *Indian Journal of Engineers*, vol. 26, Annual Number '97, pp. 21–37, 1998.

[6] Gardener, H., *The mind's new science: A history of the cognitive revolution*, New York: Basic Books, 1985.

[7] Biswas, B., Konar, A. and Mukherjee, A. K., "Fuzzy Moments for digital image matching," Communicated to *Engineering Applications of Artificial Intelligence*, Elsevier Publications, North Holland; also appeared in the *Proc. of Int. Conf. on Control, Automation, Robotics and Computer Vision*, ICARCV, '98, 1998.

[8] Bharick, H. P., "Semantic Memory Content in permastore: Fifty years of memory for Spanish learned in school," *Journal of Experimental Psychology: General*, Vol. 120, pp. 20–33, 1984.

[9] Chang, T. M., "Semantic Memory: Facts and Models," *Psychological Bulletin*, vol. 99, pp. 199–220, 1986.

[10] Winston Patrick Henry, *Artificial Intelligence*, Addison-Wesley Pub. Com, 1993.

[11] Baldi, Pierre F, Hornik, Kurt, "Learning in Linear Neural Networks: A Survey" IEEE Transactions on Neural Networks. Vol. 6, No. 4, July 1995, pp. 837–857.

[12] Carpenter, Gail, A., Grossberg, Stephen, "A Massively Parallel Architecture for a Self-Organizing Neural Pattern Recognition Machine", Computer, Vision, Graphics, and Image Processing 37, pp. 54–115. 1987.

[13] Lee, Seong-Whan, Song, Hee-Heon, "A New Recurrent Neural-Network Architecture for Visual Pattern recognition", IEEE Transactions on Neural Networks, Vol. 8, No. 2, March 1997, pp. 331–340.

[14] Pagac, D., Nebot, Eduardo M., and Durrant-Whyte, Huge, "An evidential Approach to Map-Building for Autonomous Vehicles", *IEEE Trans. on Robotics and Automation*, Vol. 14, No. 4, pp. 623–629, August, 1998.

[15] Oriolo, G., Ulivi, G. and Vendittelli, M., "Motion Planning with Uncertainty: Navigation on Fuzzy Maps." *Proc. forth IFAC Symp. on Robot Control (SY.RO.CO.'94)*, I, pp. 71–78, Capri, 1994.

[16] Dombi, J., "A General Class of Fuzzy Operators, the De Morgan Class of Fuzzy Operators and Fuzziness Measures Induced by Fuzzy Operators", *Fuzzy Sets and Systems*. Vol. 8, pp. 149–163, 1982.

[17] Asada, Minoru, "Map Building for a Mobile Robot from Sensory Data", *IEEE Trans. on Systems, Man and Cybernetics*, Vol. 37, No. 6, pp. 1326–1336, Nov/Dec., 1990.

[18] Elfes, Alberto, "Sonar-Based real-World Mapping and Navigation", *IEEE Journals of Robotics and automation*, Vol. RA-3, No. 3, pp. 249–264, June, 1987.

[19] Patnaik, S., Konar, A., and Mandal, A. K., "Map building and navigation by a robotic manipulator", *Proc. of Int. conf. on Information Technology*, pp. 227–232, TATA-McGraw-Hill, Bhubaneswar, Dec. 1998.

[20] J. Borenstein and Y. Koren, "Histogramic In-Motion Mapping for Mobile Robot Obstacle Avoidance", IEEE Trans. on Robotics and Automation, Vol. 7, No. 4, pp. 535–539, August 1991.

[21] Alberto Elfes, "Sonar-Based Real-World Mapping and Navigation", IEEE Trans. on Robotics and Automation, Vol. 3, No. 3, pp. 249–263, June 1987.

[22] Pagac, D., Nebot, Eduardo M., and Durrant-Whyte, Huge, "An evidential Approach to Map-Building for Autonomous Vehicles", *IEEE Trans. on Robotics and Automation*, Vol. 14, No. 4, pp. 623–629, August, 1998.

[23] Maja J. Mataric, "Integration of Representation into Goal-Driven Behavior-Based Robots", *IEEE Trans. on Robotics and Automation*, Vol. 8, No. 3, pp. 304–312, June, 1992.

[24] Dickmann, E.D., and Graefe, V., "Dynamic Monocular Machine Vision", International Journal of Machine Vision and Application, Vol. 1, pp. 223–240, 1988.

[25] Langer, D., Rosenblatt, J. K., and Herbert, M., "A Behavior Based System for off-Road Navigation", *IEEE Trans. on Robotics and Automation*, Vol. 10, No. 6, Dec. 1994.

[26] Murphy, Robin R., and Arkin, R. C., "Lessons Learned in Integrating Sensing into Autonomous Mobile Robot Architecture", Journal of Excperimental and Theoretical Artificial Intelligence, Vol.9, No. 2, pp. 191–209, 196.

[27] Hu, H., Brady, J. M. and Probert., P. J., "Distributed Architecture for Sensor-guided Control of Mobile Robot", The International Journal of Intelligent Automation and Soft Computing Vol.1, No. 1, pp. 63–83, 1995.

[28] Gat Erann and et. al., "Behavior Control for Robotic Exploration of Planetary Surface", IEEE Tran. on Robotics and Automation, Vol. 10, No. 4, Aug. 1994.

[29] Jain, L. C., Fukuda, T., *Soft Computing for Intelligent Robotic System*, Springer-Verlag, 1999.

[30] Patnaik, S., Konar, A. and Mandal, A. K. "Constrained Hierarchical Path Planning of a robot by employing Neural Nets," Proc. of the fourth Int. Symp. on Artificial Life and Robotics, (AROB 4th '99), pp. 690–693, Japan, Jan. 1999.

[31] Meng, H., and Picton, P. D., "Neural Network for Local Guidance of Mobile Robots", *Proc. of the Third Int. Conf. on Automation, Robotics and Computer Vision (ICARCV' 94)*, pp. 1238–1242, Singapore, Nov. 1994.

[32] Michalewicz, Z., *Genetic Algorithms + Data Structure = Evolution Programs*, 3rd edition, New York, Springer-Verlag, 1986.

[33] Kosko, B. "Bidectional Associative memories" *IEEE Transaction on Systems, Man and Cybernetics*, SMC-18, pp. 42–60, 1988.

[34] Kosko, B. "Adaptive bi-directional associative memories", *Applied Optics*, 26 (23): pp. 4947–4960, Dec. 1987.

[35] Patniak, S., Konar, A., and Mandal, A. K., "Bi-directional Associative Memory for Mobile Robot Navigation", *Proc. of the Int. Conf. on Neural Network*, Washington, July, 1999.

[36] Michalewicz, Z., *Genetic Algorithms + Data Structure = Evolution Programs*, 3rd edition, New York, Springer-Verlag, 1986.

[37] Goldberg, D.E., *Genetic Algorithm in Search Optimization and Machine Learning*, Reading, MA, Addition Wesley, 1989.

[38] Xiao, J., Michalewicz, Z., Zhang L. and Trojanowski K., "Adaptive Evolutionary Planner/ Navigator for Mobile Robots", *IEEE Trans on Evolutionary Computation*, Vol. 1, No. 1, pp. 18–28, April 1997.

[39] Jamshidi, M., Zadeh, L., Titli, Andre', Boverie, S., *Application of Fuzzy Logic: Towards High Machine Intelligence Quotient Systems*, Prentice Hall PTR, 1997.